MACROFOUNDATIONS
OF POLITICAL ECONOMY AND DEVELOPMENT

Macrofoundations of Political Economy and Development

Survival Conditions Analysis

David Goalstone

MACROFOUNDATIONS OF POLITICAL ECONOMY AND DEVELOPMENT
© David Goalstone, 2007.

Copyrights and publishing rights for the Okishio paper "Goalstone's Macro Foundation" have been granted by Professor Hiroko Hagiwara and Kobe-Gakuin University respectively.

First published in 2007 by
PALGRAVE MACMILLAN™
175 Fifth Avenue, New York, N.Y. 10010 and
Houndmills, Basingstoke, Hampshire, England RG21 6XS
Companies and representatives throughout the world.

PALGRAVE MACMILLAN is the global academic imprint of the Palgrave Macmillan division of St. Martin's Press, LLC and of Palgrave Macmillan Ltd. Macmillan® is a registered trademark in the United States, United Kingdom and other countries. Palgrave is a registered trademark in the European Union and other countries.

ISBN-13: 978–1–4039–7621–5
ISBN-10: 1–4039–7621–X

Library of Congress Cataloging-in-Publication Data

Goalstone, David, 1951–
    Macrofoundations of political economy and development : survival conditions analysis / by David Goalstone.
        p. cm.
    Includes bibliographical references and index.
    Contents: Modern macrofoundation—Classical macrofoundation—Aspects of development.
        ISBN 1–4039–7621–X (alk. paper)
        1. Subsistence economy. 2. Economic development. 3. Developing countries—Economic conditions. I. Title. II. Title: Survival conditions analysis.

HD75.G62 2007
339.5—dc22   2006050729

A catalogue record for this book is available from the British Library.

Design by Newgen Imaging Systems (P) Ltd., Chennai, India.

First edition: April 2007

10 9 8 7 6 5 4 3 2 1

Printed in the United States of America.

Everlasting thanks to the team at Newgen in Chennai.
I have learned much from you at each stage
and love your beautiful design work.
Everlasting thanks to my editors at Palgrave Macmillan.
I am very grateful for the freedom to prepare
this book as treatise, textbook, and literary experiment.

Man in this world has only three original needs: (1) that of his subsistence, (2) that of his preservation, and (3) that of the perpetuation of his species.

—Marquis de Mirabeau and Francois Quesnay, *Rural Philosophy* (1763)

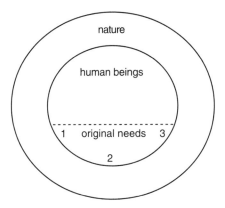

. . . we must consider the common weal in terms of its essence, and humanity as a whole in terms of its roots, *subsistence*. All moral and physical parts of which society is constituted derive from this and are subordinated to it. It is upon subsistence, upon the means of the subsistence, that all the branches of the political order depend.

—Marquis de Mirabeau and Francois Quesnay, *Rural Philosophy* (1763)

The principal object of this science is to secure a certain fund of subsistence for all the inhabitants, to obviate every circumstance which may render it precarious . . .

—Sir James Steuart, *Principles of Political Economy* (1767)

Political economy, considered as a branch of the science of a statesman or legislator proposes . . . first, to supply a plentiful revenue or subsistence for the people, or more properly to enable them to provide such a revenue or subsistence for themselves . . .

—Adam Smith, *Wealth of Nations* (1776)

CONTENTS

INTERLUDE

PART THREE—ASPECTS OF DEVELOPMENT

PREFACE

Conditions of life and death in the poorworlds differ dramatically from conditions in the first world. This is seen most starkly in the difference between life expectancy at birth and median age at death. In the first world these indicators are nearly equal. In the poorworlds there is a huge gap—with the median age at death in Africa astonishingly low. The problems of subsistence and survival are naked in the poorworlds. First-world theory will not do. For the poorworlds we need survival-conditions analysis.

1990	ESTABLISHED MARKET ECONOMIES	SUB-SAHARAN AFRICA	MIDDLE EAST CRESCENT	INDIA
life expectancy at birth	76	52	61	58
median age at death	75	5	24	37

Source: *World Development Report 1993* (New York: Oxford University Press, 1993), 200–201.

Marginal analysis and methodological individualism are powerful and useful tools in many ways. But for far too long they have dominated thinking in economics with spillovers into other social sciences. Economists and political economists have neglected macrofoundations and many even deny the 'existence' of macrofoundations. This has been to the detriment of people in the poorworlds. Their most basic difficulty—solving the perennial subsistence problem—can be usefully analyzed through macrofoundations.

Problems of mass poverty and underdevelopment are attracting a great deal of attention. The Copenhagen Consensus and the UN Millennium Project both seek to focus attention on core problems and possible remedies. I particularly admire the UN project, led by Professor Jeffrey Sachs. It draws from all social sciences, uses social accounting and indicators fully, diagnoses challenges insightfully and sets high but appropriate goals. In the UN project, we see a new and intelligent focus on solving the intractable problems in the poorworlds. I hope this book can provide useful theoretical tools for that sort of project.

In a critical way the Copenhagen Consensus demonstrates why this book is needed. That plan endorses nine projects. All of the projects are worthy but the list itself is demographically one-sided. Most of the projects would reduce death rates but none of them would reduce birth rates. Education is pointedly omitted from the list. To adopt their list would worsen population growth problems in the poorworlds. In survival-conditions analysis, demography is treated as the queen of social sciences.

In order to reach an understanding of macrofoundations, I have drawn upon economics, demography, cultural anthropology, anthrodemography, political demography, history of political economy, history of economic thought, economic history, ecology, social accounting, and financial accounting. One might expect this to lead to a complex book. I hope it is not. I have tried to achieve simplicity and directness, making the reading experience user-friendly.

I began this work 18 years ago in Kobe, Japan, with the assistance of Professor Nobuo Okishio. The model developed in Part One was brought to life there. Some of the work done in Kobe is found in Chapters 7–9. They contain the most elaborate models in the book. Chapter 8 contains Professor Okishio's algebraic interpretation of my model. I am publishing his algebra in preference to my own because it is more compact and requires fewer limiting assumptions.

In addition to Kobe, work on this book has been done, in chronological order: in Honolulu, Colombo, Dhaka, Boulder, Monterey, Seoul, Phoenix, and Durham. The first draft was prepared in Seoul, at the Graduate School of International Studies, Korea University. The manuscript was greatly expanded in Phoenix, at the Thunderbird CIBER—Garvin School of International Management. Finalizations and bibliography were prepared during a research trip to the Perkins/Bostock Library at Duke University.

Much of the book has been built upon one inequality:

net output > social subsistence

I have wanted very much to understand this relationship all of my adult life. The main goal of this book is to establish the principle of social subsistence.

I hope students and scholars with a keen interest in model building will be attracted to the analysis. In the hands of the younger generation—especially if they can be brought together through the internet—the macrofoundations based upon survival-conditions analysis can take root.

The book is rich with diagrams. About 50 diagrams are built using social subsistence as the entry point. Many of these diagrams have more than one algebraic interpretation. Mathematically inclined economists and political economists can begin to harvest this crop if they master the algebraic model found in Chapters 8 and 9.

Survival-conditions analysis is, by its nature, interdisciplinary. I hope students and scholars from the full spectrum of social sciences will benefit from this book. All fields can contribute to our understanding of survival conditions. All contributions to our understanding should be warmly welcome.

The twenty-first century has begun with a new and noble social dream: to Make Poverty History and put it in a museum. Although utopian, it is a worthy dream. We may not get there but we can get closer. And closer.

By way of dedication I would like to say that this book is written from my mind, heart, and soul for the peoples throughout the poorworlds.

David Goalstone
Phoenix • May 25, 2006

ACKNOWLEDGMENTS

I owe Professor Nobuo Okishio a special debt for being a remarkable friend and teacher. I am very pleased to publish his algebraic interpretation of my macrofoundation in order for him to receive the full credit he deserves. I thank Professor Okishio's daughter, Hiroko Hagiwara, for granting copyrights.

In America, special thanks are due to Professor Robert Grosse, a former classmate and life-long friend. His energetic and productive ways have helped many people, me included. I owe my profound thanks to him for insight, encouragement, and practical guidance.

Special thanks are also due to my mother, Jeanne Hardie. Her loving support during difficult times has made completion of this project possible.

I would like to record words of thanks to people in nine places I have called home during the past three decades. What was born in Durham and Kobe was brought to fruition in Seoul and Phoenix. With gratitude I thank and remember:

Durham: Martin Bronfenbrenner, Neil deMarchi, Edward Tower, Janet Seiz, Charles Flynn

Kobe: Nobuo and Hisami Okishio, Ryoichi Mikitani, Kazuhisa Matsuda, Takeshi Nakatani, Taiji and Hiroko Hagiwara, Takashi Okamoto

Honolulu: Deane Neubauer, Johan Galtung, Franz Broswimmer, Jody Boyne, Peter Manicas, Daniela Minerbi, Edward Reiser

The excellent staff at Hamilton Library—University of Hawaii at Manoa

Colombo: A.T. Ariyaratne, Jehan Perera, David Cracknell

Dhaka: R.I. Molla, Tanweer Akram, Oliver Martin, Woodrow Denham

Boulder/Denver: David Hawkins, Robert Urquhart, Tracy Mott, William Kaempfer, Don Roper, Phyllis and Jane Levine

Monterey: Lynette Shi, Brian Hager, Shawn Marshall

Seoul: Sang-Kyung Kwak, Inn-Won Park, Andrew Kim, Shin-Wha Lee, Peter Sylvestre

Phoenix: Robert and Christine Grosse, Tania Marcinkowshi, John Mathis, Adrian Tschogel

Durham: The fantastic staff at Perkins/Bostock Library—Duke University

Miami: Richard Weisskoff, Michael Halleran, Jackie Dixon

Finally, I have a great debt to three editors at Palgrave Macmillan: Anthony Wahl, Elizabeth Sabo, and Heather Van Dusen. They generously supported this project as a treatise, a textbook, and a literary experiment. They have earned my eternal thanks.

Those thanks also go to Maran Elancheran, and his team at Newgen. The formatting posed real challenges. They carefully reset the entire book and smoothed out inconsistencies while preserving my pagination.

INTRODUCTION

1. CONTROVERSY OVER FOUNDATIONS

While this is a book on macrofoundations, it is also, perhaps more importantly, a book on survival-conditions analysis. As such it stands outside of orthodox discourse. I have referred to that discourse only when necessary. But it might be helpful to make a comment so this book may be understood in the context of the neo-Classical/Keynesian dispute over foundations.

I believe the neo-Classical thought experiment involving constrained optimization is very useful but its extension into macro is problematic. The standard textbook takes for granted unique points of equilibrium, as depicted in supply-and-demand analysis. In the world of Marshallian micro, this seems reasonable to me. When dealing with macro issues, however, it seems to both overreach and to truncate analysis at a very interesting juncture.

In macro, points of equilibrium may be less interesting than the *areas of equilibrium* around them. All macro equilibrium are embedded in *context*. Areas of equilibrium and their context are always relevant and can be surprisingly illuminating.

I have written this book in this spirit. One of the tools used extensively here is 'relevant range analysis'. All of the diagrams beginning with social subsistence are drawn to reveal relevant ranges. The diagram 'Rich Country, Poor Country, Starving Country' is a good example because it depicts consumption possibilities in three different contexts, with three different relevant ranges and illustrates how different the three contexts are.

Perhaps the most mature use of relevant range analysis is found in Chapter 9, on real wages. The subtitle is "On a Macrofoundation of Microeconomics." The relevant range of real wages in first and third worlds are depicted, constrained by both output and survival conditions. Neo-Classical equilibrium is a sideshow there or an empty shadow. Context is the main show.

The macrofoundations literature within economics is small but it is not empty.[1] I feel significant sympathy for the views expressed in David Colander's article entitled "The Macrofoundations of Micro" (1993). He shows well the dilemma faced by the neo-Classicals when projecting up from a Marshallian base. Interdependencies make unique points of equilibrium very unlikely.

Traditions from the past have much to offer as we explore survival-conditions analysis. In this book I champion eighteenth-century Classic writings and I specially praise Sir James Steuart. There is still much to learn from them. The surplus approach is both practical and deep. Its neglect should not stop its rehabilitation. Even Marxists can be called to the party if they will modify their extremist theory of exploitation. Even neo-Classicals can contribute models. In survival-conditions analysis, everyone is invited!

2.   VICIOUS CYCLES OF POVERTY

Although some progress has been made in the poorest regions of the world, the majority of people there are still very poor. Let us consider a simple macroeconomic model that illustrates vicious cycles of poverty.[2]

We assume a closed economy without government. This allows us to use the simplest macroeconomic accounting equations:

national income − consumption = saving   and   *saving = investment*

The vicious cycle begins with consumption needs pressing upon the low level of national income. This results in low savings. Low savings will only support low investment. Low investment will only be enough for low capital formation. Low capital formation will re-enforce the existing low level of productivity. Low productivity will lead back to low income.

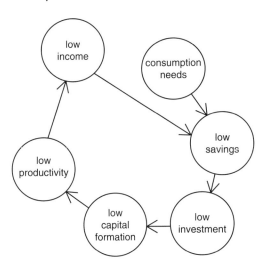

Source: James R. Kahn, *Economic Approach to Environmental and Natural Resources*, 3rd ed. (Mason, Ohio: Southwestern Press, 2005), 591.

If we introduce government, taxation and borrowing can potentially be used to finance investment in education, health, and physical infrastructure. At the same time, those funds may be invested very ineffectively. This frequently keeps the vicious cycle going.

If we introduce international trade, foreign investment, and donor assistance, new possibilities emerge for breaking the cycle of poverty. But none of them will be of any use unless human and social capital are built up, with significant productivity gains. The same principle applies to NGO activities.

The odds against economic development are reinforced when we bring some other factors into the picture. In the diagram above we said nothing about population or the environment. Let us bring them in.

In most poor countries, the birth rate remains high, while simple improvements in sanitation and public health have dramatically reduced death rates. This accounts for declines in child mortality and increases in life expectancy. It also accounts for extraordinary population booms.

With so many more mouths to feed, subsistence pressures on national income tend to intensify. *Quantity* of human life absorbs hard-earned gains that may have been made in output or productivity.

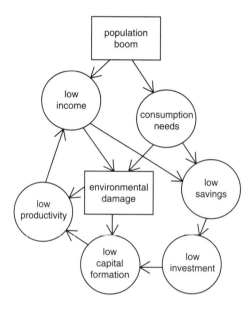

Note: See also Kahn, *Economic Approach*, 594.

At the same time, the struggle for survival greatly strains the environment. To satisfy daily needs, the natural resources of an area may be used to the point of exhaustion. Large areas may become uninhabitable deserts. In the great cities, severe pollution from industry, vehicles, and every kind of organic waste injures health. This reduces productive activity. Given the pressing survival needs of daily life, environmental concerns are frequently low priorities.

What, in fact, ought to be the highest priority? It is astonishing that we still lack a consensus on this question. In my opinion, *the first and greatest task is to solve the subsistence problem.*

The great political economists of the eighteenth century were preoccupied with this matter. Quesnay, Steuart, and Smith devoted themselves to show how the subsistence problem could be solved. Malthus came along and said the problem could never be solved! Should we accept such pessimism? As we observe poor life opportunities and low life expectancies in large parts of the poorworlds, Malthus may seem persuasive. Is there a way out? Can we finally, globally, decisively, solve the subsistence problem?

3. Executive Summary

Part One—Modern Macrofoundation

Chapter 1: We begin with the idea that a society must be able to produce a net output greater than its overall subsistence needs. Armed with both production and distribution survival conditions, five different cases are identified.

Chapter 2: The relationship between social subsistence and life expectancy is explored. Life expectancy is shown to largely be a function of the quality and distribution of social subsistence. A short story creates a context for this theory.

Chapter 3: Three sources of population crisis are identified: insufficient capital accumulation, ecological stress, and insufficient food production. Incomplete demographic transition is discussed. The genocide in Rwanda is considered.

Chapter 4: The production survival condition is fleshed out as a ratio:

$$alpha = net\ output/social\ subsistence > 1$$

Simple and complex societies are distinguished. The Euro-American transition from simple to complex is discussed using the formula for alpha.

Chapter 5: Upper and lower productivity limits are introduced. Labor productivity in the poorer parts of the world is shown to be *too low* for modern capitalism to function. They need a transitional system for development.

Chapter 6: The model is used to shed light on some topics in macroeconomics. Problems of effective supply and demand are illustrated. Ineffective investment, international trade, and poverty elasticity of growth are discussed.

The next four chapters contain or reflect the earliest work I did on macrofoundations. They may be considered the heart of the book. Chapters 7–9 are, by far, the most complex part of the book.

Chapter 7: The building of the modern macrofoundation is explained step-by-step. The Marxian theory of exploitation is critiqued. The model here is much more detailed than elsewhere in the book.

Chapter 8: Professor Okishio's algebraic interpretation of the model is printed here in preference to mine. His version is more professional and very compact.

Chapter 9: Results from Chapter 8 are used to discuss maximum and minimum real wages consistent with production and distribution survival conditions. The relevant range of real wages in first and third worlds is analyzed.

Chapter 10: Some results from Part One are brought together and some themes from my Kobe days are discussed. The Five-Worlds' Spectrum is introduced and the central diagram of the Modern Macrofoundation is constructed. This chapter is written in the spirit of Chapters 7–9.

PART TWO—CLASSICAL MACROFOUNDATION

The next section explores a macrofoundation found in the Classics of British Political Economy. This analysis is not an historical curiosity. It presupposes a largely agrarian society—a common condition, even now, in the poorworlds.

Chapter 11: The Classical preoccupation with subsistence is shown. The Classical Macrofoundation is constructed, with Sir James Steuart playing the pivotal role. Ricardo's distribution theory is illustrated.

Chapter 12: The model is used to summarize a classic of anthropology: Childe's *Man Makes Himself* (1936). We observe human development from hunter-gatherer days on. Two kinds of population booms are distinguished.

Chapter 13: A complex diagram by Galtung on the 'Rise and Fall of Rome' is rationally constructed in stages. The entire story is told in terms of two social-surplus conditions: one for the domestic economy and one for the empire.

Chapter 14: The dark side of 'man makes himself' is explored in a discussion of Browswimmer's *Ecocide* (2002). Ecocide is traced back to the megafauna extinction of Cro-Magnon days. The threat of dirty, wasteful, and violent industrialization is analyzed. The need for Green Democracy is considered.

Chapter 15: Some themes associated with 'the dismal science' are discussed. The rise of scientific agriculture is shown to be both a key to solving the subsistence problem and a vital link in the transition from Classical political economy to neo-Classical economics.

Chapter 16: The extraordinary survival-conditions analysis found at the beginning of Steuart's *Principles* (1767) is constructed step-by-step, using his own words as much as possible. His keen empirical sense is documented.

Chapter 17: The connection between Malthus and survival conditions is considered. Some of his observations on 'checks to population' are summarized. Present-day relevance and irrelevance of Malthus is discussed.

Chapter 18: Taking up the post-Malthusian theme of capital-accumulation crisis, Goldstone's *Revolution and Rebellion in the Early Modern World* (1991) is summarized. This analysis is highly relevant in today's poorworlds.

Chapter 19: To caution against the abuse of macrofoundations, the fascist surplus analysis found in Alfred Sauvy's *General Theory of Populations* (1952) is introduced. He is briefly compared with Marx.

Chapter 20: In order to help solve the subsistence problem in the poorworlds, the section ends with a plea for the rehabilitation of Classics. The current life-expectancy crisis is compared with the life-expectancy crisis common before industrialization. Diamond's *Guns, Germs and Steel* (1997) is brought in.

INTERLUDE

The next two chapters comprise an interlude using the Modern Macrofoundation. They provide additional background for Part Three.

Chapter 21: 'Guns and Butter' looks at the crisis in North Korea. That nation's decline to fifth world is discussed. Prospects for reform are considered.

Chapter 22: 'Butter and Books' looks at the role of education in solving the subsistence problem. Taiwan's great success is compared with India's relative failure.

PART THREE—ASPECTS OF DEVELOPMENT

The last section looks at development from the point of view of stages as well as some essential elements of success and failure. Agriculture, infrastructure, finance, natural disasters, and alternative development are highlighted.

Chapter 23: We begin with a summary of Rostow's *Stages of Economic Growth* (1960). It is shown to be an extension of Classical thought.

Chapter 24: Agricultural supply and demand problems are discussed. The living and working conditions of poor farmers are highlighted.

Chapter 25: Land reform in Taiwan is introduced using a book written by the architect of that successful program. 'Land to the Tiller' is the centerpiece.

Chapter 26: The building of infrastructure is considered. Insufficient and ineffective investment are discussed. Rules for public finance are formulated.

Chapter 27: The financial strains of rapid industrial development are introduced. Chain bankruptcy is analyzed. Odious debt is considered.

Chapter 28: The Asian 'Miracle' is analyzed, applying the model from Part One to Krugman's well-known paper on 'the Myth'.

Chapter 29: The macroeconomic impact of FDI on poverty reduction is explored. Demographic crisis is shown to swamp the positive impact in Africa.

Chapter 30: A natural-disaster model is set up and applied to the study of the Bangladeshi typhoon of 1991. Survival accounting is introduced.

Chapter 31: The destruction of New Orleans by Hurricane Katrina is studied using the sequence introduced in the previous chapter:

vulnerability—preparedness—events—response—recovery

Chapter 32: The book closes with an introduction to the Sarvodaya and Grameen models of 'alternative development'. Both are impressive movements. Sarvodaya's brilliant Five-Stage Model of village renewal may become a powerful way to help build 'Senian capabilities'.

4. HIGHLIGHTED CONCLUSIONS

I would like to emphasize seven conclusions from this work:

1. There are two different but related macrofoundations based upon survival-conditions analysis. One is found in Classical thought—most fully by Sir James Steuart. The other is 'Modern'. Social subsistence is central to both.
2. Life expectancy is closely related to the quality and distribution of social subsistence, modified somewhat by lifestyle factors.
3. Large declines in death rates cannot be sustained unless birth rates greatly decline too *and* capital accumulation is appropriate, sufficient, and effective.
4. Labor productivity in the poorest parts of the world is too low for modern capitalism to function. They need a transitional system for development.
5. Humanity's ecocidal tendencies can be traced back to Cro-Magnon days. This indicates the historic depth of our ecological problems.
6. Every social science can benefit by developing courses on survival-conditions analysis.
7. The Sarvodaya Five-Stage Model of village renewal has extraordinary potential. Mahatma Gandhi coined the word Sarvodaya while living in Africa. The Sri Lankan based Sarvodaya Movement might have much to offer there.

5. CHAPTER OUTLINES, DIAGRAMS, AND TABLES

While this book is a treatise on macrofoundations and survival-conditions analysis, it may also be considered a textbook. Each chapter is the length of a lecture and is built around a seven-point outline. Care has been taken to confine the discussion of a diagram or table to the page on which it appears. This has enabled readers to learn the main lessons efficiently.

Each seven-point outline reveals the story I wish to tell on the topics comprising this book. Readers can test their understanding of a chapter by thinking through the outline. This, too, has enabled readers to absorb the main lessons efficiently but it has also helped them to identify where they might be inclined to tell the story differently.

Because of the page-by-page construction of this book, each diagram and table may be known by its section heading. For example, the section heading 'Rich Country, Poor Country, Starving Country', found on page 7 (Chapter 1, Section 4), may also be used to identify the diagram there.

NOTE

Whenever possible, Classic authors are cited by book number (if relevant), chapter, and paragraph. For example, the quote on page 4 from Smith's *Wealth of Nations* comes from Book 4, Introduction, Paragraph 1—shown as (4.Introduction.1) in the text.

The online Library of Economics and Liberty, at http://www.econlib.org, has made this both possible and convenient.

Classic authors are cited by page number in only three cases, all listed in the bibliography: Meek's translation of the Physiocratic *Rural Philosophy*, Ricardo's *Essay on Profits*, and Senior's *Two Lectures on Population*. The last two items are found in original printing on microform in the Goldsmiths'—Kress Library of Economic Literature.

PART ONE

MODERN MACROFOUNDATION

In order for a society to exist and survive, it must produce a net output greater than its overall subsistence needs. This is the key concept behind the principle of social subsistence. Armed with both production and distribution-survival conditions, we can distinguish five different 'worlds'.

Demography is central to the macrofoundations built upon survival-conditions analysis. We observe this first in our studies of life expectancy and sources of population crisis.

It is important to distinguish societies according to their degree of complexity. It is also important to understand the upper and lower productivity limits confronting any social order. Labor productivity in much of the poorworlds appears to be far too low for modern capitalism to function.

Poor countries face unique macroeconomic challenges. Faced with chronic ineffective investment and great inequality, they require their own analysis of effective supply and demand.

The Modern Macrofoundation was initially conceived as a thought experiment. This is illustrated by a set of relational diagrams and formalized algebraically. It is essential to show the maximum and minimum rates of profit and real wages consistent with survival conditions.

Once we know the maximum and minimum real wages consistent with survival conditions, it is possible to shed light on a macrofoundation of microeconomics.

We end Part One with a discussion of the principle of social subsistence.

1

SOCIAL SUBSISTENCE

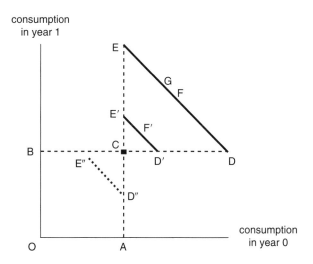

Rich Country, Poor Country, Starving Country

1.1   FOUNDATIONS OF ECONOMICS

Orthodox economics is built upon a microfoundation. Starting with the individual, orthodox economists construct neo-Classical microeconomics. From that base they build their macroeconomics. Unfortunately this dependence upon 'methodological individualism' has allowed orthodox economists to ignore factors authentically macro and independent of individual decision making.

One such factor is the main theme of this book—survival conditions. A great deal of this topic *is* authentically macro, where the individual *is* a misleading or nonsensical level of abstraction.

In this chapter we are interested in the following question:

WHAT ARE THE ECONOMIC CONDITIONS A SOCIETY MUST SATISFY IN ORDER TO EXIST AND SURVIVE?

This is not a neo-Classical question. It is, however, an important question. It is also the main subtext behind the Classics.

The great political economists of the eighteenth century were vitally interested in this because throughout human existence the subsistence problem had never been solved. Over the generations, societies constantly suffered population expansions and contractions, life expectancy increases and decreases. This made continuity of any social order difficult and often impossible.

Sir James Steuart said:

> The principle object of this science is to secure a certain fund of subsistence for all the inhabitants, to obviate every circumstance which may render it precarious . . . (1.Introduction.6)

Adam Smith said:

> Political economy, considered . . . as a science . . . proposes . . . first, to provide a plentiful revenue or subsistence for the people . . . (4.Introduction.1)

And the Physiocrats said:

> It is upon subsistence, upon the means of subsistence that all the branches of the political order depend. (Meek translation, 59)

As we see later, there is a clear macrofoundation in Classical thought. But first we begin with the initial propositions of a different and complimentary macrofoundation—one I simply call 'Modern'. Here we are looking for a macrofoundation of macroeconomics that can also shine a light on microeconomics while doing a great deal besides.

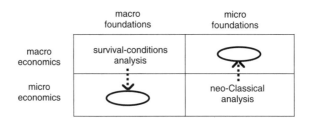

1.2   CRITIQUE OF NEO-CLASSICALS

We begin our inquiry with a version of a diagram found in textbooks. Consumption in year 0 is on the horizontal axis. Consumption in year 1 is on the vertical. Let us suppose a closed economy. It produces and consumes only corn, with a given fertility of corn seed and productivity of labor time:

corn is produced with corn seed and labor time

The maximum consumption of corn in year 0 depends upon the size of the recent harvest. This is marked by the distance OA. If none of the harvest is consumed in year 0, and all of it is planted, the size of the harvest in year 1 is marked by the distance OB. The curve AB, is the 'production-possibility frontier'. A textbook might call it a 'menu of choices'.

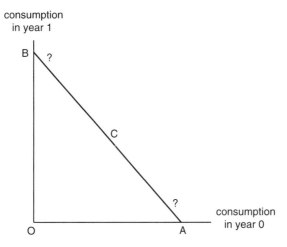

According to orthodoxy, a society will choose a point along this curve. Points inside the curve will not be chosen because it is possible to have more consumption in both years. Points beyond the curve cannot be chosen because the society lacks the productive capacity.

Point C, near the middle of the curve, is interesting. At point C consumption is the same both years. We can imagine the members of a society choosing a point near C because it represents stability.

But what about points near A or B? Something is terribly wrong with those points. Near point A almost all of the corn is consumed in year 0—almost none is planted—and everyone starves to death in year 1. That is social suicide. Near point B almost none of the corn is consumed in year 0—almost all is planted—and everyone starves to death in year 0 while the corn is growing. That, too, is social suicide.

Orthodoxy has made a false start. Its possibility frontier is invalid because it pretends there are no social-survival conditions. While this may not appear to matter in a rich country, it is a blind error when applied to poor countries. We must make an effort to build an analysis of survival conditions.

1.3 NET OUTPUT > SOCIAL SUBSISTENCE

The macrofoundation begins with a definition of subsistence,[1] from a social point of view:

social subsistence
EQUALS
subsistence consumption per person TIMES *the population*

The diagram below uses the same axes as the one on the previous page, but our ABC are different. Let us suppose that subsistence consumption per person is a given quantity of corn. Let us also suppose that the size of the population is given and unchanging, with the birth rate equal to the death rate. Then the social subsistence is the same both years. This is noted by the distance OA = OB. From these points we derive point C. Point C represents the two-year social-subsistence condition.

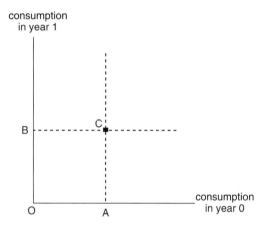

Now let us consider production. The net output is the harvest minus the replacement seed. A society will want to always produce a net output greater than point C in order to assure the availability of the social subsistence:

net output > social subsistence

There are two reasons for requiring a greater-than sign. First, if the distribution of corn food is unequal, some surplus must be produced to ensure that everyone can get at least a subsistence bundle. Second, as a precaution against natural disaster, some corn food should be set aside as an emergency supply.

Even within a corn model we can observe three distinct parts of the social subsistence: (1) corn needed for physical survival of people; (2) corn needed by workers for productive labor; and (3) corn needed by women to produce healthy children and by children to become productive workers. Therefore we have another definition:

social subsistence
EQUALS
survival needs + productivity needs + reproduction needs

1.4 RICH COUNTRY, POOR COUNTRY, STARVING COUNTRY

Now that we have identified the social-subsistence condition, we can look at some possibility frontiers. Consider the diagram below. This diagram contains the same ABC just established. We compare three countries: one rich, one poor, and one starving. They have the same population size and the same social-subsistence condition.

The rich country has a possibility frontier well above point C. We have noted it as the curve DE. What is the most relevant range of choice along that curve? Points near D involve overconsuming in year 0, with only the social subsistence available in year 1. That is the road to poverty! Likewise, points near E are unlikely because they require a great sacrifice in year 0 while there is no pressing need to sacrifice. Point F represents equal consumption both years—it permits stability *and* consumption well above the social subsistence. If people prefer constant consumption, or increasing consumption over time without too much sacrifice, they will choose points in a range like FG.

The poor country has a possibility frontier above point C, but not far above it. This is marked as the curve D'E'. Equal consumption in both years is marked by point F'. If people prefer constant or increasing consumption over time, they will choose points in the range F'E'. If growth is the highest priority, point E' will be chosen. At that point, consumption in year 0 is only the social subsistence but it is possible to consume more than subsistence in year 1.

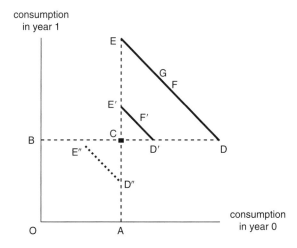

We turn to the tragic case, a country unable to meet the social-subsistence condition. This is represented by the dotted-curve D"E". Point E" falls short of the dotted line out of point B because it implies some amount of dieoff. At D" the social subsistence is available in year 0 but a short fall D"C occurs in year 1. Point D" would appear to be their 'best' choice: to live this year and to start dying off next year! While they await the famine they can pray for food-aid from outside. Some of them might migrate. We might observe a civil war, as people struggle over the inadequate means of survival.

1.5   INEQUALITY IN A SUBSISTENCE ECONOMY

Let us look now at a society producing and consuming exactly its social subsistence, but dividing it unequally. On the diagram below we have consumption per person on both axes. The distances OA and OB are subsistence consumption per person in year 0 and in year 1. (OA = OB.) The two-year subsistence-per-person condition is marked at point C.

This society is composed of five people: Persons C, D, E, F, and G. Person C gets exactly the subsistence bundle. Person D gets more and Person E gets correspondingly less. Person F gets the most while Person G gets correspondingly less. What can we say about such a society, or what might we expect? Let us group our comments into three categories:

rich . . . poor   long life . . . short life   social survival

(1) In our corn economy, the 45 degree line portrays a rich/poor spectrum. If this distribution indicates a hierarchy of decision-making power, then Person F dominates decisions while the others, down the line, obey. Under that condition, the brunt of the work will fall upon the people at the bottom. We will return to this idea in a moment.

(2) Below point C we would expect length of life to steadily decrease as we move toward the origin. At some point the level of consumption is too low to sustain life. So Person G will probably have the shortest life expectancy and person E the next shortest. Above point C we would expect length of life to increase to a maximum and then decline as obesity sets in. Hence it is not clear who would have the longest life expectancy. Person F's high consumption may be unhealthy. In addition, people below him may plan a violent coup.

(3) Lacking emergency provisions, a disaster would destroy this society. It is, however, already vulnerable. Because of undernutrition, persons G and E will have impaired productivity. If Persons C and D are the only well-nourished workers, production of the social subsistence may not be sustainable.

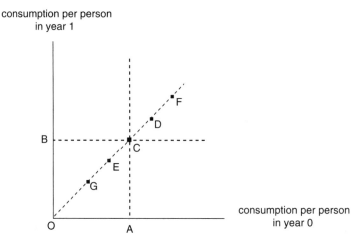

consumption per person
in year 1

B

C

D

F

E

G

O   A

consumption per person
in year 0

1.6   SOCIAL-SURVIVAL CONDITIONS

We can now gather together the conditions for social survival that have emerged from building the simplest possible model: a closed-economy corn model with zero population growth. We identified the following condition as the centerpiece of our analysis:

net output > social subsistence

We call this the production-survival condition. The survival of a society and its social order depends upon maintaining this. The following four conditions of production are necessary to assure fulfillment of this inequality:

(1) *enough corn seed* must be reserved and planted every cycle.
(2) *effective labor time* must be applied during every cycle.
(3) *enough corn food* must be produced every cycle.
(4) *adequate fertility* must be maintained from cycle to cycle.

If the net output declines below the level of social subsistence, the population will deteriorate in one or both of two ways. First, as health conditions worsen, the average length of life will decline. Second, unless the birthrate increases to compensate, the population will begin to shrink. If the suffering becomes prolonged and acute, social instability and violence will occur. Challenges to the leadership will eventually emerge. In the best case, the society will be reorganized. In the worst case, the society will suffer apocalypse.

In addition to the four conditions of production—which are generally binding—we can identify three more conditions that bind more loosely but cannot be ignored if societies are to survive over long periods of time:

(1) *emergency provisions for potential disasters*
While this condition is always present it is only revealed by the onset of a disaster. The onset can be sudden, like an earthquake, or slow, like a drought. The proper size of emergency reserves can probably be estimated from the accumulated experience of a group living in a particular location.
(2) *adequate sharing of the social subsistence*
This condition may not seem binding. The squalor of the masses can long exist within view of the pampered few. It may not even bind on a generation-to-generation basis. But eventually this condition binds; it is a long-run condition sensitive to the breakdown of the primary conditions above. An oppressively unequal social order will face the dustbin of history when put to the test.
(3) *adequate sharing of information and decision making*
Since stressful and unexpected events can occur in any society, information and decision making are also relevant survival issues. Without some threshold level of cooperation, the social fabric is worn-out and can disintegrate in times of trouble. Effective cooperation depends upon information-based decision making with useful feedback mechanisms to correct for errors and changing conditions. Social conventions are put to the test here if they become obsolete.

1.7   FIVE-WORLDS THEORY

Some of those conditions can be followed up using an algebraic model. That appears in Chapter 8. There is much for us to do with the principle of social subsistence without needing recourse to algebra.

Moreover, there is another way to get at the framework for social-survival conditions that yields a bumper crop. We need to look more closely at the archetypes. Is 'rich country, poor country starving country' a complete set? How many 'worlds' are there?

Recall the centerpiece of our analysis, the production-survival condition:

$$net\ output > social\ subsistence$$

We need to find its companion, on the side of distribution. For this we consider the position of the median person. Does this person get at least his or her share of the social subsistence?

$$consumption\ of\ median\ person \geq subsistence\ per\ person$$

This gives us a distribution-survival condition. Because of inequality—a general problem—it is possible to satisfy the first condition but fail this one.

We can now divide the world into five, because there are two archetypes between our original set of three. There is a 'middle country' archetype and an 'almost failing' archetype.

The first world country satisfies both conditions easily. The second world country satisfies both conditions, but not so easily. The third world country satisfies both conditions, but with little margin for error. The forth world country satisfies the production-survival condition but fails the distribution-survival condition. The fifth world country fails both conditions.

	PRODUCTION-SURVIVAL CONDITION	DISTRIBUTION-SURVIVAL CONDITION
first world	satisfy easily	satisfy easily
second world	satisfy	satisfy
third world	satisfy somewhat	satisfy barely
fourth world	satisfy poorly	fail
fifth world	fail	fail miserably

These are the five worlds of survival-conditions analysis. The fourth world is in a twilight, with one foot in life and one foot out of it. Most of South Asia and Africa probably fit in here. While the first condition is probably met, the second is not: the median person is undernourished, undereducated, and undercared for.

The fifth world is a bleak land of sharply falling life expectancy, and, possibly, shrinking population. Fourth worlders come and go from here.

The fourth world poor live hard lives in vicious cycles of poverty. The fifth world poor find life even more bitter. What does it take so they may have life and have it abundantly?

2

LIFE EXPECTANCY

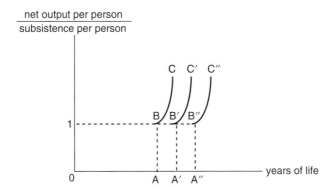

Corn + Cod + Quinine
Quality of Subsistence and the Life-Expectancy Curve

2.1 HISTORICAL PERSPECTIVE[1]

Let us begin with a handy formula from demography. If we set aside the possibility of migration, a stationary population implies a particular relationship between births, deaths, and life expectancy:

> In a *stationary population*, the birth rate equals the death rate, and they both have a reciprocal relationship with life expectancy. When we calculate in rates 'per 1000', we have:

$$\frac{1000}{life\ expectancy} = death\ rate = birth\ rate$$

We use this formula to calculate a table when birth rate = death rate, for life expectancies from 10 to 100 years, in decades. Four zones emerge:

LIFE EXPECTANCY (YEARS)	BIRTH RATE = DEATH RATE (PER 1000)	ZONES
100	10	Four: Twenty-first
90	11.1	Century?
80	12.5	
70	14.3	Three: Industrial
60	16.7	
50	20	
40	25	
30	33.3	Two: Pre-industrial
20	50	
10	100	One: Impossible

Let us inspect each of the zones.

Zone 1: Impossibly Low—Life Expectancy 10 and below. This is too low for social reproduction or survival because it is below the age of puberty.

Zone 2: Pre-industrial Age—Life Expectancy from 20 to 40. This included hunter-gatherer, agricultural, and commercial societies, up to 1800. This was of great importance to Malthus and was a cornerstone of his famous pessimism.

Exceptions above 40 can be traced to special factors. For example, in eighteenth-century Norway, most men were required to postpone marriage until after a 10-year military service. When they married in their thirties they were fit and mature.

Zone 3: Industrial Age—Life Expectancy from 50 to 80. Adoption of simple public health measures reduced child mortality sharply and life expectancy rose to at least 50. Advanced countries have achieved life expectancies near 80.

Zone 4: Twenty-First Century?—Life Expectancy 90 and above. Japanese women have a life expectancy of 85 years—largely attributed to lifestyle. Advanced countries expect gains as discoveries in medicine, biology, and genetics find application. Optimists believe life expectancy can be doubled.

I mentioned Malthus. He published his famous *Essay on Population* in 1798, completely unaware of the revolution in human longevity about to occur. He thought the laws of population were fixed, with average life expectancy quite low, even in countries like Britain. At that time, life expectancies above 40 were rare. Malthus was adamant—such a state of affairs was the human lot:

> With regard to the duration of human life, there does not appear to have existed from the earliest ages of the world to the present moment the smallest permanent symptom or indication of increasing prolongation. (9.7)

Malthus was disputing the 'speculations on the perfectibility of man and society'. Those were words of reproach to the thinkers dreaming about a dramatic increase in the average length of human life. Malthus poured scorn on this belief because he thought a scanty subsistence was an eternal prospect for most people. However, we should note the way he summarizes Condorcet:

> From the improvement of medicine . . . food . . . habitations . . . a manner of living which will improve the strength of the body . . . from the destruction of the two great causes of the degradation of man, misery and too great riches, from the . . . removal of transmissible and contagious disorders . . . rendered more efficacious by the progress of reason and of social order, he [Condorcet] infers . . . the duration between . . . birth and natural death will increase without ceasing, will have no assignable term, and may be properly expressed by the word indefinite. (9.2)

This, in fact, is a striking vision of actual developments the past two centuries. Condorcet was capable of seeing areas of human activity ripe for improvement and concluded correctly that these would extend average length of life.[2] He did not have much evidence from history to support this vision. Humanity was caught by surprise, not knowing how *hugely* the combination of discovery, education, and ambition were about to transform the world.

The most famous of the optimists was Hegel. We are reminded of this by Francis Fukuyama in *The End of History* (1992). Fukuyama approvingly quotes a passage from Hegel, spoken only eight years after Malthus wrote:

> We stand at the gates of an important epoch, a time of ferment, when the spirit moves forward in a leap, transcends its previous shape and takes on a new one. All the mass of previous representations, concepts, and bonds linking our world together are dissolving and collapsing like a dream picture. A new phase of spirit is preparing itself. Philosophy especially has to welcome its appearance and acknowledge it, while others who oppose it impotently, cling to the past. (Fukuyama quoting G.W.F. Hegel in a lecture on September 18, 1806)[3]

Spirit moves forward in a leap! Malthus was one of the clingers to the past. He thought the subsistence problem could never be solved. He was wrong, but not entirely wrong. Part of the world has moved forward in that leap, leaving Malthus in the dust. Much of the world, however, has yet to make the transition. The Hegelian and Malthusian worlds coexist. The gap may be growing.

2.2   LIFE-EXPECTANCY CURVE

In Chapter 1, when discussing inequality, we found a relationship between access to subsistence or surplus and life expectancy. Let us develop this idea.

Using our corn model, the subsistence bundle contains an amount long established for a corn worker and is associated with a particular life expectancy.

Consider the following diagram. Years of life are on the horizontal axis. The production-survival condition, in ratio *and* per-person form, is on the vertical. A ratio of one is marked on that axis. A person living at this level is consuming his/her share of the social subsistence. The distance OA shows the expected length of life for such a person. Point B is the first point on the curve.

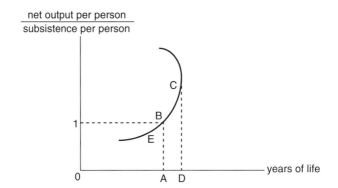

Consumption above point B will tend to extend human life, up to a certain limit. This is indicated by point C. If everyone could attain the distance CD, life expectancy would be OD. Note that AD is a fraction of the distance OA. This indicates the primary role played by subsistence in determining life expectancy.

Below point B, people get less than their share of the social subsistence. Life expectancy decreases as the bundle gets smaller. An 80 percent bundle is indicated at point E. At a certain point below E, the curve ends because the bundle is too small to support human life.

What is the shape of the curve above point C? Is it inelastic or does it bend in? In a corn model it will *always* bend in because the body has a limited ability to convert food into energy. Overeating will tend to reduce years of life.

In general it is possible to overconsume *any* subsistence good. So, as a general principle, life-expectancy curves will always bend in eventually.

Now we can state one of the main theoretical and empirical ideas in the book:

> the higher the *quality* of the social subsistence,
> and the more *equitable* its distribution,
> the longer the life expectancy.

In order to develop this idea, we need to add some high-quality subsistence goods to the usual bundle anticipated by an average worker and his/her family.

2.3 QUALITY OF SUBSISTENCE

We derived the life-expectancy curve assuming only corn is consumed. Such a diet would invariably have a relatively short life expectancy because essential nutrients would be lacking. Let us add two subsistence goods to the bundle, starting with cod, a high-protein food, found, we assume, in a local lake.

A protein-enhanced diet will feed the body and the brain in beneficial ways. First of all, the better nourishment will make human beings stronger and less vulnerable to disease. Secondly, the energy-enhanced body and mind will have more productive capacity. These changes will increase life expectancy.

Let us see this on a diagram. We will only consider the simplest case, where the impact of an additional subsistence good shifts the life-expectancy curve to the right in a *parallel* fashion. We are only interested in two points from the previously established curve: at subsistence and at the maximum benefit.

In the corn model, OA is life expectancy for subsistence-level consumption; point B is the starting point of the life-expectancy curve; and point C is the maximum benefit from consuming corn.

The introduction of cod into the subsistence bundle increases life expectancy at the subsistence level from OA to OA′. Point B shifts to point B′. Since we assume the life-expectancy curve shifts to the right in the simplest way, point C moves to point C′. Compare point B′ with point C. In this illustration, because of the wonderful protein-related attributes of cod, the new subsistence bundle supports life better than the best corn-only bundle.

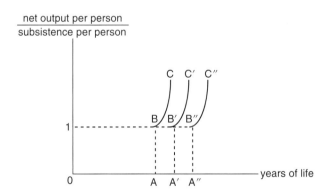

Now we introduce quinine, a potent curative, found in the bark of a native tree. When consumed in a corn mush, it relieves deadly fevers and can prevent them. When quinine is added to the subsistence bundle, life expectancy increases from OA′ to OA″. Point B′ shifts to point B″ and point C′ moves to point C″.

Once again, life expectancy was significantly extended by the introduction of a powerful subsistence good. Compare point B″ with point C′. In this illustration, because of the great impact on curing or preventing deadly diseases, the new subsistence bundle supports life better than the best corn+cod bundle.

2.4 ANTHRODEMOGRAPHY ALLEGORY

FIELD REPORT
From: Adam Godwin, PhD Candidate in Anthrodemography
To: Honorable Sensei, Professor of Anthrodemography, Highland University
Regarding: Life among the People in Trinity Valley on Sandieu Island

Dear Professor Sensei:

In my last days of fieldwork among the people of Trinity Valley, the Chief GreenThumb included me in a yearly ceremony called 'the remembering'. It took place in the village temple, which they call the 'divine storehouse'. Because of the information shared at that ceremony I am able to file this report.

Let me begin with a map of Trinity Valley. The people live in corncob houses on the west side of the village. These are clustered in roundish groups. The cornfield is in the south-central region, watered from the lake by a simple irrigation system. The lake is found on the east side. It is very rich with cod. Quinine trees grow natively on the northwest shore of the lake.

The divine storehouse is located near the middle of the valley. The corn harvest is blessed at the altar in batches. The first batch, called the 'life giver', is the seed to be set aside for the next harvest. Then they bless the corn food in small batches. Each batch is the size of the family subsistence bundle.

They also have a ceremony to bless the quinine. The Chief GreenThumb gathers the bark in small batches and removes the bitter-tasting curative salt. It is then stored in a special corncob box on the altar of the divine storehouse. The gods, themselves, are said to give the quinine its potency.

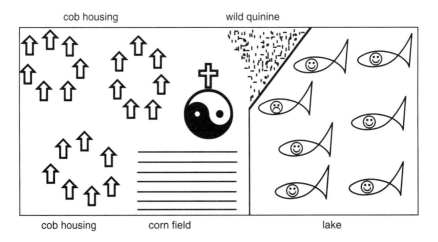

I was surprised to learn that the fish caught in the lake are not blessed in the divine storehouse. The Chief GreenThumb laughed at me, saying, "You think we should stink up the place?" He thought I must come from a crude society. "Everyone knows," he said, "that cod should be blessed at the shore."

Now: let me tell you about 'the remembering'. It was the first full moon after the spring harvest. Everyone sat in circles in the divine storehouse. The Chief GreenThumb took some very old quinine and herbs and prepared a ceremonial pipe. The tribe was silent. He held the pipe in the air and said, "Tonight we thank our gods and remember our ancestors."

Then the Chief GreenThumb lit the pipe from a fire always kept burning at the altar. A great aroma filled the room. Then the pipe was passed from adult to adult. It had a calming effect on these already calm working people.

After circulating the pipe three times, the Chief GreenThumb spoke again. "We thank our gods for our corn, our cod, and our quinine. Tonight we remember how our ancestors became civilized people.

"In the distant past we lived in another valley, five mountains away. We knew only the wild corn. We gathered, we ate. We gathered, we ate. We were few in number. Then the first Chief GreenThumb had a dream.

"In the dream he was visited by the god of corn seed. The god said, 'Plant and eat and multiply.' The first Chief GreenThumb obeyed the command. As the amount of corn increased, the tribe grew in size. At that time we learned the many uses of corncob and corn sheath. After a few generations we filled the valley with corn and with people until the land could support no more.

"Then the Chief GreenThumb was visited in a dream by the god of the lake. The god said, 'Catch and eat and live longer.' Then we ate cod with our corn. We became stronger and grew in wisdom. We could see farther, run faster and think better. By the grace of our gods we had fewer children.

"Generations passed. Then the Chief GreenThumb was struck down by the fever. Near death, the god of the quinine came to him in a dream and said, 'Arise and chew!' With his last bit of strength he walked to the quinine woods, pulled some bark, and chewed on the white area he had seen in the dream. The next day he awoke, fully restored.

"With this blessing we lived longer. But our numbers began to grow and grow. After a few generations we emptied the lake of cod. We started to live fewer moons. We started to have more children. Without the cod we were senseless."

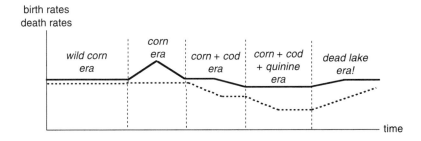

After the Chief GreenThumb said those words, everyone stood up. They walked clockwise in three circles. In unison, they cried, "Not this generation, not this generation!" Then they looked at each other and hugged. They sat down. The Chief GreenThumb spoke again.

"After the War between the Brothers we buried the dead. We started to walk towards the rising sun. We had no idea where we were going. We walked and we walked. For months we found no lake. Finally, after much suffering, with our numbers small, we came to this beautiful valley.

"That night, the Chief GreenThumb was visited by the gods. They called this place Trinity Valley. They gave it to us for all eternity. May this be so." Then the entire group stood up and said, "May this be so. The gods be with us."

Then, the Chief GreenThumb took a cod liver oil *wafer* from a box. He held it in the air and said, "This is the body of a god! Eat this wafer so a god may be in you!" Everyone walked up to the altar. The Chief GreenThumb put a wafer on each tongue. It was the most reverential moment I have ever observed.

After the ceremony, everyone gathered by the shore of the lake for a party. It seemed to me to be a charming dreamscape. While drinking a quinine tea, I sat down next to the Chief GreenThumb. I thanked him for including me.

I asked him when they adopted the sacred-wafer ritual. He replied, "My grandfather was granted that revelation. As long as we do not overfish the lake, the gods promise a bright future. The sacred wafer is the symbol and body of that covenant. For our part, we delay marriage in order to control our number."

I asked the Chief GreenThumb how they achieved the wisdom to maintain balance in Trinity Valley. He was happy with the question. "Over many moons we learned the Law of Harmony. It is possible to consume too much or too little of any good thing. For example, the quinine protects us from the fever and calms our nerves. But if we consume too much we damage ourselves.

"The fish is a greater mystery. Without it we are dull and reproduce too often. If we consume too much cod we become puffed up with our own cleverness. Then the gods punish us with sterility!" He laughed. Light radiated from his face. "Isn't it amazing? The body of a god lives in a cod?"

	Main Attributes	Under Consumption	Over Consumption	Demographic Impact When Introduced
domesticated corn	calories	underweight	overweight	higher birth rate
cod	protein	dull brain	too clever	lower death rate
	birth control	excess fertility	sterility	lower birth rate
quinine	curative	fevers	organ damage	lower death rate
cod liver oil	preventative	weak immunity	organ damage	lower death rate
delayed marriage				lower birth rate

2.5   CIVILIZATIONAL CRISES

Let us put our model building aside and consider two contemporary crises. We begin with Russia, followed by Southern Africa.

2.5.1   CRISIS IN RUSSIA

It is easy to forget the great achievements of the Soviet Union. It excelled in science, sports, and space. In arts and literature it was greatly admired. But by 1970, the Soviet Union hit its upper-productivity limits. The inefficiencies of a centrally planned economy reached a critical mass. Stagnation set in.

According to Russia's official statistics, life expectancy reached a peak in 1964–65 and gradually fell by three years for males, reaching a trough in 1979–80. During the same period, life expectancy was gradually rising in the first world.

The brief upturn in the mid-1980s is attributed to Gorbachev's antialcohol campaign. After the unpopular policy was suspended, life expectancy drifted lower again. As the Soviet Union unraveled, life expectancy of males fell dramatically. Today that figure for Russia is still below the trough of 1979–80.

LIFE EXPECTANCY IN RUSSIA	1964–65 (PEAK)	1979–80 (TROUGH)	1986–87 (PEAK)	1994 (TROUGH)	2005*
male	64.6	61.5	64.9	57.6	60.5
female	73.3	73.0	74.5	71.2	74.0
average	69.6	67.5	70.1	64.0	67.1

Source: Demographic Yearbook of Russia (Moscow: Official Statistical Handbook, 1996), 103.
CIA Factbook—Russia, http://www.odci.gov/cia/publications/factbook (accessed March 1, 2006).

The rise of the death rate in Russia tells much of the story, specially the rise between 1990 and 1995. This was driven by many factors. The failed Soviet system induced great economic and social insecurity. The healthcare system was starved for funds and deteriorated. And lifestyle habits took a turn for the worse as the depressed population increased consumption of tobacco, alcohol, and drugs, often at the expense of nutrition.

When we bring in birth rates we observe another aspect of the reversal of Russian fortunes. In 1960, Russia was reaching the end of its postwar baby boom. With the ageing of the population, death rates rose gradually, reducing the natural increase in population. But the sharp decrease in birth rates after 1985, coupled with the increase in death rates, led to a negative net birth rate. For well over a decade, the Russian population has had a tendency to contract.

RUSSIA	1960	1965	1970	1975	1980	1985	1990	1995	2000*	2005*
birth rate	23.2	15.7	14.6	15.7	15.9	16.6	13.4	9.3	9.0	9.8
death rate	7.4	7.6	8.7	9.8	11.0	11.3	11.2	15.0	13.9	14.5
net	15.8	8.1	5.9	5.9	4.9	5.3	2.2	−5.7	−4.9	−4.7

Source: Demographic Yearbook of Russia (Moscow: Official Statistical Handbook, 1996), 53.
CIA Factbook—Russia (accessed March 1, 2006).

2.5.2 *CRISIS IN SOUTHERN AFRICA*

While the Russia case is dramatic, the problem in Africa is breathtaking. Some countries there have suffered a collapse in life expectancy. Botswana and Zimbabwe are *far below* their life expectancies in 1960! They started off then much ahead of the pack in Sub-Saharan Africa, with life expectancies of a decade greater than the regional average. What happened to them?

In Botswana, life expectancy has fallen 28 years from its 1985 peak. It has been ravaged by HIV/AIDS, with an infection rate of more than a third. On the basis of mining, it is ranked as an upper-middle income country. The government can afford, and has in place, a comprehensive treatment program.

LIFE EXPECTANCY	1960 –65	1965 –70	1970 –75	1975 –80	1980 –85	1985 –90	1990 –95	1995 –00	2000 –05
Sub-Sahara	41.4	43.4	45.3	47.2	48.6	**49.4**	48.2	47.0	45.9
Botswana	51.5	53.3	56.1	60.0	63.3	**65.1**	64.2	51.9	36.6
Zimbabwe	52.4	54.0	55.6	57.7	60.3	**61.7**	56.4	43.8	37.2

Source: *World Population Prospects: The 2004 Revision Population Data Base*,
United Nations, http://esa.un.org/unpp (accessed March 1, 2006).
Note: Peak shown in bold.

Zimbabwe is complex. Life expectancy decline set in the 1980s and continued. To divert attention from AIDS and a foolish war in the Congo, Mugabe turned against the whites, renounced the racial reconciliation upon which the country was founded and gave white-owned lands to 'war vets' and cronies. Agriculture broke down. Coffin making flourished! Terror keeps Mugabe in power.

Both countries had flatout, fullon population growth for *decades*, with high birth rates and low death rates. It could not go on forever—or even very long. Death rates shot up the last decade while birth rates eased. The HIV rate is higher in Botswana, which might account for much of its lower net birth rate.

	1960 –65	1965 –70	1970 –75	1975 –80	1980 –85	1985 –90	1990 –95	1995 –2000	2000 –05	HIV RATE*
Botswana										37% in 2003
birth rate	47.9	47.2	47.5	45.5	41.9	36.6	32.0	29.8	26.7	
death rate	15.9	14.3	12.2	9.6	7.5	6.3	6.5	12.5	25.0	
net	32.0	32.9	32.3	35.9	34.4	30.3	25.5	17.3	1.7	
Zimbabwe										25% in 2001
birth rate	48.1	48.7	48.7	46.8	44.9	40.3	36.1	32.1	30.0	
death rate	15.0	13.9	12.8	11.3	9.6	8.5	10.5	17.3	22.7	
net	33.1	34.8	35.9	35.5	35.3	31.8	25.6	14.8	7.3	

Source: *World Population Prospects*. *CIA Factbook—Russia* (accessed March 1, 2006).

Both potentially face depopulation from the net birth rate going negative or from emigration. Members of the Zimbabwe regime have sometimes praised the possibility of depopulation. Life expectancy there might plunge further.

2.6   AVERAGE AND MEDIAN AGES AT DEATH

In the previous section we worked with life-expectancy figures. Usually only one figure is reported: life expectancy at birth. This obscures a great difference between the upper and lower worlds. Let us get another angle by comparing average and median ages at death.

Life expectancy at birth can also be called average age at death; that is how it is calculated. For example, suppose we get data on all the people who died in 1990 in Country β. We would sum the years they lived and divide by the number who died to calculate the average age at death. This figure would be reported as life expectancy at birth. That is its conventional, polite, name.

Median age at death is the years of life of the *median person* in that group. We would 'line them all up', from the youngest to the oldest, and identify the age at death of the fiftieth percentile person.

The chart below contains World Bank data for 1990. Three of the areas are in the poorworlds. The other two come from the first world (established market economies) and the second world (formerly socialist economies in Europe). A pattern is evident: While it makes *no difference* which indicator is used in the first and second worlds, there is a huge gap in the poorworlds.

The life-expectancy figure for Sub-Saharan Africa is probably lower now because of AIDS but the median age at death might be higher because AIDS kills many adults.

Still, a five-year median age at death in Africa should come as a shock, reminding us of ancient conditions. It is easy to see why governments in Africa do not publish it! It would be political dynamite, a stark reminder of failure.

What about the other average/median gaps? The gaps are large in the Muslim world (37 years) and in India (21 years). What determines their size?

1990	SUB-SAHARAN AFRICA	INDIA	MIDDLE EAST CRESCENT	FORMERLY SOCIALIST ECONOMIES	ESTABLISHED MARKET ECONOMIES
life expectancy at birth—years	52	58	61	72	76
median age at death—years	5	37	24	72	75
fertility rate—per adult woman	6.4	4.0	5.0	2.2	1.7
child mortality rate—per 1000	175	127	111	22	11

Source: *World Development Report 1993* (New York: Oxford University Press, 1993), 200–01.

Based upon consideration of fertility and child mortality data, we may venture a preliminary hypothesis:

(1) the larger the fertility rate, the larger the gap.
(2) the larger the child mortality rate, the larger the gap.
(3) the gap is insignificant or disappears if these rates are low.

Although beyond the scope of this book, this requires more investigation.

2.7 GLOBAL HIERARCHY

2.7.1 *THE PRINCIPLE OF SOCIAL SUBSISTENCE*

We should consider the global scene in light of the social-subsistence theory presented here and in Chapter 1. According to this theory, countries with the best quality social subsistence, well distributed, will have the longest life expectancies. Countries with the worst quality social subsistence, badly distributed, will have the shortest life expectancies.

This stands outside of the common opinion that relates life expectancy to income. For example, the *World Development Report* on Health just cited expresses the usual opinion (on page 34) and shows a rough correlation. Since social accountants do not measure social subsistence, we cannot make a similar calculation. But we can make an attempt to justify our position.

First, only countries that have solved the subsistence problem can achieve and maintain high life expectancy. This requires, at a minimum, good nutrition, widely available; access to enough education to participate intelligently in the social division of labor and in prudent household management; and, access to public health measures appropriate for different stages of the life cycle. None of these requires high levels of per-capita income. They *do* require a commitment by governments to achieve and maintain standards in these areas.

The following data illustrates the point. Costa Rica, with a *quarter* of the per-capita income of the United States has the same life expectancy. Chile and Cuba approach the American level of life expectancy.

Moreover, even though there is a huge gap between income levels in upper-middle and lower-middle income countries, they have the same life expectancy.

	GROSS NATIONAL INCOME PER CAPITA PPP BASIS— U.S DOLLARS (2000)	LIFE EXPECTANCY (1999)
United States	34,260	77
Costa Rica	8,250	77
Chile	9,110	76
Cuba	1,700*	76
upper-middle income countries	9,170	69
lower-middle income countries	4,580	69

Source:World Development Report 2002, 232–3, 240.
*CIA Factbook—Cuba (accessed May 1, 2002).

Many countries have a life expectancy greater than the United States while having per-capita incomes 10–30 percent lower. The *long* list includes (in order of life expectancy): Japan, Singapore, Australia, Switzerland, Sweden, Canada, Iceland, Spain, France, and Norway. In all of these countries, the *quality* of the social subsistence is superb and very few people are excluded. The United States also has a high quality social subsistence but it has poverty and lifestyle problems.

2.7.2   PERFECTIONISM MISGUIDED?

Although I believe the main determinant of life expectancy is found in the principle of social subsistence—reinforced or undermined by lifestyle—it is possible the centrality of social subsistence will be superseded by genetic science in the leading countries. At the turn of the century, BBC News had an exciting headline hinting at this possibility:[4]

Altered flies live twice as long

The old debate between Malthus and the perfectionists has taken a new turn. While much of the world is still incapable of solving the subsistence problem, another part continues to move farther ahead.

What, actually, has been discovered?

> The fruit flies lived for between 69 and 71 days—the [insects] would normally die after about 37 days . . . The gene mutation appears to work by restricting energy absorption on a cellular level—in effect, putting the cells on a diet . . . "This study points to the possibility that if you genetically alter metabolism, you can alter lifespan" . . .

If this research eventually translates into human applications, it would appear to be good news for those who can afford it, or inherit it, through reproduction. Right now, the pursuit of *profitable* life-extending breakthroughs is heating up. Competition for profits and for fame assures much effort in this direction.

At present we see the first world, with life expectancy near 80 years, and a slight tendency toward depopulation because of low birth rates. And we see the fourth and fifth worlds with life expectancies in the range of 30 to 60 years and high birth rates. There is great danger here.

For suppose life expectancy is actually doubled in the first world during this century, while the fourth and fifth worlds make little progress. At what point do the 'superior' groups, who struggle to maintain their numbers, look down on the teaming masses in the poorworlds as 'useless eaters'? At what point does the split in human development give rise to the notion of 'a new species'? At what point does the 'new species' decide to violently reduce the population of the 'old species'?

We cannot rule these questions out. Francis Fukuyama has warned us of *Our Posthuman Future* (2002). Vicious cycles of poverty show no sign of solution in the fourth and fifth worlds. Global pressures on natural resources—specially fresh water, forests, and fuels—guarantee tensions and unhealthy competition. There is talk of an 'optimum global population'. Websites such as dieoff.com and dismantle.org promote depopulation. The latter site recommends an 85 percent reduction in population!

Will the leading civilizations of this century go down that road?

3

POPULATION

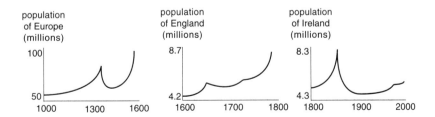

Depopulation and Repopulation

3.1   GLOBAL POPULATION EXPLOSION

The population booms of antiquity were driven by the improved capacity to feed larger numbers and support diversification in the division of labor. In recent centuries a new element has come into the picture. The discovery of simply health interventions lead to a drastic decline in death rates. The potential of a population boom was *magnified* into a population explosion.

The following chart contains the relevant global data. We observe a boom become an explosion during the second half of the twentieth century. Today the population stands at over six billion.

The annual increments have started to decrease but they are expected to add tens of millions per year for decades. We expect our seven billionth person in 2013 and our nine billionth person in 2054. That is within the lifetime of today's students. Most of these extra billions will be in the poorworlds. Is it realistic to expect that jobs and resources will be sufficient locally to assure the production and consumption of at least subsistence bundles?

FROM 1 BILLION TO 6 BILLION IN ONLY 195 YEARS.
WORLD POPULATION REACHED:

1 billion in 1804
2 billion in 1927
3 billion in 1960
4 billion in 1974
5 billion in 1987
6 billion in 1999
7 billion expected in 2013
8 billion expected in 2028
9 billion expected in 2054

Source: *The World at Six Billion* (New York: UN PDF, 1999), 8.

As we see in the following chart, the world is living in three distinct zones, now politely referred to as 'more, less, and least'. The net birth, fertility, and life expectancy indicators give a snapshot of demographic life in the zones.

The high net birth rates in the poorworlds cannot go on forever. How will it be resolved: with lower birth rates, higher death rates, or some combination? Will the poorest countries experience a stabilization of population or will some of them depopulate?

REGIONS 2000–05	BIRTH RATE PER 1000	DEATH RATE PER 1000	NET BIRTH RATE PER 1000	FERTILITY RATE PER WOMAN	LIFE EXPECTANCY AT BIRTH
more developed	11	10	1	1.6	76
less developed	24	9	15	2.9	63
least developed	36	13	23	5.0	53
world	21	9	12	2.7	65

Source: *World Population Prospects* (http://esa.un.org/unpp) (accessed March 5, 2006).

3.2 INCOMPLETE DEMOGRAPHIC TRANSITION

Thus far only a small part of the world has passed through a demographic transition to low birth and death rates. While death rates have been brought down almost everywhere, birth rates remain high in most of the poorworlds.

We should keep in mind the story from our chapter on life expectancy. When a simple medical intervention leads to a huge fall in the death rate, it does *nothing* to assure sustainable means of subsistence for that population. If they exceed the carrying capacities of their natural and social capital, they cannot complete the demographic transition—and they invite disaster.

Consider the case of India. Its population grew more than fourfold in the past century, with a current density of over 320 per square kilometer. Most of that growth was during the past half century. India is still growing rapidly. Will it complete the demographic transition or will it Malthusize?

INDIA	POPULATION (MILLIONS)	DENSITY PER SQUARE KILOMETER
1901	238	77
1951	361	117
2001*	1027	324

Source: Ashish Bose, *Demographic Diversity of India* (Delhi: B.R. Publishing Co., 1991), 48–49.
*Ashish Bose, *India's Billion Plus People* (Delhi: B.R. Publishing Co., 2001), 29 and 31.

The following table contains birth and death rates from 1911 until 2005. Although birth rates have fallen greatly during the past quarter century, population growth is still strong. It will end *eventually*. Will this come about through further declines in the birth rate, higher death rates, or both?

INDIA	1911	1921	1931	1941	1951	1961	1971	1981	1991	2005*
birth rate	49.2	48.1	46.4	45.2	39.9	41.7	41.2	37.2	32.6	22.3
death rate	42.6	47.2	36.3	31.2	27.4	22.8	19.0	15.0	11.1	8.2
net	6.6	0.9	10.1	14.0	12.5	18.9	22.2	22.2	21.5	14.1

Source: K. Srinivasan and Michael Valssoff, eds, *Population-Development Nexus in India* (New Delhi, Tata McGraw-Hill Publishing Company Limited, 2001), 36.
CIA Factbook—India (accessed March 5, 2006).

Both look likely. India may not be advanced enough to sustain the low death rates, but birth-control ideas appeal to women. If anything can save India it will be education and economic opportunities for women.

Depopulation could eventually haunt India. Population already presses against resource constraints. Caste and fundamentalism undermine development efforts. India might lack the leadership to solve these problems. The grudge match with Pakistan diverts resources from accumulation to 'defense' while many men are given to flights of nationalistic bombast. Finally—perhaps decisively—the average adult is still seriously undereducated. Such a population may not be well situated to solve grave social and ecological problems but it is a candidate for sharply higher death rates, even to the point of depopulation.

3.3   DEPOPULATION AND REPOPULATION

Bouts of depopulation were still known in medieval- and early-modern Europe. Three depopulation patterns can be observed based upon this history.[1] Let us begin with the greatest depopulation ever known there.

In 1347, the Bubonic Plague swept into Europe along trade routes from China. By 1351, one-third of Europe had perished. Oriental rat fleas carried on the back of black rats spread the plague. Fleabites initially spread it.

The sudden decline in population disrupted every aspect of life. Villages disappeared, and downsized cities were suddenly without skilled workers. Lender/creditor relations were entirely disrupted. The ranks of priests and monks were sharply reduced. There must have been a lingering mental depression because depopulation continued until the end of the fourteenth century. It took two centuries for population to reach its former peak.

By 1400, memory of the 'Black Death' was fading into history. There was a favorable land per-person ratio. The population boom *accelerated dramatically* in the sixteenth century. As we see, on the next page, this sustained population boom posed certain problems for the agrarian bureaucratic societies of the day.

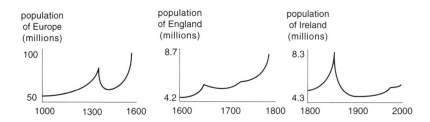

England was visited again by the Bubonic Plague in the mid-seventeenth century. The worst outbreak occurred in 1665. It started in a poor, over-crowded London neighborhood. Better-off families fled the city: 15 percent of London's population died that summer.

The first three decades of the eighteenth century saw a sharp rise in death rates correlated with a sharp rise in alcohol consumption. Cholera epidemics in 1731 and 1732 contributed to England's last-ever (brief and slight) depopulation.

The Irish case was as dramatic as the Black Death. To this day Ireland's population has never recovered. A disastrous potato blight struck in 1845 and worsened in 1846. After that, seed was scarce. Englishmen owned most of the land and most Irishmen depended upon potatoes for survival. Nonagricultural employment was very limited. The British government response was tepid and inadequate. This was a perfect-storm for mass starvation and emigration.

The depopulation continued well into the twentieth century. The shock of the Great Famine combined with British colonialism to induce waves of emigration. Birth rates declined as marriage and fertility rates fell dramatically.

3.4   CAPITAL-ACCUMULATION CRISIS

Jack Goldstone has studied deeply the problem of population growth running ahead of the accumulation of private and social capital. His book *Revolution and Rebellion in the Early Modern World* (1991) investigates this problem. With his eyes focused mainly on the seventeenth century, he observes massive challenges to state authority as country after country suffered a decline in productive and administrative capacities per capita.

The context for this is elaborated by Goldstone in the following way:

> Large states of the early modern period . . . faced certain common constraints. They needed to raise sufficient revenues to support their armies and reward their retainers. They needed sufficient allegiance from the elites to secure loyal officials for government service and, perhaps more importantly, to secure loyal local authorities in an era when centrally appointed officialdom rarely penetrated below the county level. And they needed to provide sufficient stability and sustenance for the working and cultivating population so that the latter could pay their taxes and other obligations and yet not be inclined to support rebellions. Thus any train of events that simultaneously led to fiscal deterioration, elite factionalism and disloyalty, and a major decline in popular living standards or undermining of popular traditional rights, threatened the ability of the states to maintain their authority . . .
>
> Put simply, large agrarian states of this period were not equipped to deal with the impact of the steady growth of population . . . eventually amounting to population increases in excess of the productivity gains of the land. (24)

An interpretation of his analysis appears in the following diagram. When capital per person falls steadily, crisis occurs at three levels.

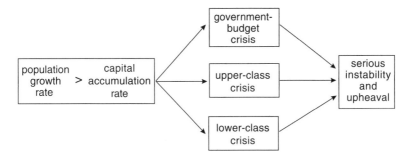

The lower classes are squeezed from several directions. Land per person shrinks as it is divided into smaller pieces each generation. Subdivisions become excessive when the land cannot provide for family subsistence. Lower classes also suffer unemployment and inflation.

The sons in upper classes wish for easy appointment to well-respected institutions. After a while there are not enough jobs to go around. Inflation eats at old wealth. At the same time, the state uses up its lines of credit and goes bankrupt. Serious suffering and instability occur. Ruin may be in the air in such strange times. Military intervention and rule is a possibility. So is breakdown.

3.5 ECOLOGICAL CRISIS

That was an exercise in 'political demography'. The problem of inadequate capital accumulation appears to haunt much of the poorworlds today. Let us get another angle on this matter by considering 'political ecology'.[2]

This analysis also begins with a population boom. But here the emphasis is on the differential effects of rapid population growth on resources and the environment. We shall follow 'upper' and 'lower' effects—the upper pertaining to the ruling classes and the lower pertaining to the lower classes.

Let us start with the lower. In the face of a population boom, existing farms are subdivided and people spread out to marginal lands in an effort to eke out a living. Such lands do not support life very well. The overcultivation of older farms may render them infertile. If efforts to cultivate fail, people will have to migrate, perhaps into urban slums or across an international border. Established social bonds are weakened in the process.

In the meantime, the elites try to figure out how to exploit whatever natural resources the country might have. If there are rich deposits of valuable resources underground, they might find foreign partners with the needed experience and capital. Any exploitation of natural resources is usually done without concern for the environment. While their eyes are filled with $-signs they are oblivious to the suffering of the lower classes.

Anything that worsens the chronic deprivation of the lowest classes will lead to a stark choice: refuge or death. If the elites fail to consider the circumstances of the poor classes, this process can eventually become confrontational. During the years the elites were consolidating their position, they used the power of the military, the police, and the courts to minimize the influence of 'antistate' forces. Gradually these antistate forces challenge the entrenched elites if they become well organized, with a source of funding.

If the balance of power seems to be shifting to the 'guerrillas'—for example, they are nearing the gates of the capital city—some of the elite will flee the country with their loot. (They may have already transferred it out of the country long before.) Other sections of the ruling classes will defend their authority with all the power at their command. The outcome of such a civil war is not a certain thing. A state of armed insurrection can last for decades if both sides have the required funds, weapons, human resources, and determination.

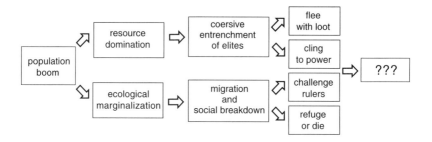

3.6   FOOD-PRODUCTION CRISIS

Per-capita food production is illustrated below using 1961 as the base year. Undernutrition was common at that time in Asia, South America, and Sub-Saharan Africa. Improvements from that date in Asia and in South America represent progress in conquering chronic undernutrition. But Africa fell behind.

Let us begin with the success of Asia and the improvement in South America. Both were in bad shape in 1961 but both improved at about the Global Average until the Oil Crisis. With Africa bringing down the average, both Asia and South America brought it up, exhibiting similar food output improvements for more than a decade. Around 1981, as China moved toward a profit-driven economy, Asia performance started to outshine South America. Scientific agriculture became a cornerstone of East Asian development.

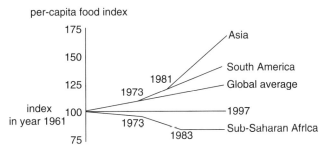

Source: Stylized version of populationaction.org/programs/afpop/afpop_fig6.htm
(accessed March 5, 2006).

By contrast, Africa floundered. Food production almost kept up with population growth until the Oil Crisis of 1973. By 1983, it stabilized at 80 percent of the 1961 figure. *Even if per capita food production could be restored to the 1961 level, it would only be restored to a past level of undernutrition.*

Why did Africa fall behind, becoming the continent of famine, war, and disease? As we just saw, in agrarian societies with feudalistic elites, population growth tends to exceed the accumulation of capital. This leads to misery and upheaval. Africa is laboring under conditions *worse* than feudalism. It has to deal with postcolonialism, corruption, and violent dictators—all layered upon tribalism. It has to adjust to nonsensical borders inherited from the colonial period. It has to survive the miseducation of the elites, who took up the false faith of Marxism-Leninism or the more subtly false faith of 'perfect competition'. And it has to pacify the Catholic and Muslim religious leaders who thunder threats of 'eternal damnation' against followers who use birth control.

The failure of scientific agriculture to take root in the minds of elites in Africa should be of great concern. So should the population boom. Africa is losing farmable acres, not gaining them by way of reclamation. If this set of circumstances continues, what will become of Africa's ability to feed itself?

With *given* technology and *limited* land, continuous population growth will not only lead to a decline in food production per person. It will eventually lead to an outright reduction in the output of food. This is illustrated on the following diagram.

Let us suppose a rural society of farmers and herders. There are three kinds of land use: farm, pasture, and wood. Suppose rapid population growth in both groups. What are we likely to observe?

First, concerning farmland, we will see the best quality land used more intensively and we will detect expansion into marginal land. Both of these will lead to a fall in output per unit of seed. Moreover, some of the expansion into land marginal from the point of view of crops will deny herders the use of land suited to their needs. So we can anticipate social conflict.

Next, the growth of herds or flocks will lead to overgrazing. This will cause soil erosion and may reduce the water table. These effects will lower productivity in the production of crops and eventually will lead to smaller herds and flocks.

Finally, the growing population will encroach upon woods and forests as the demand for fire and construction wood increases. The tendency toward deforestation will have two effects. First, it will lower the water table. Second, hillside deforestation will cause soil erosion when the rains rush unimpeded onto farmlands below. These effects will lower farmland productivity.

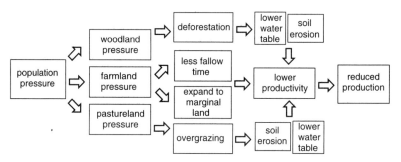

Note: Compare Thomas F. Homer-Dixon, *Environment, Scarcity and Violence* (Princeton: Princeton University Press, 1999), Figures 5.4 and 7.1.

This is a very pessimistic picture, denied by many as 'outdated'. But something nearly like this happened in Rwanda. *Traditionally*, Rwanda was a country of Hutu-farmers and Tutsi-herders. Herding requires more land per family than farming, so while the herders were a fairly small minority they controlled much of the land. However, little surplus of any kind was produced and poverty was common in both groups.

During the genocide in 1994, the Hutus were urged by their leaders to exterminate the Tutsis—the 'useless eaters'. This was a tragically classic case where *the worsening of chronic deprivation led to social disaster*. We should take a closer look at the Malthusian basis for this tragedy.

3.7   GENOCIDE IN RWANDA

Rwanda is one of the few ancient countries in Africa. Centuries ago the population was divided into farmers/Hutu and herders/Tutsi. Since herding requires more land than farming the Hutu always outnumbered the Tutsi.

When Europeans arrived, the division of land took on a different meaning. In European eyes land was the greatest source of wealth and power—something to kill and die for! In European eyes, the Tutsi were an elite minority.

Even before independence from Belgium in 1961, the resentment toward the Tutsi turned bloody. In the Social Revolution of 1959, more than 150,000 Tutsis were killed or fled into exile. The Belgians shifted support to the Hutu.

Pastureland was converted to farmland. As food availability increased, so did fertility rates. Simple health measures sharply reduced child-mortality rates.

Rwanda became the most densely populated country in Africa and the environmental pressures on the land were enormous. Daily per-capita food supply was only 82 percent of the requirement. The government squandered foreign assistance on projects in the president's home region, leaving the rest of the country to smolder in backwardness. Doom was not far away.

On April 6, 1994, President Habyarimana's plane exploded. This was the signal to the Hutu militias to begin their systematic slaughter of Tutsis.

The Malthusian basis for the tragedy can be seen in the following data. Major food crops are listed in order of output. Output in the early 1990s was not much higher than 1980 while the population was more than 2 million larger. Food availability per person in 1993 was 73 percent of the figure for 1980!

DATA FROM: AFRICAN DEVELOPMENT INDICATORS 1998–99	1980	1991	1992	1993	1994
A—population (millions)	5.16	7.15	7.35	7.54	6.23
major crops (thousands of metric tons)					
plantains	2,063	2,120	2,316	2,136	1,489
sweet potatoes	871	1,000	1,063	1,100	800
sorghum	179	205	154	109	85
maize	85	104	109	74	60
B—total major crops	3,198	3,429	3,642	3,419	2,434
per-capita food index [1980 = 100]	100	77	80	73	63

This must have been a decisive blow. Since about 90 percent of the labor force in Rwanda was connected with agriculture, the squeeze in that sector was fertile ground for a campaign to rid the country of 'cockroaches'!

About 75 percent of the Tutsi population was murdered in 100 days. The butchers were told to show no mercy—this was part of the 'Hutu Ten Commandments'. Victims were hacked to death with machetes or shot. Teachers killed student and doctors killed patients. The horror of insane hunger!

4

PRODUCTION-SURVIVAL CONDITIONS

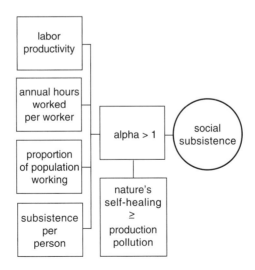

4.1 Alpha = Net Output/Social Subsistence > 1

Recall the production-survival condition:

$$net\ output > social\ subsistence$$

Let us flesh this out into a ratio analysis. Rewriting this condition as a ratio yields something we will call alpha (α):

$$alpha = \frac{net\ output}{social\ subsistence} > 1$$

Let us present it as a per-person relationship:

$$alpha = \frac{net\ output/population}{social\ subsistence/population} > 1$$

These ratios can be written for any unit of time. We will use one year as our unit. Our task is to elaborate the contents of the numerator. There are three elements, all related to labor, that belong here.

First, production always occurs within the limits of technical knowledge and hours of work. A simple economic measure of productivity is the net output relative to the *total* hours of work during the year. This includes the labor time spent replacing and expanding the capital stock. From this we define labor productivity (λ):

$$\lambda = net\ output/hours\ of\ work$$

Second, we need to introduce the number of people employed. The hours of work divided by the number of workers tells us the annual hours worked per worker (h):

$$h = hours\ of\ work/workers$$

Finally, only part of any society is engaged in production. Some of the population may be too young or too old; some may be unemployed; some may be incapable of work while others may be in a position to avoid work. So we need to know the proportion of the population engaged in production—the participation rate (ω):

$$\omega = workers/population$$

Let us call the denominator σ:

$$\sigma = social\ subsistence/population$$

We should recall from Chapter 1, the social subsistence comprises survival, productivity, *and* reproduction needs.

We may now bring the ratios together:

$$\alpha = \frac{\lambda h \omega}{\sigma} > 1$$

4.2 Alpha and Standards of Living

Let us say a bit more about each of the four components.

$$\lambda = net\ output/hours\ of\ work$$

High labor productivity is the key to high personal incomes, modest working hours, and a large middle class. This depends upon the quality of infrastructure and tools as well as the quality of labor and management. It also depends upon the rule of law, including fulfillment of contracts.

$$h = hours\ of\ work/workers$$

The length of the working year varies greatly among countries. In much of East Asia the working year is still 2,300 hours or more; in parts of Western Europe it is 1,600 hours or less. Demanding work schedules should not be confused with high labor productivity.

$$\omega = workers/population$$

In many societies about half of the population participates in the work force. The ratio is much lower in high-fertility societies because of the baby boom. It is also rather lower in societies where women are forced to remain at home.

$$\sigma = social\ subsistence/population$$

Sigma depends upon the degree of technical development. It will be small in traditional societies and large in modern societies. In Chapter 2 we studied the relationship between the *quality* of social subsistence and life expectancy.

We should bring in an environmental condition:

$$nature's\ capacity\ to\ self\text{-}purify \geq pollution\ from\ production$$

If this condition is not satisfied, the value of alpha should be *adjusted downward* in order to render environmental damage accountable.

We may be tempted to conclude that an *increase* in alpha is always desirable, or is always desirable with a given distribution. This is not necessarily valid.

For a *given* subsistence bundle (σ constant), alpha can only increase if the numerator increases. Let us suppose that productivity of labor and size of the population are unchanged. Then an increase in alpha can only occur by increasing annual hours worked per worker or the participation rate must increase.

A longer working year is generally resisted unless incomes rise significantly. An increase in the participation rate should be reckoned a gain if the unemployment rate falls but a step backward if it takes children out of schools.

In addition, an increase in alpha may be at the expense of the environment.

So we cannot use a distribution-neutral increases in alpha as an index of higher well-being without looking at the labor and environmental requirements.

4.3   SIMPLE AND COMPLEX SOCIETY

Our attention has largely focused on the numerator of the formula for alpha. We should now turn to the denominator. The denominator measures social subsistence per person. The subsistence requirements differ from community to community, and change within communities over time, specially as they industrialize. This suggests we need to distinguish *simple social reproduction* from *complex social reproduction*.

Consider a Simple community adhering to old traditions and pre-industrial technologies. The number of items in the subsistence bundle is small; it contains food, shelter, clothing, fuel, medicine, educational materials—and not much more. All of these items are derived from local resources. Very little social capital is required by the working population to maintain this society.

Now consider a Complex community; if it helps to think of a concrete example, perhaps Japan, by all means do so. This community also has the basic needs already listed. In addition, it requires schools, hospitals, roads, railways, motor vehicles, electricity, telephones, radios, televisions, flush toilets . . . and lots of watches! *All of these items* are required for the reproduction of the working population and are therefore part of the social subsistence. To maintain this system, nature is likely to be depleted in some ways and polluted—if not in the home country then in the land of some trading partners.

Let us compare two communities of equal population, the same size alpha, the same hours of work per year, and the same participation rate—but let one be Simple and the other Complex. Simple is 'underdeveloped' and 'primitive' while Complex is 'developed' and 'modern'. Which is better off?

If we look only at the social-accounting figures for aggregate consumption we may think the answer is unmistakable. Complex has more of every *thing* per person than Simple. 'Bigger is better; more is preferred to less'. This may not be the answer we would get from considering a wider set of factors. Recall:

$$\alpha = \frac{\lambda h \omega}{\sigma} > 1$$

Complex must have a higher productivity of labor (λ) to *achieve and maintain* its larger social subsistence. The people in Complex may pride themselves on their high productivity and their mass consumption and they may feel they have a duty to extend 'development assistance' to Simple.

But does this productivity advantage yield other fruit? (1) which has the longer life expectancy? (2) which is more capable of adjusting to emergency circumstances? (3) which is environmentally more sustainable? The answer to these questions is *not* certain. For example: the Amish people of Lancaster, Pennsylvania, with their horse and buggy society, may score higher on these grounds than their modern neighbors.

4.4   FOURTH-WORLD PROBLEM

It is disturbingly easy for a country to satisfy the production-survival condition—alpha > 1—but fail the distribution-survival condition.

(1) Suppose the society has 100 people, the net output equals 120 units and the social subsistence equals 100 units. Then, alpha equals 1.2.

Let us divide the population into fifths. The average output per fifth is 24 and the subsistence requirement per fifth is 20. Let us suppose the highest fifth gets 40 percent of the net output as income, the next highest fifth gets half this and the lowest 60 percent divides the remainder. This gives us clearly identifiable upper, middle, and lower classes. This is not particularly great inequality. What is the situation of the median person? Consider the numerical chart below:

	AVERAGE OUTPUT	SUBSISTENCE	INCOME	GROUP-ALPHA
highest fifth	24	20	48	2.4
fourth fifth	24	20	24	1.2
middle fifth	24	20	16	0.8
second fifth	24	20	16	0.8
lowest fifth	24	20	16	0.8

Income distribution is shown in the fourth column. We calculate *group-alphas* by dividing income by subsistence.

According to our distribution hypothesis, the highest fifth gets 48 and the next highest fifth gets 24. These groups will have alphas above one. If the remainder of the net output is equally divided, each group gets 16. The alpha of the median person will be 0.8.

Thus, in this example, with alpha of 1.2, the median person gets 0.8 of this, which is the fourth world case. We obtained this result without assuming especially large inequality.

(2) Let us now suppose the *same pattern of inequality* but with every fifth getting at least its share of the social subsistence. How high must alpha be to assure this?

In this case, the bottom 60 percent gets its full subsistence, the fourth fifth gets 30 and the highest fifth gets double that. Let us add these up: 20 + 20 + 20 + 30 + 60 = 150.

Thus, with the same pattern of inequality, in order to escape from the fourth to the third world, alpha must reach 1.5.

	AVERAGE OUTPUT	SUBSISTENCE	INCOME	GROUP-ALPHA
highest fifth	30	20	60	3
fourth fifth	30	20	30	1.5
middle fifth	30	20	20	1
second fifth	30	20	20	1
lowest fifth	30	20	20	1

4.5   ALPHA IN A POOR COUNTRY

We expect alpha to be small in very poor countries. We can make an educated guess for Bangladesh based upon poverty studies.

Recall the production-survival condition:

net output (Y_net) > social subsistence (C')

We define a similar kind of relationship in terms of aggregate poverty income:

gross income (Y) > aggregate poverty income (Y_poverty)

Gross income is greater than net output. Aggregate poverty income is the poverty line times the population. It includes survival and personal productivity needs but it *does not* include social productivity needs or reproduction needs, so it is smaller than the social subsistence. We have, therefore, the following relationship:

$$\alpha = \frac{Y_{net}}{C'} < \frac{Y}{Y_{poverty}}$$

$Y/Y_{poverty}$ sets an upper limit on the size of alpha.

The table below contains monthly figures for Y and $Y_{poverty}$ *per household* in rural Bangladesh, in 1985–86. I do not have reason to think the situation has changed much since then. The population boom has probably swamped any potential gains, specially since land per person continues to decline.

The table is organized according to land ownership, from landrich to landless. It shows average household size as well as the percent of households in each category. Variations in $Y_{poverty}$ are due to household size. $Y/Y_{poverty}$ is near one for very small landholders. It is less than 1.2 for small landholders and for the landless. It exceeds two in the families with relatively large farms.

$Y/Y_{poverty}$ is less than 1.2 for most households. This sets an upper limit on the size of alpha. Thus, *alpha was (and probably is) less than 1.2 in rural Bangladesh*. The figure for cities is likely to be better, but not much better, because slums are pervasive. This result is not surprising in the fourth world.

LAND OWNERSHIP (ACRES) 1985–86	% OF HOUSEHOLDS	AVERAGE HOUSEHOLD SIZE	Y (AVERAGE MONTHLY TAKA INCOME PER HOUSEHOLD)	$Y_{POVERTY}$ (AVERAGE MONTHLY TAKA INCOME PER POOR HOUSEHOLD)	$Y/Y_{POVERTY}$
> 7.50	3.4	9.5	7362	3397	2.17
2.50–7.49	18.4	7.1	3430	2594	1.32
0.05–2.49	46.6	5.7	1990	1671	1.19
< 0.05	0.8	3.9	1065	1004	1.06
landless	31.8	5.1	1658	1432	1.16

Source: PK. Md. Motiur Rahman, *Poverty Issues in Rural Bangladesh* (Dhaka: University Press Limited, 1994), 93.
Note: Numbers are rounded off.

4.6 ALPHA IN A RICH COUNTRY

We can also use poverty studies to help estimate alpha in a rich country. Consider the following observation by Isabel Sawhill:[1]

> [S]ome economists have argued that poverty thresholds can only be defined relative to some measure of general well-being, such as the median income, and should be indexed to changes in that measure. *One idea*, originally advanced by Victor Fuchs, *would be to define as poor all those with incomes less than one-half the median income*. In 1965, when the U.S. official poverty line was first introduced, it stood at 46 percent of the median for a family of four.

OECD follows this practice when defining and measuring the poverty line. Let us use the *inverse* of the 'one-half rule':

$$\frac{median\ income}{poverty\ line} = 2$$

We can use this to estimate the relevant range for alpha in a rich country. Let us write alpha in per-person form: average income (net of depreciation allowances) divided by subsistence per person. We can see three possibilities:

$$\frac{average\ income}{subsistence\ per\ person} > = < \frac{median\ income}{poverty\ line} = 2$$

As we know from the definition of social subsistence, subsistence per person is greater than the poverty line. So, in a rich country, alpha will systematically relate to the level '2' according to the following relation:

$$\frac{subsistence\ per\ person}{poverty\ line} \quad relative\ to \quad \frac{average\ income}{median\ income}$$

The second ratio depends upon the degree of inequality in distribution. No inequality implies the average and median are equal. Generally there is some inequality so the average is greater than the median.

Now we can see the three cases:

$= $ sign → alpha equals 2

This requires average income to exceed the median income in the same proportion subsistence per person exceeds the poverty line.

$>$ sign → alpha is greater than 2

This requires average income to exceed the median income in greater proportion than subsistence per person exceeds the poverty line.

$<$ sign → alpha is less than 2

This requires average income to exceed the median income in smaller proportion than subsistence per person exceeds the poverty line.

There is a paradox in this analysis. When poverty is defined by the 'one-half median rule', the greater the inequality in distribution the larger the alpha.

4.7   TRANSITION FROM SIMPLE TO COMPLEX

We conclude this chapter with a look at the transition from simple to complex, based upon the Euro-American experience of the pioneer industrializes. We should keep in mind this process was spread out over more than a century, as various inventions pushed the process along. (We discuss the East-Asian case of 'catch-up' in Chapters 27 and 28.)

We assume the simple society has a small social subsistence and a small alpha. We observe its transformation to a complex society with a large social subsistence and a large alpha. We can identify three phases.

$$\alpha = \frac{\lambda h \omega}{\sigma} > 1$$

Phase 1: The successful movement from simple to complex begins with an alpha above one, in order to assure an internal source of savings. With increases in the productivity of labor (λ), in annual hours worked per worker (h), and in work-force participation (ω), alpha rises. But the subsistence requirements (σ) also rise, because of the needed social and physical infrastructure. This mitigates the rise in alpha.

Phase 2: Labor organizes to reduce h—because it is abusive. This is more than offset by increases in λ; but increases in λ are, in turn, offset somewhat by increases in σ, as the new social capital required for industrial-urban society spreads to the countryside, and as the cities become more modern. Women flood into the modern work place, increasing ω. Thus, while alpha increases in the second phase, its increase is probably smaller than in the first.

Phase 3: There is again pressure on h to fall—now it is called 'demand for leisure'. The course of ω is ambiguous because the emerging ageing society might be offset by increases in the female participation rate. λ continues to move ahead but σ still follows like a shadow. Moreover, much labor must be applied to environmental matters—with a possibly significant negative impact on alpha. Thus, alpha may reach its peak in this phase.

	PRODUCTIVITY OF LABOR λ	LENGTH OF WORKING YEAR h	PARTICIPATION RATE ω	SUBSISTENCE PER PERSON σ
phase 1	up	up	up	up
phase 2	up up	down	up	up
phase 3	up up	down	?	up

Can a society *revert* to Phase 2? While it cannot 'reverse' the process, it can suffer a decline in alpha. If a society hits an upper productivity limit associated with its form of political economy, it may stagnate and decline.

The tendency toward depopulation in ageing societies may begin a new phase.

Let us look at this another way. We are especially interested in a successful escape from the poorworlds. Recall the main production-survival condition:

net output > subsistence per person × population

A few simple public health interventions lower the death rate and trigger a population boom. In order to maintain the already low level of consumption, the net output will have to grow as fast as the population. But modernization requires increasing subsistence per person: irrigation, schools, clinics/hospitals, public administration offices, roads, transportation, electricity, and communications. Thus, the net output must increase greatly for *two* reasons: larger population *and* more complex conditions of social subsistence.

Moreover, the social division of labor has an upper productivity limit determined by the extent of the infrastructure. Suppose a society has no modern form of transportation, communication, or power. Unless they specialize in artisan crafts for export, most labor will be found in agriculture. This would tend to perpetually result in simple social reproduction, as illustrated on the left-side diagram below. There, the subsistence bundle is small and social surplus per person is also small.

But suppose this society solves the basic problems of human development—eliminating undernutrition, illiteracy, and childhood diseases. The distances OA and OB (representing subsistence bundles) increase with modernization. In order to significantly improve general living conditions, labor productivity will have to increase at a much greater rate than the population and the gains will have to be spread widely.

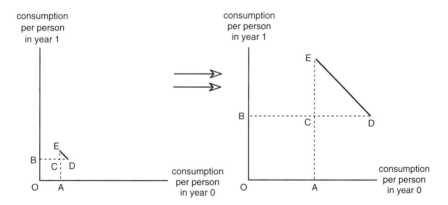

This will require effective investment in infrastructure. The right-side diagram shows a higher stage of development. The subsistence bundle is much larger but so is the capacity to produce social surplus per person. Educated people using modern infrastructure can increase productivity enough to escape from the poorworlds. Properly educated, it can be done without industrialism fullon.

5

PRODUCTIVITY LIMITS

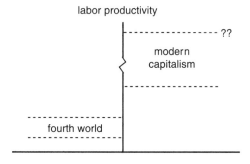

Fourth World Dilemma

5.1 SMITH AND MARX

What factors are necessary for a particular kind of society to exist, survive, and reach full maturity? To get some hints let us turn to history of economic thought.

In the *Wealth of Nations* Smith says a society's 'full complement of riches' is determined by 'the nature of its laws and institutions' as well as 'the nature of its soil and climate, and its situation with respect to other countries'. In a 'fully peopled' competitive society, this implies to Smith low wages, low profits, and low rates of interest. One can jump from here to the Ricardian conclusion that only the landlord would appear to prosper. One can get a sense of hitting an upper productivity limit—thus spelling the end of progress.

A neglected Marxian question takes a broader view: What are the upper and lower productivity limits associated with any mode of production?[1]

> (1) For any particular mode of production there is a lower limit of productivity below which it cannot exist and work at all.
> (2) Any mode of production, if it can exist and work, contains a mechanism which assures that its productivity will increase as time goes by.
> (3) Any mode of production has a certain upper limit to productivity beyond which it cannot continue to maintain itself.

Consider the case of feudalism and capitalism. The lower productivity limit in feudal society was determined by the size of the social subsistence plus the minimum social surplus expected by a landowning class. The upper productivity limit was determined by the disincentive associated with sharecropping or serfdom combined with the limitations of soil and climate.

To have a transition from feudalism to capitalism the lower productivity limit in capitalism *must overlap* the range for feudalism. To make the transition from the lower system to the higher, the *attitude toward* the use of surplus must change from desiring it for its use value to appreciating its investment value. Once the capitalistic mentality takes root, competition for profits will lead to innovation and enrichment of the division of labor.

What determines the upper productivity limit? Marx thought competition eventually ends in monopoly. With all-round monopolization he expected the great historical task of the capitalist to come to an end, followed by socialization of the means of production. This vision led humanity down a blind alley. We still await the determination of the upper productivity limits in capitalism.

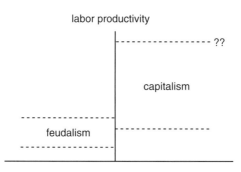

5.2   AMERICAN SLAVE SOCIETY

Fogel and Engerman, in *Time on the Cross* (1974), sought to correct common misconceptions about the economic performance of the American slave society. Let us consider this issue in our model.

From our previous discussion it would be easy to conclude that slave-based agriculture must be less productive than farms owned and run by freemen, or, even, sharecroppers. If the only factor was personal incentive this would be so. In the American case we can see other factors at play.

First of all, labor productivity in the American slave system easily exceeded European feudalism.

> By 1860 the South attained a level of per capita income which was high by the standards of the time. Indeed, a country as advanced as Italy did not achieve the same level of per capita income until the eve of World War II. (*TC*, 6)

The American South had the advantage of large, fertile lands, easily adapted to plantation production of crops greatly valued in world markets. American cotton was supplying England's textile mills; its tobacco was feeding the addictive habit of millions. Moreover,

> Slave agriculture was not inefficient compared with free agriculture. Large-scale operation, effective management, and intensive utilization of labor and capital made southern slave agriculture 35 percent more efficient than the northern system of family farming. (*TC*, 5)

The lack of *positive* incentive could be more than overcome by large-scale production combined with coercion. Given favorable trading conditions,

> Far from stagnating, the economy of the antebellum South grew quite rapidly. Between 1840 and 1860, per capita income increased more rapidly in the South than in the rest of the nation. (*TC*, 6)

The upper productivity limit in the North, however, certainly exceeded that of the South. There was no legal bar on education or labor mobility. Resources did not have to be expended to maintain a system of human bondage. The introduction of new products or technologies was stimulated purely by profit incentive. They were not held back by considerations of 'is it good for slavery?' And, they were not the heirs of a system that could be Gone with the Wind.

```
              labor productivity (1860)
                            |
                            |------------------ ??
                            |
                            |       Yankee
                            |       capitalism
                            |
                            |   -------------------
                            |
                            |       American
          -------------------       slave
                            |       society
              European     |
              feudalism     |
          -------------------------------------
          _____
```

5.3   INEQUALITY, ELITE INTENT, AND PROGRESS

Let us look at matters more abstractly in 'story form' to gain another view. Suppose a society lives under grinding poverty and great inequality. The upper-class families (H) only consider their personal comfort and social power. A small middle class (M) serves their refined needs. The huge lower class (L) is treated as fodder. This situation is shown on the left side of the diagram.

Suddenly an enlightened ruler comes to power. He reads a sentence once spoken by Adam Smith and is smitten by its words:

> Little else is requisite to carry a state to the highest degree of opulence from the lowest barbarism, but peace, easy taxes, and a tolerable administration of justice . . . (from a lecture given in Edinburgh, winter of 1750–51)

He sets out to follow this advice. He is heartened when one of his radical subjects brings to his attention a Marxian proposition:

> Any mode of production, if it can exist and work, contains a mechanism which assures that its productivity will increase as time goes by.

The Smithian Decree is promulgated. This is represented by the expansion of the circle to include as much of society as possible. Over time we would expect to see growth in the ranks of the middle and lower-middle classes. The upper class should also grow as low taxes stimulate inventive activities.

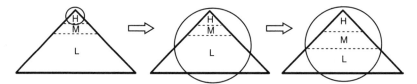

Decades pass. The wise ruler presides over a society that has grown in riches and numbers, with population still growing. Diminishing returns haunts agriculture—a boon for the landlords. Other sectors, starved for capital, stagnate. The wise ruler returns to Adam Smith and is disturbed by a powerful passage:

> [I]t is in the progressive state, while the society is advancing to the further acquisition, rather than when it has acquired its full complement of riches, that the condition of the laboring poor, of the great body of the people, seems to be the happiest and the most comfortable. It is hard in the stationary, and miserable in the declining state. The progressive state is in reality the cheerful and the hearty state to all the different orders of the society. (1.8.42)

His aging radical subject alarms him further with another Marxian proposition:

> Any mode of production has a certain upper limit to productivity beyond which it cannot continue to maintain itself.

This sounds like a grave threat to his kingdom. How can he forestall hitting this upper productivity limit? Now, at a higher level than before, the *elite intent* must be reformed or decline is round the corner. Can he even conceptualize the reforms needed to find the way ahead into another progressive period?

5.4 Hitting the Ceiling—Tokugawa Japan

The intent of elites in highly unequal societies will certainly condition the potential for development because of their control over the use of social surplus. However, the structure of social hierarchy must also be looked at. Some are better than others. East Asian history provides an interesting example.

Traditional Chinese philosophy puts scholars and farmers at the top and soldiers at the bottom. In Tokugawa Japan the warriors were firmly in control at the top, with all of the economically useful classes below them. The Chinese ideal had more productive potential than the Japanese because the military class was not in a position to make excessive demands upon the public finances.

Tokugawa society was actually designed to be a caste system. According to estimates, the warrior class was about 7 percent of the population, farmers were 80 percent and the remaining 13 percent were artisans and merchants. Since 80 percent were farmers, and they lived on a scanty subsistence, we can surmise a modest capacity to produce surplus food. The rice tax was fixed at 40 percent of output. These conditions constituted a great upper productivity limit.

Chinese Ideal	Tokugawa Japan (1603–1868)	
scholar	warrior	(7%)
farmer	farmer	(80%)
artisan	artisan	(13%)
merchant	merchant	
soldier		

Source: David Flath, *The Japanese Economy* (Oxford; New York: Oxford University Press, 2000), 24.

It is amazing that Tokugawa Japan did as well as it did. It was not only a caste system controlled by the warrior class—it was also a closed economy. Its success can possibly be traced to the ingenious way the Tokugawa family organized the national economy.

All of Japan was united under their centralized leadership, creating a unified economic space. The capital was moved from Kyoto to Edo (now called Tokyo). Once a small fishing village, by 1700 it had a million people. (Flath, 23)

The local lords were required to spend half of their time in Edo. Their families were required to live in Edo. This was a kind of gilded-hostage situation but it proved stable. It greatly stimulated economic activity inside Japan.

People and goods were constantly on the move—to and from Edo. Roads and ports were extended and upgraded. Western Japan was the most fertile area. This allowed Osaka to became a mighty center for warehousing and shipping.

The population increased from 20 to 30 million people between 1600 and 1700. It was still at that level when American gunboats arrived. They found a stagnant feudalistic society. Historians hotly dispute how and when stagnation set in.

5.5 TRASH CAN OF HISTORY—SOVIET UNION

It is easy to forget the accomplishments of the Soviet Union. Under Stalin's ruthless dictatorship, it was transformed from poverty and illiteracy into a power capable of defeating the Nazi war machine on the eastern front of World War II. Even the cold warrior, Richard Nixon, recognized its considerable achievements during his visit in 1959. By 1970, however, it achieved the 'full compliment of riches' possible within its centrally planned economy. A long stagnation set in.

Marxist economists were fond of dividing an economy into two sectors: means of production and means of consumption. By 1970, a third sector, 'means of repair', required more labor time than either of those primary sectors.

The Soviet Union excelled in areas subject to nonmarket competition: the arms and space races, athletics, and the refined arts. Market competition, however, was forbidden. According to Marx it was exploitative—always exploitative. On this basis, state-run monopolies dominated the economy. While this did make sense as a way to build and maintain the vast physical infrastructure required for an industrial society, it guaranteed inferior results in areas proven to work well under the rules of market competition.

As a secretive society, information was handled on a 'need to know' basis. All business accounting information was restricted in this way. Moreover, the accounting information sent from the factory level up to the planning office was more likely to contain the information the planning office *wanted to hear* rather than the actual conditions. After a certain point, economic data from below were nearly useless for planning the allocation of resources.

The desire to tightly control information flows proved incompatible with the development of certain mass-production technologies. Copy machines and personal computers exceeded the upper productivity limits of a centrally planned economy. To develop and produce such items in large numbers meant to undermine the power of political and economic elites. To not produce them meant to fall behind the United States forever. An 'information society' was impossible without changing the system. Rational pricing or manager autonomy—or other modest reforms—could not overcome such a fatal flaw.

While Gorbachev evidently grasped this, it was too bitter a pill for the 'true believers' educated in Marxism-Leninism. Lacking the ideological flexibility demonstrated in China, the Soviet Union simply unraveled.

Fukuyama has summarized the American triumph over Russia in these words:

[C]apitalism has proven far more efficient than centrally planned economic systems in developing and utilizing technology, and in adapting to rapidly changing conditions in a global division of labor, *under the conditions of a mature industrial economy*. (*End of History*, 91)

Neither Smith nor Marx could have said it better.

5.6   BASIC NEEDS AND INFRASTRUCTURES

People in the rich countries tend to take the development of a mature industrial economy for granted. Will people in the poorworlds ever claim such achievements for themselves?

Consider the following diagram. Successful modern society can be seen as a functional pyramid, with satisfaction of the most basic needs at the bottom and the latest additions to infrastructure at the top. The upper elements of the pyramid require adequate foundations below.

At the bottom are food, shelter, clothing, and medication. If the mass of people are *undernourished* and remain so, they will be undereducated too. In adulthood their earning power will be stunted. Until the basic needs are satisfied in general, the development of social and physical infrastructures will exist on a limited scale only, mostly for the benefit of elite families and their direct interests. Even for those families, the administrative capacities, electricity, and telephone will tend to be frustrating and unreliable.

If undernutrition can be conquered, primary education can be effective. If enough resources are devoted to basic education, illiteracy can be conquered. With these accomplishments, modernization can proceed.

The quality of physical infrastructure critically depends upon the quality of social infrastructure. A poor education system dooms everything above it. Without sufficient administrative capacities the massive demands of building and maintaining electricity and telephone grids will prove too much. If the legal system falters, the theft of electricity and telephone service will sap the finance of those industries; expansion will become unaffordable.

In the example below the internet is placed at the top of the pyramid—the greatest infrastructure achievement thus far in mature industrial economies. We should reflect again upon the Soviet experience. While they could claim some success with the lowest seven in the pyramid, their telephone grid was always inadequate. Moreover since development of personal computers exceeded their upper productivity limit, the internet would have been beyond their grasp—unless they humiliated themselves by total dependence upon imports.

		—START AT THE BOTTOM—	
		internet	x
	physical	telephone	xx
infrastructures		electricity	xxx
		legal system	xxxx
	social	admin capacities	xxxxx
		education system	xxxxxx
		income	xxxxxxx
basic needs	persons	education	xxxxxxxx
		food, shelter, clothing, meds	xxxxxxxxx

5.7   LOWER AND UPPER LIMITS IN CAPITALISM TODAY

As we saw at the beginning of the chapter, in order for capitalism to evolve out of feudalism, their productivity limits had to overlap.

The early generations of capitalism gave birth to industrialization. They grew together as applied science was married to the profit motive. Modern capitalism is the offspring of that marriage.

People in the fourth and fifth worlds aspire to better lives. Since the planned economy was discredited by Soviet experience, and China, too, abandoned that path, people tend to assume that capitalism is the only way ahead.

While this would appear to be correct it overlooks a difficult question: does the upper productivity limit in the fourth world today *even overlap* the lower limit needed for capitalism to function in the modern world? I think it does not.

At a minimum people must be well-fed and literate. The feudalists, crooks, and capitalists who dominate the ruling classes in the fourth and fifth worlds have shown little talent or inclination to conquer these problems.

Capitalistic reforms in China were not adopted until *after* hunger and illiteracy were largely eliminated. It may be necessary for the fourth world to evolve its own 'transitional socialism' as a way to solve the subsistence problem. Once this has been achieved the productive advantages of capitalism can come vigorously into play if an entrepreneurial class emerges.

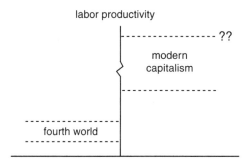

What about the upper productivity limits of modern capitalism? It is possible global oligopolies will establish their reign as global masters, thus undermining the technical progress we associate with fullon competition.

Even if competition can survive, some recent technologies are decidedly *antiprofit*. For example, CD burners give people the power to share/steal(?) music, video, computer software, and games. These technologies undermine a system based upon profit seeking by transferring reproduction capabilities to individuals. They exceed capitalism's upper productivity limits so the original producers press their claims in the courts, or booby-trap their products.

Even if antiprofit technologies do not fatally undermine global capitalism, ecology might. The motor of capitalism is profits-investment-profits-investment—continual expansion. A stationary state is impossible in modern capitalism. How much longer can we chew up the planet this way?

6

MACROECONOMICS

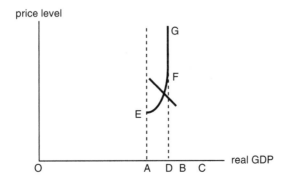

Effective-Supply Problem

6.1   PERFORMANCE OF LDCs

Taken as a whole, per capita GDP among the least developed countries changed little between 1980 and 1999. The erosion in per capita GDP in the 1980s was made up for in the 1990s but the decline in per capita food production was not.

Within the LDCs we can identify a group that expanded on a per capita GDP basis both decades and a group that contracted on that basis both decades. Among the seven growing both decades, four still have per capita GDP of less than a dollar a day. Among the seven shrinking both decades, five had per capita GDP of less than a dollar a day in 1980 as well as in 1999.

BEST AND WORST PERFORMING LDCs BETWEEN 1980 AND 1999						
	per capita real GDP growth rate (annual average %)		per capita food production growth rate (annual average %)		per capita GDP (1999 dollars)	
	1980–90	1990–99	1980–90	1990–99	1980	1999
all LDCs	−0.2	1.1	−0.7	0.3	284	288
Fastest growing						
Maldives	6.3	4.4	−1.1	−0.5	481	1359
Bhutan	4.6	4.0	−1.0	−0.3	434	733
Cape Verde	3.6	3.0	9.5	1.9	774	1389
Laos	2.0	3.7	0.4	1.4	147	259
Bangladesh	1.9	3.1	0.1	0.6	228	361
Uganda	0.7	4.3	0.9	−1.6	185	300
Nepal	1.9	2.2	1.7	0.1	142	210
Fastest shrinking						
Rwanda	−1.2	−1.3	−2.5	−2.1	322	270
Madagascar	−1.6	−1.6	−1.0	−1.7	353	241
Zambia	−1.3	−2.1	1.8	−1.4	505	370
Niger	−3.3	−0.9	−3.5	−0.2	309	199
Haiti	−2.6	−2.8	−2.4	−2.0	808	485
Sierra Leone	−1.8	−6.4	−0.5	−2.5	314	142
Congo/Zaire	−1.6	−8.3	0.0	−4.6	350	115

Source: *Least Developed Countries Report 2002* (New York and Geneva: UNCTAD, 2002), 247 and 250.

The two fastest growing countries both experienced declines in per capita food production. The Maldives more than compensated for this by expanding tourism. Bhutan more than compensated by exporting electricity to India. But in Bhutan more than 90 percent of the work force is still in subsistence agriculture and forestry. Most of the growth accrued in the few urban areas.

Among the fastest shrinking countries, per capita food production declined in five of the countries in the 1980s and in all of them in the 1990s. This gives the list a Malthusian tone. Some of these countries had violent internal problems. Vicious cycles were probably at work: poor economic performance damaged political stability that further undermined economic performance.

6.2   POSSIBILITY FRONTIER

The scanty subsistence wages earned in the poorest countries cannot rise steadily and sustainably unless capital accumulation stays ahead of population growth. Is capital per person increasing, constant, or decreasing?

growth rate of capital > or = or < growth rate of population

Let us put this in perspective by drawing a possibility frontier for a country with an alpha of about 1.3. OA and OB are subsistence per person. Point C is the two-year subsistence condition. DE is the per-person possibility frontier.

In the simplest situation, capital/output and consumption/output ratios are constant. Then we may distinguish three cases: if the accumulation rate exceeds the population growth rate, the frontier shifts out; if the accumulation rate equals the population growth rate, the frontier is unchanged; if the population growth rate exceeds the accumulation rate, the frontier shifts in.

In Section 1, the first group had improving frontiers while the second had contracting frontiers.

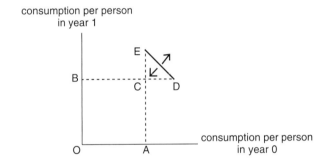

In a country with such a low alpha, an external shock can send it into severe crisis. Let us suppose an oil monopoly drastically increases prices. An orthodox economist might say: 'not to worry—this will play itself out in income, substitution, and innovation effects. Substitution will ease the pain, and, when innovation kicks in, we will be better off than before.'

He is taking a great deal for granted—assuming a well-developed market economy, among other things. Why is an economist in Dhaka not persuaded?

The income effect hurts first worlders, but it does not kill them. Poorworlders living on a scanty subsistence face a different scale of problem. Consider poor farmers near Dhaka. They are usually illiquid, nearly insolvent, often undernourished, and illiterate. After the oil shock, input costs soar and bankruptcy may force them off of the land. If they lose their land, 'substitution and innovation effects' involve finding another strategy to stay alive.

In general, in the poorworlds, the income effect is strongly felt, but alternatives are few, and innovation, operating through the profit motive, is constantly faced with a low level of effective demand. But low real incomes cannot grow without higher productivity. Let us look at the effective-supply problem.

6.3   Effective-Supply Problem

When we apply aggregate analysis to first world countries, the center of attention is 'potential output'. When we study the poorworlds, our attention should focus on the capacity to produce surplus above the social subsistence. Moreover, poor countries do not know 'full employment of labor' or 'full performance of capital'. They chronically suffer effective-supply problems.

Consider the following diagram. Real GDP is on the horizontal axis and the price level is on the vertical. The distance OA is the social subsistence. The distance OB is the level of output if all productive capacity is utilized. The distance OC is the level of output if there is full employment at the average product of labor. *BD represents output chronically lost because of waste, inefficiency, mismanagement, and fraud.* The distance OD is the *actual upper limit* on real GDP. DC indicates unemployment or underemployment of labor.

The aggregate-supply curve is constrained by OA and OD. Since that is a narrow band, it will be largely inelastic. It is represented here by the curve EFG. This effectively rules out Keynesian policies intended to induce multi-plier effects. Since aggregate supply is largely inelastic, demand-management policies will tend to be inflationary.

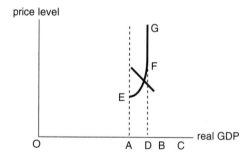

There are four sources of aggregate demand that are relevant for keeping it closer to point F than point E. Two are internal and two are external:

Internal Sources: (1) *Survival Strategies of Individuals and Families.* Since most people are living near subsistence they will do what they can to survive and get a bit ahead. (2) *Government Spending.* Governments will frequently run large deficits, specially to cover public investment.

External Sources: (1) *Donor Funds.* These are earmarked for governmental and nongovernmental organizations. (2) *Remittances from Overseas.* Citizens living abroad will send savings home, which boosts domestic demand.

We should note two problems. A fall in external sources can have a great impact since alpha is already low. This is a great dilemma facing donor-dependent countries and the organizations funding them. In addition, much of the investment spending is *ineffective.* This creates a great drag on improving the aggregate-supply curve.

6.4   INEFFECTIVE INVESTMENT

As we just saw, the aggregate supply/demand analysis for a poor country is fundamentally different from the rich country textbook. There is another issue overlooked when that kind of textbook is transplanted to the poorworlds.

Neo-Classical and Keynesian theories *take for granted* that net-investment spending (net I) will be turned into additions to capital (ΔK):

$$net\ I = \Delta K\ (orthodox\ assumption)$$

This assumes all investment spending is effectively converted into private or social capital and then utilized as such. This is a big assumption!

A hallmark of poor countries is the high proportion of investment spending that is *ineffective*. Some of it is taken as pure plunder. (Notorious bank loan defaulting comes to mind.) Much of the government investment never works according to plan. Much of the private investment never achieves profitability. Thus, instead of an equality between net-investment spending and capital accumulation, we have severely *ineffective investment*:

$$net\ I \gg \Delta K\ (poorworlds)$$

Consider the following diagram. Consumption is on the horizontal axis and net investment is on the vertical. OA is the social subsistence. OB is the highest level of consumption that can be sustained while holding the capital intact. Alpha is OB/OA. CA is the largest net investment possible while still producing the social subsistence. BC is the possibility frontier.

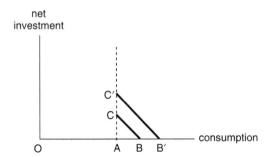

Suppose point C is chosen. If all of CA is effectively invested, the possibility frontier will shift out, to (say) B′C′. What happens if all of the net investment is ineffective? In that case, the possibility frontier will not shift at all. The social accounts will show significant net investment but the net output will be unchanged. The typical situation is likely to be between these two cases.

Chronically ineffective investment implies ineffective capital accumulation. In the face of a population explosion, this spells trouble. This is a great barrier to overcoming the vicious cycles of poverty.

6.5   EFFECTIVE-DEMAND PROBLEM

The problem from the demand side is no less daunting. Scanty subsistence incomes combine with meager collateralable assets to create two mutually reinforcing vicious cycles depressing private consumption and investment.

In the poorest countries, small incomes from wage-labor or self-employment are enough only to pay for poor nutrition, inadequate healthcare, and insufficient education. This keeps labor productivity low, which reinforces low incomes and low purchasing power. Life is a daily grind for subsistence and survival.

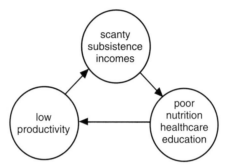

In most poor countries a significant part of the labor force is unemployed or underemployed. In order to survive, it is often necessary to create a micro-enterprise. Without physical collateral (or *certified proof* of physical collateral), credit access is greatly limited or usurious. Under these conditions, it may be possible to earn a scanty subsistence but difficult to make a profit.

Microfinance institutions have mushroomed over the past 25 years. Some follow the Grameen model based upon 'social collateral'. While this provides working-capital loans at a reasonable interest rate, gaps in the banking system make it difficult to graduate to larger loans. This can be partly overcome if housing and education loans are available from Grameen-type institutions.

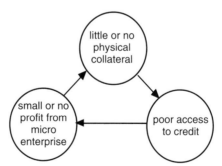

It is now widely recognized that a threshold level of human development and economic opportunity are necessary to break vicious cycles of poverty. Undernutrition, poor healthcare, illiteracy, and lack of credit are grave impediments. If these barriers to effective demand can be solved, problems on the supply side can prove less daunting because capital accumulation would have a new stimulus and the proportion of ineffective investment might be reduced.

6.6 INTERNATIONAL TRADE

It is nearly impossible for a poor country to make progress without international trade. Using the principle of social subsistence we can illustrate gains from trade as well as risks from unlimited free trade.

Let us suppose a society well known for its 'bongos'. It is also capable of producing all of its social subsistence. To what extent should it engage in trade?

Consider the diagram below. Butter is on the horizontal axis. Bongos are on the vertical. OA is the social subsistence of butter. If all resources are devoted to the production of butter, OB can be produced.

Bongos are not part of the social subsistence, so there is no subsistence quantity. However, if this country produces only the social subsistence of butter it can produce AC bongos. It can produce even more bongos if it is willing to produce less butter. In order to introduce butter/bongos exchange rates it is convenient to assume a rounded possibility frontier.

Gains from trade are easily illustrated. Suppose that this country can trade bongos for butter at the rate represented by the line through point D. In this case it can produce at point D and trade to point E. At point E it consumes more butter than OB and it consumes some bongos too.

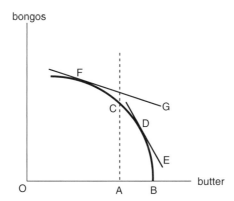

What if the butter/bongos relative price changes to the line through point F? In this case it can produce at point F and trade to point G—more consumption of butter than OB *and* many bongos. This would seem to be very desirable.

It may be desirable; it is also risky. *By producing at point D this country can assure its food security and still benefit from trade.* By producing at point F this country ties its food security to the conditions of trade. If the trading partners suddenly experience a great emergency, the sale of bongos will collapse. Production at point F will then mean too many bongos and not enough butter. That is a recipe for social upheaval. Choosing point D regardless of relative prices, and trading from there, would be a risk-averse conservative policy.

6.7   POVERTY ELASTICITY OF GROWTH

Let us end this chapter with observations on poverty and poverty reduction in LDCs. Rates of poverty are often reported on the basis of a 'dollar a day' or 'two dollars a day'. The first is a very scanty subsistence. In the chart below we use the second measure. On this basis, since 1965, the incidence of poverty has risen in the African LDCs and declined in the Asian LDCs. Rates of poverty, however, are still high in both groups.

POPULATION % LIVING ON LESS THAN $2 A DAY—1985 PPP				
	1965–69	1975–79	1985–89	1995–99
African LDCs	82.0	83.7	87.0	87.5
Asian LDCs	78.8	79.6	73.4	68.2

Source: Least Developed Countries Report 2002, 59.

The measurable reduction of poverty in the Asian LDCs would not have been possible without economic growth. This brings us to a fundamental question: If real per capita GDP grows by one percent, by what percent does the poverty headcount decline? This measure is called the 'poverty elasticity of growth'.

According to Lucia Hanmer and Felix Naschold,[1] the poverty elasticity is highly sensitive to the degree of inequality:

when inequality is 'low' (gini < 43): the poverty elasticity = −0.93
when inequality is 'high' (gini > 43): the poverty elasticity = −0.34

In the first case, a one percent growth of GDP per capita would average more than 9/10ths of a percent decline in headcount poverty. In the second case, the impact would average only a *third* of a percent.

If these estimates hold up, we can say something about the group of 'fastest growing' LDCs listed in Section 1. The *Human Development Report 2003* gives gini-index figures for four of the seven countries: Bangladesh (32); Laos, Uganda and Nepal (37). All four of these countries would be included in the group where poverty reduction is nearly unit elastic to per capita GDP growth.

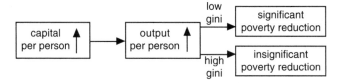

The growth-and-distribution theory of this chapter may be summarized briefly: if the effective rate of capital accumulation exceeds the population growth rate, net output per person will rise and real wages can rise. The impact of per-capita growth on poverty will depend upon the degree of income inequality. The smaller the initial degree of inequality, the larger the responsiveness of poverty reduction. High initial inequality is itself a barrier to poverty reduction.[2]

7

MACROFOUNDATION—DIAGRAMS

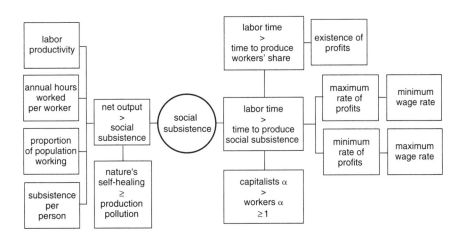

7.1 RECOGNIZING THE PRINCIPLE OF SURVIVAL

I could not have done the work on survival-conditions analysis without the assistance of someone highly skilled in math. My intuition was keen enough to grasp the main propositions in student days, but without a mathematical model it was impossible to survey the land from a suitable height. When the Invisible Hand delivered me to Japan I had no idea my much needed mentor was there.

I met Professor Nobuo Okishio in the faculty of economics at Kobe University, in September 1982. I had just joined his faculty. During my three years in that faculty, we developed a warm friendship. We discussed many topics, on campus and off campus. Professor Okishio was very well read. Discussions on religion, politics, and history dominated our first years together. We were vitally concerned about the nuclear arms race, environmental destruction, and mass poverty. In this context we had a decisive conversation.

We were walking up a hilly road in downtown Kobe, heading for a beautiful coffee shop. I made a joke about the 'three faces of Keynes' because we were discussing the models found in *The General Theory*. Just as we approached the door of the coffee shop I asked Professor Okishio, "What is the deepest principle of economics?" He replied, with one word: "Survival."

I agreed with him completely. Soon after that I showed him my critique of the neo-Classicals, the social-subsistence concept and alpha. But the presentation did not seem to leave an impression.

I left Kobe in August 1985 but returned in April 1988, this time to a private university. Upon my return, Professor Okishio asked what I wanted to work on. I said, "the subsistence problem." He immediately agreed and began producing, *on the spot*, algebraic interpretations of my words and diagrams.

That day he convinced me of the need to develop an algebraic model. My words and diagrams implied more than one interpretation. I chose the simplest model. That became the algebra for my first paper on the macrofoundation.

After that paper was written I could see the way ahead. The next paper had to develop production-survival conditions, while the third paper had to explore distribution-survival conditions. These became the three papers he refers to in his essay "Mr. Goalstone's Macro Foundation of Macro Economics."

I did not correct the 'Mr.' in the title—even though I had defended my Ph.D. dissertation long before, when I was 23 years old. The 'Mr.' reflected our relationship. He was the master and I was an apprentice.

It was an honor to work with Professor Okishio. He gave his time to me, and many others, selflessly, with constructive assistance, and good fellowship. Even when my analysis became distinctly anti-Marx—attacking the fundamental theorem of Professor Okishio's life's work—he maintained our friendship and working relationship. It was a privilege to call him *sensei*.

Now let us see the development of the macrofoundation based upon survival-conditions analysis, which I discovered with the help of Professor Okishio.

7.2   PROFESSOR OKISHIO'S ALGEBRAIC INTERPRETATION

In this book I am publishing Professor Okishio's algebra for the Modern Macrofoundation in preference to my own. His version is more professional. His algebra is compact, elegant, and exciting.

My clunkier algebra was dependent upon a stationary state. This was unsatisfactory but I should point out its one virtue. My limited skills forced me to begin with the assumption of a given population. I was later able to recognize the Classical Macrofoundation because, by its nature, it began with a variable population.

After writing my third paper, I asked Professor Okishio if he would write his interpretation. I knew it would be superior to mine because of his superior skills. When I saw it, it startled me, because it was compact. It was reassuring to see my results still hold in a corn model outside of the stationary state.

Professor Okishio's paper contains two algebraic sections plus a mathematical appendix. The first section summarizes some general conditions. The second section identifies the relevant range of real wages and rates of profits that satisfy the survival conditions when we assume that capitalists have a greater income than workers. In both sections he gets to the point quickly.

His first algebraic section identifies three core survival conditions, one each for output, labor time, and nature:

net output ≥ social subsistence
hours of work per person ≥ hours of work per subsistence bundle
nature's net capacity to self-purify ≥ social subsistence production pollution

Actually, the first two should be strict inequalities. I did not notice this until after the Kobe Earthquake. That shocking tragedy reminded me of the need for emergency supplies. Throughout this book I have written:

net output > social subsistence

However, right after identifying the three inequalities above, Professor Okishio says something amazing:

> [These] conditions are requirements for nine parameters . . . to guarantee social survival. They show that four of them . . . must be greater than certain limits and that five of them . . . must be smaller than certain limits.

This needs careful investigation by mathematical economists. I think it may contain a unifying principle.

Professor Okishio's algebraic discussion on distribution was immediately useful. I had built the relevant range for rates of profit that satisfy survival conditions, but I did not identify the range for real wages. I preferred to work in terms of working-class alphas. As soon as I saw his analysis for the relevant range of real wages, I recognized the connection with microeconomics. I wrote the first draft of the Real Wages chapter, included in this book after Professor Okishio's paper. That chapter pushes the analysis of relevant ranges ahead significantly.

7.3   SOCIAL SUBSISTENCE

The entry point is the social subsistence, subsistence consumption per person times the population. Everything grows out of this; this is the key discovery.

From there we have the primary inequality of the macrofoundation, the relationship which for most of the book is simply 'the' production-survival condition: net output greater than social subsistence. It is the most powerful relationship in the book.

To build the distribution theory of the *full* macrofoundation—something not needed in previous chapters—we need to write that condition measured in units of time: labor time devoted to production must be greater than the time required directly and indirectly to produce the social subsistence. This includes its replacement seed.

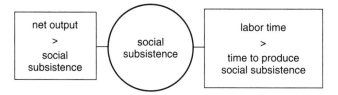

7.4   PRODUCTION-SURVIVAL CONDITIONS

Many diagrams in this book have been built upon 'net output greater than social subsistence'. In the diagram below it touches every part. Chapter 4 was devoted to the four components on the left side.

That chapter also included, very briefly, an ecological condition: nature's ability to self-purify must at least offset pollution from production. At that point we observed this as a massive challenge to modern, complex, societies.

Chapter 14, on Ecocide, deals with ecological matters in greater depth.

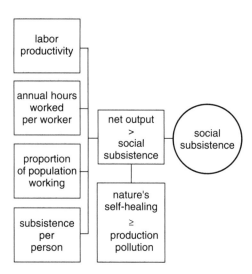

7.5 DISTRIBUTION-SURVIVAL CONDITIONS

My third paper was the decisive essay, even though I do not need to use it elsewhere in this book! It was subtitled, "On the Requirements for Social Reproduction". I particularly wanted to reveal the maximum and minimum rates of profits consistent with survival conditions. They had to satisfy the production-survival condition *plus* a simple distribution assumption:

capitalist-class alpha > alpha > working-class alpha ≥ 1

In order to establish the relevant range for rate of profits, it was necessary to first establish *existence of profits*:

$$T > tB$$

where T is the total labor time, t is the labor time required directly and indirectly to produce a unit of corn, and B is the share of output workers can buy with their wages. This is the so-called Fundamental Marxian Theorem. In a corn model this expresses existence of profits as a *residual*. We turn to my rejection of it as a theory of exploitation in a moment.

In order to establish the relevant range itself, I needed my primary production-survival condition, written in units of time:

$$T > tC'$$

where C' is the social subsistence. From this, and the distribution-inequality assumption written above, it was possible to identify the relevant range, establishing maximum and minimum rates of profits.

I also established the relevant range for the working-class alpha. While that had some value, Professor Okishio correctly saw advantages in establishing, instead, minimum and maximum wage rates.

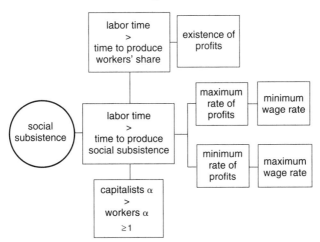

Getting to this point was a mountaintop experience. From this point I could look down and get the lay of the land. But also from this point I was able to *look up* and view another mountaintop, the Five-Worlds Theory. When I finally reached that peak, while working in Dhaka, I only needed one production- and one distribution-survival condition for much of the work.

7.6   Critique of Marx

While I needed a way to establish existence of profits, and used the simple theorem I learned from Professor Okishio, I could not accept the baggage that went along with it. As I said in my third Kobe paper:

> The Fundamental Marxian Theorem was conceived by Marx to carry two loads simultaneously. He not only wanted to shed a light on the condition for the existence of profits—which I have accepted above—he also wanted to build a revolutionary but 'scientific' analysis of exploitation. Great power was unleashed by his notion of exploitation; violently revolutionary governments were established upon it. Can the Fundamental Marxian Theorem really carry its second load?

No, it cannot:

> *First we recognize social subsistence* and the labor required to secure it, since they are the raw basis of social reproduction . . . From this first step we can have a concept of surplus product. Only after establishing these do the questions of profit and exploitation come up. Let us look at the fundamental theorems in their proper order.

From the viewpoint of existence and survival of *society* the proper order is:

$$T > tC' \qquad \textit{production-survival condition}$$
$$\textit{THEN:}$$
$$T > tB \qquad \textit{existence of profits}$$

The critique continues:

> Marx would have us believe that the subsistence requirements of the propertied class come from exploitation . . . *But subsistence consumption is required by propertied-class people as human beings—without it, they are denied life.* Even Herr Moneybags is a human being. To attribute all of his consumption to exploitation, including his subsistence bundle, dehumanizes in a thoughtless, even a violent, way.

> In the drama of twentieth-century history, this dehumanization has taken an appalling form. From Marx's analysis, propertied-class people have been depicted as 'parasites', devoid of human qualities. This depiction has had its own inner logic. For if they are 'parasites', they are seen as things, things living off of healthy bodies, things to be eliminated. How many 'revolutionary tribunals' have reached this conclusion? By following Marx's concept of exploitation to a bitter end, revolutionary Marxists stepped far beyond an analysis of class conflict, plunging into the spiritual wasteland of class hate. (May 10, 1990)

That critique was written in the context of the macrofoundation. I think there is a related flaw in Marx, equally disastrous. In his worldview *all* profits of capitalistic business come from exploitation of workers. This crude perspective is pure extremism. Workers are not the only stakeholders in private enterprise. It is astounding that brilliant people have believed exploitation theory *literally* and have tried to establish societies on the basis of outlawing private enterprise.

7.7   MODERN MACROFOUNDATION RESTATED

Now we can put it all together—the macrofoundation I discovered in Kobe with the help of Professor Okishio. I do not use the word discovery lightly. It had the feel of something inevitable, as though I were trying to transcribe a thought of God—God's corn model!

In this chapter, the social-subsistence diagram has three parts. The production-survival conditions diagram has seven parts. The Distribution-Survival Conditions diagram has nine parts. The diagram below has fifteen parts. This is the model you find in Professor Okishio's chapter.

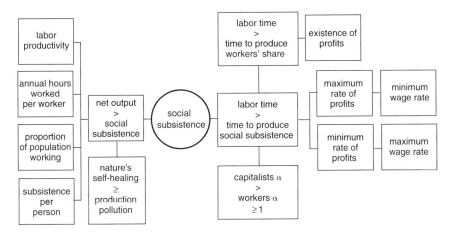

When this is combined with the archetypes 'rich country, poor country, starving country' the model takes on a three-dimensional quality. With the addition of the Five-Worlds Theory the three-dimensional quality deepens. Most of this book is based upon that.

The Life-Expectancy Theory rounds out the core propositions and is an integral part of the Modern Macrofoundation.

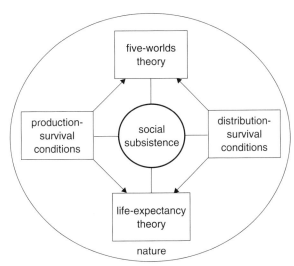

8

MACROFOUNDATION—ALGEBRA
—By Professor Nobuo Okishio—

[These] Conditions . . . are requirements for nine parameters . . . to guarantee social survival. They show that four of them . . . must be greater than certain limits and that five of them . . . must be smaller than certain limits.

Mr. Goalstone's "Macro Foundation of Macro Economics"

Nobuo Okishio

published in *Kobe-Gakuin Economic Papers* 23, no. 2 (1991) 1–11.

Mr. Goalstone, in this journal, wrote three papers that have the unfamiliar title "Macro Foundation of Macro Economics." This unfamiliar title induced me to write the present note.

8.1   Micro Economics and Macro Economics

Many people usually divide curriculum of theoretical Economics into *Micro Economics* and *Macro Economics*. Micro Economics covers choice theories of individual households and firms and General Equilibrium Theory. Macro Economics covers Keynes' Theory and neo-Classical Theory in aggregate terms.

In my opinion this division is very confusing. This division seems to be a distinction of theories by the criterion of number of variables in respective theories. In Micro Economics, for example, the number of prices is n. In Macro Economics the number of variables is, for example, two or three. However, we sometimes teach students choice theory of individual economic units only treating small number of variables. Even General Equilibrium Theory can be taught in miniature model successfully. In these cases are these classified as Macro Economics? To the contrary, we sometimes teach Keynesian Theory and neo-Classical Theory introducing n sectors. Are these to be classified as Micro Economics?

How should we define Micro Economics and Macro Economics? Clear definitions, I think, are the following: Micro Economics is the theory that treats behaviors of various economic units including households, firms, banks, governments, and so on. Macro Economics is the theory that treats movements of the social economy that are the synthesis of results of various individual economic units' behaviors. According to this definition, General Equilibrium, of course, belongs to Macro Economics.

8.2   Micro Foundation

In literatures of Economics we find "Micro Foundation of Macro Economics." In fact, any movements of the Macro Economy cannot occur without behaviors of individual economic units that constitute a social economy. In this sense, Macro Economics, the subject of which is movements of the social economy, must have Micro Foundation. For example, though Ricardo's theory is chiefly Macro Economics, still it is built on Micro Foundation. When Ricardo insists that prices of various commodities are determined so as to equalize rates of profit in every sector and that under certain conditions prices are proportionate to the amount of labor bestowed, he tacitly assumes capitalistic behavior that seeks for a higher rate of profit and bargaining patterns in the case of disequilibrium in markets. Almost everybody regards Keynes' theory as Macro Economics. However, it has Micro Foundation. He analyzes consumer's behaviors, firm's decisions of current production and new investment and financial investor's decisions for choosing securities.

Some people think that since in order to analyze behaviors of individual economic units the maximum principle becomes a necessary assumption, every theory with this Micro Foundation is neo-Classical, because the maximum principle was introduced by the neo-Classical School. Such thinking has a twofold defect. First, though the maximum principle is sometimes very useful to analyze individual behaviors, it is not a necessary thing. In some case we can get better results about individual behaviors by introducing the concept of conventional behavior supported by observations. Mr. Goalstone has insisted this in talks with me. Second: the maximum principle is not the exclusive possession of the neo-Classical School. Though some of the mathematical tools with which the maximum principle became effective were introduced by neo-Classical people, the principle itself is known from Smith. The fact that capitalists always look for maximum of profits is the most important aspect of capitalism. Therefore any theory of capitalistic economy, more or less, must reflect this aspect. The distinction between neo-Classical and Keynesian is not whether they admit the maximum principle in analyzing individual behaviors. The critical departure between them lies in whether they admit an automatic mechanism to achieve full employment in uncontrolled capitalism.

8.3 MACRO FOUNDATION

Micro Economics treats behaviors of individual economic units. This gives Micro Foundation of Macro Economics. However, Micro Economics too should have *Macro Foundation*. What kind of economic units constitute social economy? By what kinds of criteria do they behave? These questions cannot be answered without considering the characteristics of the social economy that economic units constitute.

Usually, lectures on Micro Economics start from consumer's choices under conditions: given incomes and prices. In this case, money and prices are assumed to exist from the beginning. But money and prices exist only in a society that has certain characteristics. What are these characteristics? Social division of labor and private ownership are sufficient social conditions in order for money and prices to exist. Are these also necessary conditions? This question is not a merely academic one. This relates to the hot problem of market mechanism in socialistic society.

The second part of usual lectures on Micro Economics is firm's choices under conditions: given feasible technical alternative and given prices and wage rate. In this case, a firm itself and wage labor are assumed to exist from the beginning. Moreover, the criterion of choice is assumed to be maximization of profit. The number of employed laborers is the variable to be determined so at to maximize profit. So wage laborers cannot be decision makers of firm's activities. Why are laborers excluded from decisions of production? Who grasps these decisions? Why cannot the criterion of firm's decisions help being maximization of profit? These questions again cannot be answered without considering special characteristics of the society.

Strictly speaking, we cannot fully explain individual economic units without knowing the social economy as a whole. In this sense, so called "*methodological individualism*" commits inevitable circular reasoning. As Marx said, an individual is a knot of tremendously many social relationships with others.

8.4   SURVIVAL-CONDITIONS ANALYSIS

We have mentioned Micro Foundation of Macro Economics and Macro Foundation of Micro Economics. So indirectly we arrive at Macro Foundation of Macro Economics.

$$Macro \leftarrow Micro \leftarrow Macro$$

When I heard Mr. Goalstone's title "Macro Foundation of Macro Economics," I thought this is what he wanted to say. However, what he wanted to say is quite different from this.

He insists that it is very important to reveal the conditions that any society must satisfy in order to survive. He names these conditions: A Macro Foundation of Macro Economics. This idea, he says, is found in Physiocratic writings.

Using a simple corn model we can summarize mathematically his necessary conditions for any society to survive as follows.

$$
\begin{align}
X_0 - \sigma P &\geq aX \tag{1} \\
X - aX &\geq \sigma P \tag{2} \\
h\omega P &= \tau X \tag{3} \\
A &\geq \pi X \tag{4}
\end{align}
$$

Here a unit of corn is assumed to be produced by an input a of corn as seed ($a < 1$) and an input τ of labor time. The production period is assumed to be one year. Condition (1) states that the amount of corn initially held X_0 minus society's subsistence consumption σP sets the upper limit on the amount of seed to produce corn aX in the next period, where P denotes the population and σ denotes subsistence consumption per capita. The second condition (2) means that the society can consume at least subsistence consumption forever. Because sustainable consumption (net produce) is required to be greater than the social subsistence. The third equation (3) shows that the amount of necessary labor time to produce X must be equal to $h\omega P$, where h denotes hours of work per laborer per year (which has a physical upper limit) and ω denotes the ratio of laborers to the total population. The last condition

(4) states that the amount of pollution of environment caused by production πX must not exceed nature's capacity to purify A, where π denotes the amount of pollution per unit of production.

From (1) and (2) we get

$$(1 - a)X_0 \geq \sigma P \qquad (5) \qquad \text{Appendix [1]}.$$

From (2) and (3) we have

$$h\omega \geq t\sigma \qquad (6),$$

where t denotes the amount of labor time directly and indirectly necessary to produce a unit of corn. It is defined by the following

$$t = at + \tau \qquad (7).$$

The inverse of this t gives the productivity of labor.

From (2) and (4) we know

$$(1 - a)A \geq \pi\sigma P \qquad (8) \qquad \text{Appendix [2]}.$$

Conditions (5), (6), and (8) are requirements for nine parameters X_0, σ, P, a, t, h, ω, π, and A to guarantee social survival. They show that four of them X_0, h, ω, and A must be greater than certain limits and that five of them σ, P, a, t, and π must be smaller than certain limits.

Mr. Goalstone in his papers gave great emphasis on the ratio net produce $(1 - a)X$ to subsistence consumption σP and named it α.

$$\alpha = (1 - a)X/\sigma P \qquad (9).$$

Of course α must not be smaller than one by (2). He rewrites α using (3) and (7) as

$$\alpha = h\omega/t\sigma \qquad (10).$$

This α is not smaller than one by (6).

8.5 DISTRIBUTION CONDITIONS

The conditions above are necessary for any society to survive. Why are they not sufficient? Even if these conditions are met, it is possible for society to collapse. These conditions only require the amount of corn production to be always enough for subsistence consumption. However, if this corn is not allocated properly, society cannot afford subsistence forever. If much corn is spent for luxury or military purposes, even simple reproduction becomes impossible and eventually people cannot get corn for subsistence. Moreover, society cannot survive without maintaining its social structure. For example, capitalistic society cannot reproduce itself without keeping the production relationships that characterize capitalistic society.

Though Mr. Goalstone's papers do not treat these sides of reproduction fully, in his third paper he takes up the conditions of income distribution that are required for capitalism to maintain itself. Using his corn model

$$hwP_L \geq \sigma P_W \tag{11}$$

$$r(a + \tau w)X > \frac{hwP_L}{P_W} P_K \tag{12}$$

Condition (11) states that the total real wages hwP_L must be enough for the subsistence consumption of the wage-laborer class σP_W, where w denotes the corn wage rate, P_L the number of employed laborers, and P_W the population of the wage-labor class including unemployed and dependents. Condition (12) means that total profit $r(a + \tau w)X$ must be enough to maintain a higher standard of living for capitalist-class people than wage-labor-class people, where r denotes the rate of profit and $(a + \tau w)$ is capital per unit of output. Since income per capita of labor-class people is hwP_L/P_W, the income of the capitalist class must be greater than $(hwP_L/P_W)P_K$, where P_K denotes the population of the capitalist class. He thinks that in order to keep the social status of capitalist, they must have a higher standard of living than labor-class people.

As the rate of real wage and the rate of profit have the following definitional relationship

$$(1 + r)(a + \tau w) = 1 \tag{13},$$

conditions (11) and (12) give the ranges in which the rate of real wage and the rate of profit must be confined.

$$\frac{P_W}{tP} > w \geq \frac{\sigma P_W}{hP_L} \tag{14}$$

Appendix [3].

$$\frac{1 - \left(a + \frac{\tau\sigma P_W}{hP_L}\right)}{a + \frac{\tau\sigma P_W}{hP_L}} \geq r > \frac{\frac{(1 - a)P_K}{P}}{1 - \frac{(1 - a)P_K}{P}} \tag{15}.$$

In order for the range not to be empty we must have the following condition

$$h > \sigma t \frac{P}{P_L} \tag{16} \qquad \text{Appendix [4].}$$

This condition coincides with the inequality form of (6) because $P_L/P = \omega$. If the real-wage rate w is at the subsistence level, the condition for the rate of profit to be positive is

$$h > \sigma t \frac{P_W}{P_L} \tag{17} \qquad \text{Appendix [5].}$$

This is the so-called Marxian Fundamental Theorem. Since $P > P_W$, condition (16) requires a higher h than (17) because it is the condition for the rate of profit to guarantee consumption per capita of capitalist-class people above consumption per capita of labor-class people.

8.6 STUDY MORE DEEPLY CONDITIONS FOR SURVIVAL

Mr. Goalstone's idea, I think, comes from several sources. First, he has much interest in underdeveloped countries. In such countries we face naked subsistence problem. Second, he feels anxiety about the future of developed countries. In these countries he sees enormous military preparations, ceaseless increase of silly consumption, and serious pollution of environment. Survival problem is vital in these countries too. Third, he sees some irrelevance in Marxian thinking. Though he highly appreciates Marx's contributions on reproduction problems, he does not agree with Marx's idea that even the subsistence consumption of capitalists is done by exploitation. For him this idea of Marx's has the implication that capitalists are dehumanized, that even their subsistence needs are denied, which has provoked unhumanistic occurrences in revolutionary days.

The former two sources are very understandable. Economics must study more deeply the conditions for survival and endeavor to find the way in which our economy keeps these conditions. In this sense his papers, though primitive yet, may help people to take up this problem more seriously. However, the third source does not persuade me. Marx in his *Das Kapital* clearly distinguishes the social status of capitalist from individuals who are playing capitalistic roles. Capitalists' profits come from exploitation of wage laborers, so consumption supported by profit comes from exploitation. But this does not mean that individuals who were capitalists before a revolution must not consume. These people, of course, can consume to live depending on their own labor or the labor of others, after confiscation of properties. This time, even if they depend upon the labor of others in the new society, it cannot be said that they exploit, because the allocation of social produce to support these people is decided by all members of the society.

8.7 MATHEMATICAL APPENDIX

[1] From (2) $X \geq \sigma P/(1 - a)$.
From (1) $X_0 - \sigma P \geq \sigma Pa/(1 - a)$.
So we get $(1 - a)X_0 \geq \sigma P$, which is (5).

[2] From (2) $X \geq \sigma P/(1 - a)$.
From (4) $A \geq \pi \sigma P(1 - a)$.
So we get $(1 - a)A \geq \pi \sigma P$, which is (8).

[3] From (13) we know the rate of profit r is a decreasing function of the rate of real wage. Therefore, maximum r corresponds to minimum w and

maximum w corresponds to minimum r. We denote maximum r, minimum r, maximum w, and minimum w as r_{max}, r_{min}, w_{max}, and w_{min} respectively.

w_{min} is defined by (11) as

$$w_{min} = \frac{\sigma P_W}{h P_L}; \qquad w \geq \frac{\sigma P_W}{h P_L} \qquad \text{(A)}.$$

As r_{max} corresponds to w_{min}, from (13)

$$(1 + r_{max})(a + \tau w_{min}) = 1; \qquad r_{max} = \frac{1 - (a + \tau w_{min})}{(a + \tau w_{min})}.$$

So we get from (A)

$$r \leq \frac{1 - \left(a + \dfrac{\tau \sigma P_W}{h P_L} \right)}{a + \dfrac{\tau \sigma P_W}{h P_L}} \qquad \text{(B)}.$$

r_{min} is defined by (12) and (13) as

$$r_{min}(a + \tau w_{max})X = \frac{h w_{max} P_L}{P_W} P_K$$

$$(1 + r_{min})(a + \tau w_{max}) = 1.$$

From these two equations we have

$$\{1 - (a + \tau w_{max})\}X = \frac{h w_{max} P_L}{P_W} P_K.$$

From (3) $\tau X = h P_L$. So

$$\{(1 - a) - \tau w_{max}\} = \frac{\tau w_{max} P_K}{P_W}.$$

From (7) $t = \tau/(1 - a)$. So

$$1 = t w_{max}\left(\frac{P_K}{P_W} + 1 \right) = \frac{t w_{max} P}{P_W}.$$

We know from this

$$w_{max} = \frac{P_W}{t P}; \qquad \frac{P_W}{t P} > w \qquad \text{(C)}.$$

Using this w_{max}, we can get r_{min} by $(1 + r_{min})(a + \tau w_{max}) = 1$

$$r_{min} = \frac{(1 - a) - \tau w_{max}}{a + \tau w_{max}} = \frac{(1 - a)\left(1 - \dfrac{P_W}{P} \right)}{a + (1 - a)\dfrac{P_W}{P}}.$$

Considering $P = P_W + P_K$,

$$r_{min} = \frac{\dfrac{(1-a)P_K}{P}}{1 - \dfrac{(1-a)P_K}{P}} \; ; \qquad r > \frac{\dfrac{(1-a)P_K}{P}}{1 - \dfrac{(1-a)P_K}{P}} \qquad (D).$$

By (A) and (C), we get (14). By (B) and (D), we get (15).

[4] From (14)

$$\frac{P_W}{tP} > \frac{\sigma P_W}{h P_L}$$

so we get

$$h > \sigma t \frac{P}{P_L} \qquad (16).$$

[5] If the real-wage rate w is at the subsistence level,

$$w = \frac{P_W}{P_L} \sigma \frac{1}{h}.$$

From (13) we have

$$r = \frac{(1-a) - \tau \dfrac{P_W}{P_L} \sigma \dfrac{1}{h}}{a + \tau \dfrac{P_W}{P_L} \sigma} = \frac{h - t \dfrac{P_W}{P_L} \sigma}{h\left(\dfrac{a}{1-a} + t \dfrac{P_W}{P_L} \sigma\right)}.$$

Therefore, in order for r to be positive

$$h > \sigma t \frac{P_W}{P_L} \qquad (17).$$

9

REAL WAGES

—On a Macrofoundation of Microeconomics—

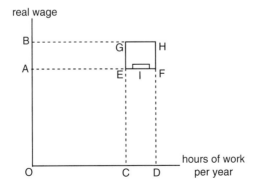

Relevant Range in the Third World

9.1 Neo-Classical Equilibrium

In orthodox economics great emphasis is placed on identifying equilibrium labor market conditions under perfect competition. The simplest model requires only a neo-Classical X—a downward sloping demand curve crossing an upward-sloping supply curve.

Equilibrium is at point A. For profit maximizing firms, the marginal product of labor equals the marginal cost of labor in equilibrium. The real wage is the distance OB. Hours of work per year are the distance OC. Real income from labor is the area OBAC.

If the real wage is above OB there will be excess supply of labor. If the real wage is below OB there will be excess demand for labor. A flexible labor market will eliminate disequilibrium. According to this analysis, minimum-wage laws create excess supply.

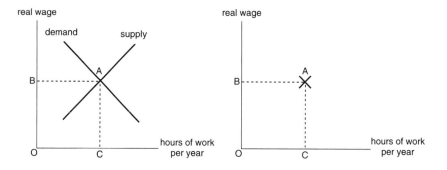

In neo-Classical thinking the relevant range of real wages is:

$$average\ product\ of\ labor > real\ wage > 0$$

This is found on a 'choice of technique' diagram depicting the relationship between the rate of profits and the real wage. For a given wage rate the most profitable technique will be chosen. A real wage near zero, however, is too low for workers to buy their daily bread. Well then, let them eat cake!

There are three interrelated reasons for doing the analysis anew.

First: As early neo-Classicals knew well, only the area around equilibrium is relevant. Why fill up the diagram with a big X? Most of it is irrelevant. A small x would be more accurate and more informative. In fact, we can act neo-Marshallian and ask what the area of equilibrium looks like.

Second: What is the social context? Is it in a rich country or a poor country? A country rising or a country sinking?

Third: Does the equilibrium real wage satisfy survival conditions? What are the implications if it fails to do so?

We deal with these issues in this chapter.

9.2   ALPHA AND INCOME INEQUALITY

We begin with the production-survival condition:

$$\alpha = \frac{\lambda h \omega}{\sigma} > 1 \qquad (1)$$

where alpha is the ratio of net output to the social subsistence, λ is labor productivity, h is hours per worker per year, ω is proportion of the population working and σ is subsistence per person. This was the centerpiece of Chapter 4.

Since we are dealing with wages and profits we have two social classes: working and capitalist. Denote proportion of the population in the working class as η_w and proportion of the population in the capitalist class as η_P:

$$\eta_w + \eta_P = 1 \qquad (2)$$

Write alpha as the weighted average of alphas for the working and capitalist classes:

$$\alpha = \alpha_w \eta_w + \alpha_P \eta_P > 1 \qquad (3)$$

Capitalists have an incentive to be capitalists and maintain capitalism only if they can maintain a higher income for their families than the income they pay out to workers for working-class families.

Thus, the capitalist-class alpha is greater than alpha. Alpha is greater than the working-class alpha. If the distribution-survival condition from Chapter 1 is satisfied, the working-class alpha is greater than or equal to one:

$$\alpha_P > \alpha > \alpha_w \geq 1 \qquad (4)$$

(4) is the key to determining maximum and minimum real wages.

9.3   MINIMUM AND MAXIMUM REAL WAGES

Working-class income must be sufficient for the subsistence needs of the working class as a whole:

$$\alpha_w = \frac{w h P_L}{\sigma P_w} \geq 1 \qquad (5)$$

where w is the wage rate per hour, P_L is the number of workers, P_w is the population in the working class (including dependents and unemployed). (5) may be rewritten:

$$w \geq \frac{\sigma P_w}{h P_L} \qquad (6)$$

Concerning the maximum real wage, from (1) and (4) we get:

$$\alpha = \frac{\lambda h \omega}{\sigma} > \alpha_w \qquad (7)$$

From (5) and (7) we get:

$$\frac{\lambda \omega P_w}{P_L} > w \qquad (8)$$

(6) and (8) can both be simplified, which gives us the relevant range of real wages:

$$\lambda \eta_w > w \geq \frac{\sigma \eta_w}{h\omega} \qquad (9)$$

(9) contains the conditions necessary to satisfy (4). (9) corresponds with (14) in Professor Okishio's algebraic interpretation of the Modern Macrofoundation.

These conditions can be written in words. Let us begin with the easier one:

average product of labor × proportion of population in working class > w

This modifies the neo-Classical upper limit. If the real wage approached this, the income of capitalist-class families would only be a bit above the income of working-class families.

The lower limit—determined by subsistence—is an unintuitive mouthful:

$$w \geq \frac{subsistence\ consumption\ per\ person \times proportion\ of\ population\ in\ working\ class}{hours\ of\ work\ per\ worker\ per\ year \times proportion\ of\ population\ working}$$

There is one surprise in this analysis. The *ratio* of maximum to minimum real wages has precise meaning. Taking that ratio, using (9), yields:

$$\frac{maximum\ real\ wage}{minimum\ real\ wage} = \alpha \qquad (10)$$

This simplifies the geometry of the relevant range.

9.4   ALPHA AND THE REPRESENTATIVE FIRM

Before drawing our diagrams we need precise concepts for a representative firm. We will use this expression in reference to an enterprise that meets both social-survival and enterprise-survival conditions.

In order to qualify as a representative firm, a firm must satisfy (4). When this occurs, the real wage rate will be found in the range defined by (9). To pay outside that range would imply either that workers live at a higher standard than the capitalists or that workers get less than their share of the social subsistence. The first would destroy capitalism. The second would undermine capitalism because effective-demand would be chronically low *or* it would indicate labor productivity is too low for capitalism to function. A representative firm in a viable capitalistic country would not do these.

When a firm satisfies (4) and (9) it will pay wages in the range defined by the size of alpha according to (10). When we draw our relevant-range diagrams this ratio will give us points A and B on a vertical axis called real wage. This is the contribution of social-survival conditions to this analysis.

9.5   Utilization of Productive Capacity

In order to find the relevant range for the horizontal axis we need to consider the utilization of productive capacity. Consider this spectrum:

full utilization . . . normal utilization . . . breakeven point . . .
shutdown point.

The full-utilization concept is useful to determine the maximum hours of employment offered in a year. What determines the lower bound?

According to the orthodox shutdown point concept, shutdown is determined by loss minimization. This is inadequate for two reasons. A firm may be forced to shutdown between the breakeven point and the so-called shutdown point in two cases related to the balance sheet. These are enterprise-survival conditions:

(1) *solvency:*   *owners equity > 0*
(2) *liquidity:*   *net current assets sufficiently > 0*

A firm incurring losses may violate (1) and go bankrupt before reaching the so-called shutdown point. This happens when leverage is high and business conditions deteriorate. A firm incurring losses may also violate (2) and find itself dissolved or transformed by the demands of its creditors. The shutdown point is too low for establishing the lower bound for the representative firm.

The breakeven point is more suitable. At breakeven, owners equity is unchanged, so the solvency condition is not violated. The liquidity condition is not quite as easy. At breakeven, income equals outgo. This would assure sufficient liquidity if the timing of income and outgo were well matched. If they are not well matched a firm may run into liquidity problems. Thus, for a representative firm in a viable capitalistic economy, the lower part of the relevant range of utilization *cannot* be below the breakeven point.

We can now define another alpha concept, this one related to the utilization of productive capacity:

$$utilization\ \alpha = \frac{full\ utilization\ of\ productive\ capacity}{breakeven\ utilization\ of\ productive\ capacity}$$

When we draw our relevant-range diagrams this ratio will give us points C and D on the horizontal axis called hours of work per year.

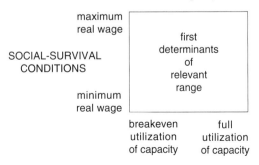

9.6   RELEVANT RANGE: FIRST WORLD

If we know alpha and the utilization alpha, we can draw a diagram for a representative firm. For a first world country, to retain simplicity, we will assume both of these are equal to two. Consider the diagram below.

The real wage rate is on the vertical axis; the hours of work per year is on the horizontal. Given the ratio approach we are using, the ratios give us the information we need.

The distance OA is the minimum real wage and the distance OB is the maximum real wage. Their ratio, OB/OA, equals two. The distance OC is hours of work at the breakeven level of production. The distance OD is hour of work at full utilization of productive capacity. Their ratio, OD/OC, also equals two. Those ratios define a relevant space by points E, F, G, and H.

Only points within the space EFHG are relevant. *The relevant space occurs in the northeast quadrant of the diagram.* Within that space can we find a smaller relevant range?

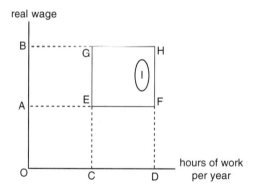

Yes, we can. With additional considerations we can perceive a relevant area I.

First, we have yet to use the concept of normal utilization of productive capacity. If rates of profit depend directly upon the degree of utilization of productive capacity, normal utilization will be much closer to full utilization than breakeven. Thus, hours of work in the representative firm will be closer to the upper limit than the lower.

The range restricting distribution is also likely to be smaller than the limits set by the maximum and minimum real wages. In a rich country, in order to maintain a high alpha, the inequality cannot be too great (effective-demand problem) nor can it be too small (capitalistic-incentive problem).

The area around I indicates the relevant space corresponding to these considerations. Under normal conditions, the neo-Classical X will be found in here. Clearly, it will not be a large X. Infact, it will be a rather small x, found in a *particular* location.

9.7   RELEVANT RANGE: THIRD WORLD

Let us now turn to a third world country. In this case we will assume an alpha of 1.3. For simplicity, we assume the same size utilization alpha.

The distance OA is the minimum real wage and the distance OB is the maximum real wage. Their ratio, OB/OA, equals 1.3. The distance OC is hours of work at the breakeven level of production. The distance OD is hours of work at full utilization of productive capacity. Their ratio, OD/OC, also equals 1.3. Those ratios define a relevant space by points E, F, G, and H.

Only points within the space EFHG are relevant. This relevant space is much smaller than the one we found for the first world country. Can we find a smaller relevant range within this space?

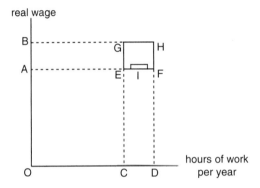

Yes, indeed. We have two reasons, which compound powerfully, for real wages to be near the bottom of the range in the third world:

* *Classical*: wage rates above subsistence encourage population growth which depresses real wages toward the subsistence level.
* *Class power*: capitalists use their decision-making advantages to maintain the inequality constrained only by the need to pay wages adequate for the reproduction of working classes.

The utilization of capacity is also different from the first world. In the third world, *every firm faces regular supply-side failures:* power cuts, poor communications, equipment breakdowns, lack of spare parts, illiteracy, and other things. So, the relevant space, I, covers a range between E and F.

There is not much room here for a neo-Classical X. Not much room even for a little x. Third world circumstances overwhelm the neo-Classical analysis.

The fourth world situation would be worse. Wages would be *below* the distance OA. In Chapter 5, on Productivity Limits, we saw that labor productivity is too low for *modern capitalism* to function in such countries.

Finally, we cannot even draw a diagram for the fifth world. It lacks *any* relevant range within survival conditions for the determination of 'equilibrium wages' because it fails survival conditions completely.

10

PRINCIPLE OF SOCIAL SUBSISTENCE

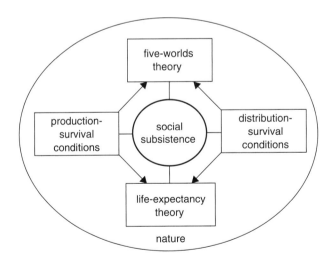

Core of the Modern Macrofoundation

10.1   THREE ORIGINAL NEEDS

Man in this world has only three original needs: (1) that of his subsistence, (2) that of his preservation, and (3) that of the perpetuation of his species.
    —Marquis de Mirabeau and Francois Quesnay, *Rural Philosophy* (1763)

The entry point for this book is found in the quote above and the diagram below. That is the first quote in the book—and the first diagram, too.

The quote identifies three 'original needs' of humanity 'in this world'. We depict this as human beings within nature, with three needs based upon species being: *subsistence, preservation*, and *perpetuation*. These are aspects of the survival problem. What can we say about them?

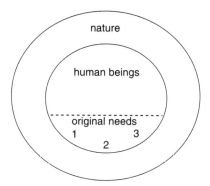

Let us consider a traditional *subsistence bundle*: food, shelter, clothing, fuel, and medicine on a continuous basis. Without these we cannot last long—as individuals, families, communities, societies, or as a species. We must produce or collect subsistence bundles or must be able to buy them from others. The nature of subsistence bundles will depend upon the technologies we use to secure subsistence goods and services. Production of the social subsistence requires a great deal of cooperation in the form of a social division of labor.

Preservation of social groups, on a year-to-year basis, requires the resources and activities needed to bring subsistence goods and services into quantities sufficient for the social subsistence. Preservation also requires the production of social surplus, in order to prepare for emergency needs and allow for inequality in distribution. If population is growing, preservation requires production of larger quantities of social subsistence.

Perpetuation of the species has three important markers: from generation-to-generation, from century-to-century and from millennium-to-millennium. How well do we stand the test of time? While our species has been fruitful and multiplied—indeed, excessively multiplied!—*social orders* rarely last more than a few centuries. This, however, does not threaten the survival of humanity. Our abuse of nature and each other is a different matter. We must overcome our ecocidal and genocidal tendencies this century or humanity has no future at all.

10.2   SOCIAL SUBSISTENCE

How can we be sure a society is capable of producing on a regular basis enough subsistence for all its members? As before, it is easiest to begin thinking within a corn model. We have a recent harvest. The replacement seed is set aside. The net output is divided into subsistence and surplus:

net output = social subsistence + social surplus

Even in a corn model, the 'weight' or content of the personal subsistence bundle is not a certain thing. It can be scanty or plentiful. A scanty subsistence bundle will tend to support a low life expectancy while a plentiful subsistence bundle will tend to support a better life expectancy.

As we saw in Chapter 1, social subsistence has three components in a corn model:

survival needs + productivity needs + reproduction needs

A scanty social subsistence would allow rations just sufficient for survival, it would impair productivity and it would tend to ignore reproduction demands. This could never be considered an adequate bundle. A plentiful social subsistence would more than allow for the daily claims of food; it would generously fuel work and assure mother and child ample food. This could be considered a normal bundle *if the society is capable of producing it.*

This provides an answer to the question above: if a country is capable of producing a plentiful social subsistence, it is capable of producing some social surplus, too. If such a society can also achieve ecological sustainability, it has solved two of the great problems plaguing humanity since our obscure origins.

Most of the time, in this book, we have had a different definition of social subsistence in mind—one based upon per capita information and analysis:

subsistence consumption per person × population

Social subsistence goes up if either the bundle or the population increases. As we saw in Chapter 4, subsistence consumption per person greatly depends upon the *complexity* of the society. A simple society will have a simple bundle but a complex society will have a complex bundle and thus a *much larger* social subsistence, even if they have same size populations.

Finally, we have the production-survival condition, written here in ratio form:

$$\alpha = \frac{net\ output}{social\ subsistence} > 1$$

Much of the book is written around this relationship. It offers an acid test of a society's capacity to persevere. If the social subsistence exceeds the net output for a few of years, the damage to the population and social order might be extensive. A population cycle is likely, as is a new social order.

10.3   Surplus theory

It is helpful to draw a picture of something central to Chapters 7 and 8. The word surplus means different things to different people. There are many valid forms of surplus analysis. I think it is best looked at pragmatically as a category of accounting and the source of much useful ratio analysis.

Social surplus refers to a residual, what is left of the harvest when both replacement seed and social subsistence are removed. This is depicted on the right side below. Usually we work from net output but here we want replacement seed in our *accounting* because it gives us rich information.

For example, what is the ratio of corn social subsistence to replacement seed? It will be high in a society with advanced agriculture and low in a society with traditional agriculture. What happens if the fertility of seeds greatly declines? The ratio declines greatly, too. If the social subsistence was plentiful, it will become scanty. Social surplus will be reduced or disappear or go negative.

surplus value	social surplus
required for reproduction of working class	social subsistence
replacement seed	replacement seed
active side	passive side

The other side of the diagram has to do with *existence of profits*. First, subtract the replacement seed, then, subtract the corn required for the reproduction of the working class. This yields 'surplus value'—the residual available for profits in a capitalistic economy. In Marxian Accounting, the shorthand for this diagram is '$C + V + S$'—starting from the bottom. This is a valid social-accounting equation, independent of Marx's discredited theory of exploitation.

Comparing the two sides of the diagram, the social subsistence is always larger than its counterpart on the left side. It allows for a subsistence bundle for all members of the society while the item on the left side calculates subsistence bundles for working-class families only.

The 'rate of surplus value'—the ratio of surplus value to the amount required for reproduction of the working class—puts an *upper limit on the size of alpha* because the proportions here will hold whenever social surplus is positive.

10.4   DISTRIBUTION THEORY

We should collect the main ideas thus far on distribution. First, let us look at some practical matters that have come up based upon inequality theory.

We have been looking at inequality from various angles. In a situation with huge inequality, the elite intent will determine the course of events. If they make decisions on the basis of self-interest only, they will perpetuate the inequality and oversee a stagnant society. If one starts with great inequality, progress depends upon investment in the poor so they can contribute to the social division of labor.

High gini coefficients are a *warning* sign. In the face of high ginis, rapid growth policies usually fail to deliver much sustainable growth or poverty reduction. High inequality itself is a barrier to reducing inequality or reversing stagnation.

If most people in a society live on a scanty subsistence, there will be chronic effective demand problems. We can observe two vicious cycles. (1) A scanty subsistence income supports poor nutrition, healthcare, and education. This perpetuates low productivity and low-earning capacity. (2) Lack of physical collateral damages access to credit. This limits earning opportunities from self-employment. These vicious cycles reinforce the inertia caused by high ginis.

Our other view on distribution has been derived from considering some algebraic inequalities. First, the distribution-survival condition from Chapter 1:

$$consumption\ of\ median\ person \geq subsistence\ per\ person$$

This made the five-worlds theory possible and contributed to the life-expectancy theory. We shall have more to say on both of these shortly. One may wonder: why choose the median person? It is possible to argue for a different measure. But this one is the simplest and it leads to various useful results when combined with the production-survival condition.

One of the original goals of the work in Kobe was to determine the maximum and minimum rates of profits consistent with survival conditions. This was one of the most important results in the relevant-range analysis done there. The maximum and minimum rates of profit had to satisfy the production-survival condition *plus* a simple distribution assumption: the families dominating the ownership of capital will live on a higher material standard than those who work for them:

$$propertied\text{-}class\ alpha > alpha > working\text{-}class\ alpha \geq 1$$

We should consider this from two angles. If the propertied class lives on a *large multiple* of the subsistence bundle, we are likely to observe high gini coefficients. If the working-class alpha is less than one, this society might be described as a 'failing country'. This brings us to the five-worlds theory. What *is* a failing country?

10.5   FIVE-WORLDS THEORY

The climax of Chapter 1 is the introduction of the five-worlds theory. The production-survival condition teamed up with a distribution counterpart to allow us to distinguish five different cases. We show this here as a relational diagram. We shall soon see this has a striking relationship with life-expectancy theory.

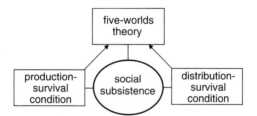

Let us review the five worlds: The first world satisfies both conditions easily. The second world satisfies both conditions, but not so easily. The third world satisfies both conditions, but with little margin for error. The fourth world satisfies the production-survival condition but fails the distribution-survival condition. The fifth world fails both conditions.

The five worlds constitute a *spectrum*. From Chapter 4 we can suggest some estimated numbers. Let us approach this beginning with 'rich country, poor country, starving country' in mind—first, third, and fifth worlds.

First World: If the poverty line is half the median income, the ratio of net output to social subsistence will be around 2.

Third World: Assuming a degree of inequality common in poor countries, we found a country might need an alpha of about 1.5 to reach the third world.

Fifth World: What is 'typical'? 0.9 suggests a net output shortfall of about one-tenth of the social subsistence—as if a tenth of the society is rubbished.

What can we say about the other two cases?

Fourth World: Based upon a Bangladesh rural poverty study, we estimated a ratio less than 1.2 there.

Second World: If it is evenly spaced between first and third, alpha would be around 1.75.

	PRODUCTION-SURVIVAL CONDITION*	DISTRIBUTION-SURVIVAL CONDITION*	NET OUTPUT DIVIDED BY SOCIAL SUBSISTENCE
first world	satisfy easily	satisfy easily	around 2
second world	satisfy	satisfy	around 1.75
third world	satisfy somewhat	satisfy barely	around 1.5
fourth world	satisfy poorly	fail	around 1.2
fifth world	fail	fail miserably	around 0.9

*Chapter 1, Section 7.

10.6   LIFE-EXPECTANCY THEORY

One of the main theoretical and empirical ideas in the book is stated in Chapter 2, right after the introduction of life-expectancy curves:

> The higher the *quality* of social subsistence,
> And the more *equitable* its distribution,
> The longer the life expectancy.

This directly confronts opinion associating life expectancy with income. I think the view in this book can prevail when social-subsistence accounting is established. This could simplify development planning in poor countries because they could concentrate on increasing the quantity, quality, and distribution of social subsistence.

The life-expectancy theory was an extension of our first inquiry into the implications of inequality. A backward bending life-expectancy curve was derived. We added two subsistence goods, cod and quinine. This gave us a sense of how the subsistence bundle, and its quality over time, is the first determinant of the center of gravity for life expectancy. Then we told the story of a mythical village as it used and ruined a beautiful valley.

The ruination of that mythical village should be pondered upon here. The village began with wild corn only. With the introduction of corn production, demographic dynamics changed. Demographic dynamics changed again two more times with the introduction of cod and quinine. However, the villagers had no sense of carrying capacity. They filled up the valley and eventually killed the lake by over-fishing. With one of their three pillars of social subsistence gone, they descended into civil war. *That story was told entirely in terms of birth rates and death rates.*

We should also ponder upon the reach of the two survival conditions from Chapter 1. They formed the basis for five-worlds theory. They can also form the basis of life-expectancy analysis. The left side of this diagram is alpha, so the production-survival condition is already here. If we have the data for the distribution-survival condition, we can predict life expectancies.

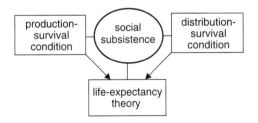

Life expectancy should be a topic in all social sciences. It is central to our species being. I hope this analysis will be useful to every sort of social scientist.

10.7 MACROFOUNDATION CORE

As we close Section 1 of this book we might reflect on the core lesson. From the point of view of the macrofoundations of economics and development, a simple relationship, developed in Chapter 4, is at the core of the book:

$$\alpha = \frac{\Upsilon_{net}}{C'} = \frac{\lambda h \omega}{\sigma} > 1$$

Υ_{net} = net output	C' = social subsistence
λ = net output/hours of work	h = hours of work/workers
ω = workers/population	σ = social subsistence/population

This is the entry point for many of our diagrams.

From the point of view of the macrofoundations of political economy, a larger perspective is required. My quest for survival conditions began with an inner *picture*—the word SUBSISTENCE in a circle, with branches in four directions. "It is upon subsistence, upon the means of subsistence that all the branches of the political order depend"—as said the Physiocrats.

Chapter 7 contains my first attempt to explore the branches. This chapter offers an additional way to explore them. I think there are more ways to explore the branches out of social subsistence.

The five-worlds theory is not surprising. Social scientists have been discussing 'three worlds' or 'four worlds' for decades. To use a simple model to extend this to five is a modest step. What *is* unexpected is how it shares common ground with life-expectancy theory. Equally surprising is the symmetry at the core of the macrofoundation. Moreover, the production and distribution branches have many branches themselves.

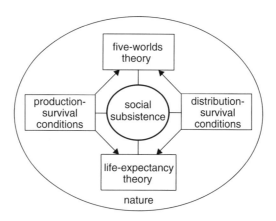

This model of a macrofoundation is a net—a web—of some social factors at the heart of political economy.

PART TWO

CLASSICAL MACROFOUNDATION

The Classics of British Political Economy contain a macrofoundation based upon the essential features of a largely agrarian society. The analysis was aimed at solving the subsistence problem. Sir James Steuart made the most important contribution to building the model. The model still plays a quiet role in anthropology and continues to be relevant in much of the poorworlds.

With the Classical Macrofoundation in hand, we witness its application to the history of civilization—*Man Makes Himself* (1936). Armed with two social-surplus conditions, the rise and fall of empires is compactly modeled. While 'man makes himself', the process has a dark side, as seen in *Ecocide* (2002).

We observe the origins of 'the dismal science' and its eventual transcendence. From an historical perspective, the rise of scientific agriculture is shown to be both a key to solving the subsistence problem and a vital link in the transition from Classical Political Economy to neo-Classical Economics.

We return to Steuart to observe in detail his construction of the Classical Macrofoundation in Book 1 of his *Principles* (1767). This allows us to consider Malthus in a new context. The post-Malthusian theme of capital-accumulation crisis is powerfully analyzed in *Revolution and Rebellion* (1991).

To caution against the abuse of macrofoundations, we consider the totalitarian use of surplus analysis.

In order to help solve the subsistence problem in the poorworlds, Part Two ends with a plea for the rehabilitation of Classics.

11

CLASSICS

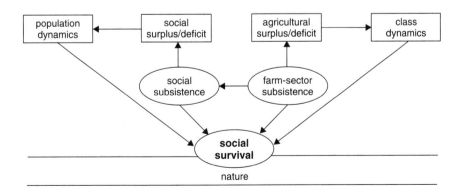

11.1   PREOCCUPATION WITH SUBSISTENCE

By 'Classical' I shall include all of the great early economists who grounded their macro work in the surplus approach. I am not interested in their price theory but in their theory of *society*. The principle of social subsistence is at the heart of these Classics. Moreover, the Classical Macrofoundation still lives in anthropology. Long banished from economics, it is needed in the poorworlds.

We begin with four quotes from the Founders.

The first is from Sir James Steuart, at the beginning of his *Principles of Political Economy* (1767; but written in exile in the late 1750s):

> The principal object of this science is to secure a certain fund of subsistence for all the inhabitants, to obviate every circumstance which may render it precarious . . . (1.Introduction.6)

This brilliant sentence expresses elegantly the still unfinished Classical agenda. The word 'subsistence' appears 258 times in the *Principles*. In my opinion, Steuart is the father of survival-conditions analysis.

Our next passage comes from the Physiocrat's *Rural Philosophy* (1763):

> [W]e must consider the common weal in terms of its essence, and humanity as a whole in terms of its roots, *subsistence*. All moral and physical parts of which society is constituted derive from this and are subordinated to it. It is upon subsistence, upon the means of the subsistence, that all the branches of the political order depend. (Meek translation, 57, emphasis in the original)

Those powerful sentences were my principle inspiration for many years. Based upon that passage I drew the diagram above, which became the entry point for my work on the Modern Macrofoundation.

The third cornerstone passage comes from Adam Smith:

> Political economy, considered as a . . . science . . . proposes . . . first, to provide a plentiful revenue or subsistence for the people, or more properly to enable them to provide such a revenue or subsistence for themselves . . . (4.Introduction.1)

The word 'subsistence' appears 162 times in *The Wealth of Nations* (1776).

Finally, in a sentence on 'Checks to Population in Siberia', in the second edition of *The Principle of Population* (1803), Malthus states with stunning compactness the production and distribution survival conditions in a corn model:

> It is not enough a country should have the power of producing food in abundance, but the state of society must be such as to afford the means of its proper distribution . . . (1.9.8)

11.2   SPECULATION ON THE ORIGINS OF SOCIETY

'In the beginning.' With these words Mirabeau and Quesnay set forth their speculation on the origins of society in the *Rural Philosophy*. They use a biblical opening intentionally, for their story is related. In the Bible we have Adam and Eve in the Garden of Eden—land of abundance. They ate the forbidden fruit and were expelled. They had to toil for their subsistence. They had children. Their first son, Cain, was 'tiller of the ground'; their second son, Abel, was 'keeper of sheep'. Let us see the Physiocratic version:

> In the beginning, man found himself faced with uninhabited spaces which, in relation to the small numbers of the first human beings, abounded in goods suitable for subsistence. At first he consumed the spontaneous gifts of nature without making any effort . . . He saw population increase, and the means of subsistence become proportionately more troublesome to acquire. Thus it was necessary for him to look for new things on which to subsist. (Meek, 60)

Three methods for obtaining subsistence were developed in order to survive:

> He had to cultivate the land . . . He had to herd together and rear domestic animals . . . And he had to hunt wild animals and set traps for them, and do the same also for fish . . . (Meek, 60)

This story differs from modern understanding. According to much evidence, human beings were hunter-gatherers for most of our existence. Domestication came late. We shall take this matter up again in Chapters 12 and 14.

But the Physiocratic story, even if inaccurate in this detail, is useful in another way. Mirabeau and Quesnay continue:

> Of these three modes of life, derived from three different kinds of subsistence, the first gives rise to settled laws, weights, measures, and everything which is concerned with determining and guaranteeing possessions . . . The second kept innocence and hospitality alive for a longer time, and devoted itself to the sciences, to astronomy and to speculation . . . The third, finally, although the most contemptible and founded on the least secure basis, was in general better adapted to natural licentiousness, to the brutish man. (Meek, 60–61)

The first was settled, the second was nomadic, and the third was warlike:

> always in accordance with the nature and kind of their means of subsistence. (Meek, 61)

Only the first could support dense populations. By nature, the land required per farmer for family subsistence was always much less than the land needed per herder or hunter for the same object.

Eventually these three intermingled and each found its place in society:

> Agriculture constituted its foundation, but the rearing and feeding of live-stock became necessary in order to link the plains with the mountains, the pastures with the crops, and the grass-lands with cultivation. The art of war, which it became necessary for it to take up in order to ensure the security of its territory, was soon bound to dominate it . . . (Meek, 62)

11.3   MACROFOUNDATION OF CLASSICAL ECONOMICS

The classical macrofoundation depends upon two demographic propositions highly relevant in pre-industrial agricultural societies. First: population is limited by the available means of subsistence. Second: nonagricultural population is limited by the size of the surplus produced in farming.

These propositions were taken for granted by classical economists. They still play an important role in anthropology. For example, V. Gordon Childe, in *Man Makes Himself* (1936), and Jared Diamond, in *Guns, Germs and Steel* (1997), could not have told their stories without them.

Sir James Steuart is the father of the classical macrofoundation. The details are found in Book One of his *Principles*, 'Population and Agriculture'. We shall leave out the details of his brilliant analysis to get to the heart of the system.

For Steuart, the first principle is found in existence and survival:

> The fundamental principle of the multiplication of all animals, and consequently of man, is generation; the next is food: generation gives existence, food preserves it. (1.3.3)

Then he identifies the principle limiting population in a state-of-nature:

> Were the earth ... uncultivated, the numbers of mankind would not exceed the proportion of the spontaneous fruits which she offers ... (1.3.5)

Under the same primitive assumption he identifies population dynamics:

> [T]he generative faculty resembles a spring loaded with a weight ... when food has remained some time without augmentation or diminution, generation will carry numbers as high as possible; if then food come to be diminished ... Inhabitants will diminish ... people will begin to be better fed; they will multiply, and ... food will become scarce again. (1.3.10)

Steuart then introduces agriculture, which allows for larger populations:

> I now suppose man to add his labour and industry to the natural activity of the soil: so far, as by this he produces an additional quantity of food, so far he lays a foundation for the maintenance of an additional number. (1.4.1)

Sir James then brings in agricultural surplus and its usage:

> One consequence of a fruitful soil, possessed by a free people, given to agriculture, and inclined to industry, will be the production of a superfluous quantity of food, over and above what is necessary to feed the farmers ... a certain number ... will apply themselves ... to ... supplying ... other wants. (1.5.19)

This leads to the emergence of the original social classes in agricultural society:

> [W]e find ... people distributed into two classes ... farmers ... and ... free hands ... (1.5.20)

This analysis, long forgotten by economists, is still relevant in the poorworlds.

Let us see the classical macrofoundation with the help of social accounting. It is easiest to build from the closed-economy corn model. We assume an agrarian society with a high ratio of agriculture labor to total labor.

Consider a recent harvest. We subtract the replacement corn seed to determine the net output. In order to identify the surplus conditions, we need to know three things: subsistence consumption per person, the total population and the population in the farm sector.

The social subsistence equals subsistence consumption per person times the population. Subtract this from the net output to get the social surplus:

$$net\ output\ -\ social\ subsistence\ =\ social\ surplus$$

The farm sector subsistence equals subsistence consumption per person times the population in the farm sector. We subtract this from the net output to get the agricultural surplus:

$$net\ output\ -\ farm\text{-}sector\ subsistence\ =\ agricultural\ surplus$$

The first condition yields *population dynamics*: if social surplus is produced, the population can expand. If less than the social subsistence is produced, the population contracts. Of course, there are other formulas possible under different assumptions of birth and death rates and subsistence quality.

The second condition yields *class dynamics*: if agricultural surplus is produced, nonfarm populations can exist and be supported. The greater the agricultural surplus, the larger the nonagricultural populations supportable from internal resources. If there is ambition, nonagriculture divisions of labor will multiple.

The farm sector requires more introduction. The right-hand side of the diagram feeds into the left-hand side through the subsistence conditions. Farmers must be able to maintain their sector or the society cannot function. Agricultural surplus is a necessary (but not sufficient) condition for social surplus.

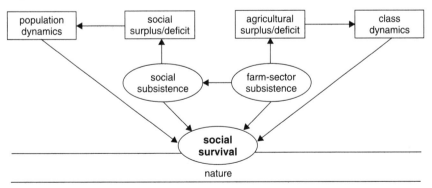

Our assumption about a high ratio of agricultural labor to total labor implies something about alpha: it will be low. For example, if the first ratio is 90 percent and the productivity of labor is equal in all uses, alpha will equal 1.1.

Social survival depends upon feedbacks from farm-sector performance, economy-wide performance, population dynamics, and class dynamics.

11.4   SCANTY AND PLENTIFUL SUBSISTENCE

In Steuart, subsistence varies from slender to full. For Smith—trying to ignore yet differentiate himself from Steuart—subsistence varies from scanty to plentiful. We shall ponder this here because the *quality of social subsistence and its distribution* played a large role in our analysis of life expectancy. Let us see what Smith has to say in the *Wealth of Nations*.

A plentiful subsistence was better for physical and mental health and this translated into higher productivity. This was a reason for wages to be 'high':

> A plentiful subsistence increases the bodily strength of the labourer, and the comfortable hope of bettering his condition, and of ending his days perhaps in ease and plenty, animates him to exert that strength to the utmost. Where wages are high, accordingly, we shall always find the workmen more active, diligent, and expeditious than where they are low . . . (1.8.43)

A scanty subsistence, on the other hand, had no redeeming quality. He expressed a blunt aversion to conditions in Canton, China, reported by travelers:

> In the neighbourhood of Canton . . . many thousand families have no habitation on the land, but live constantly in little fishing boats upon the rivers and canals. The subsistence which they find there is so scanty that they are eager to fish up the nastiest garbage thrown overboard from any European ship . . . (1.8.24)

But subsistence in China was not *too scanty* for maintaining its already huge population. It was an agrarian fourth world country, but not fifth:

> China, however, though it may perhaps stand still, does not seem to go backwards. Its towns are nowhere deserted by their inhabitants. The lands which had once been cultivated are nowhere neglected. The same or very nearly the same annual labour must therefore continue to be performed, and the funds destined for maintaining it must not, consequently, be sensibly diminished. The lowest class of labourers, therefore, notwithstanding their scanty subsistence, must some way or another make shift to continue their race so far as to keep up their usual numbers. (1.8.25)

Smith found the wages of labor in Britain adequate for family subsistence and certainly of a better standard than the 'lowest rate' for 'common humanity':

> In Great Britain the wages of labour seem, in the present times, to be evidently more than what is precisely necessary to enable the labourer to bring up a family . . . There are many plain symptoms that the wages of labour are nowhere in this country regulated by this lowest rate which is consistent with common humanity. (1.8.27)

What of the original division of labor discussed by the Physiocrats? With some irony we can observe a dialectic progression for the most violent type:

> Hunting and fishing, the most important employments of mankind in the rude state of society, become in its advanced state their most agreeable amusements, and they pursue for pleasure what they once followed from necessity. (1.10.6)

11.5   SOCIAL CLASSES

The classical macrofoundation, as presented in our discussion of Steuart, leaves open the character of the social classes that grow out of an agricultural society. Certainly there will be landlords, those who work the land, and those engaged in other activities. Steuart had his way of comprehending the social classes and Quesnay had another. It was the genius of Smith to have greater insight and foresight on this point. Referring to 'civilized society', he said:

> The whole annual produce of the land and labour . . . naturally divides itself . . . into three parts; the rent of land, the wages of labour, and the profits of stock; and constitutes a revenue to three different orders of people; to those who live by rent, to those who live by wages, and to those who live by profits. These are the three great, original, and constituent orders of every civilised society, from whose revenue that of every other order is ultimately derived. (1.11.261)

The elevation of profit seekers into the social core signaled a change of economic system: from feudalism, where the landowners dominated and desired surplus for its use value, to capitalism, where the capitalist desired 'profits of stock' in his quest to accumulate capital. 'It is glorious to get rich.'

Smith was the prophet of this doctrine. He was the first to realize that the desire to carve out new profit opportunities, maximize profits, and accumulate capital would become the mainspring of economic progress. Assuming competitive conditions, he observes the consequences of a successful innovation:

> The establishment of any new manufacture, of any new branch of commerce, or of any new practice in agriculture, is always a speculation, from which the projector promises himself extraordinary profits . . . If the project succeeds, they are commonly at first very high. When the trade or practice becomes thoroughly established and well known, the competition reduces them to the level of other trades. (1.10.46)

Successful innovation is richly rewarded. Competition tends to equalize rates of profit in similar and different uses of capital. This analysis was destined to influence every great thinker in political economy. We still live in its shadow. It is one of the few theories included as a core proposition in all of the schools.

Smith made another observation on civilized society that would become a thread in demography. While observing the 'principle of population'—that population is limited by the available means of subsistence—he insisted the horrifying consequences in civilization only apply to the 'inferior ranks':

> Every species of animals naturally multiplies in proportion to the means of their subsistence, and no species can ever multiply beyond it. But in civilised society it is only among the inferior ranks of people that the scantiness of subsistence can set limits to the further multiplication of the human species; and it can do so in no other way than by destroying a great part of the children which their fruitful marriages produce. (1.8.38)

11.6   POPULATION

In his *Essay on the Principle of Population* (1798), Malthus pounded the sunny optimism found in Smith and expressed less carefully by end-of-the-century writers who dreamed of the 'perfectibility of man and of society'. Malthus saw one main obstacle in the way. The production of social surplus tends to encourage population growth and the standard of living therefore tends toward the level of subsistence that just maintains a population. If this cannot be evaded, human and social perfection are impossible.

At the end of Chapter 7, Malthus reduces his thesis to three propositions:

> [I]ncrease of population is necessarily limited by the means of subsistence . . . population does invariably increase when the means of subsistence increase . . . the superior power of population is repressed, and the actual population kept equal to the means of subsistence, by misery and vice. (7.21)

The second and third propositions could not withstand immediate criticism so Malthus revised the set in the Second Edition (1803), putting them in Chapter 2:

> 1. Population is necessarily limited by the means of subsistence.
> 2. Population invariably increases where the means of subsistence increase, unless prevented by some very powerful and obvious checks.
> 3. These checks, and the checks which repress the superior power of population, and keep its effects on a level with the means of subsistence, are all resolvable into moral restraint, vice and misery. (1.2.22)

While the second proposition is now valid, the third was made obsolete by successful industrialization. However, it still rings true in the poorworlds.

Also of interest to us is the quote from Malthus at the beginning of this chapter:

> It is not enough a country should have the power of producing food in abundance, but the state of society must be such as to afford the means of its proper distribution . . . (1.9.8)

In just a few words he indicates the two main propositions of Chapter 1:

- production-survival condition: ability to produce social surplus.
- distribution-survival condition: effective distribution of the social subsistence.

In the quote above, Malthus is bothered by the failure of the second condition. In this passage, Malthus cuts one of the diamonds of survival-conditions analysis: the borderland between the third and fourth worlds.

We should say one more thing here. Recall the production-survival condition:

$$net\ output > subsistence\ per\ person \times population$$

When this is rearranged it *implies* the Classical principle of population:

$$net\ output/subsistence\ per\ person > population$$

We use this, along with the Classical Macrofoundation, in the next chapter.

11.7   DIMINISHING RETURNS AND DISTRIBUTION

Malthus took exception to Smith's partially formed ideas on population. David Ricardo took exception to Smith's views on the 'harmony of interests' of the three great classes in capitalistic society. For while Smith said,

> The interest of the first of those three great orders . . . is strictly and inseparably connected with the general interest of the society. Whatever either promotes or obstructs the one, necessarily promotes or obstructs the other. (1.11.262)

He also said:

> As soon as the land of any country has all become private property, the land-lords, like all other men, love to reap where they never sowed, and demand a rent even for its natural produce. (1.6.8)

There is a loophole in the Smith argument. Ricardo appears to have seen it. He produced a refinement of Malthusian population theory—with a *twist*.

This is seen in Ricardo's analysis of distribution, in *An Essay on Profits* (1815). Everyone agreed that wages were determined by subsistence—sometimes scanty and sometimes plentiful. What determined profits and rent?

Consider the following diagram. Corn is produced on land with corn seed and labor time. Landlords provide the land; capitalists provide the seed and management. The same quantity of seed and the same labor time are applied to every acre. But land differs in quality, from very productive to totally barren.

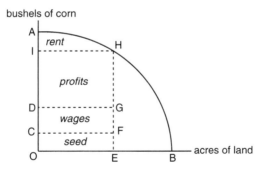

OA is the product of the most fertile acre. OB is number of farmable acres. AB is the marginal-product curve. The area OAB is the maximum production of corn. OC is the seed per acre and CD is the wage per acre.

Suppose capitalists rent OE acres for production. The seed needed is OCFE. The wage-bill is CDGF. *Agricultural surplus is DAHG.* The division of the agricultural surplus between profits and rent is determined 'at the margin' at point H. Profits are DIHG and rent is IAH.

For the next harvest, OCFE replacement seed is available, or, if the capitalists would like to sow more acres, additional seed can be got out of profits.

Suppose productivity remains unchanged and corn imports are forbidden. As population expands, additional acres will have to be brought under cultivation. Such expansion of agriculture will be at the expense of capitalists and to the benefit of landlords. This bothered Ricardo terribly. Let us see why.

The diagram below has the same points A through D but now point E has moved to the right. OE′ acres are under cultivation to feed the larger population. Agricultural surplus now equals DAH′G′. The division of surplus between profits and rent is determined at point H′. Rent has swelled to I′AH′ while profits have shrunk to DI′H′G′

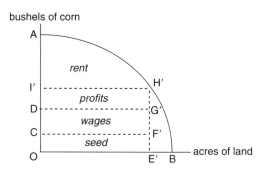

But the news gets worse. In the Ricardo model, the rate of profits in agriculture will determine the center of gravity for the general rate of profits in society:

> In this state of society, when the profits on agricultural stock . . . are fifty per cent, the profits on all other capital . . . will be also, fifty per cent. (6–7)

On the previous page the rate of profits was the ratio of profits to the sum of seed and wages. It was obviously very high. On the diagram above the rate of profits has shrunk considerably.

For Ricardo, this threatened the expansion of capitalistic society. If the average rate of profits fell too low, the incentive to accumulate capital would weaken seriously and progress would come to a halt. Ricardo was blunt in drawing an awesome conclusion:

> [T]he interest of the landlord is always opposed to the interest of every other class in the community. (20)

These were tough words. Ricardo wanted Britain to renounce Corn Laws prohibiting the importation of grain. The political power of the landowning class was still too strong. The Corn Laws sat on the books until almost the middle of the eighteenth century, until the political power of the capitalists could overwhelm the landlords on this issue. In the meantime, technical change had come to the rescue and capitalism in England was booming!

The modern poorworlds have not been so lucky. They still struggle against feudalistic thinking while facing run-away population growth.

12

ROOTS OF CIVILIZATION

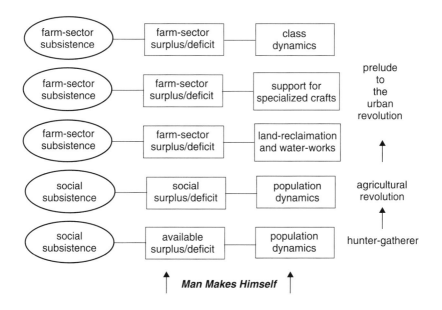

12.1   HUMAN REVOLUTION

No book quite like this has ever been written . . . we regard Professor Childe's
book as the most stimulating, original and convincing contribution to the history of civilization which we have ever read.
> —Review of V. Gordon Childe, *Man Makes Himself* (1936) by
> O.G.S. Crawford, 'Human Progress', *Antiquity* 10: 391–404

Note: all quotes in this chapter are from the 1951 American version

Jared Diamond's *Guns, Germs and Steel* (1997) has recently had spectacular
success. In that book, Diamond applies the surplus approach to study early
human development. While the book has many merits—one of which we
shall consider in Chapter 20—the use of surplus analysis does not go very far.

The classic and brilliant study of human development grounded in
surplus analysis is found in a book nearly forgotten these days. V. Gordon
Childe's *Man Makes Himself* (1936) uses the surplus approach with the skill
of a master.

Diamond begins with Yali's Question concerning 'cargo'. Childe begins
with 'progress' as measured by the capacity of human beings to control
nature and multiply. Reflecting on rapid population growth in Britain after
1750, he says:

[W]e shall be able to discern in earlier ages of human history other 'revolutions'.
They manifest themselves in the same way as the 'Industrial Revolution'—in an
upward kink in the population curve. (19)

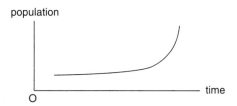

Recall the inequality that expresses the Classical principle of population:

Net output/subsistence per person > population

Childe wants to know: what extraordinary discoveries occurred in ancient
times raising the upper productivity limits *so dramatically* that ancient
humanity could *twice* experience revolutionary population booms?

In this chapter we follow Childe's story faithfully, quoting from him
extensively. It is possible for us to do so because his story may be told as an
application of the Classical Macrofoundation. Childe thought he was doing
good Marxian analysis. But most of *Man Makes Himself* is Classical in the
sense developed in Chapter 11.

I have been smitten by this beautiful little book. I hope you shall see why.

12.2   HUNTER-GATHERERS

Our hominid predecessors were endowed by nature with a weak body but a big brain. This allowed hominids to become problem-solving creatures.

In order to survive, the early hunter-gatherers made tools of wood, bone, or stone. By slightly sharpening these tools they could acquire more food—vegetable, animal, and aquatic—than was possible with their bare hands. They could also protect themselves somewhat from wild beasts.

Our ancestors evidently emerged from Africa and spread by land into Europe and Asia. Some ventured into cold climates in search of meat:

> During the Ice Ages several species of man already existed, contemporary with the mammoth; they hunted the beasts and drew pictures of them in caves . . . Instead of undergoing the slow physical changes . . . our ancestors found out how to control fire and make coats out of skin. (22)

Capture and killing of large animals required cooperation. This was essential for species development. So was the control of fire, which was epoch making:

> For the first time in history a creature of Nature was directing one of the great forces of Nature . . . The sight of the bright flame bursting forth when a dry bough was thrust into glowing embers, the transformation of the bough into fine ashes and smoke, must have stimulated man's rudimentary brain . . . He was asserting his humanity and making himself. (46)

Population was strictly limited by the available means of subsistence. This could be accessed better, somewhat, by the use of tools, made mostly of stone, and the application of fire, which increased the proportion of animal bodies that could be eaten. Changes in climate might decrease availability of plants and animals and reduce populations. So might excessive hunting-gathering.

Not all of their activity was directed at securing subsistence. We mentioned cave pictures; but Childe believes these were connected with magical ideas concerning successful hunts. What do we make of evidence of burial practices?

> More than a dozen Neanderthal skeletons have been found in France, ritually buried in the caves where their group lived. Generally attempts have been made to protect the body . . . The head sometimes rests on a stone pillow . . . their graves were placed near the hearths, as if to warm their occupants. The departed was provided with tools and joints of meat. (50)

I will venture a speculation. 'Elders'—living much longer than average—made particular contributions to the survival of the group. The hearts of the bereaved may have been stirred profoundly at the death of such an elder and they invented burial to maintain a connection between the living and the dead.

12.3   AGRICULTURAL REVOLUTION

The 'Old Stone Age' of hominids and early man lasted hundreds of thousand of years. Eventually discoveries ushered in the 'New Stone Age':

> The first revolution that transformed human economy gave man control over his own food supply. Man began to plant, cultivate, and improve by selection edible grasses, roots, and trees. And he succeeded in taming and firmly attaching to his person certain species of animal in return for the fodder he was able to offer, the protection he could afford, and the forethought he could exercise. (59)

Among the grains domesticated, wheat and barley offered special advantages: they were nutritious, yields were high, they did not require much water, the labor time was not too demanding and they could be easily stored.

Domestication had revolutionary impacts on population. It not only provided for the feeding of larger numbers; it also changed the position of children:

> To increase the food supply it is only necessary to sow more seed, to bring more land under tillage. If there are more mouths to feed, there will also be more hands to till the fields . . . children become economically useful. To hunters children are liable to be a burden. They have to be nourished for years before they can begin to contribute to the family larder effectively. But quite young toddlers can help in weeding fields and scaring off birds or trespassing beasts. If there are sheep and cattle, boys and girls can mind them. (61–62)

The population boom is attested to in the following dramatic archeological fact:

> [T]he human skeletons assigned to the New Stone Age in Europe alone are several hundred times more numerous than those from the whole of the Old Stone Age. Yet the New Stone Age in Europe lasted at the outside 2000 years— less than one hundredth of the time assigned to the Old! (63)

The Classical principle of population now operates according to a much higher productivity limit because much of the social subsistence is *produced* and social surplus is produced as well. The surplus can feed a growing population.

But an upper productivity limit is quickly reached:

> Nature soon posed a question to the first cultivators—the problem of soil exhaustion. The easiest way of dealing with the issue was to dodge it and move away . . . It was, of course, a nuisance to have to clear a new bit of forest every few years, but that was surely less trouble than thinking out a new solution . . . Yet it is a wasteful method, and ultimately limits the population, since suitable land is nowhere unrestricted. (64)

This was *one* early model of cultivation. No particular piece of land became home. Agriculture was, however, emerging in another way.

Certain locations were specially auspicious for food production. The most auspicious irrigate naturally and renew the soil by the action of nature:

> the most suitable land for cultivation is often found on the alluvial soils deposited where intermittent torrents flow out from the hills on to the plains, and in the valley of rivers that periodically overflow their banks . . . Now under such conditions the floods . . . not only water the crop, they create fresh soil . . . The silt contains the chemical constituents that last year's crop had taken from the soil, which is thus renewed and refertilized. Under conditions of natural irrigation, the cultivator need not be nomadic. (64–65)

The great civilizations, built up along the Nile, the Tigris-Euphrates, and the Indus, had these qualities. This plays an important role later in our story.

The other great aspect of domestication involves animals. Childe speculates on how man domesticated some of them. He believes that hunter-cultivators had the opportunity during droughts:

> [I]f the hunter is also a cultivator, he will have something to offer the famished beasts: the stubble of his freshly reaped fields will afford the best grazing in the oasis . . . Such will be too weak to run away, too thin to be worth killing for food. Instead, man can study their habits, drive off the lions or wolves that would prey upon them, and perhaps even offer them some surplus grain from his stores. The beasts, for their part, will grow tame and accustomed to man's proximity. (67–68)

Gradually man discovered a variety of ways the animals could yield value and soundly contribute to the social subsistence:

> At first the tame or domesticated beast would presumably be regarded only as a potential source of meat, an easily accessible sort of game. Other uses would be discovered later. It might be noticed that crops flourished best on plots that had been gazed over. Ultimately the value of dung as fertilizer would be realized. The process of milking can only have been discovered when . . . studying . . . the suckling of calves and lambs and kids. But once the trick was grasped, milk would become a second staple . . . Still later the hair of sheep or goats would win appreciation. (68–69)

We should summarize some of the consequences of the production of surplus:

> Food-production, even in its simplest form, provides an opportunity and a motive for the accumulation of a surplus. A crop must not be consumed as soon as it is reaped . . . a proportion of every crop must be set aside for seed . . . it means on the one hand forethought and thrift, on the other receptacles for storage . . . The surplus thus gathered will help to tide the community over bad seasons; it will form a reserve against droughts and crop failures. It will serve to support a growing population. Ultimately it may constitute a basis for rudimentary trade . . . (71)

Other skills were acquired in these early years of man—pottery, weaving, and spinning the most important. Just as in the case of food production, these required the pooling of experience and knowledge and the development of collective traditions. In numerous ways, human beings learned to cooperate.

12.4 PRELUDE TO THE URBAN REVOLUTION

The prelude to the second revolution can be summarized in three words: invention, specialization, and ambition. These transformed small farm villages into great cities—eventually empires—dependent upon massive foreign trade.

> The scene of the drama lies in the belt of semi-arid countries between the Nile and the Ganges. Here epoch-making inventions seem to have followed one another with breathless speed . . .
>
> Between 6000 and 3000 BC man has learnt to harness the force of oxen and of winds, he invents the plow, the wheeled cart and the sailboat, he discovers the chemical processes involved in smelting copper ores and the physical properties of metals, and he begins to work out an accurate solar calendar. He has thereby equipped himself for urban life, and prepares the way for a civilization which shall require writing . . . In no period of history till the days of Galileo was progress in knowledge so rapid or far-reaching discoveries so frequent. (87)

Previously, social surplus was simply available for the expansion of population and as a hedge against emergencies. Now, surplus food was utilized to support people withdrawn from cultivation. There were two great obstacles to the expansion of villages into cities: adequate fresh water and suitable land:

> As the human race multiplied under the stimulus of the first revolution, such became rare and valuable possessions. (88)

Great effort at land building occurred along the Nile. Swamps and reedy jungles had to be reclaimed. The same thing happened along the Tigris and Euphrates:

> The land on which the great cities of Babylonia were to rise had literally to be created . . . . Their reward was an assured supply of nourishing dates, a bounteous harvest from the fields they had drained, and permanent pastures for flocks and herds. (89)

These activities required planning; they also required some form of social control over the allocation of surplus:

> And all the works in question were collective undertakings . . . generally their execution required capital in the form of a stock of surplus foodstuffs, accumulated by and at the disposal of the community. The workers engaged in draining and embanking must be fed . . . (90)

Thus, the other half of the Classical Macrofoundation came into play:

With the development of irrigation channels, a form of social coercion emerged to keep uncooperative or antisocial farmers under control:

> the community can refuse a recalcitrant access to water and can close the channels that irrigate his fields. (90)

The sedentary life stimulated improvements in housing. Architecture slowly evolved. The invention of bricks gave permanence to buildings.

All the while there was contact between nomads and farmers. Trade in gold, stones, and shells developed, perhaps because of the magic properties attributed to them. Here was another turning point:

> The high estimation of magic substances may well have led to an active search for them . . . It would have been a principle factor in the diffusion of civilization . . . The collection of malachite, turquoise, and other colored stones accordingly caused men to frequent metalliferous regions and put copper ore into their hands. (94–95)

The Stone Ages were about to be superseded:

> The real superiority of metal is that it is fusible and can be cast. Fusibility confers upon copper some of the merits of the potter's clay . . . The only limit to size is the capacity of the mold . . . And the molds themselves can be made of potter's clay . . . the metal on cooling possesses the essential virtues of stone and bone . . . Yet it has the additional advantage of being malleable. And finally, it is more permanent than stone or bone. (96)

As the secrets of prospecting, mining, smelting, and metalwork were discovered, highly specialized crafts emerged. With the emergence of these fields, surplus relations became far more complex:

> But a community can afford a smith only if it possess a surplus of foodstuffs . . . it generally means more; it usually means the final sacrifice of economic independence. Copper is far from common; its ores are not found on the alluvial and löss plains preferred by neolithic farmers, but among wooded or stony ranges . . . the great majority had always to import the metal or its ore. In the end it had to be obtained by the production of a surplus of foodstuffs above what was needed for home consumption. (97)

Thus, the other half of the Classical Macrofoundation underwent a transformation. The production of surplus food above the needs of the food growers was made available to anyone with specialized skills. The complexity of the division of labor would then depend upon three things: farm-sector surplus, technical knowledge, and the extent of the market.

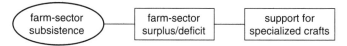

With trade over long distances a new feature of economic life, improved transport was needed:

> That meant the harnessing of animal motive power and of the winds. Both were, like the discovery of metal and the invention of metallurgy, preconditions of the second revolution and achieved before it. (99)

When man harnessed these he found himself inventing labor-saving devices. Man was making himself—and he was making life a little easier for some.

The marriage of tame but strong animals, with knowledge from leather, wood, and metal works, led to a breakthrough in agricultural productivity—the plow.

> Plowing stirs up those fertile elements in the soil that in semi-arid regions are liable to sink down beyond the reach of plant roots. With two oxen and a plow a man can cultivate in a day a far larger area than can a woman with a hoe . . . And all that means larger crops, more food and expanding population. (100)

Achievements piled up. The invention of horizontal and vertical wheels led to two great developments. First, pottery became mass-produced. Later, people and goods could be transported in wheeled vehicles drawn by animals. This greatly improved commerce and communications. The perfection of sail-boats had the same effect.

We have told this story without mentioning the dark side of human nature. Both superstition and violence were clearly present at this time and they played major roles at the end of the prelude to the second revolution.

Life itself was fearful and uncertain and always ended in death. Ideologies were formulated on the basis of superstition. Bands of priests sprang up out of this dark soil. They not only demanded resources; they demanded 'sacrifice'.

Moreover, the invention of metal stimulated the demand for weapons. Why work in a village when one can be conquered! Why conquer one village when two can be snatched! Why stop there!

With conquest came social classes—the masters and the mastered. Moreover, wars of plunder and conquest led to a shattering discovery:

> that men as well as animals can be domesticated . . . by early historic times slavery was a foundation of ancient industry and a potent instrument in the accumulation of capital. (109)

Now:

> it must be admitted that the realization of the second revolution did require an accumulation of capital in the form primarily of foodstuffs, and that accumulation had to some extent be concentrated to make it effectively available for social ends. (107)

Thus, we have a third, and decisive, transformation of the other half of the Classical Macrofoundation: the emergence of class society, with upper classes composed of priests and oligarchs, and slaves at the bottom.

Only one thing was lacking before the urban revolution could begin. Human beings had to invent methods for recordkeeping and nonverbal communication. Prehistoric times were drawing to a close. History was about to commence.

12.5   URBAN REVOLUTION

The requirements for surplus food in the new cities were colossal:

> The surplus of home-grown products must not only suffice to exchange for exotic materials; it must also support a body of merchants and transport workers engaged in obtaining these and a body of specialized craftsmen to work the precious imports to the best advantage. And soon soldiers would be needed to protect the convoys and back up the merchants by force, scribes to keep records of transactions growing ever more complex, and State officials to reconcile conflicting interests. (115)

With successful establishment of cities we observe another population boom:

> The new cities are spatially larger and can accommodate a much denser population than the agricultural villages that have been absorbed in them . . . the urban cemeteries attest not only an increase of wealth, but also multiplication of people. The change from self-sufficing food-production to an economy based upon specialized manufacture and external trade did accordingly promote a marked expansion of the population. (116)

A priesthood was the focus of capital accumulation in the Mesopotamian cities:

> The oldest . . . documents . . . are . . . the accounts of the temple revenues kept by the priests. They reveal the temple as not only the center of the city's religious life, but also as the nucleus of capital accumulation. The temple functions as the great bank; the god as the chief capitalist . . . (124)

Eventually the cities of Babylonia were united under the power of kings. Two of them are legendary—Sargon (about 2500 BC) and Hammurabi (about 1800 BC). Hammurabi established a capital city, a written law and a calendar.

Egypt followed a different political development. Instead of passing through a stage led by a corporation of priests, it was unified directly through conquest of the Delta by the king of Upper Egypt. This occurred five centuries before Sargon's unification of Babylonia. There was, however, a striking difference:

> The unification of Egypt has, in fact, evoked the same new classes and the same new professions as in the urban revolution in Sumer. But their services seem to have been devoted primarily to the conservation [and memory] of royal corpses. (130)

The urban revolution occurred at about the same time along the Indus:

> By [2500 BC] large cities had been established in Sindh and the Punjab. They may exceed a square mile in area. The houses are built mainly of kiln-fired bricks, and boast at least two stories . . . It is . . . uncertain what was the nucleus of capital accumulation . . . Both temples and palaces are so inconspicuous among the ruins that their very existence is dubious. (134–35)

	NILE	TIGRIS-EUPHRATES	INDUS
focus of accumulation	monarchy—royal corpses	priests—king	???

Once this complex system had been established in the three primary centers it spread to secondary centers, much as industrial capitalism spread to colonies and dependencies in recent centuries:

> The second revolution was obviously propagated by diffusion; the urban economy in the secondary centers was inspired or imposed by the primary foci. It is easy to show that the process was inevitable. (136)

We have examples of both types. The imperialistic way of spreading has been the subject of most historical accounts. The spread of the urban revolution by way of mutually advantageous trade is less glamorous, but it is much more instructive. Consider the case of Egypt and Lebanon.

The Egyptians had a huge appetite for high-quality wood. The cedars of Lebanon were ideal for tombs, boat building, and furniture. The port of Byblos, near Beirut, began as a community of self-sufficient fisherman and farmers. We know them by way of biblical account as Giblites. Contact with Egypt created a great, mutually beneficial, interdependency:

> The effect of the revolution in Egypt had been to make effective a tremendous demand for the raw materials Byblos could supply. In satisfying it, the Giblites had an opportunity to share in the surplus wealth of Egypt; its expenditure opened up means of livelihood to families for whom the local farming and fishing could offer no sustenance. But its acceptance spelt the final abandonment of economic self-sufficiency. Byblos would henceforth owe its prosperity to producing for a foreign market. (137)

Such an important trading outpost required the on-site skills of Egyptian merchants and administrators. The Egyptians taught the Giblites their business practices and their methods of city management. In order to feel at home, the Egyptians built a stone temple in Byblos. They were there to stay. To meet the needs of foreign trade, the Giblites learned Egyptian writing. Byblos became a booming success:

> Thus the Giblites adopted discoveries of the Egyptians, assimilated their economy to the standards of the urban revolution and increased in numbers. Their township became a city, and was soon rich enough to become a market for raw materials from other regions, a secondary center for the diffusion of the new economy. (137)

The Giblites preserved their distinct culture. In architecture, crafts, dress, and religion they stood their ground. They adopted Egyptian refinements only when such refinements could increase the functionality and beauty of Giblite culture. When they borrowed from the Egyptians they internalized it thoroughly:

> The Egyptians, for instance, improved their script with the passage of time; the Giblites preserved the archaic characters adopted under the early dynasties and kept them unchanged for nearly a thousand years. (137–38)

This was a brilliant success story. Most were not. Inferior, even comical diffusion, was more common. And violent diffusion was all too common.

12.6 UPPER PRODUCTIVITY LIMITS

The agricultural revolution, and the prelude to the urban revolution, produced more than a dozen stunning inventions. But:

> The two thousand years after the revolution—say from 2600 to 600 BC— produced few contributions . . . to human progress. (180)

The urban revolution was rich in people and glory, but science lost out to superstition and oppression. Upper productivity limits were reached and they became unbreakable ceilings. How did this come about?

We should retrace the progress of social surplus and agricultural surplus. The original production of social surplus allowed for population growth. For a long time it was *solely* applied to this end. Gradually, as various sciences developed, the other aspect of surplus began to play a role. Agricultural surplus was first applied to land reclamation and irrigation. Then it was applied to specialized crafts, like pottery, weaving, carpentry, metal works, and shipbuilding. Finally, when the contributions of farmers and artisans were ripe, dominant classes emerged in the form of priests and rulers.

With the rise of ruling classes the great surpluses could be concentrated into a few hands. These hands built mighty cities and armies. But in the process the farmers and artisans became 'lower class'. They had little incentive to innovate.

At the same time, the priests and rulers were steeped in superstition. They could hardly be expected to champion rational science. Moreover, the ruling classes had 'domesticated humans'—lots of them—at their disposal. With such a pool of cheap labor, the pursuit of labor-saving devices was not economical. Thus, powerful internal contradictions put a break on progress.

There was also an external contradiction. The supplies obtained by international trade did not satisfy the voracious appetites of priests and rulers. In their hunger for *more* they could calculate the cost of an army relative to the expected plunder. Plunder could pay—and for men of a violent nature, it was fun.

> Sargon's empire, although transitory, became the model for all Oriental impe- rialisms. Throughout the Ancient East Sargon's conquests became an ideal and the conqueror himself a hero of romance. (184)

The victims were not always willing to be 'domesticated'. Many resisted taxation. Some revolted. When the empire was essentially a 'tribute-collecting machine', collection expenses could be high, specially in the peripheries.

As empires got old they began to sag. Sometimes the glory days could be renewed. Sometimes a failing empire would fall to one on the rise. More often scruffy barbarians would pick away at the edges. Perhaps they had a leader with insight and daring. Inspired by gods or greed, he dreamed of being Sargon. He grabbed his chance. This, too, was man, making himself.

12.7   TWO KINDS OF POPULATION BOOMS

Let us close where we began. Figure 1 *of Man Makes Himself* contains a
'graph estimate of the population of Great Britain, 1500–1800'—with an
unmistakable boom after 1750. But Childe never asks if this had been driven
by a sharp increase in the birth rate, a sharp decrease in the death rate, or
some combination of these factors?

We have at hand some figures for England. They corroborate the population boom on his diagram. We can see that it was driven entirely by a decline
in the death rate.

ENGLAND	1720	1730	1740	1750	1760	1770	1780	1790	1800	1810	1820
birth rate	30.5	32.0	33.3	34.1	33.3	34.0	34.4	35.4	34.2	33.8	33.4
death rate	29.7	33.4	31.7	28.2	26.7	27.9	28.8	25.7	23.1	20.0	20.3
net	0.8	−1.4	1.6	5.9	6.6	6.1	5.6	9.7	11.1	13.8	13.1

Source: G. Talbot Griffith, *Population Problems of the Age of Malthus*
(Cambridge, UK: Cambridge University Press, 1926), 43.

This pattern is shown on the right-side diagram. Would we expect the same
pattern in the agricultural and urban revolutions from antiquity? I think not.
I think we would expect the opposite pattern, specially in the first revolution.

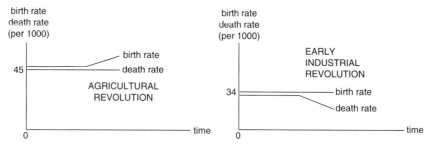

With domestication of plants and animals, irrigation, fertilizers and plowing,
many more mouths could be fed. But they did not necessarily eat better or have
greater insight concerning disease or sanitation. The left-side diagram depicts
the death rate at 45 per 1000. This implies a life expectancy of no more than
22 years, certainly high enough for the reproduction of tribes, while not much
below the 25 years estimated for life in the polluted cities of the Roman
Empire. Malthus, himself, said, "With regard to the duration of human life,
there does not appear to have existed from the earliest ages of the world to the
present moment the smallest permanent symptom or indication of increasing
prolongation." The Industrial Revolution nullified that—*extraordinarily!*

Childe discusses imperialism and the retardation of progress, but he does
not discuss carrying capacities. This is his anti-Malthusian blinder. Did any of
the ancient civilizations succumb to overpopulation or ecocide? In Chapter 14
we turn to this issue and see the dark side of Man Makes Himself. But first,
let us build a compact model depicting the rise and fall of empires under
pre-industrial conditions.

From Index—1951 U.S. Edition Mentioned Seven Times or More	Page Numbers
chemistry	13, 34, 46, 76–77, 81, 98, 120, 152
classes	116, 125, 126, 129, 135, 137, 149–50, 181–82
copper	14, 35, 95–96, 115, 121, 125, 129, 138, 142
diffusion of culture	30, 65–66, 74–75, 82–83, 102–3, 104, 135–36, 141–42, 177, 185
environment, adaptation to	16, 24, 26, 43, 53, 57–60, 105, 186–87
fishing	13, 54, 63, 70, 89, 92, 103, 114, 133–34, 137
hunting	49, 51, 53–54, 63, 71, 87, 92, 114, 133
kings	84, 86, 90, 109, 111, 122, 124–25, 126–27, 134, 182
magic	32, 43, 50–51, 54, 55, 81, 84, 93, 127, 130, 174, 175, 182
population, growth of	16, 17–18, 26–27, 34–36, 49, 51, 61, 71, 100, 116, 133–34, 137, 186
schools	56, 145, 149, 150, 152–53, 159, 161
science, applied	13, 34, 45, 51, 80, 104, 120–21, 131, 135, 136, 149, 178–79
specialization of labor	13, 35, 56, 71, 80, 87, 92, 97, 100, 102, 115, 118, 126, 134, 137, 182–83
stone tools, significance of	13, 75, 96, 99, 108–9, 138, 140, 142
surplus (of food)	13, 14, 71, 90, 92, 97, 100, 107, 110, 118, 125, 126, 131, 133–34, 137, 138, 140, 182
trade	14, 35, 54, 74, 87, 92, 94, 119, 126, 134, 137, 142, 155, 159, 183
writing	27, 120, 123, 131, 138, 139, 144–51, 177, 180

13

RISE AND FALL OF EMPIRES

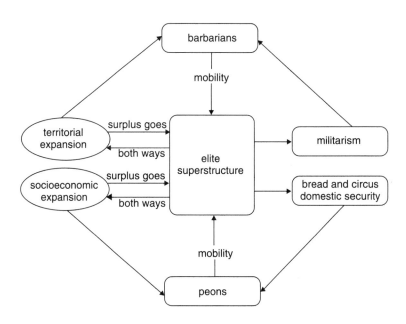

Fully Functioning Pre-Industrial Empire

13.1   EXPANSIONARY SOCIAL COSMOLOGY

In any well-developed society, some things are taken for granted by its members. This includes the prevailing philosophy regarding the nature of the society, its relationship to the divine, the dominant set of social relations, and the rules defining acceptable behavior. We call these elements of the 'deep structure' of a society its social cosmology. As long as they are taken for granted and not questioned, they will tend to be mutually reinforcing—giving people the sense of what is 'natural' and 'normal'.

Before the industrial revolution, most social cosmologies were conditioned by one fact facing almost all agrarian societies: the ability to produce agricultural surplus was greatly limited. Perhaps they could support 5–20 percent of the population outside of agriculture. A few bad harvests could make even that precarious. This had an enormous impact on the development of the social cosmology in order for it to furnish adequate survival strategies. This included strategies of self-defense against antagonistic neighbors.

On rare occasions, there arose a religion or social philosophy imbued with vast ambition. Energized by such a dynamic ideology, the people were mobilized to work harder and take full advantage of their natural resources. Following a religious prophet, a charismatic leader, or a nationalistic impulse, the society pushed militarily beyond the boundaries determined by nature and pre-industrial technology, into the domain of neighboring societies.

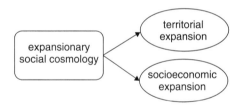

When successful, an empire was established. We are all familiar with the most famous, such as the Greek and Roman. The Greek collapsed almost as quickly as it was created, but it left behind language and access to great knowledge. Perhaps no social formation has fascinated historians as much as the Roman Empire. If it could have embraced the entire world, it would have. Rome not only conquered without loss of appetite or ambition, it Romanized, too.

In this chapter, we concentrate on interpreting a model developed by Johan Galtung, found in Galtung, Heiestad, and Ruge, "On the Decline and Fall of Empires" (1979). That long paper contains a brilliant diagram on the Roman Empire. The diagram is too complex for most readers to grasp. I build a version here bit-by-bit in order to flesh out the essence of the model.

I assume pre-industrial conditions, which imply very limited agricultural surplus. The entry point is illustrated above. Let us see the analysis unfold.

13.2   TWO SOCIAL-SURPLUS CONDITIONS

Usually we only need one social-surplus condition to analyze a society:

$$net\ output\ -\ social\ subsistence\ =\ social\ surplus$$

When we speak of empire building, it is necessary to add a second condition related to conquered territories. Since it is possible to seize both their annual social surplus and their accumulated wealth, the second condition reads:

$$net\ output\ -\ social\ subsistence\ +\ plundered\ wealth$$
$$\text{EQUALS}$$
$$social\ surplus\ +\ plundered\ wealth$$

Understanding the course of these two conditions is the key to the analysis.

Domestic socioeconomic expansion can occur without centralized control of the social surplus, if it is invested in projects expanding the national productive capacity. But ambitious territorial expansion is possible only if a small elite is able to appropriate much social surplus and apply it to conquest. The soldiers, officers, equipment, and survival rations must all be supported out the surplus. So must the bureaucracy. Centralized control of surplus makes this possible.

Once the expansion into empire is underway, the conquerors exploit the territories for annual social surplus and accumulated wealth. If ruthless, they may reduce the subsistence bundle of the alien populations to snatch more than the social surplus. However, this cannot go on very long. If they impair the work capacity of the conquered people, the territory will yield too little surplus to make the empire project sustainable. In addition, empires based upon plunder do not last very long.

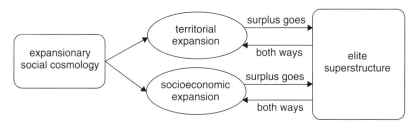

Continuous expansion of the system requires the regular investment of some of the social surplus, both at home and in empire. Part of it must be used to support the growing demands of home bureaucracy—the center of the center. Some of it must be invested in capital cities in the empire—the centers in the periphery. Some of it must be available to the intellectual and priestly classes. These are the people who articulate the social cosmology and rouse support for it.

Specially when there is population growth, the elite superstructure had a tendency to require growing amounts of surplus because carrots and sticks are both needed to buy loyalty and punish disloyalty. This must come from more intensive utilization of the existing empire or its expansion into new lands.

13.3   BARBARIANS AND PEONS

The classes composing the elite superstructure could achieve nothing without farmers, manual laborers, artisans, and soldiers. We refer to them as 'peons' if they live in the home society and 'barbarians' if they live in the empire. We use these expressions to cover the spectrum from slave to free. In the eyes of the elite, these expressions imply low and despised status.

When domestic surplus production and appropriation are functioning smoothly, it is possible for the brighter peon males to find a position in the elite superstructure. If literate, they may enter the bureaucracy; if strong and intelligent, they may rise in rank in the military. It is also possible for the prettier peon females to marry men from elite families. This mobility brings fresh blood and life into the elite superstructure.

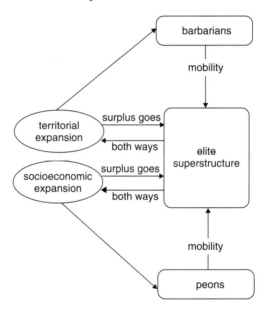

In order to control and administer the empire, barbarians must also be recruited. Some come from the local elites—not at all 'barbarian' from the point of view of the social division of labor! Their services are very valuable and are well rewarded if they prove both loyal and effective. If such men adopt the language and customs of the overlords, they are likely to gain respected status—from postbarbarian to full citizenship in the empire.

Barbarian men of lower status can also enter the elite superstructure if they have unusual talent or ambition. Ironically, entering the empire as a slave can prove to be the most effective route upward, if the person has a good head for languages, numbers, or the management of people. Of course, beautiful barbarian women of low status can rise into leisure and influence by marriage.

The numbers recruited these ways will depend upon the character of the empire. Empires based upon intricate social and trade relations will be more productive and provide for more mobility. Empires based upon plunder will offer few opportunities.

13.4 MECHANISMS OF SOCIAL CONTROL

As a consequence of the system just outlined, certain institutions of social control were necessary to protect the venture, abroad and at home. In the empire, military conquest yielded to military control. The counterpart at home was domestic security, supplemented by the pacifying and diversionary value of 'bread and circus'—to use the expression associated with Rome.

Military control in the empire need not be overt, if the conquered people appear sufficiently accepting of their status *and* if the overlords are sufficiently insightful on this matter. Overt military control can antagonize the people, creating resistance where none was likely. But, if the empire overlords use plunder of wealth and seizure of slaves as methods to augment their position, they must be prepared to spend some of it on harsh forms of social control.

Social control at home is a more delicate matter. Its forms, and the amount spent on them, will depend upon the unity of the elite and the passivity of the peons. If the elite is divided into antagonistic groups, the emperor might use some of the surplus to buy off opponents (high-class bread and circus) or might use it for intimidation (high-class 'domestic security'). Among the peons, the use of force—or threat of force—can be open and cruel, especially if they have no legal rights. Bread and circus is the more pleasant way to exert authority.

Social control, in general, might be costly, even to the point of determining the internal and external limits of empire.

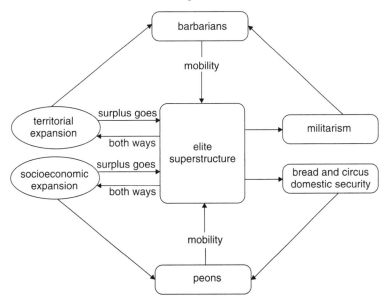

We can see here the genius of Rome, with their efforts at domestic tranquility, Romanization and the 'Roman Peace', lasting from 27 BC to AD 180. Romanization was probably the key ingredient. Conquered people felt included in something vast—symbolized by the emperor's head on coinage. Adopting the language and religion of Rome often served to create an effective link.

13.5   BREAKDOWN OF SOCIAL-SURPLUS CONDITIONS

Nonproductive takeout from social surplus has a tendency to grow continuously. This includes bureaucratic, military, religious, luxury, and social-control costs. Each of these sectors demands the proverbial *more*.

When the system hits its upper productivity limits, the growth of surplus stalls. Eventually, all of it is promised to nonexpansionary forms of expenditure. The elite superstructure absorbs and spends the surplus without the ability to invest in expansionary activities. In terms of our arrows, social surplus now goes only one way. This has an impact on some of the other arrows.

This may happen first in the domestic economy or in the empire. For a while, a weakening in one can be covered by financial strength in the other. If new sources of social surplus do not emerge, the second sector, too, loses its financial capacity for growth.

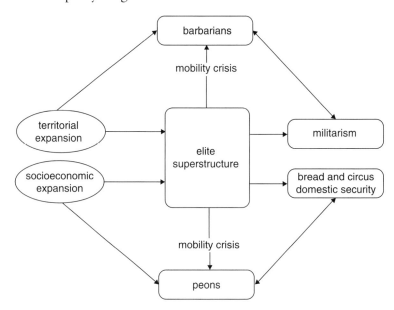

The problem is seen from 'below' as a mobility crisis. Without expansionary projects, recruitment of peons and barbarians into the elite has little purpose and cannot be afforded. As ambitious or disgruntled people of low status recognize this change, they may become restive—adding to military and domestic security costs. If this happens, it serves to deepen the budgetary problem.

When this crisis first appears, it is only an early stage of decline and may be reversed. As long as it is possible to extract the surplus needed for the functioning of most essential tasks of the elite superstructure, financial reform is doable. Budget cutting is needed. It must eliminate useless and frivolous expenditure without undermining the political authority at the top.

If there is a sharp division in the elite, this form of crisis might be used by a faction to seize control. If an ambitious man usurps power this way, he can reduce the budgets of perceived opponents and redefine overall priorities. If he can restore expansionary expenditure, he can make his mark on the empire.

13.6   Nine Conditions of Crisis

If the proper functioning of social-surplus conditions cannot be restored, cumulative crisis will follow. We shall assume the surplus extraction process has for a long time been insufficient to cover the finance of expansionary activities. What are the most likely forms of crisis? Our model suggests nine.

First, we consider a probable empire-wide crisis: ecological breakdown. Intensive exploitation of lands, forests, and mines will, at a minimum, lead to lower productivity and higher costs. If on a serious scale, it will be ecocidal.

Next, what about the lower classes? The barbarians pose the greatest danger. If bold, some of them can instigate successful rebellions in peripheral areas. If very bold, such victories can lead to barbarian conquest of lands near their home territory. If such lands are the 'periphery of the periphery', the financially weakened empire might be unable to restore its authority. If the lands are near the center, they may be compelled to use the army to restore authority. Failure here could devastate the authority of the emperor and lead to a coup.

The peons do not pose a direct danger unless they ally with internal enemies of the regime. Otherwise, their behavior is likely to be the *opposite* of the barbarians. Whereas the barbarians become bold and aggressive, the peons remain meek and passive. They have no education or experience solving problems beyond family survival issues. Mechanisms of social control have inculcated excessive passivity. Even if the regime wants to call upon them to arise to nationalistic duty, peons are unlikely to be cost effective.

At some point, all this becomes too much for the elite superstructure. Experiencing a breakdown in spirit, they flee the sinking center.

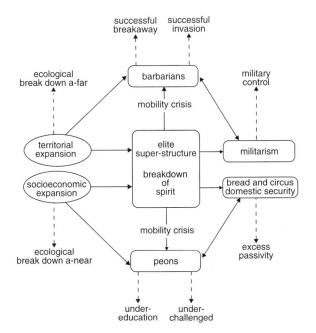

13.7 FAILING EXPANSIONARY SOCIAL COSMOLOGY

At some point, the collapse of the empire becomes irreversible. The sufficient condition for this is depicted by the *reversal* of the surplus-extraction arrows. It becomes impossible to extract surplus from the empire as it loses territory and enforcement mechanisms. It may also become impossible to extract surplus at home if environmental damage goes too far, or the tax-collecting authority stops functioning properly. For simplicity we depict the diagram this way.

The diagram used in Section 1 now appears in *opposite* form: instead of expansion, contraction and crisis. Instead of arrows out, the arrows are in.

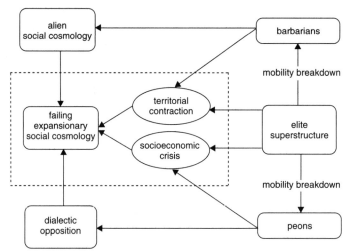

The contraction process is speeded up by the breakdown of mobility. As the elite superstructure shrinks, former barbarians and former peons are pushed (or jump) out of the elite. Some of them can pose a new threat to the failing system because they have valuable inside knowledge and connections. The more ambitious can try to grab some wealth or power based upon these advantages.

With the collapse of the spirit that animated the empire, dialectic opposition can come to the fore and play a role in determining the next social cosmology. At home this dialectic opposition can be expected to lash out at the social hierarchy and top-down rules of decision making. A populist revolution can be mounted if sympathetic intellectuals join with ambitious peons and fleet-a-foot members of the sinking elite superstructure. Such revolutions are rarely stable.

In what remains of the empire, and in the former empire, barbarians can rediscover—or reinvent—their native social cosmologies. This may be built around their traditional religions, local legends, and economic patterns. If they are aggressively asserting themselves in their own expansionary efforts, they may try to assert the superiority of their native social cosmologies over the decrepit one collapsing. If they have momentum on their side, barbarians might conquer the center of the old center.

In a rare case, like Rome, an expired empire might have a legendary afterlife for millennia, influencing history and feeding visions of grandeur.

14

ECOCIDE

And they were sawing off the branches on which they were sitting, while shouting across their experiences to one another how to saw more efficiently. And they went crashing down into the deep. And those watching shook their heads and continued sawing vigorously.

—Bertolt Brecht, *Exile III*

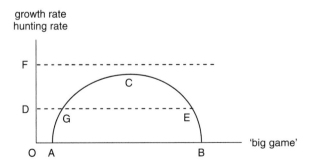

Stone-Age Megafauna Extinction

14.1 *HOMO ESOPHAGUS COLOSSUS*

During the past 500 million years, the natural rate of species extinction was about 100 per 500 years. Under the Dominion of Man the rate is now about 100 *per day*. In addition, we devour nonrenewable resources without restrain.

Franz Broswimmer, in *Ecocide* (2002), details the dark side of Man Makes Himself. This crucial story comprises the longest chapter in the book.[1]

Even during the Stone Ages we had the tendency to trash our habitats. The pattern of being 'future eaters' is as ancient as our development of language. It makes us appear to be a cancer on the face of the earth. This should trouble us deeply. Do we have the capacity—and time—to reform?

Somehow we never grasped the interdependence of living things: we depend upon other species for our existence:

> [O]ther species produce the oxygen we breathe, absorb the carbon dioxide we exhale, decompose our sewage, produce our food, maintain the fertility of our soil, and provide our wood and paper. Humans are not only part of biodiversity, but also profoundly dependent on it. (6)

The following chart is representative of our current plunder of natural resources. We could call up legions of statistics all indicating the same thing: our current patterns of resource consumption and abuse are unsustainable.

LIQUIDATING OUR ASSETS	
topsoil created by nature each year	0.4 billion tons
topsoil lost to erosion each year	25.4 billion tons
global consumption of the equivalent of 22 million tons of oil	1 day
time it took the planet to create this energy	10,000 days
time it took to lose 1% of world's forests before Industrial Revolution	100 years
time it takes to lose 1% of world's forests now	1 year

Source: Broswimmer, Table 28.

Our hunger for exploiting nature is so extraordinary Broswimmer believes we should be renamed *homo esophagus colossus.*

According to Broswimmer, ecocide can be traced to three root causes:

(1) *The development of language and culture*, which facilitated colonization of the planet. As we spread across the globe into virgin lands we killed off most of the megafauna. This created a food crisis solved by:

(2) *The agricultural revolution*, arising when megafauna extinction combined with climate change and population growth to induce the development of plant and animal domestication. This resulted in the population booms so famously analyzed in *Man Makes Himself.*

(3) *The rise of modernity*, based upon the application of scientific thinking to complex divisions of labor, driven forward by the profit motive and the nation state. This resulted in industrialization and globalization.

14.2   STONE-AGE MEGAFAUNA EXTINCTION

Cro-Magnon were the first *homo sapiens sapiens*. Their culture surpassed the Neanderthals because of better capacity for speech. Among their achievements, Cro-Magnon invented complex fire hearths, spear tips, harpoons, and animal traps. Armed with weapons and an increasingly complex social organization, they were the first humans capable of killing off their own source of livelihood.

And they did. Let us see this in the species-growth-and-endangerment model. 'Big game' is on the horizontal axis. Their population growth rate and the rate at which they are hunted are on the vertical.

The distance OA represents the smallest number of big game needed to maintain genetic and biological viability. The distance OB represents the carrying capacity of the environment if none of the big game is hunted. Point C represents the highest natural rate of growth of this species when it is not pressing upon the carrying capacity. A smooth curve, ACB, connects the points.

Suppose a band of Cro-Magnon migrates to this area. The land has long supported OB big game. Let us suppose they hunt at the rate OD, which yields a good amount of calories and protein. This reduces the big-game population from OB to DE. If they maintain this level of hunting, the big-game population stabilizes at the level DE. This rate of hunting is a fraction of the entire stock.

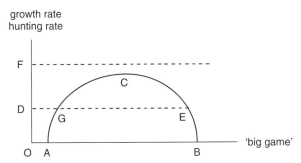

As the Cro-Magnon establish themselves in this area they experience a population boom because they have a good supply of meat. In order to maintain meat consumption per person the hunting rate rises. After a certain point population growth pushes them to hunt above the level represented by point C.

In this example, when the Cro-Magnon population doubles they need to hunt OF per year to maintain meat consumption per person. This exceeds the highest natural growth rate of the big game. They are on a path to extermination.

Eventually the stock of big game is reduced to the level DG. This yields an insufficient amount of meat for the Cro-Magnon group, which constitutes for them a Malthusian crisis. While they annihilate the remaining stock they must secure a *reliable substitute*. If their habitat does not stock sufficient 'little game' alternatives they must migrate in order to survive as meat eaters. Demographic success in another location repeats this destructive process.

This struggle for subsistence became, in fact, a *war on* subsistence. As social organization, weapons and language evolved, humans gained the capacity to kill far more meat than they could eat. Without reflection on consequences, they would:

> encircle great numbers of animals and drive them over a cliff . . . at the bottom of a cliff . . . one can find a vast accumulation of bones estimated to contain the remains of more than 100,000 horses. (23–24)

The extermination of megafauna by humans represents the first time a species of earth could disrupt ecosystems because of its social capacity to organize.

The largest herbivores disappeared entirely. Only the smaller and faster herbivores were likely to survive the migration of humans into their habitats.

LATE PLEISTOCENE MEGAFAUNA EXTINCTION BY WEIGHT AND PERCENT	
1000 + kg herbivores	100%
100–1000 kg herbivores	75%
5–100 kg herbivores	41%
<5 kg herbivores	<2%

Source: Adapted from Broswimmer, Table 7.

Whenever *homo sapiens sapiens* entered virgin territories, mass extinction of megafauna followed as an unintended consequence. If we exterminated the herbivores, the carnivores dependent upon them followed them to extinction.

> In most cases, the megafauna extinctions began shortly after the first arrival of prehistoric humans. If we compare the number of genera of large mammals lost on various continents, we find that Australia lost 94 percent, North America 73 percent, Europe 29 percent, and Africa south of the Sahara 5 percent. (24)

All of this damage occurred when less than 10 million humans roamed the earth. Moreover, it generally preceded any systematic human knowledge of plant or animal domestication. Agriculture itself is only 10,000 years old.

ONSET DATES OF MAJOR EXTINCTION EPISODES	
Africa	50,000 years ago
Southeast Asia	50,000 years ago
Australia	45,000 years ago
North America	11,000 years ago
South America	10,000 years ago

Source: Adapted from Broswimmer, Table 8.

Language played a central role. Whereas the Neanderthal might have been able to point and exclaim the equivalent of "Dude, meat!" our ancestors could communicate more effectively, brainstorm, devise better tools, and learn from their mistakes—except for that disturbing pattern of unintentionally killing off their source of livelihood!

A man-nature imbalance worse than any imagined by Malthus was let loose! We, *homo esophagus colossus*, are still pulling that caboose!

14.3 ANCIENT ABUSE OF LAND

Our species lived as hunter-gatherers during most of its existence. Small bands of people spread across the globe before they applied any of the secrets of domestication. As natural abundance gave way to scarcity and unintended extinctions, human beings had to innovate or die. With the discovery of agriculture far larger population and population densities could be supported. By the time of the Caesars, hunter-gatherers were a minority.

However, all was not well:

> Human history is replete with accounts of early ecocidal activities of great empires such as Babylonia, Egypt, Greece, Rome, ancient China and Maya, all of which destroyed their forests and the fertility of their topsoil and killed off much of the original fauna through a combination of 'their linear thinking and their insatiable drives for material wealth'. (32)

We can illustrate the process of deforestation. Trees are on the horizontal axis. Growth and harvest rates are on the vertical. The distance OA represents the smallest mass of trees needed for a viable woodland habitat. The distance OB represents the largest mass of trees in the area if none is harvested. A virgin forest size OB supports an interconnected habitat of plants and animals.

The shape of the curve depends upon growth characteristics. Are the trees slow growth or fast growth? A fast-growth curve is narrow and high; a slow-growth curve is wide and not so high. The curve ACB represents a slow-growth case.

Suppose a neolithic village regularly harvests OD trees from this forest. This does not endanger the forest because it can maintain itself at the level DE.

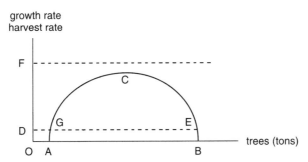

Suddenly the village is incorporated into an empire in need of wood for fuel, construction, transportation, and weapons. The yearly harvest rate jumps to OF. This exceeds the rate at which the forest can self-replenish. Before long the forest is thinned out. After a while it is reduced to DG. After that it vanishes.

Deforestation was the elephantiasis of ancient empires, driven by their greed and militarism. It deprived distant villagers of their wood supply and threatened their ability to grow food because of soil erosion. They were further impoverished by the loss of biodiversity. And, with the exhaustion of 'its' forest, the empire turned its ravenous attention elsewhere hunting the big wood.

Such ecocidal activity was the by-product of hierarchical-expansionist societies, where social surplus was largely controlled by a small elite. In such societies,

> maximization of economic output replaced the mix of social and economic goals that characterized communal peasant farming societies. (39)

Mesopotamia offers an early and great example. It was famous for large-scale land reclamation with a giant system of irrigation canals, dams, and reservoirs. A small elite of priests and rulers lorded over slaves, farmers, and artisans. Enough surplus food was produced to support 10 percent of the population outside of farming. But this intensified farming greatly overtaxed the ecology.

Let us see this in our corn model. In the simplest model we *implicitly* assumed no difficulty because of water or land issues. Let us introduce these.

OA and OB are subsistence per person in years 0 and 1. Point C is the two-year subsistence condition. Given the capacity to produce surplus food, let us assume the possibility frontier DE. During normal years the elites consume in the area F while the vast majority of people are undernourished in the area G.

What happens if there is too much water, or too little?

> Waters cresting too high would destroy settlements and grain stores; waters too low would yield poor crops, food shortages or famine. (37)

Those were perennial problems in Mesopotamia—and in all hydraulic societies. Another difficulty—salinization—developed over time. As river water evaporated it left behind salt deposits. The natural fertility of the soil declined. At first the Mesopotamians tried to solve the problem by allowing weeds to grow during fallow years. Eventually they switched to a more salt-tolerant crop. That gave only temporary relief and they often had to abandon farmlands.

> The accumulating salts drove crop yields down more than 40 percent, resulting in shrinking food reserves for an ever-increasing population. (38)

This spelt the decline of the southern empire. Political power shifted to the north because saline soils were less common. Most of Mesopotamia, however, eventually succumbed to deforestation.

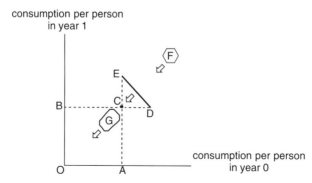

Much of it is desolate to this day.

Lone philosophical voices in antiquity sounded the alarm of ecocide, to no avail. In China, Mencius observed the environmental ruin clearly:

> There was a time when the trees were luxuriant on the Ox Mountain. As it is on the outskirts of a great metropolis, the trees are constantly lopped off by axes. Is it a wonder that they are no longer fine? With the respite they get in the day and in the night, and the moistening by the rain and dew, there is certainly no lack of new shoots coming out, but then the cattle and sheep come to graze upon the mountain. That is why it is as bald as it is. (33)

Plato observed in Greece:

> What now remains compared with what then existed is like the skeleton of a sick man, all that fat and soft earth having wasted away, and only the barest framework of the land being left. (41)

Seneca, the Roman, said:

> If we evaluate the benefits of nature by the depravity of those who misuse them, there is nothing we have received that does not hurt us. You will find nothing, even of obvious usefulness, such that it does not change over into its opposite through man's fault. (42)

Even a brief discussion of the Ancients should mention a unique Roman practice. They ransacked their empire for big game—to torment and kill by the thousands in their gladiatorial arenas.

> The poor conditions of capture, transport, and housing of these animals must have meant that for every animal that died entertaining the masses, dozens or even hundreds of others must have perished before reaching the arena. The Roman Empire was probably responsible for the greatest annihilation of large animals since the Pleistocene megafauna mass extinction. (42)

14.4   RISE OF CAPITALISM

After the fall of the Roman Empire, Europe largely withdrew into small feudal states. Towns still existed as centers of specialized crafts but the overall level of economic activity was a shadow of the glory days of Rome.

Gradually trade picked up. A new expansionist ethic was emerging. It was seen in a shift of attitude toward profit: from a focus on use value to accumulation potential. The emerging capitalistic ethic whispered its powerfully hypnotic song: 'It is Glorious to Get Rich'. All sorts of people heard the call.

At the same time, scientific thought came out of the shadows of reactionary religious dogma to claim a place for itself. This liberated some of the best minds of the age. If it was glorious to get rich it was also glorious to understand and use God's creation scientifically. But instead of developing an organic philosophy of science, the founders of 'the scientific method' chose a mechanical view—the world as divine machine. The cold, lifeless mechanics of heavenly bodies supposedly revealed the divine better than familiar life.

The marriage of profit motive to applied science unleashed a powerful dynamic. In the process nature was banished from the sacred and relegated to commercial interests. Accumulate! Accumulate! That became the highest value.

Broswimmer is scathing in his assessment of this turn of events:

> [O]f all its core features, the systemic growth imperative is perhaps the most destructive dimension of the capitalist ethos.
>
> There have been few more important changes in human history than the abandonment of the last few seeds of the sense of intimate dependence on nature to the exaggerated feeling of absolute free will and human autonomy.
>
> The desire for accumulation of wealth is the cultural impetus that originally drove Europeans into the New World, and then corporations into all corners of the earth in search of new markets and resources. (58–59)

The decisive year was 1492, when Columbus 'discovered America'. The Portuguese and Spanish immediately plundered the Americas for gold and silver. The Amerindian suffered apocalyptic depopulations, cut down by germs more often than by guns. And massive international trade emerged, linking Europe, Africa, and the Americas. The system of 'Triangular Trade' was simple as long as millions of slaves could be acquired as cheap labor.

In the first leg, Europeans traded various goods for slaves, including firearms and rum. The slaves were packed into vessels for the Americas. The survivors of the journey were sold to plantation and mine owners. Finally, the products of slave labor were shipped to Europe. There was a lot of profit in this triangle. It continued for centuries. In the eighteenth century, at the height of the slave trade, more than 6 million Africans were exported into slavery.

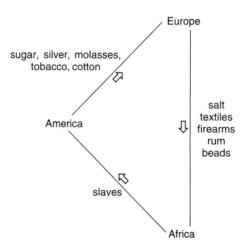

Patterns of underdevelopment and dependency took shape. For example, in the sixteenth century, Brazil had more than 120 sugar mills and the best land was devoted to sugarcane production—but they grew no food for their own subsistence!

> "They imported it, just as they imported an array of luxury articles which came from overseas with the slaves and the bags of salt." (61)

Let us consider the fate of the Amerindians once they became participants in the international fur trade. The following diagram illustrates this sad story.

Let us assume an Indian nation had two subsistence goods: corn (for calories and sheath) and critters (for protein and furs). Let us further assume a constant human population. The distance OA is their subsistence corn. The distance OB is their subsistence critters. Point C is their social subsistence. Point D is the largest amount of corn they can produce if they specialize in that activity. Their possibility frontier is depicted as a curve passing through points E and F.

Before the arrival of the Euro-Americans, they would generally try to consume near point E, getting some surplus of both corn and critters.

The Euro-Americans, however, had a mighty taste for the profits they could earn from fur trade. We can imagine one of the clever white guys drawing part of this diagram and saying: "Look! Right now you consume near point E. We can offer you an exchange rate shown by the line passing through point F. You can hunt at point F and trade with us to point G. At point G you will have your usual amount of corn and a huge surplus of critters, the distance EG. You can use that surplus for further trading. You will be far better off. What have you got to lose?"

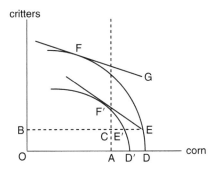

At first the leaders of the Indian nation were cautious. They limited the fur trade to a side activity so they could retain control over the production of their social subsistence. Gradually, they moved up the possibility frontier toward point F.

Time passed and the situation turned decidedly against the interests of the Amerindians. Points D and E shifted to D' and E' because their agricultural capacities deteriorated due to neglect. The possibility curve caved in at the top because excessive hunting seriously thinned out the stock of critters.

The effects of competition in the industry led to a change in the terms of trade. One day that clever white guy announced a new price for furs, represented by the line passing through points F' and E. Now the Amerindians could only achieve point E through trade. "It's nothing personal," said the clever white guy, "Just business." Eventually the stock of critters was exhausted and the clever white guy abandoned the Trading Post. "Unprofitable" read the farewell sign.

Excessive hunting of animals in Europe, to meet upper-class demands, preceded the situation in America just described.

> Several hundred squirrel pelts were needed to make one cloak, so the numbers killed were enormous. Eventually the population of fur-bearing animals in Western Europe was almost exhausted . . . (63)

As other forms of fur hunting declined, seal hunting in Canada became a new growth industry. Often they were clubbed to death when they came ashore to breed. The newborn seals fetched very high profits because their pure white fur was specially desirable. Eventually the herds were reduced by about 80 percent.

The North American bison barely escaped extinction. When the Europeans first arrived perhaps 75 million of these buffalo roamed a large part of the land.

> Migrating seasonally, often following the same routes year after year, bison always sought the easiest paths around obstacles and across terrain. Their trails were later used as the basis for most of [United States'] railroads and modern highways . . . By 1891 the bison population in the United States had been reduced to a mere 541 animals. (66)

The mass slaughter of buffalo was evidently intended to cripple the Indians' way of life and force them onto reservations. But killing buffalo was considered good sport, too. Professional hunters slaughtered them for fun.

Some time after these shameful episodes, in 1913, the American government issued the 'Indian head nickel'—a five-cent piece with a buffalo on one side and an Indian head on the other. The word LIBERTY was written above the Indian's face. Although attractive to look at, the coin was of inferior quality. Regular use would rub the design out of existence!

14.5 MECHANIZED WAR

When capital replaced land as the central factor of production, the rate of profit on capital became the primary criteria for economic decisions. Wave after wave of technical innovations proved profitable and spread.

As the Industrial Revolution picked up steam, the colonial powers "pillaged the ecologies and societies of the conquered territories" (72) in a scramble for the resources needed to feed the new machines.

> The global assault on the planet's species and environment is the logical extension of the violence inherent in colonialism and imperialism. (72)

The weapons of imperialism were improved as warfare was industrialized.

Arms production was highly profitable and it did not depend upon the whims of consumer markets. It did depend upon government demand, so arms producers and merchants had an interest in seeing enemies and plots everywhere. Paranoia became a great marketing tool.

Kill-rates became the scientific measure of weapon efficiency. Was it big enough to 'take out the enemy'? The distinction between civilian and soldier was blurred out of existence. Dynamite upped the kill-rate significantly but it was only a taste of things to come.

With the invention of airplanes and complex bombs, the kill-rate could be measured 'by the city'. Thanks to Yankee ingenuity, it was possible in early 1945 to burn down a city in an evening. By the summer of 1945 it was possible to burn down a city in a few minutes. Oh, and leave a nasty radiation behind.

The earliest alleged ecocidal war was waged by the Romans against the North African city of Carthage. After destroying the city they covered the surrounding land with salt in order to destroy their enemy's means of subsistence.

Twentieth century technology allowed for larger assaults. In 1938, the Chinese dynamited a dike on the Yellow River to halt the advancing Japanese army. The tactic worked, drowning several thousand Japanese soldiers.

> In addition, the resulting flooding ecologically ravaged three provinces and inundated several million hectares of farmland. The human costs were staggering: eleven cities and 4,000 villages were flooded, killing several hundred thousand civilians and leaving millions homeless. (75)

United States used ecocide as a deliberate policy in its war against Vietnam. The brutal use of air power perfected in World War II was now aimed at forests and jungles. American B-52s dropped 13 million tons of bombs on Southeast Asia—triple the tonnage dropped in World War II.

Heavy doses of herbicides and pesticides were inflicted on forests and farmlands. Nearly a million acres of prime farmlands were poisoned, along with the people living there. Giant 'Roman plow' bulldozers were used to clear ancient tropical forests, and flatten uncooperative villages.

By the end of the war, more than half of South Vietnam's mangroves were destroyed, 5 million acres of tropical forest were heavily damaged and 20 percent of the people were environmental refugees living in the cities.

This created an ecological *domino effect*: starving hill tribes descended to the plains to use contaminated rice fields. Displaced farmers turned to logging. The trauma to nature was so severe that "Deforestation, erosion, dried-up water sources, and flooding have increased drastically since the war ended" (77).

In the meantime, the Superpowers prepared for Armageddon. The cold war period was probably the worst ecodisaster in the past 10,000 years. The production, testing, and storing of enormous stockpiles of nuclear, biological, and chemical weapons has made vast areas unfit for habitation—in addition to the lingering dangers from the weapons and the materials involved. The veil of secrecy allows governments to keep citizens in the dark on these matters.

Perhaps up to 30 percent of all environmental degradation is military related.

14.6   TERMINAL GRAND BUFFET?

Human beings emerged from the hunter-gatherer state only 480 generations ago. We now number more than 6 billion. Half of that increase occurred in the past 40 years. Population is expected to increase by billions this century, much of it in the world's last remaining areas of rich biodiversity.

Perhaps the best measure of the demographic threat to biodiversity is found in the global expansion of human and livestock biomass:

> In 1850, humans and their livestock represented perhaps 5 percent of total terrestrial animal biomass . . . currently [it] is somewhat more than 25 percent . . . This . . . occurs at the expense of wildlife biomass . . . (82)

About 20 percent of the world's population consumes 80 percent of the resources. United States leads the way, consuming over 25 percent.

At least 2 billion people live on less than two U.S. dollars a day. People living this way will do anything to survive. The toll on nature takes many forms: soil erosion, loss of soil fertility, desertification, depleted game and fish stock, massive loss of species and their natural habitats, depletion of groundwater resources, and pollution of rivers and other bodies of water.

In the past decade poorworld debts soared while foreign aid shrank. In order to service this debt they have had to accelerate natural resource exports. The debt crisis deepens the correlation between poverty and environmental degradation.

Indonesia is a telling example. In the past 20 years more than a million hectares of forest were cut down—one of the world's richest genetic storehouses. In the late 1970s, President Suharto bluntly recognized the relationship between Indonesia's debt and deforestation, when he said:

> "We do not have to worry our heads about debts, for we still have forests to repay those debts." (90)

Since 1970, the world's forests have declined from 4.4 square miles per 1000 people to 2.8 while a quarter of the world's fish stock has been depleted.

Our patterns of consumption and population growth have left us in a state of *ecological overshoot*. This implies eventual depopulation. Consider a classic case from the animal kingdom—reindeer on St. Mathew Island in Alaska:

> In 1944 a population of 29 animals was moved to the island, without concern for its impact on the local ecosystem. Within two decades, the reindeer population swelled to 6,000, only to 'crash' within three years to a total of 41 females and one male, all in miserable condition. Klein estimates that the carrying capacity of the island was about five deer per square kilometer. At the population peak, there were 18 reindeer per square kilometer. After the crash, there remained only 0.126 animals per square kilometer. (92)

Our species is engaged in what may be the Terminal Grand Buffet. Only part of the species, that is. Billions of people clearly consume too little for decent life.

This state of affairs is presided over ideologically by the neoliberal agenda for 'free markets' and 'free trade'—to 'get the governments off our backs'. Efficiency is the goal; 'equity' in this worldview, refers to the interests of shareholders. It has nothing to do with justice or fairness or any human value.

This ideology nearly deifies transnational corporations—organizations obsessed with costs and profits and markets. Of the world's 100 largest economic systems, 47 are corporations. Each has more wealth than 130 countries.

> In many ways, TNCs define our progressively ecocidal world, and they do so by effectively silencing, trivializing or legitimizing their exceedingly damaging social and ecological practices. (87)

Profits-investment-profits-investment-profits-investment: this is the motive *and* the motor of our global economy. Global capitalism must expand continually or face crisis. This contradicts the basic conditions of global ecology.

Captains of industry freak out if there is even a minor recession. The only 'sustainability' they are concerned with is good quarterly profits forever!

While profits are not forever, extinction is. As our leaders obsess over profits, the specter of mass extinctions should induce us to measure a new kind of account while we can. Consider the following incomplete but revealing chart.

The vast majority of threatened extinctions are due to habitat loss and overexploitation. Species introduction accounts for most of the remainder. As we devour more forests and destroy more bodies of water the toll will climb.

FACTORS RESPONSIBLE FOR SOME EXTINCTIONS AND THREATENED EXTINCTIONS
PERCENT DUE TO EACH CAUSE*

	habitat loss	over-exploitation	species introduction	predators	other	unknown
Extinctions						
mammals	19	23	20	1	1	36
birds	20	11	22	0	2	37
reptiles	5	32	42	0	0	21
fish	35	4	30	0	4	48
Threatened Extinctions						
mammals	68	54	6	8	12	—
birds	58	30	28	1	1	—
reptiles	53	63	17	3	6	—
amphibians	77	29	14	—	3	—
fish	78	12	28	—	2	—

Source: Broswimmer, Table 18.
*Some species may be influenced by more than one factor.

We move ever closer to gigantic human dieoffs unless we do something about overconsumption in the rich world, underconsumption in the poorworlds and the population bomb ticking away in the poorworlds. We must change our political economy or dieoff.com will be the defining theme of this century.

14.7   GREEN DEMOCRACY

Few students are exposed to systematic thinking about environmental challenges so few have grasped the depth of the global problem. 'Everyone' knows about global warming, the holes in the ozone layer, the increase in species extinctions, and the greater frequency of extreme weather events. How many understand the sources of these crises? How many are familiar with the actors, institutions, and processes involved?

> An emancipatory political ecology, then, would have to begin with a relentless critique of ecocide, loss of biodiversity, and the globalization of environmental degradation. (97)

The Green Party in West Germany was founded upon the principles of ecology, pacifism, and postpatriarchal values. The growing movement for Ecological Democracy is rooted in those same principles. The practical agenda, however, must be understood by sound environmental and economic goals:

> The challenge of an ecologically sustainable form of global social development is to safeguard what remains of the biological heritage of the planet. In addition, the task is to provide people all over the world with a broad mix of stable jobs, goods, and services that meet human needs in ways that promote equity, efficiency, and environmental protection. (98)

This requires a new set of values—nothing less than an ethical revolution.

The rise of democracy a few centuries ago, against the mainstream of hereditary authority, was brought forth by way of ethical revolution. 'All men are created equal'. 'Liberty, equality, fraternity'. We need a *deepening* of democracy.

On the horizon we can perceive a new model of political economy based upon ecology, markets, and social justice—green social market economy. Perhaps Germany will show us the way. They brilliantly blended Christian and Social Democracy. With vision they can blend in Green Democracy, too.

The powerful corporations have hijacked democracy to do their bidding. The great media outlets are not particularly profitable but they protect the profits of the worst industries by focusing on something else, on anything else. But global death by ecocide would be terrible for profits. There is hope.

In order to protect the greatest of global commons, the atmosphere, we need to rapidly develop and globalize solar and hydrogen energy technologies. If they had received the subsidies of the oil and nuclear industries, we might be near that goal. How long can we allow the interests of oligopolists to rule the world?

Homo sapiens sapiens is an adaptable species. We had better be so. All our talents are needed in order to realize a meaningful form of Green Democracy.

We slander dinosaurs when we ridicule them. They ruled the earth for millions of years. They never threatened the balance of nature. Unless we change our ways, we shall be but a terminally bitter moment in the life of a beautiful planet.

15

DISMAL SCIENCE—YES *THEN* NO

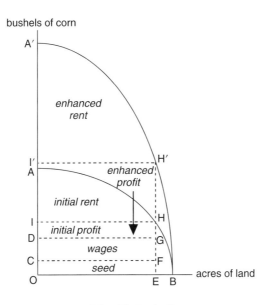

Scientific Agriculture

15.1   BRUTAL ROOTS OF CIVILIZATION

> In the highest stage of social prosperity, the great mass of citizens will most
> probably possess few other resources than their daily labour, and consequently
> will always be near indigence . . .
>
> —Jeremy Bentham, *Principles of the Civil Code* (Part 1, Chapter 14)

Steuart, Quesnay, and Smith analyzed the subsistence problem in order to find
a lasting solution through the establishment of Social Science. In Bentham's
quote we find a bald expression of the naysayer version—the Dismal Science.

According to Bentham, civil law had four distinct objects: subsistence, abundance, equality, and security. That would seem to be the logical order since the
others are not possible without an adequate social subsistence. However,
Bentham believed *natural law* was the only needed authority over subsistence:

> What can the law do relative to subsistence? Nothing directly . . . Want, armed
> with every pain, and even death itself, had commanded labour, had sharpened
> courage, had inspired foresight, had developed all the faculties of man . . .
>
> The force of the physical sanction being sufficient, the employment of the
> political sanction would be superfluous. (*Civil Code*, Part 1, Chapter 4)

This appeal to natural law in the form of animal hunger driving man to secure
subsistence or die found company in 'the principle of population' and the
'law of diminishing returns'. In the first, unrestrained human reproduction
would tend to outrun food production. In the second, nature was simply
stingy.

Joseph Townsend made Bentham's point bluntly in his *Dissertation on the
Poor Laws* (1786):

> Hunger will tame the fiercest animals, it will teach decency and civility,
> obedience and subjugation, to the most brutish, the most obstinate, and the
> most perverse. (Section 4)

This brutal naturalism became the soil into which the Malthusian branch of
economics was planted. Smith actually stated the principle of population
carefully and correctly, even if briefly:

> Every species of animals naturally multiplies in proportion to the means of their
> subsistence, and no species can ever multiply beyond it. But in civilized society
> it is only among the inferior ranks of people that the scantiness of subsistence
> can set limits to the further multiplication of the human species; and it can do
> so in no other way than by destroying a great part of the children which their
> fruitful marriages produce. (1.8.38)

Unlike Townsend, Smith distinguished between animals and humans. But
Malthus ruled British Political Economy for more than a generation too
often emphasizing the *first* of these sentences. Educated Brits, after the
French Revolution, were willing to see the poor masses as potential revolu-
tionaries and wished to understand the 'natural laws' in order to protect
themselves.

15.2 ADVANCING, STATIONARY, OR DECLINING?

The actual threat to the social order from the principle of population and the law of diminishing returns depended upon a broad macro assessment of the situation. Was the society advancing, stationary, or declining?

How was this to be determined? According to Smith, the best evidence would be found in the prevailing subsistence. Was it 'liberal, moderate or scanty'?

> [The money price of corn] regulates the money price of labour, which must always be such as to enable the labourer to purchase a quantity of corn suffi-cient to maintain him and his family either in the liberal, moderate, or scanty manner in which the advancing, stationary, or declining circumstances of the society oblige his employers to maintain him. (4.5.12)

Of course, the advancing was most desirable, the declining the least desirable:

> [I]t is in the progressive state . . . rather than when it has acquired its full com-plement of riches, that the condition of the labouring poor, of the great body of the people, seems to be the happiest and the most comfortable. It is hard in the stationary, and miserable in the declining state. The progressive state is in reality the cheerful and the hearty state to all the different orders of the society. The stationary is dull; the declining melancholy. (1.8.42)

Smith had little else to say about the declining state but he has a deep insight into the stationary state. He tells us, in his chapter on "the Profits of Stock":

> In a country which has acquired that full complement of riches which the nature of its soil and climate, and its situation with respect to other countries allowed it to acquire; which could therefore advance no further and which was not going backward, both the wages of labour and the profits of stock would probably be very low. (1.9.14)

This analysis has a Ricardian ring to it. Smith continues:

> In a country fully peopled in proportion to what either its territory could main-tain or its stock employ, the competition for employment would necessarily be so great as to reduce the wages of labour to what was barely sufficient to keep up the number of labourers . . . In a country fully stocked in proportion to all the business it had to transact . . . competition . . . would everywhere be as great, and consequently the ordinary profit as low as possible. (1.9.14)

This clear analysis must have been read by Ricardo, feeding his anxiety about the stationary state. In the next paragraph Smith sets the stage for Ricardo's famous struggle against the Corn Laws which forbade importation of grains:

> A country which neglects or despises foreign commerce, cannot transact the same quantity of business which it might do with different laws and institutions. (1.9.15)

Smith's analysis was in the context of a world filled with agrarian societies, where commercial societies were rare. That, however, was starting to change.

15.3   POPULATION AND CAPITAL

By the time Ricardo wrote his *Essay on Profits* (1815) the progress of Britain's agrarian society toward capitalism was advanced enough for the analysis of capital to emerge. Smith's distinction could be reinterpreted:

$$capital\ accumulation\ rate > or = or < population\ growth\ rate$$

An advancing state requires the greater than sign, a stationary state is represented by the equal sign and a declining state suffers the less than sign.

Francis Place, in *Illustrations and Proofs of the Principle of Population* (1822), took the gloomy view on the relation between population and capital:

> When the population of any country increases, one of two things invariably takes place; either a proportional increase of capital as fast as that of the people, or a deterioration in the circumstances of the great body of the people. (Place, 259)

Invariably? To our eye there is a logical error here: it should also be possible for capital to increase faster than population. But Place has in mind a largely agrarian society expanding into land with average or inferior fertility, or, working old land more intensively. Place then drew a Malthusian conclusion:

> If population increase without proportionate increase of capital . . . the real wages of labour will fall. In course of time, the people will be reduced to extreme poverty and misery . . . in this state, a bad harvest or two will cause dearth or famine, and produce pestilential diseases. (Place, 261)

This sort of oppressive pessimism did not go unchallenged. Nassau Senior, the first Drummond Professor of Political Economy at Oxford, thought that capital was *obviously* growing faster than population in England, easing the subsistence problem:

> I have nothing to do at present with those portions of capital which consist of the materials and implements of labour. That they *have* increased far more than in proportion to the increase of population, is almost too obvious for remark. My present subject is the relative increase of *subsistence*. (*Two Lectures on Population* (1828), 46, italics in the original)

As Donald Winch has observed, Malthus was becoming less relevant in the more advanced societies. Ricardo had founded a Political Economy Club in 1821. A decade later, long after his death, Ricardo was taken to task there for following Malthus on population. Winch quotes a meeting of the Club in 1831:

> [I]t is clear from the progress of social improvement and the bettering of the conditions of the people in the greater part of the civilized world, that Capital, or the means of Employment—the fund for labour—increases in greater ratio than population. [Quoted in Winch (2001), 424.]

Here we see, for the first time since 1798, the eclipse of Malthus and the adjustment of Classical thinking to the possibility of open-ended progress.

15.4 AGRARIAN SOCIETY IN DECLINE

Ricardo left us a simple model for analyzing stationary and advancing economies but not economies in decline. Even Malthus failed to do so. Fortunately, Professor Jack Goldstone has brilliantly filled in this gap in his book *Revolution and Rebellion in the Early Modern World* (1991).

With his eyes focused mainly on the seventeenth century, Goldstone observes challenges to state authority as country after country suffered the effects of population growth exceeding the productive and administrative capacities. The context for this is elaborated by Goldstone in the following way:

> Large states of the early modern period . . . faced certain common constraints. They needed to raise sufficient revenues to support their armies and reward their retainers. They needed sufficient allegiance from the elites to secure loyal officials for government service and, perhaps more importantly, to secure loyal local authorities in an era when centrally appointed officialdom rarely penetrated below the county level. And they needed to provide sufficient stability and sustenance for the working and cultivating population so that the latter could pay their taxes and other obligations and yet not be inclined to support rebellions. Thus any train of events that simultaneously led to fiscal deterioration, elite factionalism and disloyalty, and a major decline in popular living standards or undermining of popular traditional rights, threatened the ability of the states to maintain their authority . . .

> Put simply, large agrarian states of this period were not equipped to deal with the impact of the steady growth of population . . . eventually amounting to population increases in excess of the productivity gains of the land. (24)

An interpretation of his analysis appears in the following diagram. When (social and private) capital per person falls steadily, crisis occurs at three levels.

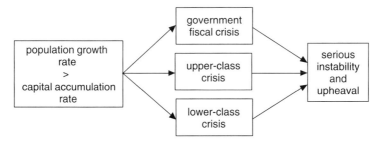

The lower classes are squeezed from several directions. Land per person shrinks as it is divided into smaller pieces each generation. Subdivisions become excessive when the land cannot provide for family subsistence. Lower classes also suffer unemployment and inflation.

The sons in upper classes wish for easy appointment to well-respected institutions. After a while there are not enough jobs to go around. Inflation eats at old wealth. At the same time, the state uses up its lines of credit and goes bankrupt. Serious suffering and instability occur. Ruin may be in the air in such strange times. Military intervention and rule is a possibility. So is breakdown.

15.5 DREADED STATIONARY STATE

If a fully peopled society could become less agrarian and more capitalistic, it would face the problem analyzed in Ricardo's *Essay on Profits* (1815). Suppose productivity remains unchanged and corn imports are forbidden— the situation at that time. As population expands, additional acres will have to be brought under cultivation. This will be at the expense of capitalists and to the benefit of landlords. Ricardo—the hypercapitalist of his day—was alarmed by this possibility. He assumed competitive market conditions where rates of profit would be equalized. In his model:

> [B]y bringing successively land of a worse quality . . . rent would rise on the land previously cultivated, and precisely in the same degree would profits fall; and if the smallness of profits do not check accumulation, there are hardly any limits to the rise of rent, and the fall of profit. (9–10)

We assume corn is produced with corn seed and labor time. Equal doses of both are applied to every acre, but acres vary in quality from highly fertile to totally barren. The subsistence wage—a corn bundle—is given and unchanging.

OA is the productivity of the best acre. OB acres are available for corn production. The maximum production of corn is the area OAB. Seed per acre is OC; wages per acre are CD. Suppose OE acres are farmed. The seed used is the area OCFE. Wages are the area CDGF. The remainder is agricultural surplus.

What determines the division of this surplus between profit and rent?

> The general profits of stock depend wholly on the profits of the last portion of capital employed on the land. (20)

Extend the perpendicular out of point E up to point H. Agricultural surplus is DAHG. Profits are DIHG. The residual, area IAH, is the rent. The rate of profit on capital is the profit divided by the 'circulating capital'—wages plus seed.

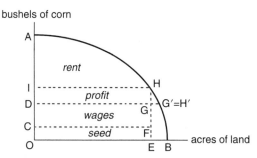

In Ricardo's model, *this* rate of profit determines the average rate of profit in society. If it falls too low, the incentive to accumulate capital will fade away, economic growth will end and the all-powerful landlords will impede progress.

Profits will *disappear* if cultivation is extended by only GG' acres, to DG'. In that case, point G' also represents H' and rents swell to DAH'. Thus, to cope with population growth, corn must be imported or productivity must increase.

15.6 SCIENTIFIC AGRICULTURE

Malthus, who put no faith in technical change, recognized the impact it could have if applied to agriculture:

> If new and superior modes of cultivation be invented . . . it is obvious that inferior land may be cultivated at higher profits than could be obtained from richer land before; and . . . may, for a long period, more than counterbalance the tendency of . . . a great increase of capital to yield smaller proportionate returns. (3.10.25)

The diagram below uses the same points A through I as before. Let us assume a huge breakthrough in the *quality* of seeds, greatly increasing yield per acre. This is represented by the new marginal-product curve A'B.

Suppose the simplest case: the number of acres sown, the quantity of seed, and the labor time are unchanged. Then, all of the additional output will accrue to profit and rent. Profit will increase to DI'H'G. Rent will swell to I'A'H'. The rate of profit has increased greatly, from DIHG/ODGE to DI'H'G/ODGE.

Agricultural surplus has increased extraordinarily. A greatly enlarged number of workers can be supported in other sectors. Domestically generated conditions for *transcending* agrarian society are emerging. Moreover, these special seeds can be adopted in other corn economies, spreading the social transformation!

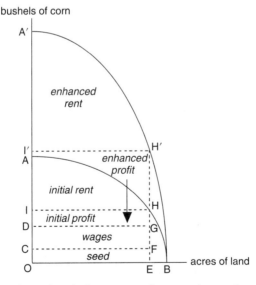

In order for this to be realized, the new surplus must be used to create jobs and businesses and expand the banking system. Landlords will divide their share between consumption and savings and might try their hand at capitalistic business. Capitalists will divide their share between consumption, financial savings, and productive investment. The rate of growth in such an economy will depend upon the rate at which the new surplus is (successfully) invested domestically in new productive capacity. If yields per acre can be greatly increased again, this process can repeat, until agrarian society is only a memory.

15.7   BEYOND SUBSISTENCE

By the time we get to John Stuart Mill's *Principles* (1848), the shift from a *theoretical* emphasis on subsistence found in Steuart, Smith, and Malthus, to an emphasis on postagrarian conditions, is nearly complete even though it looks blurry. Mill is still Classical when he writes in his "Preliminary Remarks":

> The production of wealth; the extraction of the instruments of human subsistence and enjoyment from the materials of the globe, is evidently not an arbitrary thing. It has its necessary conditions. (paragraph 30)

Steuart or Smith could have written that. Moreover, Mill continues to use the logic of the Classical Macrofoundation. For example, he writes:

> It is evident that every labourer who extracts from the land more than his own food, and that of any family he may have, increases the means of supporting a non-agricultural population. (1.9.35)

But he chides other writers for thinking Malthusian conditions still exist in England limiting nonagricultural populations to a fraction of overall activity:

> But although the gross produce of the land is greatest, caeteris paribus, under small cultivation, and although, therefore, a country is able on that system to support a larger aggregate population, it is generally assumed by English writers that what is termed the net produce, that is, the surplus after feeding the cultivators, must be smaller; that therefore, the population disposable for all other purposes . . . must be less numerous . . . This, however, has been taken for granted much too readily . . . In France it is computed [1848] that two-thirds of the whole population are agricultural. In England, at most, one-third. (1.9.32)

France is still living under the conditions explored in the Classical Macrofoundation but England has transcended them!

Even Malthus can be seen in a softer light than usual. While he never retracted:

> Population is necessarily limited by the means of subsistence. (1.2.22)

he had no idea how correct his loophole was:

> the progress of civilization naturally tends to counteract . . . (1.2.22)

In the last paragraph of his opus, Malthus appears to be saying: The roots of society shall always be grounded in social subsistence but we can climb well above it through additional progress of civilization, even enough to reduce the gap between asset owners and workers and improve their social relations:

> A strict inquiry into the principle of population obliges us to conclude that we shall never be able to throw down the ladder by which we have risen to this eminence [of civilization]; but it by no means proves, that we may not rise higher by the same means. The structure of society, in its great features, will probably always remain unchanged. We have every reason to believe that it will always consist of a class of proprietors and a class of labourers; but the condition of each, and the proportion which they bear to each other, may be so altered, as greatly to improve the harmony and beauty of the whole. (4.14.14)

An online library allows us to count the number of paragraphs in which a word appears. I have used that site to count the paragraphs containing 'subsistence' in important works by Classical and neo-Classical British economists.

The word is central to Steuart, Smith, and Malthus. By the time we get to Mill and Senior, it is a less-frequently used *side* category, no longer requiring for Britain the depth of Steuart and missing the sting of Malthus. A generation or two later, it has nearly disappeared. In Marshall its context is historical. Subsistence makes only a cameo appearance in Jevons and Wicksteed.

What about the multimillionaire Ricardo? He scarcely uses the word even though he accepts Malthus on population. In this regard he is the first modern economist—an abstract thinker incapable of relating to the subsistence problem.

SUBSISTENCE	
	# of paragraphs in which it appears
British Classical Economists	
Malthus, *Essay on Population*—6th ed. (1798 . . . 1826)	196
Smith, *Wealth of Nations* (1776)	104
Mill, *Principles of Political Economy*—7th ed. (1848 . . . 1909)	75
Senior, *Political Economy*—3rd ed. (1850 . . . 1854)	51
Ricardo, *Principles of Political Economy*—3rd ed. (1817 . . . 1821)	11
British Neo-Classical Economists	
Marshall, *Principles of Economics*—8th ed. (1890 . . . 1920)	14
Jevons, *Theory of Political Economy*—3rd ed. (1871 . . . 1888)	4
Wicksteed, *Common Sense of Political Economy* (1910)	2

Source: Library of Economics and Liberty, http://www.econlib.org/library (accessed May 1, 2002).
Note: Steuart is not published at this website. Elsewhere I have cited a word count.
'Subsistence' is found 258 times in Steuart's *Principles* (1767) and 162 times in Smith's *Wealth of Nations*.

While Steuart told us in Book 1 of his *Principles*, 'Population and Agriculture':

> The principle object of this science is to secure a certain fund of subsistence for all the inhabitants, to obviate every circumstance which may render it precarious . . . (1.Introduction.6)

a century later, Jevons gives economic science its modern form, dismissing population problems from economics with the wave of a hand:

> The science of Political Economy rests upon a few notions of an apparently simple character. Utility, wealth, value, commodity, labour, land, capital, are the elements of the subject . . . (1.1)

> The doctrine of population has been conspicuously absent, not because I doubt in the least its truth and vast importance, but because it forms no part of the direct problem of Economics. (8.2)

The neo-Classicals won the day in Britain because they were in tune with changing conditions in that nation. But Steuart, Smith, and Malthus *were still* highly relevant in less-developed nations. They will continue to be relevant in poor countries until we can put Steuart's definition of the science in a museum.

16

STEUART

I present this enquiry to the public as nothing more than an essay which may serve as a canvass for better hands than mine to work upon.

(Preface, Paragraph 18)

The wandering and independent life I have led may naturally have set me free, in some measure, from strong attachment to popular opinions.

(Preface, Paragraph 30)

—*An Inquiry into the Principles of Political Economy* (1767)

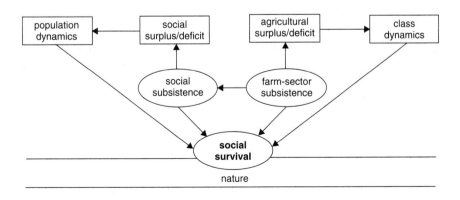

16.1   BOOK 1 OF *PRINCIPLES*

The principal object of this science is to secure a certain fund of subsistence for all the inhabitants, to obviate every circumstance which may render it precarious . . . (1.Introduction.6)

[W]hile subsistence is upon a precarious footing, no statesman can turn his attention to any thing else. (1.4.13)

[T]he principal care of a statesman should be to keep all employed . . . (1.13.17)

The chapter on the Classical Macrofoundation gave the briefest glimpse into Steuart's contribution to the history of economic thought—just enough to state the theory. Here, we will let Steuart speak to us on this topic at greater length.

His effort is concentrated in Chapters 3–8 of Book 1 of his *Principles*. The chapter titles below are interpretations of Steuart's *wordy* titles. Chapter 7, on slavery, has been omitted because it is not essential for telling the story. Steuart, himself, said Book 1 is intended to accomplish the following things:

This first book shall . . . set out with taking up society in the cradle . . . I shall here examine the principles which influence their multiplication, the method of providing for their subsistence, the origin of their labour, the effects of their liberty and slavery, the distribution of them into classes . . . (1.2.33)

As I said before—and demonstrated in the chapter on Roots of Civilization—the basic *structure* of this analysis still lives in cultural anthropology. It will be relevant to development economics as long as agrarian or semi-industrial societies exist and struggle to solve the subsistence problem.

BOOK 1: POPULATION AND AGRICULTURE
CHAPTERS CONTAINING THE CLASSICAL MACROFOUNDATION

3. Population in a State of Nature
4. Natural and Immediate Effects of Agriculture on Population
5. Political and Extended Effects of Agriculture on Population
6. Human Wants and Human Multiplication
8. Proportion Necessary for Agriculture/Proportion Available

Book 1 was written in exile in Germany during the late 1750s. Although brilliant, its lack of good editing has made it taxing for all but persistent readers.

Steuart's moral passion for his topic rises to the surface from time to time. For example, he considered it a scandal for England to export food while people died of hunger or the diseases of hunger. He sought to remedy this:

Those who cannot buy, are exactly those who . . . die for want of subsistence . . . my principal point in view . . . is to find out a method for enabling the indigent to buy up [the] quantity which is at present exported. (1.15.21)

Steuart has been underappreciated for centuries. Let us see, in his own words, the unfolding of the Classical Macrofoundation—a survival-conditions analysis.

16.2   STATE OF NATURE

Steuart is deliberate in the systematic unfolding of what should be called a thought experiment. He starts with existence and survival:

> The fundamental principle of the multiplication of all animals, and consequently of man, is generation; the next is food: generation gives existence, food preserves it. (1.3.3)

In the state of nature, population is strictly limited by means of subsistence available from gathering fruit and vegetables and from killing animals:

> Were the earth . . . uncultivated, the numbers of mankind would not exceed the proportion of the spontaneous fruits which she offers for their immediate use, or for that of the animals which might be the proper nourishment. (1.3.5)

The human carrying capacity of the earth in the state of nature, before any form of agricultural knowledge or activity, is designated as (A):

> There is therefore a certain number of mankind which the earth would be able to maintain without any labour: allow me to call this quantity (A). (1.3.6)

If we think of this not globally but *locally*, population (A) is the center around which a dynamic process can be understood. Gradually, a certain territory is populated, then overpopulated, then depopulated then repopulated:

> Those who are supposed to be fed with the spontaneous fruits of the earth, cannot . . . multiply beyond that proportion; at the same time the generative faculty will work its natural effects in augmenting numbers. The consequence will be, that certain individuals must become worse fed, consequently weaker. consequently, if, in that weakly state, nature should withhold a part of her usual plenty, the whole multitude will be affected by it; a disease may take place, and sweep off a far greater number than that proportioned to the deficiency of the season. What results from this? That those who have escaped, finding food more plentiful, become vigorous and strong. Generation gives life to additional numbers, food preserves it until they rise up to the former standard. (1.3.9)

This brings us to the paragraph celebrated by Malthus in the second edition of his *Essay on Population* (1803).

> Thus the generative faculty resembles a spring loaded with a weight, which always exerts itself in proportion to the diminution of resistance: when food has remained some time without augmentation or diminution, generation will carry numbers as high as possible; if then food come to be diminished, the spring is overpowered; the force of it becomes less than nothing. Inhabitants will diminish, at least, in proportion to the overcharge. If, upon the other hand, food be increased, the spring which stood at 0, will begin to exert itself in proportion as the resistance diminishes; people will begin to be better fed; they will multiply, and, in proportion as they increase in numbers, the food will become scarce again. (1.3.10)

As we shall see, Steuart—to a much greater extent than Malthus—was inclined to modify this principle of population when analyzing agrarian societies.

16.3 AGRICULTURAL SECTOR

Steuart then introduces agriculture as a human-devised method for procuring food to support a population larger than (A):

> [S]uppose man to add his labour and industry to the natural activity of the soil . . . as . . . he produces an additional quantity of food . . . he lays a foundation for the maintenance of an additional number. This number . . . call (B). (1.4.1)

(A) + (B) signifies the emergence of social classes: hunter-gatherers and farmers:

> [W]e find mankind . . . divided into two classes; those who . . . live upon the spontaneous fruits of the earth . . . those . . . obliged to labour the soil. (1.4.2)

He detects another far-reaching social distinction. With the invention of food *production* emerges the existence of a man-made surplus. A successful farmer, by producing a surplus above the needs of his family, can hire the services of people less skilled in the arts of survival. But he adds an ominous observation:

> The others [of inferior skill] . . . will very naturally become their servants; as this method is . . . the most easy to procure subsistence . . . Those who become servants for the sake of food, will soon become slaves: for slavery is but the abuse of service . . . and men who find no possibility of subsisting otherwise, will be obliged to serve upon the conditions prescribed to them. (1.4.3)

While analyzing population in the state of nature, the principles of animal reproduction sufficed. With the emergence of agricultural society, the dynamic is influenced by something unknown in the animal kingdom—employment:

> Multiplication will . . . go forward, not in proportion to the generative faculty, but according to the employment of the persons already generated. (1.4.6)

The establishment of agricultural lands depends upon its own complex division of labor, requiring the feeding of construction workers for extended periods of time. Once the lands are fit for farming, those workers need new employment in order to procure subsistence for themselves and their families:

> To make an establishment in a country not before inhabited, to root out woods, destroy wild and venomous animals, drain marshy grounds, give a free course to water, and to lay down the surface into corn fields, must surely require more hands than to cultivate the same after it is improved. (4.12)

Even though agriculture is the foundation of population and survival, Steuart does not want this turned into a fetish. Man does not live to eat—he eats to live. Thus, he urges the appreciation of advanced agrarian societies capable of supporting many professions out of their agricultural surplus:

> Nobody can dispute that agriculture is the foundation of multiplication, and the most essential requisite for the prosperity of a state. But it does not follow from this, that every body almost in the state should be employed in it; that would be inverting the order of things . . . The duty and business of man is not to feed; he is fed, in order to do his duty, and to become useful in his profession; whether agriculture, art, or science. (1.4.14)

16.4 NONAGRICULTURAL SECTOR

If a large agricultural surplus is produced a diversified division of labor becomes possible. The central task of a wise leader will be the creation of jobs:

> The statesman must . . . find . . . a method to make the [agricultural surplus] circulate downwards, so as to relieve the wants of the most necessitous: Otherwise, the plenty produced, remaining in the hands of those who produced it, will . . . perish . . . (1.5.4)

> If he acts . . . with [the] spirit of liberty . . . he has . . . to contrive different employments for the hands of the necessitous, that, by their labour, they may produce an equivalent which may be acceptable to the farmers . . . (1.5.6)

Thus, *effective demand* between the two great economic sectors plays a role in determining both social tranquility and population size:

> These are the reciprocal wants which the statesman must create, in order to bind the society together . . . Agriculture . . . will augment population, in proportion only as the necessitous are put in a situation to purchase subsistence with their labour. (1.5.9)

If subsistence is naturally easy to come by, ambition will not take root in the minds of people and the division of labor will remain simple:

> If the soil be vastly rich, situated in a warm climate, and naturally watered, the productions of the earth will be almost spontaneous: this will make the inhabitants lazy. Laziness is the greatest of all obstacles to labour and industry. Manufactures will never flourish here. (1.6.12)

If people have to face four seasons, survival will depend upon developing suitable skills and products. In such a country, the more ambitious and skillful the people, the greater the division of labor and the larger the population:

> It is not in the most fruitful countries . . . that we find the most inhabitants. It is in climates less favoured by nature, and where the soil produces to those only who labour, and in proportion to the industry of every one, where we may expect to find great multitudes . . . even these multitudes will be found greater or less, in proportion . . . to ingenuity and industry. (1.6.15)

Over time such a society can develop refinement—the hallmark of civilization. This acts as a virtuous cycle for economic and demographic expansion:

> In such countries where industry is made to flourish, the free hands . . . will be employed in useful manufactures, which, being refined upon by the ingenious, will determine what is called the standard of taste; this taste will increase consumption, which again will multiply workmen, and these will encourage the production of food for their nourishment. (1.6.16)

Steuart highly esteems a refined agrarian society because it can create and sustain high levels of productive employment:

> Let it . . . never be said, that there are too many manufacturers employed in a country; it is the same as if it were said, there are too few idle persons, too few beggars, and too many husbandmen. (1.6.17)

16.5   MACROFOUNDATION RESTATED

In the chapter on the Classical Macrofoundation, we built the diagram via short quote from Steuart and two social-accounting equations. The diagram can be built up, step-by-step, from the previous three sections of the current chapter. But I would much rather reproduce it in the context of three of Steuart's most brilliant paragraphs where he summarizes the macrofoundation for a *simple agrarian society*. He does this as a series of three interconnected principles.

First: agricultural surplus. To the extent this is produced, nonagricultural populations can exist and satisfy the nonagricultural demands in the society:

> First, One consequence of a fruitful soil, possessed by a free people, given to agriculture, and inclined to industry, will be the production of a superfluous quantity of food, over and above what is necessary to feed the farmers. Inhabitants will multiply; and, according to their increase, a certain number of the whole, proportional to such superfluity of nourishment produced, will apply themselves to industry and to the supplying of other wants. (1.5.19)

Next: social classes. The society is divided into two classes based upon the division of labor: farmers and those outside of agriculture—*free hands*:

> Secondly . . . we find the people distributed into two classes. The first is that of the farmers who produce the subsistence, and who are necessarily employed in this branch of business; the other I shall call free hands; because their occupation being to procure themselves subsistence out of the superfluity of the farmers, and by a labour adapted to the wants of the society . . . (1.5.20)

Finally: population dynamics. The crude principle of population in a state of nature is superceded by one based upon ample employment being available to support the free hands and their families while also limiting their reproduction:

> Thirdly, If . . . both money and the luxurious arts be supposed to be unknown, then the superfluity of the farmers will be in proportion to the number of those whose labour will be found sufficient to provide for all the other necessities of the inhabitants; and, so soon as this is accomplished, the consumption and pro-duce becoming equally balanced, the inhabitants will increase no more, or at least very precariously, unless their wants be multiplied. (1.5.21)

In this rendering of the macrofoundation, the equilibrium of production and consumption evidently guarantees sufficient feedbacks for social survival.

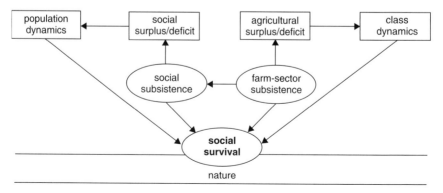

16.6 SOCIAL ACCOUNTING

Given the central importance of understanding an agrarian society by its two main sectors—agricultural and nonagricultural—Steuart tried to estimate some social accounts for England using bits of old data. His effort, in Chapter 8, is confusing. We will try to reconstruct part of it in a compact way.

The annual product of corn-lands was £9 million while the annual product of 'pasture-lands' was £12 million—summing to £21 million. Pasture-lands production included dairy, meat, hides, wool, hay, horse breeding, and forestry.

Rent from corn-lands was £2 million; rent from pasture-lands was £7 million. The residual in both categories was poorly defined. For consistency sake, we will call them 'consumption by farmers' and 'consumption by herdsmen', even though they include replacement of capital goods used up during the year. Steuart appears to assume their consumption equaled their income—which implies farmers and herdsmen kept their capital intact but did not add to it.

Steuart tried to measure the ratio of farmers to herders using this data:

> as the consumption upon corn-farms is 7/9 and that upon pasture 5/12, the proportion of these two fractions must mark the ratio between the populousness of pasture-lands, and those of tillage . . . as 84 to 45 . . . (1.8.20)

PRODUCT ACCOUNT • ENGLAND, LATE SEVENTEENTH CENTURY DATA • MILLIONS OF £			
Product of Lands		**Claims on Product of Lands**	
corn-lands	9	consumption by farmers	7
		rent from corn-lands	2
pasture-lands	12	consumption by herdsmen	5
		rent from pasture-lands	7
Product of Lands	21	**Claims on Product of Lands**	21
		income of farmers and herdsmen	12
		rent from corn-lands and pasture-lands	9

For Steuart, the vital demographic estimate was the proportion of agricultural to nonagricultural populations. As a first approximation, he appears to assume farmers and herdsmen only bought products of land, and, rent was only used to employ free hands, yielding the 12 to 9 proportionality calculation below. However, we can adjust the spending pattern sensibly and get the same result.

England's pasture-lands generated a huge surplus allowing it to support a large nonagricultural population—43 percent—an unusually large one for that era.

POPULATION ACCOUNT • ASSUMING 5.6 MILLION PEOPLE IN ENGLAND			
Steuart's Assumptions			
all of ag. income spent in ag. sector	12 to 9	**Steuart's Calculation**	
all of rent spent in nonag. sector	proportionality	total population	5.6 (100%)
Alternative Assumptions		agricultural sector	3.2 (57%)
3/4 of ag income spent in ag. sector	12 to 9	nonagricultural sector	2.4 (43%)
2/3 of rent spent in nonag. sector	proportionality		

16.7 PLENTY AND SCARCITY

While England produced a good agricultural surplus, it produced a fairly small *social surplus*. This was not generally understood. Steuart, however, thought a good year only produced enough food for fourteen months:

> Nothing is more common than to hear that an abundant crop furnishes more than three years' subsistence . . . I am, on the contrary, apt to believe, that no annual produce of grain ever was so great in England as to supply its inhabitants fifteen months . . . a very good year . . . produces full subsistence for fourteen months; and crops which much exceed this are . . . very rare. (1.17.3)

Let us suppose the nonagricultural sector produced the same ratio of product to necessities. Then the ratio of net output to the social subsistence would be 14/12 or 1.2. In our classification this would make 1750s England fourth world.

Steuart believed England could always produce much more than half of its required food. Otherwise, because of the small surpluses produced in Europe, a bad crop in England would lead to a level of famine unknown there:

> I am apt to believe, that there never was a year of such scarcity as that the lands of England did not produce greatly above six months subsistence . . . Were six months of the most slender subsistence to fail, I imagine all Europe together might perhaps be at a loss to supply a quantity sufficient to prevent the greatest desolation by famine. (1.17.5)

To support these assertions, he refers to export and import data to show that England produced neither great social surpluses nor great social deficits:

> [T]he greatest exportation ever known in one year [1750] . . . is equivalent to about 46 days' provision only.
>
> [T]he greatest importation ever known . . . in the year 1757 . . . is equivalent to [England's] subsistence for 4 days 2 hours and 24 minutes. (footnote 8)

Steuart concluded that *no society* on earth produced huge social surpluses:

> I must conclude . . . that the best corn country in the world . . . does not produce wherewithal fully to maintain, as in years of plenty, one third more than its own inhabitants . . . (1.17.10)

Thus, even the most advanced societies were still subject to subsistence cycles:

> If it be true, that a crop in the most plentiful year is nearly consumed by the inhabitants, what becomes of them in years of scarcity? For nobody can deny, that there is a great difference, between one crop and another . . . In years of plenty every one is well fed; the price of the lowest industry can procure subsistence sufficient to bear a division; food is not so frugally managed; a quantity of animals are fatted for use; all sorts of cattle are kept in good heart; and people drink more largely, because ale is cheap. A year of scarcity comes, the people are ill fed, and when the lower classes come to divide with their children, the portions are brought to be very small; there is great economy upon consumption, few animals are fatted for use, cattle look miserably, and a poor man cannot indulge himself with a cup of generous ale. (1.17.9)

17

MALTHUS: CHECKS TO POPULATION

AGE OF MALTHUS	
first world	
second world	
third world	Norway
	France
fourth world	France
	Siberia
	Africa
fifth world	France
	Siberia
	Africa
	American Indians

17.1   FUNDAMENTAL THEOREMS

> It is not enough a country should have the power of producing food in abundance, but the state of society must be such as to afford the means of its proper distribution . . .
>
> ("Checks to Population in Siberia," 1.9.8)

In these well-chosen words, Malthus approximates the fundamental theorems in Chapter 1:

production-survival condition: ability to produce social surplus.
distribution-survival condition: access to a share of social subsistence.

In the quote above, Malthus is concerned about the failure of the second condition—when a society lacks the will or ability to widely provide the means of subsistence. This is the defining characteristic of the fourth world. When the production condition is also violated—which in Malthus' day generally implied depopulation—we are in the realm of the fifth world.

For Malthus, the nucleus of the principle of population was self-evident: no species can multiply beyond its means of subsistence. This is implied by the production-survival condition. That condition says:

$$net\ output > social\ subsistence$$

Since the social subsistence is defined as subsistence per person times the population, dividing both sides by subsistence per person yields:

$$net\ output/subsistence\ per\ person > population$$

In a closed-economy corn model, this is a precise way of saying a population size is limited by the means of subsistence. If birth control is common, that will be the effective limiting factor. If the society can produce huge surpluses, the inequality above is simply a curiosity. But Malthus believed—and wanted to prove—that human populations usually, and carelessly, tended to push the limit.

In this chapter we find it convenient to use the formula for life expectancy in a closed economy when population is stationary:

$$\frac{1000}{life\ expectancy} = death\ rate = birth\ rate$$

Although this formula from demography was unknown to Malthus, he understood a similar logic to it and frequently worked with its main implication:

> If we suppose a country where the population is stationary . . . the annual mortality will accurately express the expectation of life. (2.11.3)

With this background, let us look at five case studies from Malthus on 'checks to population'—'all resolvable into moral restraint, vice and misery'. As we proceed we may ponder upon their progress since the Age of Malthus.

17.2   SIBERIA

> Such countries seem to be under that moral impossibility of increasing which is
> well described by Sir James Steuart. If either from the nature of the govern-
> ment, or the habits of the people, obstacles exist to the settlement of fresh farms
> or the subdivision of the old ones, a part of the society may suffer want, even in
> the midst of apparent plenty. It is not enough a country should have the power
> of producing food in abundance, but the state of society must be such as to
> afford the means of its proper distribution . . . ("Checks to Population in
> Siberia," 1.9.8)

In this quote, Malthus was in the middle of discussing a paradox found in the
demography of Southern Siberia. Life was poor and population thin, even
though the soil was extremely rich—'as to not require or even bear dressing':

> The mode of agriculture . . . require[s] very few labourers. The buck-wheat . . .
> sown very thin, yet one sowing will last five or six years, and produce every year
> twelve or fifteen times the original quantity. The seed which falls during the
> time of the harvest is sufficient for the next year. (1.9.8)

Under these conditions, a varied division of labor was perpetually stillborn.
Huge surpluses could be produced, but the local demand for labor was
insufficient to generate purchasing power. Larger markets were distant and
transportation was poor. This allowed much fallow time for land as well as for
labor. With little demand for agricultural labor, and few opportunities in
manufacturing or services, population stagnated.

Malthus identified three circumstances necessary for progress: (1) the
availability of complimentary resources, such as wood and water; (2) legally
secure purchase of land in small lots; and (3) habits of industry and accumulation. However, since the third had never developed, the settlement of fresh
farms was rare:

> [T]he redundant labourers of Siberia would find it extremely difficult to collect
> such funds as would enable him to build a house, to purchase stock and utensils,
> and to subsist till he could bring his new land into proper order and obtain an
> adequate return. (1.9.14)

The story of Northern Siberia is even starker. Subsistence in those 'inhospitable
regions' had long been based upon hunting and fishing. Surviving long winters
required preparation and strength. Famines were common but smallpox might
have been the 'principle check to their increase':

> The extraordinary mortality of the small-pox among these people is very naturally
> accounted for by the extreme heat, filth and putrid air of their underground
> habitations. Three or four . . . families are crowded together in one hut . . .
> They never wash their hands, and the putrid remains of the fish, and the excre-
> ments of the children are never cleared away. (1.9.4)

Kamtschatka, evidently, lost three-fourth of its native population to smallpox.

17.3 AFRICA

> If accurate registers of mortality were kept among these nations, I have little doubt that . . . 1 in 17 or 18 at the least dies annually, instead of 1 in 34, 36, or 40, as in the generality of European states. ("Checks to Population in Africa," 1.8.22)

This statement, which pertains to the Horn of Africa, may be translated into modern death rates. To deepen the contrast, we may also compare approximate life expectancies in the Age of Malthus with recent figures. The two-to-one ratio of old has nearly been retained.

MALTHUS' STATEMENT	DEATH RATE (PER 1000)	STATIONARY STATE LIFE EXPECTANCY	RECENT LIFE EXPECTANCY
Horn of Africa '1 in 17 or 18'	56–59	17 or 18 years	Ethiopia 42 years
Europe '1 in 34 to 40'	25–29	34–40 years	Switzerland 80 years

Malthus, to some extent, accepts a geographic determinism:

> [I]t seems agreeable to the analogy of nature to suppose that, as the natives of hot climates arrive much earlier at maturity than the inhabitants of colder countries, they should also perish earlier. (1.8.4)

By colder countries he had in mind Western Europe, not Siberia.

One needs to ask what manner of society can exist if life expectancy is only 17 years? Certainly this must be close to an absolute minimum if a group of people is to have any capacity to preserve and reproduce a culture. Evidently, in Abyssinia (Ethiopia) "the checks of war, pestilential diseases and promiscuous intercourse, all operate in an excessive degree" (1.8.21).

Malthus reports on a twofold pattern of violence—open warfare between small petty states and postharvest plunder. The insecurity of property has a dreadful impact on economic activity:

> [A]s there are not many opportunities of turning to advantage the surplus produce of their labour, we cannot be surprised that they should in general content themselves with cultivating only so much ground as is necessary for their own support. (1.8.3)

Warfare and plunder were also used to acquire slaves. In some societies, slaves outnumbered free men. Periodic famines drove people to sell themselves or their children. What was the price of a child?

> "Observe that boy . . . his mother has sold him to me for forty days' provisions for herself and the rest of her family." (1.8.6)

Malthus believed the most essential reform needed in Africa was the security of property, as understood by Europeans.

17.4 AMERICAN INDIANS

> The very extraordinary depopulation that has taken place among the American Indians, may appear to some to contradict the theory which is intended to be established; but it will be found that the causes of this rapid diminution may all be resolved into the three great checks to population ,which have been stated . . . ("Checks to Population among the American Indians," 1.4.39)

This chapter poses a particular difficulty. Malthus summarizes various reports from observers who both disdain the Indians and are oblivious to the roles played by Europeans in the long, drawn out depopulations. Only in the *last paragraph* of the chapter does Malthus recognize this point:

> [I]t should be observed that almost every where the connexion of the Indians with Europeans has tended to break their spirit, to weaken or give wrong direction to their industry, and in consequence to diminish the sources of their subsistence. In St. Domingo, the Indians neglected purposely to cultivate their lands in order to starve out their cruel oppressors. In Peru and Chili, the forced industry of the natives was fatally directed to the digging in the bowels of the earth, instead of cultivating its surface . . . The number of wild animals, in all the know parts of America, is even more diminished than the number of people. (1.4.40)

Frequent and widespread depopulations by smallpox is discussed, but Malthus did not seem to realize it was introduced into the Americas by the Europeans.

Pressure toward depopulation not only came from a high death rate; among many tribes, the birth rate was unusually low. The observed 'want of ardor in the men toward their women':

> probably exists in a great degree among all barbarous nations, whose food is poor and insufficient, and who live in constant apprehension of being pressed by famine or by an enemy. (1.4.3)

Thus far we have not identified their means of subsistence. Although agriculture was well established in the larger nations before the arrival of Europeans, most groups lived by hunting, gathering, and fishing. This alone would limit the size of the tribes but it would require them to acquire their subsistence over a large territory.

This frequently bought tribes into conflict, specially over hunting grounds. The growth of one tribe was felt by the other as added competition for game. In such conflicts there were three possible outcomes: an equilibrium with both suffering losses, emigration by the losing side, or extermination of the defeated group. With the stakes so high, a 'ferocious spirit of warfare' developed.

> Their object in battle is not conquest, but destruction. The life of the victor depends upon the death of his enemy . . . (1.4.19)

Such life was harsh by European standards in the Age of Malthus. But this brings us to a prime question: what were the European standards at that time?

17.5 NORWAY

Norway, during . . . the last century was . . . exempt from the drains of people by war. The climate is remarkably free from epidemic sicknesses; and, in common years, the mortality is less than any other country in Europe . . . The proportion of the annual deaths to the whole population . . . is only as 1 to 48. ("Checks to Population in Norway," 2.1.2)

With such a low mortality rate, Norway probably had the longest life expectancy in Europe. It also had a low birth rate. Since the 'positive checks'—vice and misery—were low, and the geography did not easily yield a plentiful subsistence, the preventive check was the dominant factor:

[W]e . . . find from the registers that the proportion of yearly marriages to the whole population is as 1 to 130, which is a smaller proportion of marriages than appears in the registers of any other country, except Switzerland. (2.1.3)

A modern case! Marriage was delayed for a few principled and pragmatic reasons. The first was found in the compulsory military service:

Every man in . . . Norway born of a farmer or a labourer is a soldier . . . The difficulty, and sometimes the expense, of obtaining . . . certificate and permission [for marriage], generally deferred those who were not in very good circumstances . . . till their service of ten years was expired . . . (2.1.4)

Commanding officers preferred to take men at least 25 years old, finding younger men weaker and immature. As a consequence, healthy men generally delayed marriage until their mid-30s or later. Although this system was eventually relaxed, the positive effects of delayed marriage remained because men were prudent about starting family life.

Marriage was delayed for another important reason. The division of useable land into farm estates was old and changed slowly. An estate would employ a fixed number of married laborers as 'housemen', setting them up with a house, a plot of land for family subsistence and a small income. Other employees would remain unmarried servants until a houseman's place became vacant.

This constraint was considerable. The social division of labor (and thus nonfarm job opportunities) was surprisingly small for a people reasonably well off:

Almost all the wants of domestic economy are supplied in each separate household. Not only the common operations of brewing, baking, and washing, are carried on at home, but many families make or import their own cheese and butter, kill their own beef and mutton, import their own grocery stores; and the farmers and country people in general spin their own flax and wool, and weave their own linen and woolen clothes. In the largest towns . . . there is nothing that can be called a market. (2.1.10)

Such a disciplined and skilled nation was close to solving the subsistence problem!

17.6 FRANCE

According to the returns of year 9 [after the Revolution], the proportion of the births, deaths . . . to the whole population, are as follows:

BIRTHS	DEATHS
1 in 33	1 in 38.5

("Checks to Population in France," 2.7.2.)

The stability and progress in Norway can be starkly contrasted with the upheavals in France. France was 'fully peopled', with about 28 million in 1800. During the eighteenth century depopulations occurred due to famine, disease, and conflict. The first school in economics, the Physiocrats, arose in Paris specifically to solve the subsistence problem. The smoldering monarchy was too selfish and too feeble to change. It was smashed in a revolution.

The demographic figures above come from about 1800. The gap between births and deaths is too great to apply our life-expectancy formula but we can surmise it was between 33 and 38 years. The data below confirms this. It also shows the sorry human condition during the 'old regime'. Given the high level of culture in France, a life expectancy of 25 years is evidence to condemn that regime.

FRANCE	LIFE EXPECTANCY
1740–49	25
1770–79	29
1800–09	34

Source: Massimo Livi-Bacci, *Population and Nutrition*
(Cambridge [England]; New York: Cambridge University Press, 1990, 70).

The revolution was replaced by Napoleon and his wars. The loss of life, during revolution and war, was in the millions. In this context a striking piece of political demography was written. Malthus, quoting one of his sources, writes:

> Supposing that, of the whole number of men destroyed, only two millions had been united to as many females . . . these two millions of couples ought to bring into the world twelve millions of children, in order to supply, at the age of thirty-nine, a number equal to that of their parents. (2.6.19)

Malthus found fault with the conclusions drawn by the author but not with the empirical suppositions. They imply six children per married woman—only one-third of the children surviving to age 39.

The revolution had a positive impact upon land distribution and agriculture. Large estates, previously owned by the nobles and clergy, were divided and sold. 'Parks and chases' were brought into cultivation. This increase in output could feed better an existing population and allow for a growing one. But the revolution greatly impaired manufacturing by destroying the social class accustomed to their purchase. Thus, the social division of labor suffered a setback. The Napoleonic wars postponed the solving of internal problems.

17.7 Upper and Lower Worlds

If the principles which I have endeavoured to establish be false, I most sincerely hope to see them completely refuted; but if they be true, the subject is so important . . . that it is impossible they should not in time be more fully known and more generally circulated . . . ("Rational Expectations Respecting Future Improvement of Society," 4.14.9)

From the obscure emergence of human beings, until the appearance of Malthus' *Essay*, no society had successfully solved the subsistence problem. He thought it 'incontrovertible' that population would always tend to press upon the means of subsistence, unless fertile adults practiced moral restraint.

The dominant factors of production had *always* been land and labor. He could not imagine a civilization where only a small part of the population was needed on the land and the expansion of capital, in the hands of educated people, could yield abundance. Malthus did not have a clue that some nations were on the verge of solving the subsistence problem through public education, public health measures and profit-driven applied science.

Malthus did, however, divide his world into upper and lower. The upper was populated by the 'Different States of Modern Europe', the lower contained the 'Less Civilized Parts of the World'. Both were subject to distressing episodes of widespread agony and suffering, but these occurred less often in the upper world. The upper world distinguished itself by the high culture of small groups of elites, the skills of various craftsmen, the institutional role of Christianity, and the capacity to dominate parts of the lower world.

In our review of case studies, only Norway had convincingly achieved the third world state. Even that country had not achieved the second world state because a climatic problem could still induce starvation. France had periods in third, fourth, *and* five worlds—episodes of empire building, mass deprivation, and depopulation. Siberia and Africa oscillated between fourth, and fifth worlds. Malthus thought this was a common pattern, in most of the world, throughout the ages. American Indians, as a whole, suffered *centuries* of depopulation, with many tribes disappearing fully.

Age of Malthus	
third world	Norway
	France
fourth world	France
	Siberia
	Africa
fifth world	France
	Siberia
	Africa
	American Indians

Malthus thought his trump card against idealistic dreamers was the brute reality of life expectancy. A certain sentence appears in every edition of the *Essay*:

> With regard to the duration of human life, there does not appear to have existed, from the earliest ages of the world to the present moment, the smallest permanent symptom or indication of increasing prolongation. (3.1.18)

When discussing Africa—where he thought life expectancies of 17 were likely—he identified the 'normal range' in Civilized Europe as between 34 and 40 years. In fact, elsewhere, he perceived 40 as high. Recalling that 'average age of death' is statistically the same as 'life expectancy at birth', we note Malthus saying in the context of a fertility analysis:

> In a country, the resources of which will allow of a rapid increase of population . . . the average age of death may be extremely high . . . In such a country we might suppose the average age of death to be 40 . . . (2.11.13)

Extremely high? The Norwegian case implied a life expectancy of almost 48 years. Norway was pushing the envelope. Not just Norway. An Alpine parish in Switzerland was known for its pure air, wholesome food, healthy pastoral employment, and delayed marriage. Citing a source from 1766, Malthus writes:

> From the calculations of M. Muret, the accuracy of which there is no reason to doubt, the probability of life in this parish appeared to be so extraordinarily high as 61 years. (2.5.19)

Malthus, the hard-headed realist, considered this a unique case rather than an expression of human potential. One wonders if Malthus, the ordained minister, spent much time pondering on a verse from Psalms, attributed to Moses?

> The days of our life are seventy years, or, if we are strong, perhaps eighty. Even then, their span is only toil and trouble, they are soon gone and we fly away.
>
> (Psalm 90:10)

Such life expectancy was never an empirical reality for entire nations until the last generation of the twentieth century! Solving the subsistence problem and releasing humanity from a low range of life expectancy were two sides of the same process of liberation—a great revolution in human existence. The Land of Milk and Honey has been reached in the upper worlds and we expect the progress to continue, even possibly accelerate. What of the lower worlds?

Here we need to wonder. In the Age of Malthus, and long before, the population-food ratio tended to be precarious, regardless of governance. Now we have to worry about numerous ecological complications and mind-numbingly bad governance in most of the poorworlds. Malthus is still around.

LIFE EXPECTANCY		
	Age of Malthus	2000 AD
upper worlds	40s and lower	80 and lower
lower worlds	17 and higher	30s and higher

18

REVOLUTION AND REBELLION

I think God Almighty hath a quarrel lately with all Mankind . . . for within these twelve years there have the strangest Revolutions and horridist Things happen'd not only in Europe but all the world over.

—James Howell, quoted on page 1 of Jack Goldstone,
Revolution and Rebellion in the Early Modern World (1991)

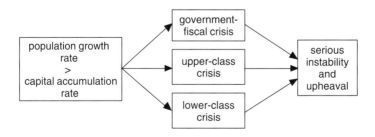

Theory of State Breakdown

18.1   POST-MALTHUSIAN PERSPECTIVE

One of our themes has been the problem of population growth exceeding effective accumulation of capital. Jack Goldstone's *Revolution and Rebellion in the Early Modern World* (1991) sheds a bright light on this theme.

Goldstone's book is focused on answering the following historical question:

> [W]hy was state breakdown . . . on a worldwide scale, clustered in two marked 'waves', the first culminating in the mid-seventeenth century, the second in the mid-nineteenth, and separated by roughly a century . . . of stability? (3)

For the seventeenth century, he anchors his answer in a period of steady population growth following a long period of killer diseases. This work contains exceptional insight into postfeudalistic agrarian societies groaning under layers of bureaucracy, patronage, a standing army and a religious hierarchy—something still all too familiar.

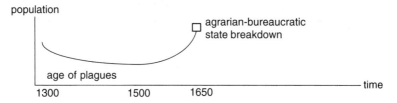

A strong feature of the analysis highlights the role of marginalized groups. Suppose a society has a population of 100, 90 of whom have adequate resources for their 'station in life' and ten of whom who do not. Suppose this does not cause social stress. What happens if the population doubles? (33)

With a *given* set of resources, *all* the additional population finds itself *marginalized*. Assume constant returns to scale. If the resource base increases by half, half of the new population can have resources while half are excluded. This is shown as an increase from 90 to 140 and from 10 to 60. Even though resources increase by half, when the population doubles the marginalized population increases *sixfold*. If we assume diminishing returns to scale, the disproportionate growth of the marginalized population would be even larger.

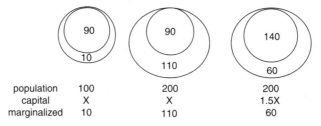

Without exception, throughout northern Eurasia, economic and administrative capacities fell behind population growth in the agrarian-bureaucratic societies of the early modern world. They suffered distributional dilemmas eventually culminating in challenges to state authority. Goldstone has given us a striking post-Malthusian alternative to Marxian theory. Development economists can learn much from his demographic-structural analysis. Let us see why.

18.2   POPULATION, FOOD, AND PRICES

[L]ong-term changes in population size before 1850 were dominated by *independent movements of mortality.* (27)

[M]ortality shifts were independent of changes in harvest . . . or . . . income. (85)

Centuries of recurring killer diseases in northern Eurasia ended by 1500 and populations doubled during the next century or so. Population growth greatly exceeded improvements in agricultural technology, marketing, and new crop acreage. Food production per person declined, with far-reaching consequences.

The diagram below, depicting some of these consequences, is best understood in three layers. In the first layer, the disappearance of some killer diseases reduced the death rate enough to trigger steady population growth. The demand for food generally grew faster than the supply of food and food prices rose regularly. This is the central econodemographic idea in the book.

The next layer depicts two direct impacts of the population boom exceeding expansion of food production. First, with population at least doubling, the load upon governments grew greatly. With larger administrative and military demands, both the bureaucracy and the army had to grow. Taxation systems lagged behind this process. This greatly strained public finance. Second, the supply of labor grew faster than the demand for labor and real wages fell.

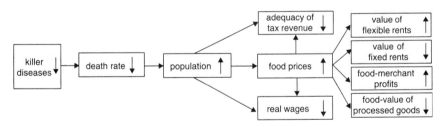

The third layer depicts six indirect impacts of the population boom through the price and social systems. First, the higher cost of feeding government workers and the army increased the budget burden per government employee. Since the ability to raise taxes was limited, governments had to sell land, borrow money, and issue debased currency. Second, money wages, if they increased at all, increased more slowly than food prices, depressing real wages.

The other impacts affected landowners, merchants, and artisans. Some rent contracts were longterm, based upon intergenerational relationships. This was specially true of lands owned by monarchs. The value of these rents fell ruinously. Renegotiable rent contracts favored the landowners. Here we can see the basis for social mobility, up and down, among landowning classes.

Food merchants also benefited from food-price inflation. Some were able to convert higher profits into land and climb the social ladder. Artisans found the domestic terms of trade tilt against them and they suffered smaller real incomes.

18.3 Theory of State Breakdown

With his eyes focused mainly on the seventeenth century, Goldstone observes challenges to state authority as country after country suffered the effects of population growth exceeding the productive and administrative capacities. The context for this is elaborated by Goldstone in the following way:

> Large states of the early modern period . . . faced certain common constraints. They needed to raise sufficient revenues to support their armies and reward their retainers. They needed sufficient allegiance from the elites to secure loyal officials for government service and, perhaps more importantly, to secure loyal local authorities in an era when centrally appointed officialdom rarely penetrated below the county level. And they needed to provide sufficient stability and sustenance for the working and cultivating population so that the latter could pay their taxes and other obligations and yet not be inclined to support rebellions. Thus any train of events that simultaneously led to fiscal deterioration, elite factionalism and disloyalty, and a major decline in popular living standards or undermining of popular traditional rights, threatened the ability of the states to maintain their authority . . .
>
> Put simply, large agrarian states of this period were not equipped to deal with the impact of the steady growth of population . . . eventually amounting to population increases in excess of the productivity gains of the land. (24)

An interpretation appears in the following diagram. When population growth exceeds the accumulation of public and private capital over a long period, crisis eventually occurs at three levels. Let us start at the bottom.

The lower classes are squeezed from several directions. Land per agrarian family shrinks as it is divided into smaller pieces over generations. Subdivisions become excessive when the land cannot provide for family subsistence. Surplus sons must fend for themselves. Inflation hurts rural workers and artisans alike.

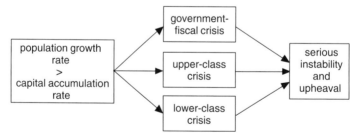

The sons in upper classes wish for appointment to well-respected institutions. After a while there are not enough jobs to go around. Inflation eats at old wealth. Old rentiers lose social position as a new class of landed rich arises, leading to severe intraelite conflict.

At the same time, the state uses up its lines of credit, sells land to cover debts and eventually goes bankrupt. State crisis occurs when there is widespread belief the government is ineffective, unjust, or obsolete.

> The crucial factors that lead to state breakdowns are state fiscal crisis, elite opposition, and intra-elite conflicts . . . Paupers do not make revolutions. (86)

18.4 LOWER-CLASS CRISIS

England's population grew from about 2 to 5 million between 1500 and 1640. Goldstone's book tells in great detail the story of the prelude to the Revolution of 1640. We can offer only a glimpse into this intricate analysis. Let us look at the three levels of crisis, starting at the bottom.

According to Marxian writers, the growing landlessness in England was caused by enclosures designed to displace subsistence family farms with large commercial ventures. But such enclosures sharply declined more than a century before the revolution. What alternative hypothesis can explain the growth of landlessness in the generations prior to the revolution?

First, some data. The percent of rural laborer families with only a cottage and garden rose from 11 to 40 percent in three generations. The total percent with access to less than one acre rose from 42 to 63 percent during that same period.

DISTRIBUTION OF LANDHOLDINGS OF ENGLISH LABORERS
DATA FROM 447 HOLDINGS ON 28 MANORS
% OF HOLDINGS BY ACRES

	cottage with garden	under 1 acre	1–1.75	2–2.75	3–3.75	4–5
Before 1560	11	31	28	7	11	11
After 1620	40	23	14	8	7	7

Source: Goldstone, 72. Based on: Everitt, "Farm Laborers," in *Agrarian History of England and Wales, vol. 4: 1500–1640* (Cambridge: Cambridge University Press, 1967), 402.

According to Goldstone, population growth and land division are *sufficient* to account for the data. His simulation assumes an empirically sound net reproduction rate of 1.2. It also assumes land is divided for all surviving sons.

SIMULATION
100 FAMILIES IN 1535 • NET REPRODUCTION RATE 1.2 • WITH PARTIBLE INHERITANCE

	cottage with garden	under 1 acre	1–1.75	2–2.75	3–3.75	4–5
c. 1540	11	31	28	7	11	11
c. 1630	41	26	19	7	3	3

Source: Goldstone, 72. *Note*: numbers rounded for simplicity.

This simulation *slightly overstates* the decline for families with a cottage and garden, or, under an acre. This can be adjusted by modifying the second assumption: the division of landholdings is reduced if some of the younger sons have to fend for themselves or choose to leave. Since holdings of two acres or more shrank much less than the simulation, this probably happened. Thus, the post-Malthusian hypothesis completely explains the data. As Goldstone says,

> The view that demographic increase could not have accounted for the changes fails to understand that landlessness was a property of the marginal population; and it is a simple arithmetic rule that in any instance of population growth on a limited resource, the *marginal* population will grow many times faster than the whole. (73)

18.5   UPPER-CLASS CRISIS

> In the century before the revolution, the reproduction rate of the peerage rose
> even more rapidly than that of the population in general, and large surviving
> families became more common . . . Thus "one necessary result was a down-
> ward social mobility among non-heirs which caused intense competitiveness
> and divisiveness among the British upper class." (110)

In the simulation on the lower class, Goldstone assumes a net reproduction
rate of 1.2 over three generations. In a simulation on the gentry, he assumes a
net reproduction rate of 1.3, also over three generations. (Both cases assume
autonomous declines in death rates.) Let us see the impact on the gentry.

Suppose the gentry have 100 families. Suppose all of them produce an heir
and 10 of them produce another surviving son. Suppose half of the 'surplus
sons' achieve gentry status through work or connections and half drop out.
If this pattern holds for three generations, the number of gentry families will
rise by 10 percent and the number of surplus sons will grow from 10 to 11.
This is bad luck for about five surplus sons each generation but it is not a
social problem.

SIMULATION: SURVIVAL OF SURPLUS SONS IN THE GENTRY

generation	net reproduction rate	# of gentry families	# of surviving surplus sons
1	1.1	100	10
2	1.1	105	10.5
3	1.1	110	11
4	1.3	116	35
5	1.3	133	40
6	1.3	153	46

Source: Goldstone, 111.
Note: Numbers rounded for simplicity, except in the second generation.

Suppose the net reproduction rate in the gentry rises to 1.3 for three
generations. The growth of this class and its surplus sons accelerate greatly.
On average, each generation produces about 40 surplus sons. If we assume
the same pattern—half achieve gentry status and half drop out—an average of
20 surplus sons fall into the lower class each generation! One can expect much
tension within these families as well as tension between old and new gentry.

With limited resources in the society, the growth of the gentry was not easily
absorbed. The creation of new estates or new positions could not keep pace
with expectations, causing excess competition. When population growth accelerated, families owning fixed rent lands lost relative position to the new gentry
issuing flexible rent contracts. Moreover, large upper-class families had to sell
land to maintain expected levels of consumption. The combined demographic
and inflationary problems lead to some displacement of old elites.

Demographically induced crisis in the upper class was a problem for the
Crown. This problem grew into a system-wide crisis when combined simultaneously with deprivation in the lower class and government bankruptcy.

18.6   GOVERNMENT-FISCAL CRISIS

Crown lands were sold every decade from the 1530s, until Crown holdings shrank from a high of 20–30 percent of England's land in the 1530s to roughly 5 percent in the early seventeenth century. With its capital shrinking and operating deficits growing, the Crown was forced into more extensive and regular borrowing. (98)

Let us draw a picture. In 1500, before the population boom, the Crown was the major landowner in England, receiving rents at a fixed rate. Current assets were adequate to meet any nonwar obligations. Most of the claims against assets were pure net worth. This was a AAA balance sheet, impeccable to creditors.

By 1640, the Crown's real assets were a fraction of their size a century before. Crown lands were a shadow of their former quantity, the treasury was depleted and the sovereign could not meet some of its most pressing obligations. It was bankrupt, for all to see, with a negative net worth. This was a FFF balance sheet, a catastrophic nightmare to Crown and creditors alike.

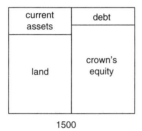
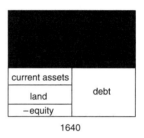

1500   1640

We have already seen the circumstances that turned a AAA monarchy into a deadbeat FFF. Under the relentless pressure of population growth, it could not easily maintain its larger armies (needed to control Scotland and Ireland and fight the Catholic powers nearby) *and* maintain a growing system of patronage needed to retain support in the upper class. Under food price inflation, these budget demands were multiplied, requiring the Crown to invent ways to raise revenue or return regularly to the bankers in London. It took decades to overcome the disadvantage of old but obsolete long leases on Crown lands.

Attempts to increase land taxes were easily deflected. In the 1540s, assessments were 80 percent of market value. By the 1590s, assessments were 3 percent of market value. The Crown lacked the leverage to change this.

Before the revolution, economic and religious interference in Ireland and Scotland backfired, increasing military costs. Control over the Isles was shaky.

Thus, in sum:

The crisis of 1640 was of revolutionary import precisely because its roots lay in the failure of the entire structure of Crown revenues to keep pace with a century and a half of inflation, during which time Crown assets and credit had already been pressed to exhaustion. (102)

18.7 POLITICAL EARTHQUAKE

> My claim is that the mid-seventeenth century was exceptional in that *all* of these factors, being driven by the underlying force of population growth the proceeding century and a half, created synergistic stress that caused the breakdown of state power. (142)

To test the theory, Goldstone brings together the three sources of crisis in a 'political stress indicator'—psi (Ψ).

Fiscal stress is indicated in a scale from 1 to 5. Below I use our AAA—FFF spectrum since it conveys the idea viscerally. This is the most critical indicator because an excellent rating suggests the resources to solve problems while a weak rating shows vulnerability to demands from elites and the masses.

Mobility and competition in elite circles is indicated by university enrollments.

The potential for mass mobilization is a composite index based upon real-wage history, urban growth, and age structure (the ratio of people age 10–29 to those age 30 or more). If real wages are below the historic norm for a long period, the other factors are destabilizers; but if real wages are above the historic norm for a long period, the other factors are stabilizers.

political stress indicator	(Ψ) =	fiscal stress	TIMES	mobility and competition	TIMES	mass mobilization potential
		credit rating AAA . . FFF		university enrollments		wage index TIMES (urban growth TIMES age structure)

All three components peaked in the 1630s. The upper-class index peaked once before, a few generations earlier. The lower-class index peaked once before, a few decades earlier. Only in the 1630s did all three peak simultaneously.

The fiscal distress of the Crown in 1640 was matched by lower-class misery. Real wages reached their lowest point since 1300! Between 1500 and 1640, London grew from 50,000 people to 400,000. Many were escaping the lack of jobs in the countryside. To feed the urban masses, grain was diverted from southeast England to London, causing food riots in villages. London lacked legal and police capacities and was ungovernable. It became a fertile breeding ground for dangerous ideas and troublemakers. In the 1630s, the ratio of people aged 10–29 to those aged 30 and over also reached a peak.

Parliament extracted concession out of the Crown when it begged for money to pay for blunders in Scotland. Compounded by a rebellion in Ireland, events got out of hand and the king lost his head. This was not inevitable. But his bankruptcy occurred at a time of *all-round crisis* making upheaval certain.

Meanwhile, under a similar set of pressures, state breakdown stalked Eurasia!

19

ABUSE OF MACROFOUNDATIONS
—ALFRED SAUVY'S FASCIST SURPLUS THEORY—

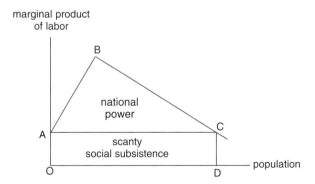

Sauvy's 'Power Optimum'

19.1   MACROFOUNDATIONS RUN AMOK

During the dying days of the Soviet Empire I attended a conference in Budapest. One of the participants asked about my research interests. I replied: "macrofoundations of economics." With a look of shock that could not be masked, he blurted out, "Oh! we tried that! It doesn't work!" I tried to calmly assure him that I respected the importance of both micro and macro foundations. He was too agitated to listen: "We tried that! It doesn't work!"

To what was he referring? He had in mind the legacy of Bolshevism. An insightful diagnosis of Bolshevism can be found in some words by Grand Duke Alexander of Russia. In an interview, in exile, in the late 1920s, the Grand Duke had this to say:[1]

> Lenin was an idealist . . . But he chose the wrong way. He exalted the body and debased the soul. Bolshevism is the negation of the soul. It signifies the destruction of individuality . . . it lacks spirituality. It denies the spiritual values . . .
>
> Some earnest souls believe that from the red flower of Bolshevism may issue the fruit of a new civilization. Such people are wrong. Bolshevism is incapable of evolution . . . It cannot blossom because its essence is barren . . . Bolshevism is the incarnation of hate. I do not believe in a personal Devil. But if there were a personal Devil I would say his name was Bolshevism.

If the Grand Duke had been interviewed a few years later, he could have said the same things about the Nazi movement, its leader, and his use of power. As in the Soviet Union, individuality was denied and social analysis ignored the individual—he/she was assumed away. Indeed, he/she was more than assumed away! Nazism, like its Bolshevik enemy, was soul-less materialism. Both were examples of societies built upon macrofoundations run amok.

The Soviet economy was erected, in part, upon Marx's analysis of surplus value and social reproduction. Hitler's economy was built more intuitively. Some years ago I came upon an extraordinary 'general theory of population' that contains a clear and unashamed *fascist* analysis based upon a surplus approach. It is a stunning and lucid book, largely unknown in the English-using world because of its French origins.

What is equally stunning is the prestige of its author. He was possibly the most important French demographer in the twentieth century. The following is a translation from the title page of the first edition, issued in 1952:

GENERAL THEORY OF POPULATION
by Alfred SAUVY

President—United Nations Population Commission
Director—National Institute of Demographic Studies

19.2 BIOGRAPHY OF ALFRED SAUVY

Alfred Sauvy died on 30 October 1990, the day before his 92nd birthday. He was one of France's most renowned scientists and a prominent member of the international community of economists and demographers during the twentieth century.

So begins the five-page obituary published in *Population Studies*.[2] His career was impressive. "Sauvy served as the French representative on the UN Population Commission from its inception in 1947 until 1974, and was its Chairman for the first two sessions." He founded the National Institute of Demographic Studies "one of the world's leading centers of demographic research, which he directed from 1945 to 1962." He wrote dozens of books and numerous articles. "He was awarded the UN Population Prize in June 1990 . . ."

The same obituary affirms that "Sauvy was a man of science and . . . took an interest in public affairs throughout his life . . ." He was advisor to Paul Reynaud, Jean Monnet, Pierre Mendes-France and Charles de Gaulle. While remaining a political independent, "by temperament he was a man of the left inclined towards socialism, but to a socialist system that was nowhere realized."

"Sauvy was not wedded to any particular doctrine. His principle interests . . . focused on two questions with which he had an almost obsessive preoccupation: demographic aging . . . and Malthusianism . . ."

"Sauvy was an opponent of racism . . . It is, however, surprising that in all his work there is not a single reference to genocide [sic] . . ."

"The germ of his ideas can be found in the first of his books *Richesse et Population* (1943) which had a sensational reception, and his ideas and theories were further developed in what might be considered his *magnum opus* the *General Theory of Population*, first published in 1954 [sic] . . ."

His first book, written in Nazi-occupied France, had a 'sensational reception'?

I have quoted from this obituary at length because few of my readers are familiar with Sauvy. But there is another, deeper, reason.

We look in particular at his two-part surplus analysis.[3] His economic-surplus analysis is called the 'power optimum'. His sociological-surplus analysis is called 'getting rid of the unwanted'. In that chapter he had mouthfuls to coldly say about genocide. The raw fascism of these chapters will show-up all the more starkly against his brilliant CV.

SAUVY'S *GENERAL THEORY OF POPULATION* (1969 ENGLISH TRANSLATION)	
PART 1: ECONOMICS OF GROWTH	PART 2: LIFE OF POPULATIONS
ch 5 Economic optimum	ch 5 Social factors of mortality
ch 6 Power optimum	*ch 6 Getting rid of the unwanted*
ch 7 The first interpretation . . .	ch 7 Social factors of fertility

19.3   JB Clark's Theory of Distribution

Sauvy's 'power-optimum' uses the concept of marginal productivity. He presents it in a diagram similar to one from neo-Classical economics. To show the connection, we begin with the neo-Classical diagram.

John Bates Clark is the father of the diagram below. He wanted to express, in the simplest diagram, the idea of income distribution determined by marginal productivity. While his diagram is simple, his explanation is certainly not. I retell the story in an easier way.

Clark's analysis assumes a downward sloping marginal-product-of-labor curve and a given supply of workers working with a given quantity of capital. (For this to hold together as a distribution analysis we also need to assume perfect competition in product and labor markets as well as profit maximization.)

A numerical example will illustrate. Suppose the first unit of labor produces 200 units of output; the second produces half as much; the third, half of the second. Total product is 350.

Units of Labor	Marginal Product	Total Product
1	200	200
2	100	300
3	50	350

Consider the following diagram. The marginal product of labor is on the vertical axis and labor is on the horizontal. The product of the first worker is the distance OA. The number of workers is OB. The last worker, at point B, has a marginal product of CB. Each worker gets the same wage, equal to CB. Total wages equals the area ODCB. Total product equals the area OACB. The residual, a surplus called 'interest' by Clark, equals the area DAC.

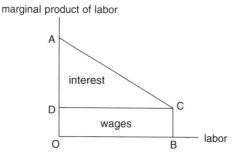

Note: See also 'Figure 1' of: Clark, *Distribution of Wealth* (New York: Macmillan, 1899), 201.

Let us use our numerical example. The marginal product of the last unit of labor is 50; this is the wage rate. Since there are three units of labor, wages are 150. Since total product is 350 the residual—'interest'—is 200. (Lucky capitalist).

19.4 'POWER OPTIMUM'

Sauvy's 'power optimum' can be understood as an ingenious variant of the Clark Diagram, influenced by the Nazi creation and use of power. Like that diagram, it can be expressed with only four points—A through D. The power-optimum chapter opens with these words:

> In history, power has often had the edge over individual welfare as an aim. It is therefore worthwhile asking which numbers ensure the greatest power in a given territory . . . Power does not necessarily mean military power—it represents a collective aim which may or may not take the form of armament. (51)

Sauvy makes three assumptions: (1) all members of society work; (2) subsistence is fixed by the energy required for production; (3) marginal product starts at a low level, reaches a maximum, and falls again to a low level.

Under these conditions, what size population yields the largest surplus product? This is Sauvy's 'power optimum'. His answer is found on this diagram.

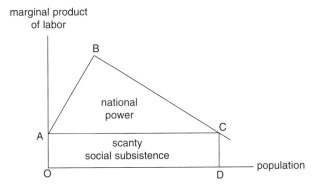

The horizontal axis represents both population and labor. The vertical axis is the marginal product of labor. Subsistence consumption per person is the distance OA. For convenience, the marginal product of labor also starts at point A, rises to a maximum at point B and declines again to the subsistence level at point C. The population that maximizes surplus is determined at point C.

> The optimum population ensuring the highest power is thus [OD]. Any extra inhabitant above this figure, not producing enough supplies for himself, would not be useful since he would need part of the output of others to feed him, thus diminishing the power of the group. (52)

Total product is measured by the area OABCD. The (scanty) social subsistence is the area OACD. The surplus, which Sauvy calls 'power', is the area ABC.

Sauvy says that this 'power' may be applied to any 'collective aim'. He elaborates on only one: the war economy. We should look at this.

19.5   MILITARIZED SOCIETY

By levying men for military purposes the factors defining the optimum are altered; non-productive soldiers will be supplied out of the surplus output of active workers, which we have called 'power'. . . *The optimum population is therefore increased by the number of non-productive soldiers.* (53)

The revisions to the power-optimum diagram follow directly from this.

The following diagram uses the same A, B, C, and D from the previous page. Total output OABCD and surplus output ABC are unchanged. But subsistence needs are increased and the use of 'power' is now given a concrete form.

Suppose the number of soldiers equals the distance DE. For their subsistence they will need the area CDEF. This will be supplied out of 'power'. Find an area AGHC equal to the subsistence needs of the soldiers. The remaining area GBH is available for use as 'armament'. In this use of social surplus we have the following relationship:

national power = subsistence for soldiers + armament.

Sauvy does not say how the surplus available for armament will be changed into weapons—or by whom. But this is almost a quibble. The starkness of the diagram is too impressive to be diminished by such complications.

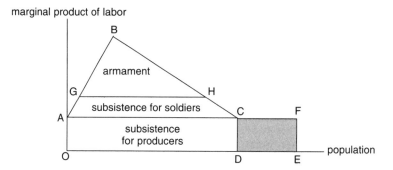

He does, however, deal with a different complication of interest. Subsistence needs vary from country to country, even in a war economy. How far can subsistence consumption be reduced if required to face a national crisis? He gives a clear historical answer:

During the Second World War . . . [subsistence] was higher in the United States than in Germany, and higher in Germany than in the USSR.

In the USSR perhaps even the lower limit was crossed: if the life of a nation is at stake, it may be in its interest to encroach into basic subsistence requirements, even if output suffers a little. If a 10 per cent decrease in supplies only leads to a 3 per cent drop in output, power will still be increased. This seems to have happened in the USSR. (55)

ABUSE OF MACROFOUNDATIONS

19.6 SAUVY AND MARX COMPARED

Sauvy's power optimum can be expressed as a ratio. This will bring to light its relationship to Marx's 'rate of exploitation'.

When defining his power optimum, Sauvy assumes that all members of society work. Under this assumption, his producers' subsistence will exactly correlate with Marx's 'socially necessary labor time'. Moreover, the surplus product Sauvy calls 'power' is, under his simplifying assumptions, that which is produced by Marx's 'surplus labor time'. *Thus, in ratio terms, Marx's rate of exploitation and Sauvy's power optimum are equivalent.*

MARX	SAUVY
surplus labor time	power
necessary labor time	producers' subsistence
'rate of exploitation'	'power-optimum ratio'

Let us recall the numerical example from Section 3. Wages were 150 and the surplus was 200. Suppose those wages cover the producers' subsistence, with nothing left over. Then the ratio, 200/150 (or 4/3) can be used by a Marxian to express the 'rate of exploitation' while a follower of Sauvy can call that figure the 'power-optimum ratio'. A great crime worthy of revolutionary justice to one, a great heroic sacrifice to the other! In both cases the ratio is used to express an extremist view of the world.

A Marxian would be alarmed by the role of population in Sauvy's analysis. Usually, Marxian analysis assumes a given population size and analyzes how surplus value is created and appropriated. Sauvy's analysis treats population size as a variable, with the population yielding the greatest surplus product considered an 'optimum'—all the while assuming a stingy social subsistence.

19.7 'GETTING RID OF THE UNWANTED'

Sauvy begins his spectacularly hard-hearted chapter on 'Getting Rid of the Unwanted' with the following words:

> Physical organisms eliminate unwanted toxins and dangerous or useless bodies in order to preserve their life or their good working order. Human society too tends to eliminate unwanted members, either useless or dangerous, more or less discreetly, more or less unintentionally. The useless ones are those who cannot contribute to economic and social life: the old the ill, the invalids, the unwanted new born, ect; the dangerous ones are the criminals, the degenerate, the anti-social, the madmen, or even sometimes political enemies, the members of other races or other religions. (341)

Sauvy then takes up a number of topics. Here are his section headings, (along with the number of paragraphs devoted to each topic):

Child Exposure (4)   Prisoners, invalids, madmen (3)
Outcasts and maladjusted (2)   'Innocent' genocide (4)
The secret button (4)   Selection of the strong (4)
The elimination of degenerates (8)   Social elimination (2)

We sample only two of these. First of all, *'innocent' genocide:*

> The American Indians, the Australian Aboriginees, and others were recently exterminated in all innocence . . . If these populations had avoided being unwanted, by agreeing to work for the rulers, they would have survived and perhaps even multiplied as did the Negroes in the United States or in South Africa . . . International ethics are such that while colonization is frowned upon, murder is allowed, providing it is discreet and not publicly announced. (344)

Sauvy manages to mention Nazi gas chambers and Stalin's work camps in this section on 'innocent' genocide! But this was just a warm up for a grand vision of exterminism. In the next section, on *'the secret button'*, he speculates on murdering by the hundreds of millions:

> Opinion in the West is now conscious of the fast demographic growth in the Third World . . . If a public opinion poll were to ask whether a few hundred millions should be exterminated with napalm or atomic bombs, only a minute number would answer yes. It would however be very different if one asked, with full guarantee of secrecy, the following question:

> 'If by merely pressing a button, you could cause the death of a hundred million Indians and two hundred million Chinese, with no suffering, and in entire families so that there would be no human distress, what would you do? I leave you before this box and you are free to put a white or a black ball into it'. (344–45)

'No human distress?' No vaporization or collapse of institutions and infrastructure? Why did he include such thinking in his *opus*? Compare this numbing inhumanity with a passage recording Native Hawaiian depopulation:

> We do not have anything tangible to look at yet or to give us any hope to increase our population, because this situation [of depopulation] continues annually. This depopulation has robbed parents of their children, men and women of their friends. It has destroyed families and the concept of community life. It has emptied schools, where once they were full of school children and students; it has emptied churches, where once they were swelled up with people, and also the fields [are emptied]. Depopulation has affected the royal families down to the commoners, and many have died. The birth rate has dropped. If this trend continues it may become impossible to find alternative health care, medicines or other ways of living to prevent further depopulation. If no alternative can be found, then what will become of us? Shall we just stand by and watch in despair and cry?[4]

These words were written in 1867, after repeated and prolonged periods of epidemic-induced depopulation—'collateral damage' from contact with Europeans. Sauvy would have probably filed this under 'innocent' genocide.

20

REHABILITATION OF CLASSICS

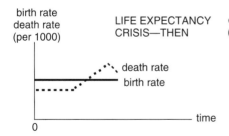

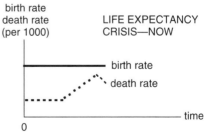

20.1   STEUART AND SMITH

Adam Smith pointedly ignored Sir James Steuart in the *Wealth of Nations*. Both men came from Scotland but Smith was pro-English while Steuart was a nationalist. Steuart supported the rebellion in 1745 and paid for it with an 18-year exile. Because of Smith's influence, Classical economists disregarded Steuart. Smith thought he was protecting the world from 'Steuart's errors'. In fact, he was denying the world the chance to learn survival-conditions analysis.

At the beginning of his *Principles*, Steuart defined the science of political economy in the following words:

> The principal object of this science is to secure a certain fund of subsistence for all the inhabitants, to obviate every circumstance which may render it precarious . . . (1.Introduction.6)

As we survey the poorworlds today we should mourn the failure of political economy and economics to recognize these words and bring them to fruition.

The word 'subsistence' appears 258 times in the *Principles*. It appears often in Book 1—home of the Macrofoundation. It is found 148 times in Book 2, 'Trade and Industry'. Maybe his mercantilism is subtler than people have supposed?

	STEUART: *PRINCIPLES OF POLITICAL ECONOMY* (1767)	WORD COUNT: SUBSISTENCE
Book 1	Population and Agriculture	69
Book 2	Trade and Industry	148
Book 3	Money and Coin	—
Book 4	Credit and Debts	6
Book 5	Taxes, and of the Proper Application of their Amount	35
		258

Adam Smith's definition of political economy is clearly related to Steuart's:

> Political economy, considered as a . . . science . . . proposes . . . first, to provide a plentiful revenue or subsistence for the people, or more properly to enable them to provide such a revenue or subsistence for themselves. (4.Introduction.1)

The word 'subsistence' appears 162 times in Smith.

	SMITH: *WEALTH OF NATIONS* (1776)	WORD COUNT: SUBSISTENCE
Book 1	Causes of Improvement in the Productive Powers of Labour	65
Book 2	The Nature, Accumulation, and Employment of Stock	10
Book 3	Different Progress of Opulence in Different Nations	35
Book 4	Systems of Political Economy	35
Book 5	Revenue of the Sovereign or Commonwealth	29
		162

The Scottish Enlightenment produced two great political economists with different but vital contributions. One of them was sidelined for possibly petty reasons. Both of them are needed in the poorworlds.

20.2   MALTHUS AND STEUART

Steuart's name did not appear in the first edition of Malthus. In that book Malthus attributed understanding of 'the principle' to Smith. He was probably referring to a famous sentence in the *Wealth of Nations*:

> Every species of animals naturally multiplies in proportion to the means of their subsistence, and no species can ever multiply beyond it. (1.8.38)

This can be interpreted more than one way. One possibility reads: Population size is limited by the available means of subsistence. I think this is what Malthus meant by 'the principle'.

In the second edition, published in 1803, Steuart is recognized as a master of the subject. Right before Malthus summarized his three main propositions (found in our chapter on the Classical Macrofoundation), he says, in a footnote:

> In the first book of his Political Economy, he [Steuart] has explained many parts of the subject of population very ably. (1.2.note 11)

That is high praise. Why was Steuart ignored by the Malthusians? We may never be sure but I think he was overlooked largely because of the lingering effect of the Smithian ban.

In another remarkable passage, Malthus invokes Steuart's authority while analyzing a seriously *underpopulated* society. Referring to Siberia, he says:

> Such countries seem to be under that moral impossibility of increasing which is well described by Sir James Steuart. If either from the nature of the government, or the habits of the people, obstacles exist to the settlement of fresh farms or the subdivision of the old ones, a part of the society may suffer want, even in the midst of apparent plenty. It is not enough a country should have the power of producing food in abundance, but the state of society must be such as to afford the means of its proper distribution . . . (1.9.8)

This is a pure statement of survival-conditions analysis—clear and penetrating.

Marx looked back at the Classical School and accused Malthus of plagiarizing Steuart. This does not appear to be correct. The first edition of the *Essay* does not resemble Steuart or his analytic framework.

After Malthus published the first edition, Steuart came to his attention *somehow* and Malthus read him. He saw that Book 1, on 'Population and Agriculture', was pathbreaking. He penned the high praise seen above. Malthus had no control over the literary interests of his readers or the Malthusians.

There is irony here. Because of Smith's cold-hearted feeling toward Steuart, economists in the twenty-first century can experience the excitement of tracing the footsteps of discovery. In Steuart we have the opportunity to read and unfold a forgotten classic, understand anew its period, and learn its current applications.

20.3 BOOK 1 OF STEUART

When we carve away the excessive verbiage of Steuart's chapter titles—which I have done here quite *liberally*—we find his unique contribution in outline form. Book 1 not only contains his version of survival-conditions analysis, it also contains what Sir John Hicks called *The Social Framework* (1943).

This brings us to one of the most important academic controversies of the past century: what topics should receive pride of place in introductory economics? Sir John believed we should *begin* with the social accounts. He believed students could only use economic theories intelligently if they were grounded in the complex realities of their societies. In this he was a great Classical.

To some extent the first edition of Samuelson's *Economics* (1948) conformed to this view, with sizeable space devoted to accounting. Over time new developments in economics competed for space, squeezing it out. Today social accounting is held in low esteem and economists sneer at the subject.

This has led to a serious undereducation of economists. As you read through the list of chapters in Book 1 of Steuart, ponder on what has been lost—in the poorworlds *especially*—by failing to learn from Sir James and Sir John.

BOOK 1: POPULATION AND AGRICULTURE
WRITTEN IN EXILE IN GERMANY IN LATE 1750s

---

1. Governments of Mankind
2. Spirit of the People
3. Population in a State of Nature
4. Natural and Immediate Effects of Agriculture on Population
5. Political and Extended Effects of Agriculture on Population
6. Human Wants and Human Multiplication
7. Slavery
8. Proportion Necessary for Agriculture/Proportion Available
9. Geographic Distribution of the People
10. Farmers, Free Hands, and Dwellings
11. Distribution of Inhabitants into Classes
12. Advantages of Well-Digested Theory
13. Necessity of Population Accounting
14. Abuses of Agriculture and Population
15. Population in Great Britain
16. Populousness
17. Effects of Plenty and Scarcity
18. Causes and Consequences of Being Fully Peopled
19. Introduction of Machines
20. Miscellaneous Observations
21. Recapitulation of the First Book

20.4   LIFE-EXPECTANCY CRISIS THEN

Steuart was born in 1713. We have some demographic data from his childhood and youth, up until his exile. The population appears nearly constant during this period. Using the formula (from Chapter 2) for stationary populations we may estimate life expectancy in England during this period:

1000/life expectancy = 31.75 . . . such that . . . life expectancy = 31.5 years

ENGLAND	1720	1730	1740	20-YEAR AVERAGE
birth rate	30.5	32.0	33.3	31.9
death rate	29.7	33.4	31.7	31.6
net	0.8	−1.4	1.6	0.3

Source: G. Talbot Griffith, *Population Problems of the Age of Malthus*, 43.

Although Steuart did not have access to very good data, his empirical sense was remarkably keen. In Chapter 13, where he discusses the Necessity for Population Accounting, he tells us:

> In England, one marriage produces four children at a medium. If you reckon 6,000,000 of people in that country, and that 1/30 part dies annually, then to keep up the stock it is sufficient that 200,000 be annually born . . . (1.8.7)

If a thirtieth dies annually in a stationary population, life expectancy is 30 years. Steuart thought the English population was growing *slightly* so his figure is quite close to our estimate. Moreover, he says in the same chapter:

> It is computed that one half of mankind die before the age of puberty in countries where numbers do not augment . . . (1.8.12)

We can see the logic in estimating four children per marriage in England. If half die before puberty at least four *are* required to maintain a population.

That quote continues with something rather striking. What happens if smaller child mortality rates occur while the production of food is unchanged?

> If methods . . . are fallen upon to render certain diseases less mortal to children, all the good that will be got by it . . . will be to render old people of the lower classes more wretched; for if the first are brought to live, the last must die. (1.8.12)

This has a modern ring in fourth and fifth worlds. Population explosions have come about through higher child-survival rates, but the societies cannot cope.

One more thing. Sir James observed one-sixth of Britain's crop exported while the population was stationary or nearly so. He attributes the latter to mass poverty, and reveals the real intent of his 'mercantilism':

> Those who cannot buy are exactly those who I say die for want of subsistence; could they buy, they would live and multiply, and no grain perhaps would be exported. This is . . . my principal point in view, throughout this whole book . . . to find out a method for enabling the indigent to buy up this very quantity which is at present exported. (1.15.21)

20.5   LIFE-EXPECTANCY CRISIS NOW

We should note a critical difference between then and now. Poor countries, since their independence, have experienced revolutionary population booms because of greatly reduced child mortality rates. But fifth world conditions now operate differently from classical and ancient times. Previously it meant lower life expectancy *and* depopulation. Now the second effect is often absent.

The left-side diagram illustrates a population cycle where a population increase is offset by a sharp increase in the death rate. The right-side diagram has the same curves but *the initial gap is much greater*. This is typical in the fastest growing parts of the poorworlds. In this case, the dieoff and sharp decline in life expectancy *do not* halt population growth—they only slow it down for a while.

This builds up a great demographic pressure. Unless birth rates are permanently reduced, the old pattern is going to reappear in the poorworlds— or much worse.

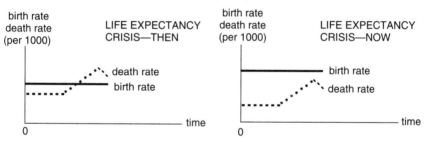

Another way to look at the present life-expectancy crisis is contained in the following table. This data appeared in Chapter 2. Perhaps we can appreciate it better now.

In the high-fertility regions, child mortality rates are high and median ages at death are remarkably low. *This is a grave humanitarian crisis.*

The world has never before known such great inequality in median age at death, child mortality rates, and fertility rates. This alone should serve as a marker that the economic, political, and social analysis of rich and poorworlds ought to be greatly different—on the basis of different foundations.

How can one expect modern institutions to function well, if at all, under the primitive demographic conditions found in Africa?

1990	LIFE EXPECTANCY AT BIRTH	MEDIAN AGE AT DEATH	CHILD MORTALITY (PER 1000)	TOTAL FERTILITY (PER ADULT WOMAN)
established market economies	76	75	11	1.7
formerly socialist—European	72	72	22	2.2
India	58	37	127	4.0
Middle East Crescent	61	24	111	5.0
Sub-Saharan Africa	52	5	175	6.4

Source: World Development Report 1993 (New York: Oxford University Press, 1993), 200–01.

20.6   DIAMOND ON 'FATES OF SOCIETIES'

Before closing this section of the book, I should include a recent use of the Classical Macrofoundation. Jared Diamond, in *Guns, Germs and Steel* (1997), writes an account of why and how agriculture and civilization took root in some places; and how civilizations spread. He tells a version of the story we saw in Chapter 12, on Roots of Civilization—*Man Makes Himself.* Diamond innovates in geographic analysis. By way of interpretation here, it is called the *seeds and soils of subsistence, surplus, and survival.*

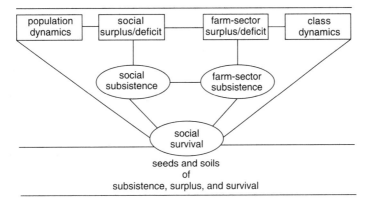

The seeds were the plants and animals provided by nature. The soils were their locations. Endowments differed everywhere. Some were richly endowed per acre and some were empty. *Successful movement of domestications to other locations operated more smoothly on the east-west axis than on the north-south.* The initial endowments and relative locations held the clues to which parts of the globe were likely to develop early civilizations and which were not.

Some plants were easy to domesticate; most were not or could not be. The best plants yielded a large net harvest of quality nutrients. The more mouths an acre could feed, the greater the population density or trade it could support.

Few animals were easy to domesticate. Most were not—each in its own way! Domesticated animals needed to have greater value than the cost of their feed and upkeep. This was done through their work, their meat, their parts—or their companionship. Animals, unfortunately, carried deadly diseases. Virgin exposure was often fatal. And early man killed off *many* potential candidates for domestication before learning the arts of domestication.

On this basis, Eurasia had the greatest natural advantage. Lush initial endowments combined with a broad east-west axis to allow easy adaptation of domestications to similar climatic conditions. The Americas were most disadvantaged. Their long north-south axis acted as a barrier to diffusing climate-sensitive domestications. Africa, with its north-south axis, was also disadvantaged.

20.7   REHABILITATION OF CLASSICS

The neo-Classical and Marxian schools have been unable to provide macro analysis tailored to the pressing needs found in the poorworlds. They lack a good solution for the productivity limits and life-expectancy crises. They lack the tools to solve the subsistence problem. The neo-Classical school cannot handle macro challenges because it ignores macrofoundations. The Marxian school stumbles in mean-spirited analysis and critique.

Classical Political Economy was crushed under the weight of economics and lost its identity when it was divided into specializations during the past century. This division of labor was useful for a time, but it is not eternal. It is now old and long in the tooth. It can change during the coming decades as faculties of social studies regroup. In this regrouping the Classics can make a comeback.

It would be welcome. Many teachers, students, and field workers are tired of time and energy wasted defending the old lines. Some people sense the breadth and power in the Classics: they were *born* to help solve the subsistence problem and lead us on the path of humane society. They have not yet achieved their purpose. Survival-conditions analysis can no longer be neglected.

In terms of the ideological wars of the twentieth century, the Classicals are promarket, proliberty, and prodemocracy—while being aware of the potential misuses of these three desirable goals and methods. Classical Political Economy is a fount to good sense and reason. Perhaps its best days are ahead.

In the twentieth century we learned many hard lessons about survival conditions on a planet achieving globalization. Billions of human beings were born into poverty. The world decolonized but postcolonial governments failed almost everywhere. Natural disasters increased in frequency and in power at an alarming rate. The leading nations developed weapons capable of killing the entire planet. And our economic systems grew in their ecocidal capacities.

We are now in a new century. As the century matures outdated dogmas might be overcome with better-grounded theory. Intellectual dissatisfaction among younger scholars might lead to new creativity. Thinking, teaching, and learning can become more in-tune with pressing global, regional, national, and local problems, as old lines are refined or superseded. The surplus approach can have time to mature and social accounting can finally become a cornerstone science.

Sir James Steuart may be an honored guest from the past as we enter the new century. An historical wrong ought to be corrected. Malthus said it plainly:

> In the first book of his Political Economy, he has explained many parts of the subject of population very ably. (1.2.note 11)

Now, will we put poverty in a museum and visit the stars? This is a fresh century. Can we make broken things new? Can we reach new heights?

INTERLUDE

The next two chapters comprise an interlude using the Modern Macrofoundation. They provide additional background for Part Three.

'Guns and Butter' looks at the crisis in North Korea. That nation's decline to fifth world is discussed. Prospects for reform are considered.

'Butter and Books' looks at the role of education in solving the subsistence problem. Taiwan's great success is compared with India's relative failure.

21

GUNS AND BUTTER
—NORTH KOREAN ECONOMY IN CRISIS—

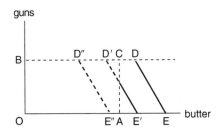

Decline from Third to Fifth World

21.1 COLLAPSE OF A STALINIST ECONOMY[1]

Most experts agree that probably more than one million and perhaps as many as three million have died prematurely since the food shortages began.
—*New York Times*, December 10, 1998

The 1995 floods in the Democratic People's Republic of Korea signaled a spiral course toward famine. Poor harvests most of that decade devastated the nation. GDP per capita fell by at least half during the 1990s.

North Korea is today nearly incapable of reform—a smoldering death trap held together by an evil Personality Cult. The people have seen better days. At one time North Koreans were decently fed and educated, based upon a modified version of the Soviet Union's rapid industrialization.

Indeed, Joseph Stalin placed Kim Il Sung into power following World War II. USSR also provided the training and equipment for the North Korean Army to attack South Korea on June 25, 1950. Throughout the war, the Soviet Union provided support. After the war they extended North Korea a large amount of aid, became the principle trading partner and heavily subsidized oil imports.

A China connection was also strong. Kim Il Sung was educated in China and spoke Chinese. China came to North Korea's aid during the Korean War, saving it from certain defeat at the hands of United States. After the war China was a reliable trading partner and a good neighbor.

In 1987, the winds began to blow against North Korea when Gorbachev required repayment of some of the Soviet Union's aid. As part of *perestroika*, oil subsidies ended. Reform-minded Chinese leaders took an interest in economic ties with South Korea. By the time the Soviet Union collapsed, North Korea's trading options had shrunk drastically. The country was left to stand on its own.

'Great Leader' Kim Il Sung died suddenly in July 1994. His son, 'Dear Leader' Kim Jong Il, replaced him in a slow-motion dynastic succession. North Korea appeared to lack the ability to recover from its desperate situation. After more than a decade of deindustrialization, this assessment is still compelling.

Efforts to calculate the extent of the famine by relief organizations have been impeded by the government. Travel and communications are closely regulated and monitored. Despite receiving food aid, North Korea's ability to feed its people remains in doubt. It certainly cannot feed its people without massive assistance. From all accounts by foreign observers, the once-proud Stalinist society of more than 20 million is in an advanced state of collapse and ruin.

The ruling ideology is called *juche*—self-reliance. We should be struck by this macho fantasy. It best sums up the lie that is at the heart of the country. North Korea was never self-reliant. It was built with Soviet aid, kept the machines running with subsidized oil, and now depends upon food aid from old enemies.

21.2 Statistical Overview

The North Korean government has always been secretive and their data are rarely reliable. Even identifying the onset of the natural disasters is unclear. Some reports say 1994 while others say 1995. It is easily shown, however, that the collapse began before 1994, with the collapse of the USSR.

Our first statistic is dramatic. Consumption of fertilizer started to decline in 1990. It fell by nearly half between 1989 and 1994. By 1998, fertilizer consumption was one-sixth the figure for 1989.

(Nutrient Tons)	1989	1990	1991	1992	1993	1994	1995	1996	1997	1998
fertilizer usage	650	600	520	480	410	350	290	170	120	110

Source: 'FAO/WFP Crop and Food Supply Assessment Mission to the DPRK',
November 12, 1998 (Estimated).

This shines a light upon the state of the economy. Agriculture was highly industrialized, depending upon irrigation, chemical fertilizer, and machinery. All of these, including the production of fertilizer, were severely constrained by the sudden shortage of oil. The fertilizer statistic may be seen as a proxy for the collapse of the industrial sectors as well as a sure precursor of bad harvests.

Much has been made of the natural disasters. This diverts attention from the mind-numbing abuse of the land under the heavy-handed planned economy. Deforestation and excessive use of nasty chemicals have ruined much soil. Under these conditions, minor droughts or floods have had major impacts.

As recently as 1990, North Korea was a net exporter of rice. The decline in rice production since that year has been devastating. By 1993, production had fallen by a quarter. This is consistent with the fertilizer statistic above. They have required imports ever since, much of it in the form of aid.

The table understates the fall in production. Huge amounts were imported in 1995 and 1996. The sum of imports plus production far exceeds the rice available in 1990. *From this we conclude that the production figures for 1995 and 1996 are greatly inflated. Otherwise there would have been no famine.*

Rice (1000 Metric Tons)	1980	1990	1993	1994	1995	1996
production	1,765	2,057	1,534	1,668	1,427	1,534
export	219	42	0	1	0	0
import	0	26	278	95	1,022	1,043

Source: Food and Agricultural Organization of the United Nations, www.fao.org.

While the rest of the economy was collapsing, the military budget was fully maintained. This statistic highlights the Stalinistic grip on the country and suggests the key characteristic of our centerpiece diagram.

(Billion of U.S. Dollars)	1990	1991	1992	1993	1994	1995	1996
defense expenditure	5.5	5.5	5.5	5.3	5.6	5.2	5.4

Source: The Military Balance, (The International Institute for Strategic Studies, 1990–1996).

21.3   GUNS AND BUTTER MODEL

We now develop a simple variant of a famous model. We should see the garden-variety diagram before drawing the one peculiar to North Korea.

Butter is on the horizontal axis and guns are on the vertical. The distance OA is the social subsistence of butter. The distance OB is the maximum consumption of butter, if no guns are produced. This society is capable of producing surplus butter AB. The distance CA is their maximum production of guns while still producing the social subsistence of butter. BC is the possibility frontier.

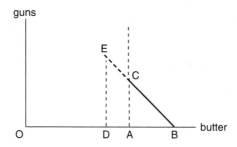

If this nation were suddenly attacked it could increase production of guns above CA—but this would require a sacrifice of butter. For example, by sacrificing AD butter it could increase guns production to DE. Since less than the social subsistence would be available, vulnerable citizens would be undernourished or would starve. (During World War II the Soviet Union made this kind of sacrifice.) After winning the war, the society could reestablish its normal production of butter if the land and capital are not too severely damaged.

The North Korean case is unique because the society is organized around the military sector. This dramatically affects the diagram. While OA is still on the butter axis, OB is now on the guns axis!

The North Korean leaders will sacrifice everything else to maintain the military. Point C represents the satisfaction of the military priority while just producing the social subsistence of butter. In the 'happy days' before the collapse of the Soviet Union, North Korea had a possibility frontier like DE. But given their fixation on the military sector, the only point they were interested in was D.

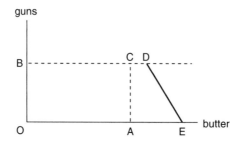

21.4 DECLINE TO FIFTH WORLD

Let us trace the decline of North Korea from third to fifth world. As we just saw, in the 1980s, North Korea was able to achieve a point like D—meeting the military objective while also producing more than its Spartan idea of social subsistence. Then a two-stage decline set in.

Decline to Fourth World: With the loss of subsidized oil and the decline in trade with Russia and China, North Korea experienced a collapse of its possibility frontier, to D'E'. It was not as self-reliant as its leaders had supposed. By choosing point D' the median person was suddenly getting less than a subsistence bundle. North Korea had declined to the fourth world.

The inability to afford imported oil was the driving force toward deindustrialization. Idle factory machines and tractors began to rust. Infrastructure began to deteriorate. North Korea produced few items of value on international markets so there was nothing to break the fall.

Harvests were poor from 1990 to 1992. A flood in 1992 severely damaged that year's crop along with portions of the road network in the countryside. The rapid decay of roads and other aspects of the infrastructure made distribution to and from rural areas difficult.

The government distributed food and medicine to the people most essential to its political survival—an old pattern. Those farthest away from the base of political power received what was left over. The position of the weak and vulnerable became critical, setting the stage for what was to come.

Decline to Fifth World: The floods in 1995 had a devastating impact on crop yields and further damaged the already dilapidated road network. North Korea then made a rapid transition to the fifth world. As the possibility frontier collapsed to D"E" undernutrition changed into mass death. During the next three years millions died.

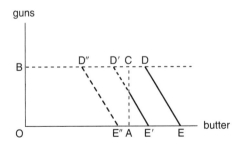

Ox cart drivers and charcoal diggers have taken the place of factory workers. Perhaps nothing can save this smoldering heap of a country from itself. If businessmen are interested in throwing money away, and suffering chronic frustration along the way, North Korea offers a unique opportunity.

21.5   Inequality and Starvation

In the late 1960s, the leaders created a Personal Classification System based upon class background: 'Core' (20–30 percent), 'Unstable' (40–50 percent), and 'Hostile' (at least 20 percent). In the face of economic collapse, this inequality became deadly.

Consider the following diagram. Consumption per person in year 0 is on the horizontal axis and consumption per person in year 1 is on the vertical. The distances OA and OB represent the subsistence bundle. Point C represents the two-year subsistence condition.

Points C, D, E, and F represent four groups in North Korean society. Point C represents the military; point D, the political/military elite; point E, the civilian-urban population; and point F, the civilian-rural population. The median person is somewhere between E and F. We briefly discuss each group.

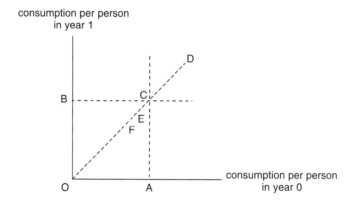

Political/Military Elite (less than 2 percent): The Party rewards the top elite with luxury goods. Party members expect a regular subsistence bundle. Food, healthcare, and heat are distributed to party members first.

Military (1.2 million soldiers): To remain in power the Kim Dynasty maintains a strong and loyal military. As we saw, military spending is kept steady no matter what setback befalls the economy. Generally, home production is used to feed the military first but reports suggest an occasional breakdown in subsistence distribution to the lower ranks.

Urban Civilians (less than 62 percent): City dwellers in the south and west receive more food and other necessities than their rural counterparts or their counterparts in the northeast. This is practical as well as politically expedient.

Rural Civilians (less than 38 percent): Villagers, specially in the north and east, are hardest hit by famine and infrastructure collapse. Insufficient food aid reaches these areas and many flee starvation by crossing into China.

In recent years this situation has changed somewhat because villagers are now allowed personal gardens, giving them an advantage over high-rise dwellers.

21.6   DEPOPULATION

Although there is no consensus regarding deaths between 1995 and 1997, middle-range reports suggest 10 percent of the population died. This would yield an average of 3.3 percent per year during that period. That would be a death rate of 33 per 1000. This should be compared with the 'official' figure for 1993 of 6 deaths per 1000. Since that strains belief, let us round it up to 10.

The official birth rate for 1993 was 22 per 1000. As we shall see, the birth rate fell by half in the most severely affected region. So let us hypothesize a decline of the national rate national to 15 per 1000.

With these guesstimates we can draw a crude but suggestive diagram.

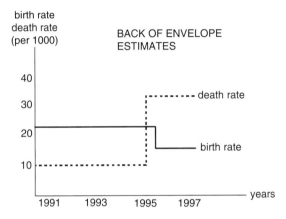

The table below is based upon a Johns-Hopkins study of North Korean families who migrated to China. Most of the migrants were from the northeast province of North Hamkyong, where the distress is said to be the most severe.

440 adult migrants were interviewed during the summer of 1998. They were asked about births, deaths, and migration patterns of their households as well as their relatives who stayed behind.

On average these figures are more dramatic than our nationwide guesstimates above—as they should be since they pertain to the most severely damaged region. They do not contradict the estimate of 10 percent dead nationwide during the period 1995 to 1997 and may, in fact, tend to reinforce it.

SURVEY OF MIGRANTS TO CHINA FROM NORTHEAST AREA OF NORTH KOREA			
	birth rate (per 1000)	death rate (per 1000)	net migration rate (per 1000)
1993 census	22	6	—
1995	13	29	16
1996	13	46	15
1997	7	56	20
3-year average	11	44	17

Source: W. C. Robinson, M. K. Lee, K. Hill, and G. M. Burnham, "Mortality in North Korean Migrant Households," *The Lancet*, vol. 354 (June 24, 1999), 292.

21.7 END OF NORTH KOREA?

The prospects for North Korea are not promising. Let us begin with the most optimistic scenario—reform along the lines of China. 'Dear Leader' Kim has hinted approval of such a possibility. Is it realistic?

Chances of success are dim. When China began its long road to reform, many people were ready, willing, and able. North Koreans are not. They are like a nation of battered children in need of care for trauma. It will take a long time to undo the mental, emotional, and physical damage of the Personality Cult.

The ruling class seems also unprepared for reform. They have botched or impeded every single joint project with South Korea since the Summit in June 2000. Although much of this can be traced to political sources, a good deal of it is sheer incompetence. The failure to reestablish rail links should serve as example because it is so obviously of economic advantage to the North.

We should not forget North Korea's terrible track record with investment from Westerners. In the 1970s, 'Great Leader' Kim borrowed large sums from Europeans and defaulted on everything. That was at the height of North Korean competence. Can anyone expect better under today's far worse conditions?

Let us look at the opposite end—collapse of the Personality Cult in a military coup. While this could begin the process of clearing away the greatest obstacle to reform, it would probably accelerate the disintegration of North Korea. Since the collapse of the public distribution system in the mid-1990s, regional and local interests have begun to fill in the vacuum. Like Humpty Dumpty, this egg may not fit back in the shell very well.

Which brings us to the possibility of unification with South Korea after the demise of the dictator. The nationalistic impulse in the South would push for this, at the earliest moment. If recent investment experience in the North is any guide, it would lead to the bankruptcy of South Korea.

In the event the Personality Cult falls, South Korea would be wise to insist upon two different administrations and currencies—with tight immigration controls—until the North shows clear signs of coming up toward the level of the South. Such a financially prudent policy would have regional support.

Will North Korea come to a violent end? President Bush, in his 'axis of evil' speech, hinted at the possibility of attacking the North. This could trigger a military response. If the leaders in the North fear imminent destruction *anyway* they might not go down quietly. On the other hand, it could give the 'Dear Leader' an excuse to visit Seoul and turn South Korea against United States.

Would North Korea initiate war against the South? It has the capacity to act aggressively but it does not have the capacity to sustain a war. Such aggression would be suicidal. Any suicidal outburst would probably be aimed at Japan, too.

22

BUTTER AND BOOKS
—EDUCATION AND THE SOCIAL SUBSISTENCE—

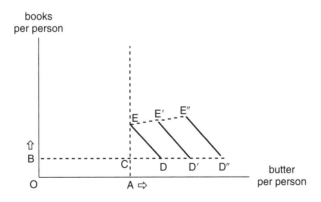

Taiwan's Solution

22.1   SOLVING THE SUBSISTENCE PROBLEM

In most of South Asia and Africa the subsistence problem remains unsolved. In these regions, undernutrition and undereducation coexist with failing political structures and explosive population growth. Many African countries lurch from tragedy to tragedy. The countries of South Asia could experience the same. Armed with nuclear weapons, two of them could experience worse.

In some countries, the majority of people live on less than a dollar a day. Four of these countries are grouped together here. They are arranged by order of literacy. In this group India is the best performer. But with such severe undereducation how can any of these countries develop?

	% ADULT LITERACY 1995	% LIVING ON LESS THAN $1 PER DAY PPP BASIS 1981–95	LIFE EXPECTANCY AT BIRTH 1995
India	52	53	62
Senegal	32	54	50
Nepal	27	53	55
Niger	14	62	47

Source: World Development Report 1997 (Table 1: Basic Indicators).

Inspired by the analysis of guns and butter, in this chapter we look at the world of butter and books.

In order to gain some insights, we compare Taiwan and India. Taiwan is widely recognized as a great (and unexpected) economic success. It excels in cutting-edge industries. Although recent progress in India is impressive, the problems affecting India at the time of independence still remain: overpopulation, low income, and low literacy rates. It is mired in a caste system and may someday have a tryst with deadly fundamentalism.

While both had leaders who used the political rhetoric of education, the actual policies could not have been much different. Leaders in Taiwan resolutely pursued education policies in their Manpower Development Plan useful for highly productive human capital development. They set serious literacy goals and they met them. They increased funding whenever they could. Competition for best-quality schools set in motion family spending on education.

Indian leaders paid lip service to the role of education in economic development. Their literacy goals were vacuous and insincere.

Taiwan and India were both very poor countries in 1960. At that time, the GNP per capita was US$154 in Taiwan and US$206 in India. Since 1960, Taiwan has outperformed India in almost every economic category. Income per person in Taiwan will soon top $25,000, with a highly literate and ambitious population. India is still a poor country with approximately 500 million illiterates. What educational policies helped Taiwan solve the subsistence problem and develop while India did not?

22.2   ENHANCING THE SOCIAL DIVISION OF LABOR

Let us look at the microfoundation for education. How much should a parent be willing to pay for? How much should a government be willing to finance? Consider the following diagram.

We have education (in years of schooling) on the horizontal axis. Marginal benefits and costs are on the vertical. Suppose the cost of a year's education is OA and suppose the cost is the same for any number of years of schooling. Then we have a horizontal marginal-cost curve (MC).

Suppose the benefit of the first year of education is OB. It will be rational for parents to educate a child as long as the marginal benefit exceeds the marginal cost. In this case we have a *private* marginal-benefit curve (MB$_p$) sloping downward. It intersects the marginal-cost curve at point C. It would be rational for parents to pay OACD for OD years of education—if they can afford it. The net private benefit would be ABC.

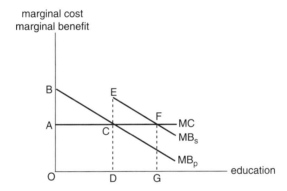

But there are *positive externalities* from such an investment in education. If the person educated OD years enters the workforce, that person will contribute to the productivity of others through enhancing the social division of labor. The distance CE illustrates this. The social benefits of education are greater than the private benefits.

The *social* marginal-benefit curve (MB$_s$) cuts the marginal-cost curve at point F. The optimal level of education for this person is OG years. Given the spillover effects, it would be rational for a child's family to pay for OD years and for a government to pay for DG. However, if the family could not afford to pay, it would be rational for the government to absorb all of the expenses.

This is an orthodox and conservative analysis. Many would argue that basic education should be free for all because the diagram overstates the private benefits of early education while it understates the social benefit of literacy.

For example, it leaves out the tendency for literate women to control family size. Thus, education for females has a double benefit—economic *and* demographic. This is monumentally important in the poorworlds.

22.3 EDUCATION IN INDIA

By any standards, the majority of Indians are undereducated. At the university level they are often miseducated. Let us look at some statistics.

We begin with years of schooling by gender. Males in India average only 3.5 years while females average less than one year. This spells illiteracy for the average man because literacy requires at least a full primary education. It reflects the harsh reality of gender inequality against females.

1992	PAKISTAN	INDIA	BANGLADESH
mean years of schooling for males	2.9	3.5	3.1
mean years of schooling for females	1.2	0.7	0.9

Source: Human Development in South Asia, 1997, 144.

According to *India Today*, annual expenses incurred by parents can be less than 400 rupees per child. Suppose a family has three school-age children. The yearly education expense might be less than 1,200 rupees. If daily family income were only 40 rupees (about a dollar a day), education expenses would equal a month's income. Many poor families cannot afford this.

PUBLIC SCHOOL EXPENSES PER CHILD	(RUPEES PER YEAR)
uniform/clothing	175
books and stationary	112
other expenses	79
total	*366*

Source: India Today, "Class Struggle," October 13, 1997, http://www.india-today.com/itoday/13101997/agenda.html (accessed January 7, 2007).

And they may refuse to spend the money because of substandard schools. Public schools are frequently in poor condition. Imagine education when more than 60 percent of the roofs leak! The teachers are often overworked and generally underpaid, with high student-teacher ratios.

% OF GOVERNMENT SCHOOLS IN INDIA WITH SPECIFIC FACILITIES	
functioning toilets	11
nonleaking roof	37
drinking water	42

Source: India Today, "Class Struggle," October 13, 1997, http://www.india-today.com/ itoday/13101997/agenda.html (accessed January 7, 2007).

In higher education the problem is different. The top students study medicine, engineering, and business; the rest are trained in 'the arts'. Few of these students will prepare for a 'vocation'. The glut of arts graduates has been severe for decades. Unemployment is common in this group.

SCHEDULE CASTE ENROLMENTS	UNDERGRADUATE (%)	POSTGRADUATE (%)
Arts	57	78
Science	12	8
Commerce	13	9
Education/Medicine/Law	13	3
Other	5	2

Source: W.H. Taylor, "India's National Curriculum," Comparative Education 27, no. 3 (1991): Table 3.

22.4   EDUCATION IN TAIWAN

The Taiwan case is vastly different. Literacy was a paramount national priority. By 1960, six years of schooling were mandatory; this was increased to nine years in 1967.

By 1990, Taiwan's primary and secondary enrolment rates had reached the level in Japan, with a similar budgetary commitment.

	SINGAPORE	TAIWAN	JAPAN
literacy rate (1990)	88	90	99
primary school enrolment, % of age group (1991)	100	100	100
secondary school enrolment, % of age group (1991)	69	95	96
public expenditure on education as % of GNP (1991)	3.4	5.5	5.8

Source: Paul Morris, "Asia's Four Little Tigers: A Comparison of the Role of Education in Their Development," Comparative Education 32, no. 1 (March 1996): 97.

The long-term commitment to education can be seen in the following table, comparing a per capita GNP growth index with the growth of education expenditure. The chart uses 1952 as the base year. Education expenditure grew much faster than GNP per capita every decade—generally twice as fast. Both growth rates were spectacular between 1972 and 1982.

	(A) PER CAPITA GNP INDEX (1952 = 100)	(B) EDUCATIONAL EXPENDITURE INDEX (1952 = 100)	(B)/(A)
1952	100	100	1
1962	447	849	1.9
1972	1,834	4,160	2.3
1982	11,012	36,900	3.4
1987	19,070	56,005	2.9

Source: Yang Yi-Rong, "Education and National Development: The Case of Taiwan," Chinese Education and Society 27, no. 6 (November/December 1994): Table 2.

Moreover, the mix of academic and vocational training at the secondary level has been adjusted to meet the needs of industry and commerce. Until 1970, it was about 50–50. Since then the mix has been shifted to vocational training. This reveals a very pragmatic aspect of Taiwanese public education. It is also highly suggestive theoretically and will play a significant role in our analysis.

TAIWAN ENROLMENTS (%)	ACADEMIC HIGH SCHOOL	VOCATIONAL HIGH SCHOOL
1950	53	47
1960	52	48
1970	50	50
1980	34	66
1988	32	68

Source: After: Cheng, Tun-jen, "Dilemmas and Choices in Educational Policies: The case of South Korea and Taiwan," Studies in Comparative International Development 27, no. 4 (Winter 1992/1993): 62.

22.5 BUTTER AND BOOKS MODEL

Let us try to capture the essential issues in a simple diagram. 'Butter' is on the horizontal axis, representing consumption goods. 'Books' are on the vertical, representing education.

OA is the social subsistence of butter. OB is the social subsistence of books needed to pass on the knowledge essential to maintain the social-economy. Point C represents the satisfaction of both conditions.

Point D is the maximum production of butter while still producing the social subsistence of books. Point E shows the maximum production of books while still producing the social subsistence of butter. DE is the possibility frontier.

Leaders in a foolish country could decide to forgo production of books in order to produce butter beyond point D. This is indicated by point F. This point cannot be sustained. If it is selected the possibility frontier gradually shifts in.

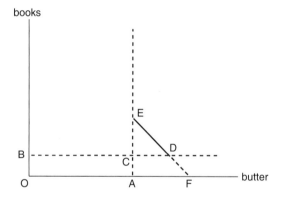

Let us suppose members of a society would like to rapidly improve their possibility frontier. Would this be assured by choosing point E?

No, it would not. The level of books AE can be divided into various parts:

books-oriented books	*butter-oriented books*
Bibles-oriented books	*bribes-oriented books*

An increase in the ability to produce butter depends upon investment in butter-oriented books—it requires *effective investment* in such books.

Suppose all of CE goes into books-oriented books. The population may benefit in nonmaterial ways from a boom in dramas, lectures, and conversations on intellectual or literary topics. But the possibility frontier will not budge.

Suppose all of CE goes into Bibles. This may feed the soul or it may feed self-centered paranoiac hate—who knows which? It will not improve the possibility frontier and it may distract needed attention from it.

Suppose all of CE goes into bribes. Only the thieves and their cohorts will benefit from the theft, in part by using their plunder to import gourmet butter.

22.6   INDIA'S PROBLEM

The Indian case can be represented on a diagram almost identical to the one just developed. Here, however, we have to allow for population growth. The easiest way to do this is by converting the diagram to per-person form.

Butter per person is on the horizontal axis and books per person is on the vertical. OA is the individual subsistence of butter. OB is the individual subsistence of books. Point C represents the satisfaction of both conditions.

Point D is the maximum production of butter per person while still producing the individual subsistence of books. Point E shows the maximum production of books per person while still producing the individual subsistence of butter. DE is the per-person possibility frontier satisfying both conditions. Point F represents a total neglect of books, which would damage the possibility frontier.

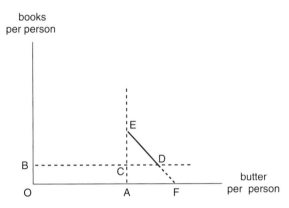

Much of India is near point D. Hundreds of millions of people are illiterate and that is not going to change for many of them. This can been deduced from the poor quality of school facilities, the high student-teacher ratios, and the dropout rates. One observer has likened government primary schools to a 'glorified child-detention center'. The government provides the minimum—if that.

Such undereducation at the primary level is compounded by miseducation at the secondary and tertiary levels—where they get 'books-oriented books'. The vast majority of university students get degrees in 'the arts'.

The per-person frontier might have shifted inward in the 1990s:

> The government's resolve to increase education expenditure to 6 per cent of GDP . . . has gone hand in hand with a decline in public expenditure on education . . . from 4 per cent in 1991–92 to 3.1 per cent in 1995–96.

> Similarly, the teacher-pupil ratio has been steadily falling in recent years. In 1981, there were 26 primary school teachers for every 1,000 pupils. In 1996 there were only 21. (*India Today*, "Class Struggle," October 13, 1997)

Only Kerala and Himachal Pradesh have achieved basic literacy goals. But human development in those states is not yet matched by economic opportunity.

22.7 Taiwan's Solution

The Taiwanese case is far better. We begin with the same points A through E as in India, but end up with a greatly different result because of a sincere and intelligent commitment to education.

Based upon our statistical overview we may suppose the leaders in the Republic of China decided to develop from point E, pouring their surplus into books—butter-oriented books. We also observed their resolve to steadily increase the budget for books as they grew. The successful implementation of this policy can be observed in the shifting out of the possibility frontier.

At the beginning of decade 0 they had the frontier DE. By investing EA in mostly butter-oriented books they shifted the frontier to D'E' during the decade. At point E' they were able to enjoy the consumption of some surplus butter.

Then, by investing in butter-oriented books at point E', they were able to shift the frontier out again. By decade 2 they had a possibility frontier D"E".

Not only that, during this process of development they improved the *quality* of their social subsistence. Thus, point A moved to the right and point B moved up. An increase in the quality of subsistence will increase the average length of life. Thus, significant life-expectancy gains occurred.

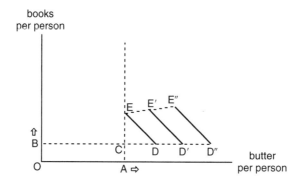

The commitment of the Taiwanese government to education was remarkable. Decades ago development economists emphasized the accumulation of physical capital. However, when human capital is lacking, investment in physical capital is often ineffective. Taiwan demonstrated a virtuous cycle of effective investment, starting with education.

The increase of human capital improved the productivity of existing physical capital and gave rise to new profit opportunities. This stimulated more complex divisions of labor and encouraged would-be entrepreneurs. A thrifty nation made many sacrifices to rapidly build a strong economy and improve standards of living. Today, Taiwan is the laptop computer 'bread basket' of the world.

PART THREE

ASPECTS OF DEVELOPMENT

Stages of Economic Growth (1960) is a modern extension of Classical thought and an apt introduction to some basic aspects of development.

We are particularly concerned with various sides of the agriculture problem. After reviewing supply and demand challenges to agriculture in the poorworlds, we summarize the brilliant *Land Reform in Taiwan* (1961).

Lack of infrastructure is another vital weakness holding back most of the poorworlds. Investment is often both insufficient and ineffective, leading to a chronic capital-accumulation crisis.

Even if a country can overcome weaknesses in agriculture and infrastructure, rapid development tends to require high physical and financial leverage. This exposes the country to chain-bankruptcy risk. It also creates opportunities for corrupt governments to create large-scale odious debt.

The Asian 'Miracle' or 'Myth' is depicted using the main model found in Part One. The model is also used to consider macroeconomic impacts of foreign direct investment on poverty reduction in the least developed countries.

Natural disasters impose extraordinary suffering in the poorworlds. We analyze both the Bangladeshi typhoon of 1991 and the destruction of New Orleans by Hurricane Katrina in 2005.

The book closes with an introduction to the Sarvodaya and Grameen models of alternative development. Sarvodaya's brilliant Five-Stage Model of village renewal may become a powerful way to help build 'Senian capabilities'.

23

STAGES OF GROWTH

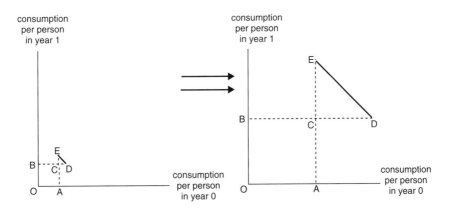

From Traditional Society to High Mass Consumption
(Diagram borrowed from 4.7)

23.1 'NONCOMMUNIST' MANIFESTO

When W.W. Rostow published *The Stages of Economic Growth* (1960), the Soviet Union was flying high. A few years earlier, the USSR was the first to launch a satellite into space. It was getting ready to put the first man into orbit. The Soviet leader had famously told a group of Western ambassadors in Moscow, 'Whether you like it or not, history is on our side. We will bury you'.

Rostow took the threat seriously. He knew the Soviet Union was a capable military foe of America. But were Khrushchev's brash words possible? Was the Soviet system of central planning a superior model of political economy?

In this context, Rostow wrote the *Stages*. He believed the Marxist approach to history and society was flawed. Since Marxists had a communist manifesto, Rostow wanted to counter it with a well-reasoned noncommunist manifesto.

Looking back we can see that Rostow correctly identified the central weakness in the Soviet model of central planning: it could not produce and deliver 'high mass consumption' without systemic reform. Central planning was well suited for rapid military-industrialization based upon nineteenth-century heavy-industry technologies—steel, cement, chemicals, oil, electric power, and machine tools. But without domestic economic competition and allocation of credit based upon perceived profit potential, it could not deliver high-quality mass production or develop cutting-edge civilian technologies.

Echoing what we saw in Chapter 5, on Productivity Limits, Rostow wrote in 1990, in the preface to the Third Edition:

> Ironically, we have witnessed an extreme version of a Marxist clash between technological change and an out-moded economic, social and political superstructure. (xiii)

This alone would warrant consideration of Rostow. But there are other reasons to devote a chapter to the *Stages*. Rostow's analysis of the development process compliments both the production-survival conditions and the Classical Macrofoundation. Although Rostow did not identify with the Classics, he recognized the food problem as the *first* task in very poor countries:

> First, food production must increase, almost always requiring an increase in agricultural productivity. The classical political economists took for granted that an increase in agricultural production was necessary to supply the enlarged working capital a growing urban, industrial system demands. A lively sense of this vital link was, for a time, lost among a good many development economists . . . (3rd ed., xxiii)

Rostow did not come to this conclusion by way of the Classical Macrofoundation. He came to it through his extensive use of sectoral analysis. Thus, Rostow is for us a fine link between our work on the Classics and our discussion of certain issues in development economics.

23.2 TRADITIONAL SOCIETY

As we saw in 'Roots of Civilization' (Chapter 12), there were two great revolutions in human existence before the Industrial Age—the agricultural and the urban. Both of these revolutions required scientific knowledge but neither of them led to science-based civilization. For Rostow—whose understanding of traditional society is very Classical—the turning point is Newton:

> Newton is here used as a symbol for that watershed in history when men came widely to believe that the external world was subject to a few knowable laws, and was systematically capable of productive manipulation. (4)

Prescientific societies were subject to severe productivity limits. While production functions were not set in stone, occasional improvements in technical knowledge never lead to a process of systematic and cumulative change:

> [T]he central fact about the traditional society was that a ceiling existed on the level of attainable output per head. (4)

This leads directly to Malthus:

> Population—and, within limits, the level of life—rose and fell not only with the sequence of the harvests, but with the incidence of war and plague. (4–5)

Thus, traditional societies were trapped entirely within the scope of the Classical Macrofoundation:

> Generally speaking, these societies, because of the limitations on productivity, had to devote a very high proportion of their resources to agriculture; and flowing from the agricultural system there was an hierarchical social structure, with relatively narrow scope . . . for vertical mobility. (5)

This entrapment in low output per person, unpleasant population cycles, and severe social hierarchy fed a 'long-run fatalism'. Probably this fatalism can be traced back to the dawn of human existence!

Land was the main source of wealth, the central factor of production. The struggle to acquire and retain land animated family dramas. It was a determining factor in politics and was at the heart of many violent struggles between neighboring societies. Ownership or control of land was *power*:

> the centre of gravity of political power generally lay in the regions, in the hands of those who owned or controlled the land. (5)

This sketch of traditional society is only a brief stepping-stone for Rostow on the way to his discussion of the development process. For us it has more significance. Today's fourth and fifth world countries continue to exhibit these characteristics. Low productivity limits, Malthusian demographic concerns, impoverished divisions of labor, and a lingering feudalistic mentality are the order of the day in the poorest of the poorworlds.

23.3   PRECONDITIONS FOR TAKE-OFF

From a purely macroeconomic perspective, the primary condition requires a steady rise in the rate of investment sufficient to persistently increase the per capita stock of capital. In a traditional agrarian economy, internally generated changes in attitudes and new divisions of labor must be brought about.

Existing agricultural surplus must be diverted, as much as possible, from consumption to investment in two priority sectors: improved *agriculture* and *social overhead capital*—mostly roads, communications, and schools. If landownership is concentrated in the hands of a small class of families, they must submit to higher taxation, land reform, or both. If the country has extractable resources, this may contribute greatly if the profit from expanding such industries is effectively invested in the priority sectors.

Well-educated people must come forward in both private enterprise and government service, willing to mobilize savings and take risks in pursuit of private profit and general modernization. The immediately relevant science and technologies must be learned or acquired from abroad. Wealthy families must be willing to lend money on long term, often at high risk. Agricultural workers must be willing to accept the demands and uncertainties of rapid change.

> In short, the rise in the rate of investment—which the economist conjures up to summarize the transition—requires a radical shift in the society's effective attitudes toward fundamental and applied science; toward the initiation of change in productive technique; toward taking of risk; and toward the conditions and methods of work. (20)

Demands on the agricultural sector are enormous. Unless an extractive industry can supply most of the working capital for expansion—*and* finance the fixed capital needs, mostly know-how and capital goods—these burdens are likely to fall on agricultural surplus. Rapid population growth will certainly diminish agricultural surplus.

> Put another way, the rate of increase in output in agriculture may set the limit within which the transition to modernization proceeds. (23)

> Agriculture must supply expanded food, expanded markets, and an expanded supply of loanable funds to the modern sector. (24)

This is a main reason Rostow has a low opinion of aggregate growth theory. It entirely misses the connection between agricultural and industrial growth.

The other priority sector is social overhead capital. Physical infrastructure has three problematic traits. The construction period is long and the payoff period is very long. The investment is 'lumpy'—it is pointless to build a road halfway from 'A to B'. And the payoff often returns to the community as a whole rather to the initiating entrepreneurs. For these reasons, the governments must play the central role in the preconditions period—and probably beyond.

23.4 TAKE-OFF

> The take-off is defined as an industrial revolution, tied directly to radical changes in methods of production, having their decisive consequences over a relatively short period of time. (57)

Take-off has three primary requirements:

(1) The rate of investment must rise high enough to support a *continual process* of higher capital per person *and* higher output per person. The threshold to achieve this will depend upon the population growth rate, the capital-output ratio and the degree to which investment spending is well targeted.

(2) In the absence of a huge natural resource, the society must develop at least one rapidly growing manufacturing sector geared for the international market. This presupposes supplies of electricity, decent roads, ports or railways, properly trained workers, financial credit at reasonable rates of interest, and a high reinvestment rate of profits.

(3) Modern institutions geared to growth must emerge and supersede traditional institutions. Educational, financial, judicial, and administrative organizations must achieve a threshold level of competence, honesty, and effectiveness.

In the poorworlds today, high rates of population growth make satisfaction of the first and third requirements very challenging. Failure of the third requirement has often spoiled a temporary victory in the first. Educational and governance failures have repeatedly negated a promising investment climate.

All of these requirements depend upon the emergence of an entrepreneurial class. Entrepreneurial elites—in agriculture, industry, and public sectors—often come from small groups denied prestige and power in traditional societies.

Take-off is impossible without leading sectors. Primary growth sectors must create an *impulse* activating growth in other sectors. Moreover, growth can only be sustained by a succession of leading sectors because each leading sector is subject to deceleration over time.

Historically, the introduction of the railroad has been the most powerful initiator of take-offs. The railroad has three major impacts on growth:

> First, it has lowered internal transport costs, brought new areas and products into commercial markets and ... performed the function of widening the market. Second, it has been a prerequisite ... of a major new and rapidly enlarging export sector which, in turn has served to generate capital for internal development ... Third, and perhaps most important for the take-off itself, the development of railroads has led on to the development of modern coal, iron, and engineering industries. (55)

When Rostow wrote this, decolonization was incomplete. Outside of East Asia, no former colony has taken to railroad building—a point one might ponder.

23.5 DRIVE TO MATURITY

During the drive to maturity, growth becomes self-sustaining as long as the expansion of credit and reinvestment of profits are sufficient. Even the occasional excess-capacity crises in rapidly growing sectors only temporarily dent the momentum toward maturity. The profile of leading sectors differs between countries, determined by the pool of technology, the nature of resource endowments, the points of entry into the international economy, the preferences of lending institutions, and the policies of governments.

Arrival at maturity is achieved when a society has absorbed all the main available technology, applying it over the whole front of its economic activity. The technology frontier has changed greatly several times since the first industrial revolution in Britain, altering the content of 'maturity'.

Using approximate and symbolic dates, Rostow identifies both take-off periods and arrival at maturity for the first three 'Graduating Classes'. We include a subset of these below. In each of these cases, the period from take-off to maturity is about 60 years. Why that period of time?

> [I]t may be that when we explore the implications of some six decades of compound interest applied to the capital stock, in combination with three generations of men living under an environment of growth, elements of rationality will emerge. (60)

South Korea is an exception to the 60-year period, going from take-off to maturity in less than 40 years. Maybe Rostow could call this case compound interest on steroids! We consider East Asia in more detail later.

	BRITAIN	UNITED STATES	GERMANY	SWEDEN	JAPAN	RUSSIA	CANADA
	CLASS 1	CLASS 2			CLASS 3		
take-off	1783–1802	1843–60	1850–73	1868–90	1878–1900	1890–1914	1896–1914
maturity	1850	1900	1910	1930	1940	1950	1950

In every case, business and government leadership was at the heart of success:

> [T]hese were all societies run by men who know where they were going. They were caught up in the power of compound interest and in the possibility of transforming one sector after another of the society by extending the tricks of modern technology. (70)

During the process, the character of business leadership changed. Aggressive entrepreneurs were replaced by professional managers and grand bureaucracies.

Technological maturity does not necessarily imply high per capita income or the emergence of a consumer-oriented society. Sweden and Canada applied their maturity toward a welfare state. Japan and Russia concentrated capital accumulation on military-industrial sectors. So, we face the question:

> [H]ow shall this mature industrial machine, with compound interest built into it, be used? (72)

23.6   HIGH MASS CONSUMPTION

When technological maturity is reached, the balance of attention in a *free* society shifts from supply to demand—from the problems of production to the problems of consumption and human welfare. In such societies, the lure of militarism is usually low. But the process of industrialization is harsh and demanding. With technological maturity accomplished, the 'reward for waiting' must be distributed and exposure to business cycles must be limited.

In democracies, there have been two main responses: the *right-wing*, based upon individualism, low taxes, and 'free markets', and, the *left-wing*, based upon comprehensive social services, high taxes, and 'social markets'. Some countries—like Sweden—were purely of the second type. No country was purely of the first type because the traumas of the Great Depression made that road politically unattractive. Every industrial society had to adopt progressive taxation, a shorter workweek, unemployment insurance, and social security.

The United States was historically suited to largely follow the right-wing path—but in zigzags. It was the first country to move rapidly from technological maturity to high mass consumption. However, this did not occur until after a progressive phase that included laws to curb abuse by giant corporations and the establishment of labor union rights.

In the 1920s, Americans in large numbers acquired cars, single-family suburban houses, and the first wave of electrical appliances—radios and refrigerators. Rural populations shrank while professional people and office workers grew much faster than other parts of the labor force.

The Great Depression started as a normal excess-capacity cycle but soon took on its dark character when institutions of credit spectacularly failed. According to Rostow, the length of the Depression had to do with the nature of modern leading sectors—specially when contrasted to leading sectors in previous eras:

> When, in earlier historical stages, the momentum of growth hinged on the continued extension of railroads, or the introduction of other cost-reducing industrial processes—on the side of supply—investment could be judged profitable at relatively low levels of current consumer demand. But when investment comes to be centred around industries and services based upon expanding consumption [cars, homes and electrical gadgets], full employment is needed, in a sense, to sustain full employment . . . (78)

Here we have an insight into the effective-demand failure diagnosed by Keynes. In post–World War II America, consumerism flourished, in part, because effective demand was always strong—and kept strong by government policy.

The other technically mature countries—with more compact geographies, greater urbanization, and much more exposure to Socialist ideals—were less inclined to spring fullon into an automobile culture of sprawling suburbs.

23.7 LATECOMERS

Rostow expected high mass consumption to become 'universal' sometime this century (166–67). While I do not think this is a possible or a desirable goal, we will confine ourselves to the modernization challenges faced by the latecomers.

Similarities: Just like those who modernized before them, the latecomers have to devote much of their resources to three sectors before they can fully enter take-off: agriculture, social overhead capital, and a foreign exchange earnings sector. They can speed up the process if they can produce and export items with a high income or price-elasticity of demand. This, however, is problematic: how many countries can successfully do this simultaneously?

They must also shift the use of traditional sources of surplus from consumption to investment and shift businessmen from trade and money lending to industry. The 'reactive nationalism' must be channeled toward modernization goals. This is a tricky task because traditional elites can use nationalistic feelings against the 'foreign pollution' introduced by the modernizers.

Basic education must also be introduced. In every field a willingness to learn and use better techniques must be accepted. Corps of technicians, civil servants, police, and professionals must be trained and put to productive work. Entrepreneurs must rise to the occasion. And they all must be:

> reasonably content with their salaries, oriented to the welfare of the nation and to standards of efficient performance, rather than to graft and to ties of family, clan or region. (140)

We have constantly seen poor countries stumble on this condition.

Differences: The postwar introduction of low-cost public health measures drastically reduced death rates in the poorworlds, leading to unprecedented population growth. This creates much greater strain on agriculture, social overhead capital, and basic administration. It also creates a tendency toward high underemployment of young men—an insidious source of instability.

Latecomers can often have access to assistance from richer nations. This takes the form of technical assistance, scholarships, soft loans, and grants. Rich countries are currently pledging to expand such assistance. Foreign direct investment can also play a constructive role. Development, though, is largely an internal process. It must be lead by local elites or it cannot be done:

> In the end, however, the task of development must be done by those on the spot. The non-Communist literate elite in these transitional societies bear a heavy responsibility for the future of their peoples. They have the right to expect the world of advanced democracies to help on an enlarged scale, with greater continuity; but it is they who must overcome the difficulties posed by the rapid diffusion of modern medicine, and ensure that the humane decision to save lives does not lead to an inhumane society. (144)

24

AGRICULTURE

FROM *THE DAILY STAR*—DHAKA

FOOD FOR THOUGHT

editorial   2 August 1997

Calorie intake per head in this land has come down by 250 in 32 years' time . . . What is in store for this country if this downward slide continues? Absolute disaster . . . This tale of nutritional deprivation going on unchecked, Bangladesh runs the risk of being known as a land of morons.

'CURSE' OF THE BUMPER CROP

editorial   11 September 1997

With losses on both the rice and jute harvest, disposal [sic] income in the hands of our farmers went down dramatically leading to a weakness of effective demand over-all . . . We will never be able to go for higher level of agricultural output if we do not ensure a fair price for our farmers.

24.1 FOOD-PRODUCTION CRISIS

Recent decades were not kind to the fortunes of the 49 countries designated least developed by the UN. Taken as a whole, per capita food production was lower in 1999 than in 1980 while per capita GDP was stagnant.

According to UNCTAD, between those years at least 17 of the LDCs suffered falling per capita food production *both decades.* This list includes: Bhutan, Burundi, Comoros, Equatorial Guinea, Gambia, Haiti, Lesotho, Madagascar, Maldives, Mauritania, Niger, Rwanda, Samoa, Sierra Leone, Somalia, Tanzania, and Vanuatu. During those decades, per capita GDP fell in all of those countries except Bhutan, Lesotho, and the Maldives.

Bhutan was able to increase per capita GDP through electricity exports to India; Lesotho via the growth of a Taiwanese-dominated textile industry; and the Maldives by way of tourism. But, in both Lesotho and Bhutan, almost 90 percent of the domestic workforce was engaged in subsistence agriculture. Per capita GDP increases did not trickle down to these people. The fall in food production per person more closely reflected their economic situation.

Anti-Malthusians wish to deny the existence of a food-production crisis in the poorworlds. The facts from Africa and elsewhere tell us otherwise. If farmers cannot produce enough food to feed a growing population decently while the country has little to trade, how can such a nation avoid living in the pit?

	% of labor force in agriculture*	per capita food production annual average growth rate %		per capita GDP (1999 dollars)	
		1980–90	1990–99	1980	1999
all 49 LDCs	—	−0.7	0.3	284	288
Burundi	93	−0.1	−3.6	131	107
Niger	90	−3.5	−0.2	309	199
Rwanda	90	−2.5	−2.1	322	270
Tanzania	90	−0.2	−2.0	307	268

COUNTIES DEEP IN THE CLASSICAL-MACROFOUNDATION TRAP

Source: The Least Developed Countries Report 2002 (Geneva: UNCTAD, 2002), 247 and 250.
* www.mapquest.com/atlas.

The situation is most problematic in countries with entirely stunted divisions of labor—where about 90 percent of the labor force is agricultural. Burundi, Niger, Rwanda, and Tanzania all face this dilemma. All of them have experienced both falling per capita food production *and* falling per capita GDP for *decades.* In Burundi, how can material standards get any lower?

The prospects are bleak in these and similar countries unless they can manage to increase agricultural productivity, expand nonagricultural divisions of labor, and control population growth—the three core requirements for progress in the Classical Macrofoundation! In this chapter we try to sort out some essential agricultural issues in the poorest of the poorworlds.

24.2 SUPPLY AND DEMAND

We can build a crisis taxonomy based upon supply and demand. A supply-side crisis is defined by an availability deficit. A demand-side crisis is defined by an intake deficit. Nutritional requirements include calories, protein, and micronutrients. This implies a variety of items are produced and widely consumed. There are three levels of crisis: undernutrition, starvation, and death.

	SUPPLY-SIDE CRISIS	DEMAND-SIDE CRISIS
	availability deficit	intake deficit
undernutrition	x	xx
starvation	xx	xxxx
death	xxx	xxxxxx

Every supply-side crisis implies a demand-side crisis, but the opposite is not true. If there is an availability deficit, intake will also be in deficit. But intake deficits are individual and group, and occur in spite of availability, when acquiring power is too low. Moreover inequality in distribution of acquiring power is common, so a supply-side crisis will be *amplified* on the demand side.

To see this better we can identify food by sources and uses, based upon an annual T-account. During the year there are four sources: carryover, production, imports, and aid. During the year there are six uses: inventories, seed, consumption, hoarding, exports, and wastage. Sources equal uses.

If sources are insufficient to meet nutritional requirements, there will be a crisis. If sources are sufficient to meet nutritional requirements, a crisis might still arise if uses are distorted by hoarding, exports, wastage, or low acquiring power of the poor. If sources depend upon imports, nonagricultural exports must be sustainable to cover the bill. If sources depend upon food aid, we must reckon the country in the throws of both supply and demand-side crises.

SOURCES	USES
carryover	inventories
production	seed
imports	consumption
aid	hoarding
	exports
	wastage

Consider the Bengal Famine of 1943. As we have learned from Professor Sen, production and carryover were adequate in 1942 and 1943. This is evidence against a supply-side crisis. Our T-account illustrates its demand-side origin.

During the famine period, large amounts of food were diverted by the British for the war effort and speculative hoarding was strong. This *drastic change in uses* upset consumption in the villages. The reduction of village supply pushed village food prices above the purchasing power of vulnerable groups. Calcutta boomed while the villages collapsed. Millions of people died.

24.3   CURSE OF THE BUMPER CROP

The average farmer in the poorworlds has little liquidity and small net worth. Being fed properly may become secondary to paying the bills. At the top of these bills are debts to moneylenders and input suppliers. Suffering from illiquidity and only modest solvency, losses on the next crop can be disastrous.

In steps the bumper crop. If output is too high in the national market, the price will be depressed below the cost of production. The already belea-guered farmer must increase his debt or lose his land. This is the curse of the bumper crop.

Producers of crops—specially primary crops—do not know how to stay in the profitable range of output. It is a moving target, beyond their control.

Consider the following diagram. Rice is on the horizontal axis and the price of rice is on the vertical. Suppose farmers cannot afford storage and must sell the harvest quickly. The supply curve will thus appear to be perfectly inelastic.

The distance OA is unit cost of production for the average farmer when he produces an average yield per acre. The distance AB is the opportunity cost of inputs per unit of rice. OC is the size of the recent harvest—a bumper crop! *The size of each harvest is different and difficult to accurately predict in advance.* A downward-sloping demand curve is marked.

Equilibrium price is DC. This entails a loss DE on every unit of rice. How will farmers pay input suppliers and moneylenders? If they own the land, will moneylenders seize it? If they rent the land, will they lose their lease?

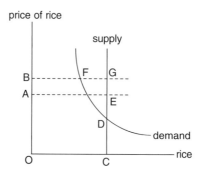

This problem is well recognized and most governments accept the principle of price supports. If a government guarantees the price OB to farmers, only BF will be sold in the market. The excess supply FG will have to be purchased by the government. Some of it can be stored for emergencies, some can be sold at a subsidized price to poor families, and some can be traded internationally if the needs of home consumption have already been met.

Governments in the poorworlds exhort farmers to 'feed the growing masses'. Without price supports, farmers often have trouble feeding themselves.

24.4   UNDERNOURISHED FARMERS

Let us consider some old but still useful and suggestive information from Bangladesh, concerning caloric intake of farmers. This chart lists them in order of food intake per person, from the highest to the lowest.

Average intake in the society—then as well as now—is significantly below the daily requirement. At the time of this survey, 72 percent of the population was in agriculture. That figure has fallen less than 10 percent during the past generation. I do not think the modest improvements since the survey was taken invalidate using it here to get a view on undernutrition among farmers.

I have calculated, from the original table, the percent of farmers in each group.

BANGLADESH (1976–77)	% OF POPULATION	% OF FARMERS*	DAILY CALORIES PER PERSON	% OF DAILY CALORIE REQUIREMENT (2,039)
large farmers	10	14	2,150	105
very large farmers	4	6	2,087	102
median-owner farmer	13	18	1,956	96
Social Average	100	—	1,782	87
median-tenant farmer	12	17	1,764	87
small farmers	12	17	1,638	80
landless farm workers	21	29	1,519	74

Source: Based on S. R. Osmani, "The Food Problems of Bangladesh," *Political Economy of Hunger: Selected Essays* (Oxford: Clarendon Press, 1995), 334. *not in the original table.

Let us inspect this chart in three parts:

Above the Daily Caloric Requirement: Only 20 percent of the farmers exceed the daily requirement! This figure probably overstates the proportion achieving good nutrition. In general, protein consumption in the country-side is low and the diet has little variety. Thus: only a fraction of the top 20 percent of the farmers has an adequate diet.

Around the Social Average: The 'median-owner farmers' are above the social average, while the 'median-tenant farmers' are below it. Together they comprise 25 percent of the population and 35 percent of the farmers. Even the owner-median farmer is somewhat undernourished.

Below the Social Average: This comprises the small farmers and the landless farm workers. Together they are a third of the population and 46 percent of the farmers. They are very calorie deficient—getting 80 percent or less of the daily requirement. Their protein and micronutrient deficiencies are probably extreme. Landless farm workers nearly starve.

This gives us an alarming picture of nutritional deficiencies among the various farming classes responsible for feeding the entire nation. Poor nutrition directly reduces both mental and physical efficiencies depressing the performance of farmers. Unless the agricultural base of the society is made strong and secure, sustainable national progress is nearly impossible.

24.5   LIQUIDITY AND SOLVENCY

We have seen our poor, undernourished, farmer faces the occasional curse of a bumper crop—which shrinks his net worth and might bankrupt him. We can sharpen our ideas with a balance sheet. Let us assume his initial condition is not too bad: he has a land title and his debts to moneylender are a fraction of assets.

On the asset side, his savings are so small we need to represent them by a thin black sliver. The land (with a small house) constitutes more than half of his assets. Since he is not mechanized, his tools are few and modest. The bulk of his current assets are tied up in crop inputs and the fund for family subsistence.

Even though he has a positive net worth, as drawn here, his debts to moneylenders equal the value of his land and house—a fact probably known to creditors. This puts him in a weak position even though he is not in a classic sense facing insolvency. He is, however, chronically illiquid and may have to sometimes dip into the family-subsistence fund to pay interest or principle.

assets	claims
family subsistence	debts to moneylenders
crop inputs	
tools	
land (with small house)	
	net worth

Each time he applies crop inputs and labor time to the land, it is a throw of the dice. He cannot accurately predict crop yields, the weather at harvest time, or the market price. Revenue from the harvest must be sufficient to pay moneylenders and renew his current assets. Otherwise, his financial condition will weaken.

He may be beset with four kinds of crisis. First, a family emergency or special occasion might divert resources from farming or may incur additional liabilities. In poor countries, with high birth rates and high death rates, this is a common problem. Second, a natural disaster might ruin everything. Without government assistance, this is sure to wreck his balance sheet because he will have no way to satisfy creditors. His fate will depend upon the policy of those creditors.

The other two crises are a matter of degree: poor or catastrophically poor revenue from the harvest. In the first case, in order to maintain current assets, current debt will have to increase and equity will shrink. In the second case, it may not be possible to maintain current assets and he might face bankruptcy. Even if he can keep his land, the family subsistence bundle might have to shrink and crop-enhancing inputs might be skimped on or skipped entirely.

We have been considering crisis as faced by farmers owing small amounts of land. Tenant farmers and landless workers are more exposed and vulnerable.

24.6   PROPERTY RIGHTS

In order to illustrate a balance sheet, it was convenient to assume a small-scale farmer had legal title to his land. As we have learned from Hernando de Soto, this is very often not the case. In a survey of four poor countries, he found 'formal landholding' in rural areas ranged between 3 and 33 percent.

RURAL LANDS		
	formal landholding (%)	informal landholding (%)
Philippines	33	67
Peru	19	81
Egypt	17	83
Haiti	3	97

Source: Hernando de Soto, *The Mystery of Capital* (New York: Basic Books, 2000), 251–54.

Referring to land as a whole, he writes:

> In every country we researched, we found that some 80 percent of land parcels were not protected by up-to-date records or held by legally accountable owners. Any exchange of such extralegal property was therefore restricted to closed circles of trading partners, keeping the assets of extralegal owners outside the expanding market. (83–84)

Without titles, land may not be used as collateral for loans in the formal banking system. This often leaves the farmers at the mercy of local money-lenders who can charge interest rates high enough to create perpetual debt bondage. Also, without the legal security embodied in land titles, incentive is lacking to improve the land and acquire better tools.

The property rights of tenant farmers are also problematic. Historically, they have had to pay about half of the harvest to the person recognized locally as the landowner. Generally, contracts have been verbal and worthless if the landowner changed his mind. Without a long-term guarantee of access to the land, the tenant farmer has had little incentive to make land improvements.

Referring to the extralegal use of government land, de Soto tells us:

> In Haiti, one way an ordinary citizen can settle legally on government land is first to lease it from the government for five years and then buy it. Working with associates in Haiti, our researchers found that to obtain such a lease took 65 bureaucratic steps . . . all for the privilege of merely leasing the land for five years. To buy the land required another 111 bureaucratic hurdles . . .

> In fact, in every country we investigated, we found that is nearly as difficult to *stay* legal as it is to *become* legal. (21)

Thus the uncertainties of market-driven agriculture are compounded by inse-cure property rights. Governments in the poorworlds need to establish and enforce clear and streamlined rules for land ownership, land use, contracts, and bankruptcy. In the *Wealth of Nations*, Adam Smith referred to the 'sacred rights of private property'. We should be happy to just secularize them.

24.7   GREEN REVOLUTION

The emergence of modern society in the nineteenth century would have been impossible without dramatic technical change in agriculture, in order to free up labor for other purposes and feed growing populations. This was embodied in agriculture's first industrial revolution—mechanization. The colossal population boom during the twentieth century induced a second revolution, designed to radically improve the fertility, and disease resistance, of seeds. I end this chapter with a bit of this great story.

The Green Revolution is identified with one of its pioneers, Norman Borlaug, a specialist in plant pathology. In 1943, the Rockefeller Foundation established a program in Mexico to transfer new farming ideas from America. Borlaug went to direct the wheat project. He was soon involved in path-breaking innovations.

> One was 'shuttle breeding,' a technique for speeding up the movement of disease immunity between strains of crops. Borlaug also developed cereals that were insensitive to the number of hours of light in a day, and could therefore be grown in many climates.
>
> Borlaug's leading research achievement was to hasten the perfection of dwarf spring wheat . . . Bred for short stalks, plants expend less energy on growing inedible column sections and more on growing valuable grain. (Gregg Easterbrook, "Forgotten Benefactor of Humanity," *Atlantic Monthly (January 1997)*, 77)

The productivity gains were amazing. In 1943, Mexico produced 750 kilograms of wheat per hectare; by 1970, output increased to almost 3000 kg/ha. Other projects in Mexico targeted potatoes and maize; in East Asia rice was the subject of intensive productivity-enhancing innovations.

Inspired by the success of this project, Borlaug began to argue for the introduction of high-yield dwarf wheat into India and other poor countries. This was resisted on scientific grounds ('they are not native crops') and on sociological grounds ('they will upset traditional relationships'). And they were resisted on economic grounds because the high-yield seeds needed irrigation and fertilizer, both costly inputs in poor countries. Although opposition was fierce, Borlaug was not going to be derailed.

In 1963, the Rockefeller Foundation sent Borlaug to India and Pakistan. Both countries were in the early stages of famine. Borlaug failed to convince the government-established seed monopoly. But by 1965, the situation became desperate; both governments decided to give the high-yield seeds a try.

> Finally the seed ship sailed . . . "I went to bed thinking the problem was at last solved, and woke up to the news that war had broken out between India and Pakistan". . . . "if it hadn't been for the war, I might never have been given true freedom to test these ideas." (Easterbrook, "Forgotten Benefactor," 78)

Borlaug's seeds took root and grew. So did his ideas. By the end of the 1960s, the productivity advantages were well established in South Asia.

His long years of toil suddenly came to the attention of the world. In 1970, Norman Borlaug was awarded the Nobel Peace Prize.

In his Nobel speech, in December 1970, Borlaug told his audience:

> Man can and must prevent the tragedy of famine in the future instead of merely trying with pious regret to salvage the human wreckage of the famine, as he has so often done in the past. We will be guilty of criminal negligence, without extenuation, if we permit future famines.

Borlaug then refers to a previous Nobel Laureate, John Boyd Orr:

> Perhaps no one in recent times has more pungently expressed the interrelationship of food and peace than Nobel Laureate Lord John Boyd Orr . . . with his famous words, 'You can't build peace on empty stomachs' . . .

> To ignore Lord Orr's admonitions would result in worldwide disorders and social chaos, for it is a fundamental biological law that when the life of living organisms is threatened by shortages of food they tend to swarm and use violence to obtain their means of sustenance.

As the use of high-yield seeds spread, opposition to the Green Revolution grew into a powerful political force. Environmentalists objected to the dependence upon chemical fertilizers, chemical pollution of water sources, pesticides, and the gradual elimination of seeds native to various locations. As Borlaug tried to branch out into Africa the donors got cold feet.

> Borlaug, once an honored presence at the Ford and Rockefeller Foundations, became, he says, "a tar baby to them politically, because all the ideas the greenies couldn't stand were sticking to me." (Easterbrook, "Forgotten Benefactor," 79)

Borlaug retired. A reformed fascist, Ryoichi Sasakawa, and a former American President, Jimmy Carter, persuaded him to forget retirement and spread the green revolution to Africa. It has not been easy. In an interview, he said:

> Supplying food to sub-Saharan African countries is made very complex because of a lack of infrastructure . . . the lack of roads is one of the biggest obstacles . . . I think roads also have great indirect value. If a road is built going across tribal groups . . . in seven or eight years you'll hear people say, "You know, that tribe over there, they aren't so different from us after all, are they?" (Ronald Bailey, "Billions Served," *Reason Online*, April 2000 http://www.reason.com/news/show/27665.html) (accessed November 16, 2006)

The last section of his Nobel lecture refers to the 'Population Monster':

> The Green Revolution has won a temporary success in man's war against hunger and deprivation: it has given man a breathing space . . . But the frightening power of human reproduction must also be curbed; otherwise the success of the Green Revolution will be ephemeral only.

The call has gone out for a Second Green Revolution—to give humanity another 'breathing space'. Discoveries in genetics and in biotechnology can increase both output per acre and nutrient qualities. The poorworlds are hungry for protein and Africa is just plain hungry. Will that hunger ever be satisfied?

25

LAND REFORM
—In Taiwan—

We are sincerely sorry for our failure to carry out Dr. Sun Yat-sen's land-to-the-tiller ideal while we were still on the mainland. Though that failure may be partly attributed to internal disturbances and foreign invasion, it was due mainly to the selfishness of a small minority of people, to their shortsightedness and lack of courage.

—Chen Cheng, Architect of Taiwan's Land-Reform Program

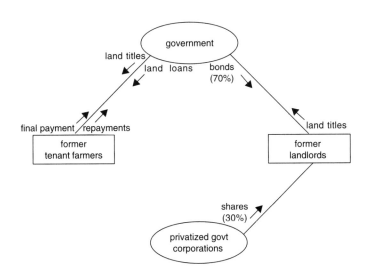

25.1   BREAKING THE MALTHUSIAN CYCLE

Mencius said: In years of plenty the farmers live a miserable life; in years of scarcity they cannot escape starvation and death.

Quoted by Chen Cheng, *Land Reform in Taiwan* (1961), 2.

Nationalists retreated from mainland China to Taiwan in utter defeat at the hands of the communists. Their defeat had been deserved. During their rule over China they all but ignored their founder's call for 'equalization of land rights'. Fortunately for the Nationalists, their new governor in Taiwan, Chen Cheng, was a true and insightful disciple of Sun Yat-Sen.

This chapter is *his story*, as the architect of the brilliant land reform in Taiwan. He begins his account with history:

> A study of Chinese history for the last 2,000 years shows recurring patterns of war and peace. Many causes may be listed, but the most important is inability to maintain a proper balance between land and population for any length of time. (ix)
>
> [Y]ears of civil commotion arising out of a poor harvest far outnumber the years of peace. Eight or nine out of every ten such disturbances have been caused by our failure to find a thoroughgoing and permanent solution of the land problem. (4)

His diagnosis of contemporary conditions and needs was simple and clear:

> [T]he best way to effect changes in an agrarian economy is to develop industry and trade. However, in a country where the economy is predominantly agricultural, capital investment in land and the exploitation of human labor constitute great impediments to such development. We must begin by setting capital and labor free through land reform. (ix)

The absolute scarcity of arable land on Taiwan was a challenge no smaller than the harsh feudalistic social relations. At the start of land reform there were only 0.27 acres of cultivated land per person. There were only three acres of cultivated land per farm family. This figure understates the problem because land distribution was highly unequal.

Taiwan experienced a great population boom. By 1959, cultivated acres per person fell to 0.2. Governor Cheng was correct: without land reform Taiwan was destined to *Malthusize*. Fortunately, he had had some experience with land reform while governor of Hupeh on the mainland. Even before the communist victory in China, he started to put that experience to great use in Taiwan.

YEAR	AREA CULTIVATED (1000s OF ACRES)	POPULATION (1000s OF PEOPLE)	CULTIVATED ACRES PER PERSON
1949	2,019	7,397	0.27
1954	2,077	8,749	0.24
1959	2,104	10,431	0.20

Source: Adapted from Cheng, Tables 1 and 2, page 307.

25.2 RENT REDUCTION

The backbone of agriculture was sharecropping; 65 percent of the farm families fell into three categories: tenant farmers with some land ownership (24 percent), tenant farmers (35 percent), and farm hands (6 percent).

The conditions of tenancy were harsh. Land rents ranged between 50 and 70 percent of gross yields. Leases were usually oral and subject to sudden cancellation. "Extraordinary extortions in the form of security deposits, guarantee money, and payment of rent in advance were also demanded and caused the tenant farmer to suffer unbearable hardships" (9).

The first step in land reform was rent reduction. In 1949, Cheng resurrected a dead 1930s law from the mainland fixing a rent ceiling at 37.5 percent of yields.

Rent reduction was intended to achieve three goals: improve yields per acre, increase the income of tenant-farm families, and reduce farm-land prices.

After signing 37.5 percent leases, yields increased 19 percent by 1952:

YEAR	YIELD OF RICE PER CHIA	INDEX FOR YIELD PER CHIA
Before rent reduction	10,249	100
1949	10,714	105
1950	11,360	111
1951	11,729	114
1952	12,192	119

Source: Adapted from Cheng, Table 5, page 309 [yield in pounds • *chia* = 2.4 acres].

Income of tenant farmers grew by 65 percent:

YEAR	YIELD OF RICE PER CHIA	FARMLAND RENT (%)	TENANT— FARMER'S SHARE (%)	INDEX FOR TENANT— FARMER'S SHARE
before rent reduction	10,249	5,637 (55.0)	4,612 (45.0)	100
1949	10,714	4,017 (37.5)	6,697 (62.5)	145
1950	11,360	4,260 (37.5)	7,100 (62.5)	154
1951	11,729	4,398 (37.5)	7,331 (62.5)	159
1952	12,192	4,572 (37.5)	7,620 (62.5)	165

Source: Adapted from Cheng, Table 5, page 309. *Note*: Calculation errors in the original corrected Based upon standard production of one *chia* on grade-nine paddy field in Taoyuan County.

Land prices fell by *far more* than half throughout rice country.

VALUE OF FARM LAND AFTER ESTABLISHING THE 37.5% RENTAL CEILING
BASE YEAR: 1948

Year	7th grade paddy field	10th grade paddy field	16th grade paddy field	22nd grade paddy field
1948	100	100	100	100
1949	65	71	67	65
1950	67	63	57	41
1951	56	48	42	38
1952	38	43	35	27

Source: Cheng, Table 6, page 310.

25.3   SALE OF PUBLIC LANDS

The government owned about 21 percent of all farmland. Most of that land had been the property of the colonial Japanese administration, Japanese nationals, or Japanese corporations. With the return of Taiwan to China in 1945, normalizing the use of that land was a high priority.

In 1947, a new leasing system was introduced for public lands. Preference was given to the formation of cooperative farms. *Rents were fixed at 25 percent of gross yields.* To sweeten things for cooperatives, 20 percent of the rent was earmarked for production improvements and public welfare.

Much to the surprise of the authorities, the program was a failure. The cooperative approach proved unpopular. Moreover, subleasing was common, undermining the goal to improve the lot of tenant farmers. In light of this failure the government decided in 1948 to sell the land to farmers, and be done with it.

That was put on a back-burner when the rent-reduction program for private lands became an urgent priority of the new governor, Cheng. In 1951, after the success of the 37.5 percent rental rate, a program to sell public lands was drafted. It had taken on new meaning, as part of a coherent plan for land reform:

> The Government, by taking the initiative in sale of public farm lands, set an example for private landowners. This served as a harbinger for the compulsory purchase of private farm land for resale to farmers and thereby paved the way to realization of the land-to-the-tiller ideal . . . Speaking of governing, Confucius said the essential point was 'first to lead the people and then ask them to render services.' The sale of public land was actually intended to lead the people. (56)

As an example, about 80 percent of the land owned by the Taiwan Sugar Corporation was sold to incumbent tenant farmers. The land retained for public use comprised roads, waterways, windbreaks, experimental farms, and offices.

The farm-size purchased, as well as the financial terms, were calculated to protect the purchaser-farmer from taking on additional financial burdens. The purchase price—2.5 times the yield of the main crop, repaid interest-free over 10 years—was fair and affordable. Given the time factor, it was less than a 25 percent rental rate. Production loans were assured. To avoid distortions from inflation, repayments were made in-kind, after harvests. Leasing to a tenant was forbidden. In the event the purchaser-farmer could not fulfill the terms of the purchase-contract, the land reverted to the state, for resale.

LAND PURCHASE TABLE—DESIGNED TO SUPPORT A FAMILY OF SIX MEMBERS

purchase price: 2.5x annual yield of main crop   •   repaid in 10 interest-free annual installments

	superior quality	medium quality	inferior quality
paddy fields	0.5 chia	1 chia	2 chia
dry land	1 chia	2 chia	4 chia

Source: Based upon: Cheng, 58–59.

25.4   LAND-TO-THE-TILLER

With great success of both rent reduction and public-land sales, the government prepared its Land-to-the-Tiller program. It was based upon three principles:

(1) *Justice for Tenant Farmers*: The sale of public land had shown the way. The same 2.5x land-pricing formula was applied to private lands. The government extended loans, repayable over 10 years. Production loans were also provided by the government. The purchaser-farmer was responsible for paying taxes, but the overall burden was no more than the 37.5 percent rental.

(2) *Justice for Landlords*: The landlords had acquired the land lawfully and were entitled to compensation. Following the 2.5x land-pricing formula, they were paid in bonds (70 percent) and shares (30 percent).

Bonds were paid over 10 years, earning 4 percent per year. They were denominated in rice or sweet potato, depending upon the kind of land. This method was chosen to avoid the ruination of former landlords through inflation—a disease that badly infected Japanese land reform. Shares were paid immediately in four recently privatized government corporations.

Former landlords were allowed to retain enough land to remain active as farmers.

(3) *Sound Finance*: The system had to be self-financing, with minimal inflationary effects, but the up-front costs to the government when buying the land *all at once* were huge. The best solution was to cover those costs immediately through privatization of important government corporations. With shares in the hands of the former landlords they could wait for annual payments of bonds financed by the repayments of the purchaser-farmers.

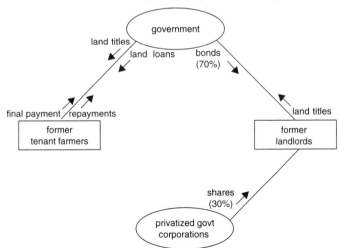

It was the hope of the government that the formerly feudalistic class would be transformed into capitalists. They were encouraged to develop new businesses, with access to advice and credit. In this way the land-reform program was truly far reaching in vision. Rather than crush the feudalists, their human potential was appreciated. They became the backbone of industrialization.

25.5 MEASURES OF SUCCESS

Implementation began in July 1953. The following data is based upon the records for 284,590 former-tenant farming families.

First, long-term capital improvements were extensive and grew steadily every year. This included water supplies, natural fertilization, soil protection, animal shelter, and postharvest processing.

	July 49–June 53 *annual* average	July 53–June 56 *annual* average	July 57–June 60 *annual* average
ENHANCEMENTS TO FACILITIES AND STRUCTURES			
water pumps bought	78	621	638
wells sunk	281	1,086	1,727
windbreaks planted (feet)	109,000	277,000	431,000
—*repaired or constructed*:			
compost houses (sq. ft.)	0.7 million	2.8 million	2.9 million
animal shelters (sq. ft.)	0.5 million	1.5 million	1.5 million
drying grounds (sq. ft.)	3.2 million	4.9 million	14 million

Source: Cheng, Tables 2 and 3, 85–86.

Complimentary tools, for each stage of the agriculture cycle, were acquired in growing numbers. Draft cattle became ubiquitous.

	July 49–June 53 *annual* average	July 53–June 56 *annual* average	July 57–June 60 *annual* average
INCREASE IN IMPLEMENTS AND DRAFT CATTLE			
deep-furrow plows	13,750	21,808	27,749
ox carts	169	2,518	4,451
sprayers	391	1,082	7,289
threshers	4,035	7,654	11,086
draft cattle	18,388	38,141	40,278

Source: Cheng, Table 3, 86.

There were also notable improvements in living conditions. Undernutrition, previously common, was conquered—for the first time in Taiwan's history. Improvements in housing and clothing were widespread. The purchase of bicycles and the forming of new families grew steadily, at nearly the same rate.

	July 49–June 53 *annual* average	July 53–June 56 *annual* average	July 57–June 60 *annual* average
IMPROVEMENT OF FARMERS' LIVING CONDITIONS			
new houses (sq. ft.)	0.4 million	1.1 million	1.9 million
repaired houses (sq. ft.)	1.4 million	3.2 million	4.0 million
new clothes (piece)	7.8 million	12.0 million	11.8 million
sewing machines bought	2,484	7,564	17,847
new bedding	3,009	7,204	43,503
bicycles bought	10,795	21,543	27,633
marriages	10,665	24,709	25,448

Source: Cheng, Table 4, 88.

25.6 COMPARISON WITH COMMUNIST METHODS

The communist revolution was a war on private property. A cornerstone was all-out war on landlords. This was a monstrously violent process in China:

> Farmers were forced to engage in struggle and liquidation of landlords, to create a reign of terror, to divide the lands of landlords, to destroy the families of landlords, and even to demand their heads . . . (127)

> As a result of liquidations and struggles, 1,200,000 of our brethren were slaughtered and more than 20 million were either driven from their homes or sent to concentration camps in the name of 'reform through labor'. (114)

All farmland became the property of the state. Between 1952 and 1957, 117 million farm families were organized into agricultural cooperatives. This was intended to both destroy family farming as the basic unit of rural production, and to create a new basic unit of rural production that could also serve as the center of rural administration.

The cooperative system gave the central government a convenient way to extract all agricultural surplus for use by industry and the military.

> For toil day in and day out the year round, farmers can receive only a third of the total income . . . Farmers have never suffered so much and been exploited to such an extent since the beginning of agriculture in China. (116)

Not content with that degree of collectivization, the communist government introduced 'people's communes' in 1958. Up to this point cooperatives were organized rationally according to divisions of labor: production, supply and marketing, credit, handicrafts, and transportation. In addition, farmers were allowed to retain houses, trees, and animals. Now, the cooperatives were merged into giant communes and the last elements of private property were socialized. On average a commune included about 5,000 families. The communes were

> a basic unit with multiple purposes including trade, agriculture, commerce, education, and military affairs. All productive materials and labor were placed at the disposal of the commune. (118)

Public mess halls, nurseries, and sewing teams replaced family activities. Thus, in addition to the collectivization of production, all aspects of daily life were collectivized.

Indeed, able-bodied adults were required to join the 'labor army of workers, peasants, and soldiers'. On rotation they were sent off the commune to production sites (like mines) in need of labor. In addition, all able-bodied adult men were required to join the militia. They were given military training and required to take up duties when assigned.

According to Chen Cheng, the commune system had three outstanding characteristics: slavery, productivity loss, and deterioration of living conditions—the opposite of land reform in Taiwan.

25.7 PRINCIPLES OF SUCCESSFUL LAND REFORM

Governor Cheng was inspired by Sun Yat-Sen's equalization-of-land-rights doctrine. He not only managed to fulfill the ideal, he also began the process of transforming the feudalistic class into capitalists. He was an intuitive genius of rare talent, outshining a generation of development economists.

Let us summarize the principles of land reform that emerge from the remarkable experience in Taiwan. This will give us an opportunity to mention some vital factors left out of the above, economic, narrative.

(1) *Land to the Tiller*: This must be the centerpiece of land reform. This is easiest to apply in the case of tenancy because farmers have a particular relationship with certain plots of land. But there should be ways of assuring the application of this principle for long-term farm workers on large farms, such as in Zimbabwe or South Africa.

(2) *Progressive Stages*: The three stages—rent reduction, sale of public lands, and purchase/resale of private lands—built up systematically, one upon the other. The rent reduction stage was not only needed to reduce exploitation of tenants and induce higher productivity. It was also essential for deflating land prices kept high by outrageous rents. This paved the way for establishing a land-pricing formula fair to former tenants and landlords alike.

(3) *Complete and Honest Record Keeping*: Each stage required comprehensive collections of information as well as preparation of legal documents. Public officials administering the program had to be incorruptible.

(4) *Democratic Input*: Organizations were set up by the government: island-wide, regional, and local. All relevant parties were included. A local-level system was designed for resolving conflicts. Governor Cheng was proud to say the land reform was 'of the people, by the people, and for the people'.

(5) *Legal Separation of Tenant from Landlord*: The government bought the land, en masse, from the landlords and resold it to the former tenants. This both facilitated the rapid enactment of Land-to-the-Tiller and accelerated the breakdown of feudalistic relationships.

(6) *Opportunities for Former Landlords*: Having established a 'just price' for the land, the former landlords were compensated by an ingenious combination of inflation-proof bonds and shares. While retaining farming rights they also had new opportunities as capitalists.

(7) *Sound Finance*: Land reform had to be financed without causing inflation or requiring foreign assistance. Taiwan had avoided the ravages of the war and could privatize some valuable government monopolies. Some of those shares provided the 30 percent 'down payment' to the former landlords. After that, tenant repayments to the government covered the bonds.

Land reform continues to be a pressing issues in much of the poorworlds. Although conditions vary greatly from place to place, the Taiwanese experience establishes the gold standard for land reform design and implementation.

26

INFRASTRUCTURE

POPULATION AND INFRASTRUCTURE IN GLOBAL PERSPECTIVE—2000

countries	population share (%)	infrastructure share (%)
high income	16	60
middle income	45	28
low income	39	13

COMPOSITION OF INFRASTRUCTURE STOCK—2000 (%)

countries	roads	electricity	water and sanitation	rail	telecom	total value $ trillions
high income	45	40	5	4	6	9
median income	28	48	10	7	7	4
low income	51	26	15	7	2	2

26.1 SOLID FOUNDATION FOR DEVELOPMENT

The land reform in Taiwan solved several serious problems simultaneously. One of the most important was the chronic undernutrition. When this success was coupled with dedicated attention to basic education, the leaders of Taiwan had laid a solid foundation for industrial development.

—TAIWAN—	1949	1951	1953	1955	1957	1959
% of children attending school	79.1	81.5	87.8	92.3	94.6	95.4

Source: Cheng, *Land Reform in Taiwan*, Table 13, 314.

South Korea fared much worse in the 1950s. Not only was the country devastated by war with the North, it also had an ineffectual government. When Park Chun Hee took power in a coup in 1961, South Korea was as poor as India and well behind its bitter enemy in the North.

President Park made education a high priority. By 1965, undernutrition was greatly relieved and the younger generation was becoming literate. During the next 20 years South Korea made steady progress in human development. In 1988, South Korea was able to host the Olympic Games.

—SOUTH KOREA—	1965	1970	1975	1980	1985
daily caloric intake (cal)	2189	2370	2390	2485	2687
daily protein intake (gm)	57	61	71	74	87
average education (years)	5.7	6.6	7.6	8.6	9.5
population per physician	2609	1773	1801	1485	1230
life expectancy (years)	55	58	61	66	69

Source: Byung-Nak Song, *Rise of the Korean Economy* (Hong Kong; New York: Oxford UP, 1990), 182–83.

The primary foundations for a modern social economy depend critically upon adequate nutrition, basic literacy, and good public health measures. If these are achieved it is possible to build properly the needed physical infrastructure *if a country has both government and business elites dedicated to the task.*

There are five grids associated with modernization: water, sanitation, transport, power, and telecom. Without these very expensive components of physical infrastructure, the upper productivity limit will be stuck at a low level. With them, a country can potentially enjoy a comfortable material life with a good margin of safety above the social subsistence.

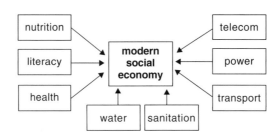

26.2   FROM SIMPLE TO COMPLEX

Industrialism is essentially the condition where educated people use modern infrastructure and tools to *magnify their productivity* far beyond what was possible in pre-industrial times.

Let us recall alpha and consider the simple-to-complex story again:

$$\alpha = \frac{net\ output}{subsistence\ per\ person \times population} > 1$$

At the beginning, alpha is not much greater than one. Suppose the story begins with public health interventions that greatly lower the child-mortality rate. (This has been typical worldwide since World War II.) Since the birth rate initially remains high, the much lower death rate will trigger a population boom. For this reason alone net output must rise—simply to keep alpha from falling under the weight of great population pressures.

But modernization requires increasingly complex conditions of social subsistence. The content of 'the subsistence bundle' depends upon productivity needs as well as survival and reproduction needs. To the extent that modern infrastructure is required by students and workers to perform their essential tasks, those infrastructure are part of the social subsistence.

The idealized picture is depicted below, written in terms of consumption per person. We have seen this diagram before—in Chapters 4 and 21. On the left-hand side, subsistence per person is low, the possibility frontier is small, and there is little surplus per person. This represents a typical pre-industrial agrarian society. On the right-hand side, subsistence per person is much larger, the possibility frontier has expanded greatly, and surplus per person is almost as large as subsistence per person. This represents a fully industrial society.

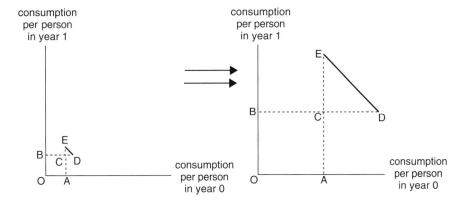

26.3 STOCK OF INFRASTRUCTURE

That diagram suggests great inequality in the distribution of infrastructure stock, with complex countries having the lion's share. Fay and Yepes have made a heroic effort to estimate this globally.

While high-income countries comprise 16 percent of the world's population, they have about 60 percent of the world's infrastructure. Put another way, this table implies that infrastructure per person in low-income countries is a small fraction of that found in high-income countries.

POPULATION AND INFRASTRUCTURE IN GLOBAL PERSPECTIVE—2000

countries	population share (%)	infrastructure share (%)
high income	16	60
middle income	45	28
low income	39	13

Source: Marianne Fay and Tito Yepes, "Investing in Infrastructure,"
World Bank Policy Research Working Paper 3102, July 2003, 2.

That is not surprising. More revealing is the composition. Roads and electricity play the dominant role. At any level of development, no less than 75 percent of the infrastructure stock is found in these two categories. But while roads dominate in low-income countries, electricity dominates in the middle income. The construction of power stations and a distribution grid is hugely expensive. In the push toward modernization, it dominates infrastructure budgets.

Water and sanitation demand a smaller share of the infrastructure as one moves up the development ladder. In median- and low-income countries, they comprise the third largest category. While they provide essential services, they also play a role in improving public health.

Compared with a century ago, railroads play a small role. Long distance trucking, buses, and private vehicles have replaced most rail transport. By contrast, telecom is a rising star. But poor countries can afford very little.

COMPOSITION OF INFRASTRUCTURE STOCK—2000 (%)

countries	roads	electricity	water and sanitation	rail	telecom	total value $ trillions
high income	45	40	5	4	6	9
median income	28	48	10	7	7	4
low income	51	26	15	7	2	2

Source: Fay and Yepes, 2.

This chart does not convey two things of great importance. First, the equipment for building infrastructure is produced in a small number of countries so the poorer countries usually must import it. Second, in countries identified as middle or low income, infrastructure shortfalls are severe or very severe: there is *never* enough electricity or phones, most roads and railways are in poor condition (as are most vehicles), and the sanitation problems are legion.

26.4   THE 'MISSING MIDDLE'

Although we often divide countries into high, middle, and low, according to levels of income, the middle label can be very misleading. The gap in income between high and upper-middle is huge. Upper-middle income is about a *third* of high income. Moreover, few people live in countries between the 24,000 and 8,000 dollar range. There is a 'missing middle'.

POPULATION AND INCOME DISTRIBUTION—GLOBAL VIEW

countries	population (millions)	per capita income 1999 PPP dollars
high income	891	24,430
upper-middle income	573	8,320
lower-middle income	2,094	3,960
low income	2,417	1,790

Source: World Development Report 2000/2001 (New York: Oxford University Press, 2000), 275.

This should not be surprising. Most of the world faces vicious cycles of poverty and low productivity limits associated with meager infrastructure. The following data tells part of the story.

The income gap we just observed is largely mirrored in electricity per capita. Upper-middle income countries have less than a third of electricity per person found in high-income countries.

Paved roads illustrate even better the 'missing middle'. Upper-middle income countries must devote so many resources to electrification that road improvement tends to be postponed.

COUNTRIES	ELECTRICITY PER CAPITA KILOWATT HOURS	PAVED ROADS % OF TOTAL
	1997	1998
high income	8,238	94
upper-middle income	2,434	47
lower-middle income	1,042	44
low income	357	19

Source: World Development Report 2000/2001, 295 and 309.

This picture is reinforced by statistics for the ownership of infrastructure-dependent products. In every category, a chasm exists between high and upper-middle. Although upper-middle income countries are in the 'take-off stage', their 'drive to maturity' is stunted by insufficient investment in infrastructure.

PER 1000 PEOPLE BY COUNTRY	RADIOS	TVs	LANDLINE PHONES	MOBILE PHONES	PCs
	1997	1998	1998	1998	1998
high income	1,286	661	567	265	311
upper-middle income	493	285	176	76	53
lower-middle income	322	250	90	18	14
low income	157	76	23	2	3

Source: World Development Report 2000/2001, 311.

26.5 INSUFFICIENT INVESTMENT

The history of Ceylon/Sri Lanka may serve as a pointed example of insufficient investment in infrastructure. Programs for human development had been a great success but the country faced a revolutionary situation in 1971. Educated young men—unemployed, radical, and angry—nearly toppled the government.

The Ceylonese government had underinvested in three essential areas: power, transport, and telecom. Such investment would have soaked up unemployed men, generated incomes, and increased productivity. But the socialist government lacked financial and managerial resources; and it was blinded by the belief that capitalistic business was 'outdated'.

The chart below compares Sri Lanka with India during the 1990s. Sri Lanka exceeds India in income per person, life expectancy, and adult literacy—by large margins. But it is *well behind* India in electricity and paved roads. Sri Lanka is only a bit ahead in telephones.

Clearly, the income differential is *not* due to superior infrastructure! It may be explained by human development factors.

	SRI LANKA	INDIA
* GDP per capita—PPP$ (1993)	3,030	1,240
** GNP per capita—PPP$ (1999)	3,056	2,149
* life expectancy—years (1993)	72	61
* adult literacy—percent age 15+ (1993)	90	51
** electricity per capita—kilowatt hours (1997)	227	363
** paved roads—percent of total (1990)	32	47
** landline phones—per 1000 (1998)	28	22
** radios—per 1000 (1998)	209	121
** TVs—per 1000 (1998)	92	69
** PCs—per 1000 (1998)	4	3

*Sources: Human Development in South Asia, 1997**
*World Development Report 2000/2001***

We can infer something else. *Sri Lanka reached an upper-productivity limit because of inadequate infrastructure.* It got as far as it could on the basis high levels of literacy, fairly high levels of nutrition, and good public health.

Starting in the mid-1990s, a government composed of 'reformed socialists' understood this. In the face of huge annual budget deficits—in the area of 7 percent of GDP—it turned to private enterprise, offering 'Build, Operate, Own' or 'Build, Operate, Transfer' contracts. The largest projects have been in transportation (ports and highways) and in thermal power.

That government was replaced by a probusiness coalition that desired to expand such projects. Recently, the 'reformed socialists' returned to power, but with a hard-line Marxist partner. If the long-running civil war is settled, we might see efforts to catch-up with neighbors like Thailand or Malaysia.

26.6 INEFFECTIVE INVESTMENT

In addition to underinvestment in infrastructure, ineffective investment is a notorious problem in the poorworlds. Let us see this diagrammatically.

Consumption is on the horizontal axis and net investment is on the vertical. OA is the social subsistence. OB is the highest level of consumption sustainable while holding the capital intact. CA is the largest net investment possible while still producing the social subsistence. BC is the possibility frontier.

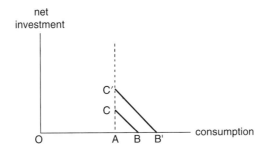

Suppose point C is chosen. This would indicate an aggressive attitude toward growth. If all of CA is effectively invested in infrastructure projects, the possibility frontier will shift out, to (say) B′C′. But, if all this net-investment spending goes down the drain, the possibility frontier will not shift at all. *The social accounts will show significant net investment but sustainable output will be unchanged.* The typical situation is likely to fall between these two cases.

The electricity sector is infamous for ineffective investment. The data below show some electricity-starved nations. Consumption of electricity is a fraction of the average in *low-income countries!* This probably reflects a tremendous waste and corruption of budgets for that sector. In addition, the 'systems loss' in transmission or in theft averages over 25 percent in this electricity-starved group. Such a great loss of revenue further undermines the ability to expand the grid. Without reliable electricity, development gets turned off.

	ELECTRIC POWER			
	consumption per capita kilowatt-hours		transmission and distribution losses % of output	
	1990	1997	1990	1997
Angola	60	64	25	28
Bangladesh	43	76	34	15
Haiti	61	42	31	42
Mozambique	35	47	16	31
Myanmar	43	57	26	35
Nepal	28	39	29	28
Nigeria	77	84	38	32
low-income country average	373	357	13	17

Source: World Development Report 2000/2001, Table 18.

26.7   COMMON SENSE OF PUBLIC FINANCE

Private finance of infrastructure grids is generally impractical. Local businessmen are not usually in a position to gather the huge funds needed—governments are. To what extent should infrastructure be deficit financed?

It would be nice if we could adopt the European Union rules for fiscal policy: a deficit/GDP ratio of 3 percent and an accumulated debt/GDP ratio of 60 percent. These rules, however, are not relevant in the poorworlds. They are based upon wiggle-room for fiscal policy, assuming the great task of infrastructure building has matured into a maintenance issue.

Let us look at matters another way, based upon social accounting:

government expenditure = current expenditure + capital expenditure

We can express two 'common sense' rules:

Current expenditure should be financed out of current revenue (with wiggle-room for economic downturns). *Capital expenditure* can be debt financed using bonds maturing during the lifetime of the investment.

Article 115 of the German constitution is close to this, although it does not mention depreciation periods. If these conservative rules are followed, and if public investment is effective, then government deficits will never be a concern.

The chart below tells three stories. First you have governments with high rates of capital expenditure but excellent budget discipline. (Singapore runs a large overall surplus because of its forced-savings program.)

Next you have EU governments with huge public sectors and a great difficulty following our rules—let alone the more restrictive European Union rules.

Finally, you have three laggards, chronically underinvesting, chronically suffering from ineffective investment, and chronically running deficits well in excess of capital expenditure. These stories are likely to have bad endings.

	PERCENT OF GDP—GOVERNMENT ACCOUNT					
	current expenditure		capital expenditure		surplus/deficit	
	1990	1998	1990	1998	1990	1998
—*Leaders*—						
Malaysia	23.3	15.2	7.3	4.5	−2.1	2.9
Singapore	16.4	11.8	5.1	5.1	10.8	10.8
—*Wannabes*—						
Greece	48.9	28.4	4.1	4.3	−23.2	−8.4
Italy	43.8	42.2	4.0	2.4	−10.3	−3.3
—*Laggards*—						
India	14.2	12.8	1.8	1.6	−7.5	−5.2
Pakistan	19.8	18.8	2.6	2.5	−5.4	−6.3
Zimbabwe	24.5	33.6	2.8	2.1	−5.3	−5.0

Source: World Development Report 2000/2001, Table 14.

27

LEVERAGE AND BANKRUPTCY

Recapitalization versus Downsizing

27.1 CLASSIC PICTURES OF HEALTH

In order to gain some understanding of our topic it is useful to begin with a bit of accounting history. Lenders have always faced risks and with the rise of capitalism they had to develop systematic methods for dealing with them. This lead to the development of accounting and ratio analysis.

The original lending convention, or *covenant*, was simple: the borrower should 'own and much as he owes'. In a model with only current assets this has a logical implication. On the following diagram, all assets and all debts are current. In accordance with the simple ownership convention, owner's equity equals current debts. This *implies* current assets are twice current debts.

A current-ratio of two was the centerpiece of ratio analysis for generations. Modern observers think it was a bit irrational but in its original historical context it made good sense. If a borrower should 'own as much as he owes', the lender could verify this by checking the state of current assets and debts.

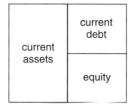

Those ratios became the core of lending covenants. A risk premium would be charged, or loans would be denied, if they were not established and maintained.

The diagrams below introduce noncurrent assets and debts. The one on the left shows a 'labor intensive' or 'inventory intensive' business—like a software producer. The one the right shows a 'capital intensive' business—like railways or airlines. Both diagrams satisfy our two ratios. Evidently this is difficult to achieve when physical leverage is high because retained profits or the sale of new shares might not be adequate to cover new fixed assets that are lumpy and large.

<table>
<tr><td>current
assets</td><td>current
debt</td></tr>
<tr><td></td><td>noncurrent
debt</td></tr>
<tr><td>noncurrent
assets</td><td>equity</td></tr>
</table>

<table>
<tr><td>current
assets</td><td>current
debt</td></tr>
<tr><td></td><td>noncurrent
debt</td></tr>
<tr><td>noncurrent
assets</td><td>equity</td></tr>
</table>

low-physical leverage   *high-physical leverage*

As recently as 1970, these ratios played a role in America. But when accounting information is reliable they tend to require excessive liquidity and excessive solvency. They also put a drag on the pace of business expansion.

27.2 LEVERAGED INDUSTRIALIZATION

The principles of conservative finance played a positive role in both United Kingdom and United States. The original industrialization process was unstable, with frequent excess-capacity crises. There was a tendency to hide debts or overstate earnings. Moreover, bankers got caught up in the excitement over new technologies and threw caution to the wind. The conservative-ratio analysis constrained these tendencies to some extent. Without it, the pioneer countries might have gone bankrupt.

Those who played catch-up, however, saw matters differently. They were inclined to have the state play an aggressive role in financing and developing all aspects of industrial society—not just the public utilities. In this case the conservative rules of finance were thrown out the window. Catch-up was the imperative—rules of finance had to be adjusted to facilitate that great goal.

Since the burden of noncurrent assets was immense, banks—both private and government—stepped in to provide long-term debt financing. Great political pressure was applied to private banks to cooperate. 'You would not want to lose your charter, would you?' In exchange, the banks would insist on protection in the event the industrial projects failed.

Under these circumstances, owners' equity might be a fifth or a tenth of assets. The condition of liquidity might be very tight, too. Current assets had to exceed current debts because it was necessary to pay bills as they came due. But if current assets were not liquid enough, managers would have to go to their main creditor bank to get temporary liquidity loans.

For this system to work well there had to be a high degree of trust between the main financial stakeholders, and little corruption. There was also little room for concern about workers. In their fury workers organized to gain concessions.

current assets	current debt
noncurrent assets	noncurrent debt
	equity

multileveraged

Under these rules of the game, catch-up could proceed at a much faster pace than the one set by the pioneer industrializers. Success depended upon continuous macroeconomic growth—it had to feed itself in a sustainable way. The margin for error was small because any recession, if prolonged, could trigger liquidity and solvency crises—and threaten the entire banking system.

27.3 CHAIN BANKRUPTCY IN EAST ASIA

Alas, accelerated-leveraged industrialization *is* a high-wire act. If internal circumstances are out of whack a large shock can cause chain bankruptcy. This occurred in East Asia in 1997. As we can see from these estimates of non-performing loans and recapitalization costs, the damage was extraordinary.

	PROBLEM LOANS		RECAPITALIZATION	
	amount ($ billions)	as % of total loans	cost ($ billions)	as % of GDP
Indonesia	36	61	17	31
Thailand	80	48	39	31
South Korea	122	33	58	19
Malaysia	35	33	12	17

Source: "Problem Loans in East Asia," *Far Eastern Economic Review* (October 15, 1998), 12.

The outside world became aware of the unfolding drama when the Thai baht collapsed in the summer of 1997. That, however, was the culmination of a story begun years before. Serious bubbles built up in both the stock and real estate markets. In early 1996 the Thai stock market crashed; it crashed again before the currency crisis. The bubble in the real estate market, too, began to deflate. The central bank wasted billions of dollars defending the baht. Probably they were trying to protect the largest businessmen who had borrowed dollars massively and would find repayment in weak baht difficult.

The crisis spread to Indonesia, Malaysia, and South Korea. All four countries were following the path of highly leveraged growth. They seemed to share some weaknesses. Perhaps the most serious was the widespread political influence on credit allocation. Coupled with this was the practice of financing plant and equipment with short-term loans from foreign sources. These poor practices occurred in the context of implicit guarantees the governments would protect large lenders and borrowers if anything went seriously wrong.

When these weaknesses were compounded by excess capacity and ridiculous asset prices, all the ingredients for a colossal crisis were in place.

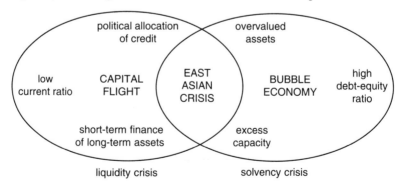

Note: An elaboration of a diagram at: Marcus Miller, "Tell me the truth about Thailand" [www.warwick.ac.uk/fac/soc/CSGR/current/thaild.pdf].

27.4 SOCIALIZING THE LOSSES

With the banking systems on the brink of collapse, the first priority was the nationalization (or renationalization) of the private banks brought low. This was necessary to reassure local depositors and avoid a run on the banks. To make good on this, infusions of capital from the government were necessary.

But the socialization of business losses did not end there. The main creditors were urged to infuse new funds into their important nonperforming borrowers, with implicit guarantees from the government. This was not only used to protect the richest families; it was also used to protect jobs at major corporations. In the face of poor, or no, unemployment insurance, this was understandable. Small businesses, however, received no protection and were starved for credit. For these people, the 'safety net' was their family.

None of the countries were prepared *at all* for system-wide failure *even though they were playing the leverage game fullon*. Garden-variety corporate failure was handled via social contract rather than bankruptcy process. Insolvency was remedied along a spectrum: from nationalization to government-funded recapitalization to debt-equity swaps to sale-of-business. Downsizing was strongly resisted—to avoid trouble with labor. Insolvent firms, main creditors, and the government would 'work things out'. There was no 'plan B'.

current assets	current debt				
		assets	debt	assets	debt
noncurrent assets	noncurrent debt				
	equity		−equity		equity

dangerously leveraged	*negative net worth*	*recapitalization*

Turning matters over to professionals in a bankruptcy-court environment was alien. This is seen in the way the South Korean government decided to get tough on excessive leverage—a war on leverage *by decree*:

> Large companies with debt-to-equity ratios of 200 percent and higher . . . will be designated as 'potentially insolvent' . . . a top financial regulator said . . .
>
> Banks will thus be required to set aside up to 30 percent of their loans to large companies with over 200 percent debt-to-equity ratios as loan-loss reserves under the new criteria and be barred from extending fresh loans . . .
>
> Under government pressure, the nation's top five *chaebol* have agreed with their main creditor banks to lower their debt-to-equity ratios below 200 percent by the end of this year. (*Korea Herald*, 09.29.99)

As 1999 was drawing to a close, it was possible to report 'significant progress':

> The first half [Jan-June] debt-to-equity ratio of 247.2 percent was a sharp reduction from the 303 percent posted six months earlier and was the lowest debt-equity ratio figure since the end of 1968 when it tallied 207.5 percent . . . . (*Korea Herald*, 11.11.99)

27.5   CLASSIC MEDICINE

Socialization of losses perpetuates inefficient credit allocation—to the most *needy* rather than the most *ready*. It establishes a drag on macro performance and probably condemns the country to an inferior upper productivity limit. Japan is the recent poster child. In United States, it is the option of last resort.

In recent decades, though, financial leverage has become common in Unites States. Whereas insolvent firms were rarely found on the Fortune 500 a generation ago, 3 percent had negative net worth in 1994! Although some of them were extremely insolvent, creditors agreed to keep them alive. Airlines and supermarket chains dominated this list.

FORTUNE 500 COMPANIES (1994—VALUES IN MILLIONS)	ASSETS (K) BOOK VALUE	EQUITY (E) BOOK VALUE	E/K %	EQUITY MARKET VALUE
Supermarkets GH	1,134	−1,301	−115	NA
Flagstar	1,582	−1,063	−67	223
Kroger	4,708	−2,154	−46	3,080
Grand Union Holdings	1,394	−645	−46	NA
AmeriSource Distribution	712	−301	−42	NA
Jefferson Smurfit	2,759	−730	−26	1,790
American Standard	3,156	−798	−25	1,867
Owen-Corning Fiberglass	3,274	−680	−21	1,592
Northwest Airlines	8,070	−1,371	−17	2,288
U.S. Air Group	6,808	−897	−13	371
Eckerd	1,342	−123	−9	943
TWA	2,793	−172	−6	28
UAL	11,764	−316	−3	1,306
Borden	3,822	−92	−2	NA
USG	2,124	−8	−0.4	1,037

The *classic medicine* consists of a bankruptcy process, such as America's Chapter 11. It is supposed to be free from political pressure. Reorganization is designed on economic grounds, with expert guidance. It generally requires downsizing—selling off assets and firing workers. This is taken for granted in United States because the government provides a safety net for workers. The rehabilitated company has to *earn its way back to solvency*. This approach probably supports a superior productivity limit to the ones in East Asia.

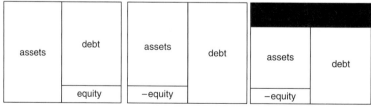

dangerously leveraged   negative net worth   downsizing

Full liquidation is applied only if creditors insist. We may wonder how Kroger could be so far in the hole and yet retain the confidence of the stock market? This is an interesting case. In order to fight unfriendly takeover bids in 1988, Kroger's management 'restructured' finances, turning the company into a 'poison pill'. It took about a decade to climb out of that hole.

27.6   ODIOUS DEBT

Let us turn our attention to some debilitating issues plaguing the poorworlds. One of them is 'odious debt'—liabilities incurred by an illegitimate regime for illegitimate purposes. The doctrine is traced back to the Spanish-American War (1898). Unites States repudiated Cuba's debt with Spain because it was imposed upon the Cubans without their consent and by force.

The next milestone was a legal battle in 1923 over collection of debt incurred by the former dictator in Costa Rica. U.S. Supreme Court Chief Justice Taft took the case as arbitrator, without fee. He rejected the bank's claim because it could not prove the loan was made for legitimate purposes.

The doctrine of odious debt was given its best-known form by Alexander Sack, a one-time minister in Tsarist Russian and a law professor in France. He wrote:

> If a despotic power incurs a debt not for the needs or the interest of the State, but to strengthen its despotic regime, to repress the population that fights against it, ect., this debt is odious for the population of all the State.

> This debt is not an obligation for the nation; it is a regime's debt, a *personal* debt of the power that has incurred it. It falls with the fall of this power. (1927)
> *Note*: See [www.odiousdebts.org] and Patricia Adams:
> [www.probeinternational.org/probeint/OdiousDebts/doctrine.htm]
> (accessed June 1, 2002)

The word kleptocrat was coined to characterize the despicable Mobutu—a true godson of King Leopold! This was a pure case of western enablers feeding an African addict! 'Would you like some millions sprinkled on your billions?'

In 1978, the IMF placed Edwin Blumenthal in the Central Bank. He resigned two years later, saying: "there is no chance, I repeat no chance, that Zaire's numerous creditors will ever recover their loans." The IMF ignored him. When Mobutu was overthrown in 1997, the debt was $13 billion. Zaire was bankrupt.

	DICTATOR'S DEBTS (BILLIONS OF $)
Indonesia—Suharto	126
Philippines—Marcos	27
Zaire—Mobutu	13

Source: http://www.jubilee2000uk.org/analysis/reports/
dictatorsreport.htm (accessed June 1, 2002).

How much of such debt should survive the demise of a dictator? The following accounting equation might clarify matters:

$$\textit{dictator's debt} =$$
$$\textit{effective investment} + \textit{ineffective investment} + \textit{plunder} + \textit{repression}$$

The last item should be repudiated entirely. The unrecoverable portion of the plunder should be repudiated, too. Some elements of ineffective investment are really corruption rather than incompetence, poor training, bad luck, or natural hazards, and should be deemed odious. If international lenders had to make this sort of calculation—and face cross-examination—they might be cautious with their decisions and recognize their share of the moral hazard.

27.7   A SMOKING GUN

It is not only brand-name dictators who manage to—may I say it? *privatize*—a central bank. Bit players can do so too if they are well placed and the culture tolerates almost any degree of corruption. Bangladesh has been such a case.

Bangladesh has long suffered from financial plunder. By some estimates, $30 billion has been 'borrowed' and misused since independence in 1971. This should be compared with the annual donor budget of about $2 billion.

This was such easy picking the development of natural gas was ignored for decades, even though those reserves were proven in the days of East Pakistan.

We have some hard evidence from internal documents at the Central Bank. Tanweer Akram was given permission to cull bank records for a study included in his Ph.D. dissertation at Columbia University. Out of the mountain of data he collected, I include here a smoking gun.

This 1998 data pertains to 'large borrowing'—loans in excess of 100 million taka, ($2 million). This is a large sum of money in Bangladesh. Over 80 percent of these loans were overdue in both the public and private sectors.

OUTSTANDING AND OVERDUE LOANS—TAKA 100 MILLION AND ABOVE
IN MILLIONS OF TAKA

sector	large borrowers	total outstanding	total overdue	% overdue
public	27	24,970	20,550	82
private	165	43,720	36,720	84
total	192	68,690	57,270	83

Source: Bangladesh Bank (1998). See: Tanweer Akram, "Ineffective Privatization of Public Enterprises: The Case of Bangladesh" (Working Paper, Columbia University, October 31, 1999).

Such information helps explain why land in Dhaka, in 1997, was over $500,000 an acre, with embassy-neighborhood land going for $2 million an acre. (Flood pumps and power-generators not included!) It does not take much imagination to convert booty into land. Where there is no fear of punishment, why not?

By ordinary standards we would conclude the Central Bank is insolvent. We might guess the same for the mostly nationalized-commercial banks. They are not, however, illiquid. Fresh dollars flow in continually from overseas. In addition to funds from international donors there is an inflow of cash from Bangladeshis working abroad, mostly in better-off Muslim countries. If these sources dry up, asset markets and the banking system will collapse.

This data is disappointing news for the apostles of privatization. The public and private sectors are equally corrupt! Bangladesh needs to get control over corruption before it can even begin to climb out of the fourth world. Where is their salvation? If only they had a Mother who would send those selfish plunderers to bed without their supper!

28

ASIAN 'MIRACLE'

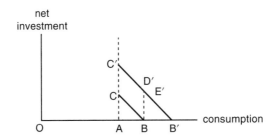

Sacrifice versus Efficiency versus Borrowing

28.1 MEIJI JAPAN

The Father of all Asian efforts at modern growth is found in Meiji Japan. Near the end of the Tokugawa era, in 1853, American warships were used to convince the Japanese to accept an unequal trade treaty. Ruinous inflation followed. When the last shogun died without an heir, chaos broke out. After a decade of this dangerous condition, the ancient emperor system was restored in 1868 in a military coup. Suddenly, Japan had a 15-year old emperor-god.

The first generation of contact with westerners left a bitter taste. Euro-American imperialism was a threat to national survival. Catch-up was an urgent task.

Reforms were needed in order to get control over public finance. In order to increase revenues, private ownership of agricultural land was formalized. In order to decrease expenditures, the *samurai* stipend was converted into bonds and then eliminated. This heralded great changes in the ruling classes.

While the older *samurai* resented this loss of status and dispossession, some of their sons had the honor of acquiring the education from overseas needed for rapidly modernizing the social and physical infrastructures.

Under the banner 'increase production, encourage industry', the Meiji government hired foreign advisors to assist with agriculture, education, factories, railways, and communications. The Japanese learned quickly.

Cotton and silk goods were the first industries mechanized for international trade. By the end of the century they accounted for half of Japan's exports even though they required one-thousandth of the labor force.

The sacred goal was 'rich country, strong army'. Following the lead of foreign powers, Japan tried its hand at imperialism. Taiwan was seized from China in 1895—only 27 years after the Meiji Restoration. Japan then picked a fight with Russia and won an expensive war. After that, Korea was colonized.

The table below understates Japan's meteoric rise. A self-isolated group of island people transformed themselves in a few decades. By the end of the Meiji era in 1912, Japan was a major power. It was also a dual economy with inefficient domestic sectors combined with aggressive international industries. Minus the militarism, Meiji Japan became the economic lodestar for the region.

CONDITIONS AT THE START OF MODERN ECONOMIC GROWTH

		GNP per person (1958 $)	adult literacy (%)	urbanization (%)	growth rate of real GNP per person first 50 years (%)
Britain	1780	1210	53	21	0.4
France	1830	1077	46	11	1.0
United States	1840	1461	not available	9	1.5
Germany	1850	1050	70+	27	1.4
Japan	1886	738	50	13	1.8

Source: David Flath, *The Japanese Economy* (Oxford; New York: Oxford University Press, 2000), 39.

28.2   ACCELERATED GROWTH AND PRESERVATIONISM

The path selected by Meiji leaders came to a bad end when imperial dreams turned into national catastrophe. After World War II, United States insisted on three reforms: renunciation of war, abolition of feudalism, and limited monarchy. These were enshrined in a democratic constitution.

The people of Japan set out to restore their dignity, honor, and well-being by pouring themselves into economic reconstruction. Savings, investment, and financial leverage were mobilized to the greatest extent possible.

The government subsidized capital investment in many industries. Coal, marine transport, agriculture, and electricity were subsidized for decades. Textiles, machinery, iron and steel, and chemicals also received large assistance.

Fears of excessive domestic competition led to government-authorized cartels. Imports were limited to things needed for reconstruction or the export sectors. Domestic industries were inefficient and overstaffed while export sectors had to improve constantly in order to succeed. Brilliant entrepreneurs were very keen to build world-class corporations and no obstacle could stand in their way.

This led to a dual economy with social-market characteristics. Small businesses and farmers were well protected. The higher consumer prices this required was the price people had to pay for full employment and social harmony.

The ministries responsible for industrial policy did not always see eye-to-eye. After World War II, the Ministry for International Trade and Industry (MITI) wanted to promote the production of cars. The Bank of Japan was opposed. MITI got its way. They controlled foreign exchange for imports so they restricted foreign exchange for cars. Besides import protection, the industry got tax breaks and low-interest loans. Eventually Japan was beating all competition.

Industrial policy targeted products with large income elasticity of demand, such as cars, chemicals, and steel. This allowed them to ride in the front seat of global growth. These industries eventually attracted global excess capacity. Japan could keep up in cars but became a high-cost center.

As analyzed persuasively by Richard Katz in *Japan the System that Soured* (1998), the downside of industrial policy began to bite at the end of the high-growth era. Inefficient compromises persisted well past their use-by date. This was papered over until asset-market bubbles burst, threatening the financial system.

Then things went sour. Fiscal and monetary policy were stretched to the limit just to avoid depression. Instead of using the fiscal deficits for something useful—like decentralization or modernization of education—they paid construction companies to build roads and bridges to nowhere. Socialization of losses in banking occurred repeatedly. Monetary policy fell into a liquidity trap. Mired in political paralysis, vested interests blocked efforts at structural reform. To some extent, they still do. (Tigers beware. Someday, this could be you.)

28.3   KRUGMAN ON 'THE MYTH'

Let us put Japan's woes aside and consider the rapid growth of the Tigers. We begin with a piece of social accounting:

$$output\ growth = input\ growth + improvements\ in\ output\ per\ unit\ of\ input$$

Input growth refers to increases in the capital stock and in labor. The second item, efficiency growth—commonly known by the ugly and confusing name, 'total factor productivity'—includes any applied knowledge that improves the contribution of a given amount of inputs. This factor is measured as a *residual* once output and input growth have been identified.

As the Tigers roared ahead it was taken for granted that growth in capitalistic economies includes a healthy portion of the second factor. This assumption was fed by the glamor of the meteoric rise from utter poverty, in a single leap. In 1994, Paul Krugman demythologized the 'miracle' of accelerated Tiger growth. Citing empirical studies by Alwyn Young, among others, Krugman argued that the Tigers were very short on efficiency growth. Moreover, he likened the Tigers in this regard to the old Soviet Union. Ouch, that has got to hurt.

He was not comparing standards of living; he was comparing factors that influence both the mobilization of resources and the upper productivity limit:

> Rapid Soviet economic growth was based entirely on one attribute: the willingness to save, to sacrifice current consumption for the sake of future production . . . (63)

> Economic growth that is based on expansion of inputs, rather than on output per unit of input, is inevitably subject to diminishing returns. It was simply not possible for the Soviet economies to sustain the rates of growth of labor force participation, average education levels, and above all the physical capital stock . . . (63)

With Young's data at hand Krugman said:

> Popular enthusiasm about Asia's boom deserves to have some cold water thrown on it . . . the future prospects for that growth are more limited than almost anyone now imagines. (64)

One country was singled out for particular scorn: "Singapore grew through a mobilization of resources that would have done Stalin proud." This witty jab at the island nation's humorless leader provoked interest in Young's estimates of efficiency-less growth in Singapore.

The measurement problems are legion. Overestimating capital and/or labor will underestimate the residual, 'efficiency'. The common neo-Classical assumptions (constant returns, perfect competition, unit elasticity of substitution, Hicks-neutral technical change) embed their own biases. But these biases cannot hide the general validity of Krugman's thesis. Tigerland was built heavily on the backs of would-be consumers and real workers.

28.4 SACRIFICE VERSUS EFFICIENCY VERSUS BORROWING

A simple diagram can illustrate some of the main issues. Let us return to our corn model, where corn is produced with corn seed and labor time. Consumption is on the horizontal axis and net investment is on the vertical.

OA is the social subsistence of corn. OB is the maximum consumption of corn if only the replacement seed is set aside and planted. OB/OA is fairly small, indicating a poor country. AC is the maximum net investment of corn seed while still consuming the social subsistence. BC is the possibility frontier.

Let us assume for now none of the seed is stolen, incorrectly planted, or subject to natural hazards. If point B is chosen, the possibility frontier will remain unchanged. If point C is chosen, the possibility frontier will shift out to (say) B'C'. For a point in-between, the possibility frontier will shift out more or less, depending upon its proximity to points C or B. Let us look at three cases.

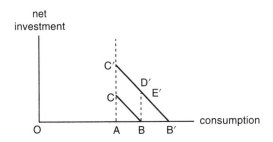

First: the leader of the Sacrifice Union declares, "Comrades, your glorious sacrifice of present consumption at point C will give us the victory of moving to point C' next year. If we dedicate ourselves this way for a decade we shall have the greatest possibility frontier in the world!" This is a pure case of growth based upon more inputs and will be disappointed as diminishing returns set in.

Next we visit the Efficiency Union. They were inclined to choose point B when a clever lad said to the ruling council: "Listen! I know how to get greater output from a unit of corn seed!" They were astonished by his insight and experiment and adopted it. With this efficiency gain they were able to improve the possibility frontier and shift to point B'. Note well: the people of EU got to enjoy the advantages of a better frontier while the people of SU did not.

Finally we visit the Borrowers Union. Their dictator, Suharcos, was inclined to choose point B to minimize social dissent and he borrowed seed from overseas equal to the distance AC. Suharcos considered defaulting on the loan, which would have allowed consumption at point D'. However, he came to his senses, paid the interest, and renewed the loan—which is depicted by point E'—or so he told the press! Behind the scenes Baby Suharcos pinched much of the seed and gambled it away. That explained the actual sluggish performance and how the post-Suharcos government got stuck with an odious debt.

28.5   INTERNATIONAL COMPARISONS

Let us compare the best of Tigerland with the most outstanding growth records after World War II. The real GDP per person figures tell the broad story: (1) Rapid growth for West Germany, France, and especially Japan, before the oil shock—slow down after that. (2) Impressive rags-to-riches growth in Tigerland over two generations. By 1996, Singapore had caught up fully, on this measure of success, while Taiwan and South Korea had the goal in sight.

	REAL GDP PER PERSON		
	1950	1973	1996
Japan	1,873	11,017	19,582
West Germany	4,281	13,152	19,622
France	5,221	12,940	18,207
Taiwan	922	3,669	14,222
South Korea	876	2,840	12,874
Singapore	2,038	5,412	20,983

Source: Crafts, "East Asian Growth before and after the Crisis," *IMF Staff Papers*, 46, no. 2 (June 1999), Table 1 (1990 $ international), 141.

We are fortunate to have estimates for the sources of growth. Since these figures all depend upon the same neo-Classical assumptions they are all subject to the same biases. The most significant point emerges immediately: efficiency growth was the largest component for the first group while accumulation of capital was the largest factor in Tigerland.

Efficiency gains accounted for more than half of the growth in Germany and about three-fifths of the growth in France. Capital accumulation accounted for about half of the growth in Tigerland. This required humongous investment/GDP ratios—lots of sacrifice there. Only one-fifth of the growth in Tigerland was from efficiency gains.

Japan and the Tigers all had large labor components. This was due to their stage in the demographic transition and the rapid increases in education levels. West Germany and France were at a more mature stage of demographic transition and depended very little upon growth of labor.

GROWTH AND ITS SOURCES (% PER YEAR)				
	Output	Capital	Labor	Efficiency
1950–73				
Japan	9.2	3.1	2.5	3.6
West Germany	6.0	2.2	0.5	3.3
France	5.0	1.6	0.3	3.1
1960–94				
Taiwan	8.5	4.1	2.4	2.0
South Korea	8.3	4.3	2.5	1.5
Singapore	8.1	4.4	2.2	1.5

Source: Crafts: Table 5, 150.

28.6   LABOR AND POPULATION

It is useful to recall the numerator of the production-survival condition:

$$\frac{net\ output}{population} = \frac{net\ output}{hours\ of\ work} \frac{hours\ of\ work}{workers} \frac{workers}{population} = \lambda h\omega$$

where λ is labor productivity, h is annual hours worked per worker and ω is proportion of the population working. Real GDP per person, from the previous page, can be used as a proxy for net output per person. If we can find figures for h and ω, we can shed some light on labor productivity and its context.

We have exact figures for working hours. There is a vast difference between the groups, with Europeans outright slackers compared with East Asians. The workplace colonization of time in Tigerland is extensive *through-out* the period. (This is paralleled in the colonization of children's time by the schools K-12.) 'Labor-leisure trade-off? No time to talk about that!'

We use a demographic statistic as a proxy for the proportion of the population working. The Tigers had a *huge* rise in the percent of the population of working age. This statistic declined in Europe during their accelerated-growth phase.

	ANNUAL HOURS WORKED PER WORKER		SHARE OF POPULATION 15–64 (%)	
	1973	1996	1950	1973
Japan	2,201	1,898	56.8	64.0
West Germany	1,865	1,558	62.7	58.4
France	1,904	1,666	61.1	57.8
			1965	1990
Taiwan	2,690	2,339	52.5	66.7
South Korea	2,428	2,453	51.2	69.4
Singapore	2,410	2,318	52.0	70.8

Source: Crafts: Tables 6 and 7, 151–52.

These figures make it clear: a great deal of Tigerland performance was based upon colonizing the time of a rapidly expanding portion of the population. Labor productivity gains were unimpressive compared with the Europeans.

This points to a great social challenge. The people of Tigerland will eventually insist on more of the fruits of economic success. The demand for leisure will be coupled with a decline in the proportion of population working. In order to maintain net output per person, labor productivity will have to rise sharply. This will require efficiency gains. Perhaps they shall do so in the IT digital revolution. Otherwise the time-colonization problem might remain unsolved.

A SCORECARD—MID-1990s				
	net output/person	λ	h	ω
Western Germany		high	low	low
France	about the same	high	low	low
Singapore		low	high	high

28.7   AN ASIAN CENTURY?

There is no point in dealing with this question from a narrow perspective. United States may stumble under poor leadership and European Union might fail too, giving East Asia the chance to take center stage. But the question brings to my mind something broader and deeper and darker.

Let us start with China. It may become the largest economy in the world, and gain much influence that way, but there are other possibilities. The financial system might suffer repeated crises as the socialization of losses in the socialist sector is coupled with the maladies of capitalism. Hyperinflation or depression could threaten the grip of the Communist Party. If it loses power, regional forces could tear the country apart. Even democratization could do that.

Or there is the opposite problem—an expansionist China. Taiwan is not the only issue. The best-kept open secret in this part of the world is the gradual movement of Chinese people into the borderlands of Asiatic Russia. Asiatic Russia is dying. Interior villages are depopulating, leaving only the old behind.

Will China seize the day, grab some 'living space' (and all its resources) and plunge the world into war? China has a large gender imbalance because of the one-child policy. Unless Russia gets its house in order, the temptation to use the surplus men militarily might be too great for Chinese leaders to resist. As long as China does not threaten European Russia, a conventional struggle over Siberia and the Far East is possible, with Russia highly disadvantaged.

In fact, I *am* fearful that this *will be* an Asian Century—one notorious for wars. North, South, East, West, take your pick in this overpopulated and politically immature continent. They all have ancient enemies ready for a scuffle.

Poverty and ecological stress, mixed with religious fervor, is an explosive combination. We are witnessing deadly varieties of messianic expectations in the Muslim, Hindu, Jewish, Christian, and 'Kim' worlds. Some variant on 'Kill a Commie for Christ' is infecting all of Asia except the commercially minded parts of the East. The United States is making its contributions to this deadly mixture and seems to have a government willing to light half of the matches!

Let me end by referring to South Asia. The expanding populations are pressing against severe natural resource constraints. India and Pakistan may both fail to keep the accumulation of social and private capital ahead of population growth. The historic grudge match diverts resources from accumulation to 'defense'. Lip service is still paid to education goals in much of the subcontinent. If India *eventually* faces depopulation *anyway*, perhaps some leader will decide they should 'die for something'—like the destruction of Pakistan.

The prospects of an Asian Century are unsettling, specially if our globalized economy suffers repeated growing pains.

29

FOREIGN DIRECT INVESTMENT
—CAN *FDI* REDUCE POVERTY IN *LDCs?*—

	FDI INFLOW AS A PERCENT OF GROSS FIXED CAPITAL FORMATION					
	average	1996	1997	1998	1999	2000
Angola	48	9	21	72	105	35
Lesotho	46	52	48	60	38	31
Gambia	41	22	29	31	64	60
Cambodia	29	36	35	28	24	23

29.1   CONSUMPTION POSSIBILITIES AND DISTRIBUTION

Points A-E in the following diagram have appeared various times in this book. Here we use the diagram to depict two views on development. The upper arrow represents raising the per-person possibility frontier through capital accumulation and technical change. The lower arrow represents empowering the poor through education, healthcare, and financial services. Can foreign direct investment (FDI) contribute to shifting upward *both* arrows in the least developed countries (LDCs)?

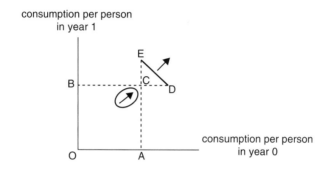

Let us use a bit of macro accounting, reckoning all components in real terms:

$$C + (I - D) + G + (X - M) = Y_{net}$$

where, C is household consumption, I is gross capital formation, D is consumption of fixed capital, G is government consumption, X is exports, M is imports, and Y_{net} is the net output or 'net domestic product'.

In order for FDI to positively impact the upper arrow, it must make a significant contribution to net investment $(I - D)$. In order for FDI to positively impact the lower arrow, it must augment household consumption C through new earned incomes of at least some of the impoverished members of the society.

The first condition can be met if the rate of capital accumulation exceeds the rate of population growth. The second condition would require poverty-reducing impacts of FDI exceed any unintended externalities (such as environmental damage, rent increases, or destruction of less-competitive jobs).

If the first condition is not met the second condition is unlikely to be met. This simplifies our task. It will be convenient to first identify the least-developed countries where FDI is a large part of overall real investment activity.

More than 90 percent of FDI in the least-developed countries is real investment activity, in new plant and equipment or new business services. As such, it directly contributes to capital accumulation, although it may entail competition for existing local firms. In light of two serious demographic complications—population booms and AIDS—has FDI been enough to matter on a per-capita basis in any of the LDCs?

29.2   FOREIGN CONTRIBUTION TO CAPITAL ACCUMULATION[1]

The UN Conference on Trade and Development (UNCTAD) publishes a volume entitled *FDI in Least Developed Countries at a Glance: 2002*. It is a valuable document. The capital-accumulation crisis in the least developed nations is not going to end on its own. UNCTAD is right to identify FDI as a desirable component of investment in the poorworlds. That document provides significant FDI information and can be used in efforts to harness FDI to the development process.

Compared with other macro figures, FDI in the 49 LDCs is small. In the late 1980s it averaged less than a billion dollars per year; in the late 1990s it averaged 3.7 billion dollars per year. Four of the LDCs are oil exporters (Angola, Equatorial Guinea, Sudan, and Yemen). Their share of the FDI rose from less than 10 percent in the late 1980s to about 40 percent in the late 1990s.

For the LDC group as a whole, FDI averaged less than 10 percent of gross fixed capital formation during the late 1990s. That figure is probably too low to have a measurable impact on poverty reduction.

The table below identifies eight impoverished nations where FDI inflows are more than 20 percent of gross fixed capital formation between 1996 and 2000. From the oil-exporter group, only Angola made the list. If FDI can have a positive impact on poverty reduction in LDCs, it may be found within this list.

FDI INFLOW AS A PERCENT OF GROSS FIXED CAPITAL FORMATION						
	average	1996	1997	1998	1999	2000
Angola	48	9	21	72	105	35
Lesotho	46	52	48	60	38	31
Gambia	41	22	29	31	64	60
Cambodia	29	36	35	28	24	23
Guinea-Bissau	24	2	18	17	23	60
Zambia	22	8	14	37	29	23
Malawi	22	20	9	36	27	20
Togo	22	14	11	19	35	29

Source: FDI in Least Developed Countries at a Glance: 2002.
(New York and Geneva: UNCTAD, 2002): see p. 1 and country-specific pages.

For simplicity and convenience we focus on the top four countries, with FDI ratios ranging from 29 to 48 percent during that five-year period. The same source allows us to calculate averages for the period 1990–2000. For those four countries, FDI averaged 20 percent or more of gross fixed capital spending over the decade. How well did they perform macro economically?

Before looking for evidence of positive per-capita impacts in macro data, we should learn a bit about each country. They are briefly introduced on the next page in rank order from the highest.

LESOTHO
FDI INFLOW AS A PERCENT OF GROSS FIXED CAPITAL FORMATION

1990	1991	1992	1993	1994	1995	1996	1997	1998	1999	2000	average
26	39	39	56	57	48	52	48	60	38	31	45

This mountainous country is surrounded by South Africa and 31 percent of adults are HIV+. Life expectancy is only 37 years. Under current trends, the death rate will soon rise to the birth rate. 85 percent of adults are literate; among women, the literacy rate is 95 percent.

In recent years, at least 90 percent of FDI has been in labor-intensive export-oriented textiles made from imported materials. This sector favors female employment.

ANGOLA
FDI INFLOW AS A PERCENT OF GROSS FIXED CAPITAL FORMATION

1990	1991	1992	1993	1994	1995	1996	1997	1998	1999	2000	average
−29	42	138	22	14	50	9	21	72	105	35	44

Civil war raged between 1990 and 1994 and again between 1998 and 2000. Less than 3 percent of the land is arable but the country is rich in natural resources. Life expectancy is 37 years—very low for a country with an HIV rate of 6 percent. The adult literacy rate is 42 percent.

FDI rates have been volatile. In recent years American interests in oil and gas expanded while French companies made large investments in the same sector. FORTUNE Global 500 investors include Johnson and Johnson, and Sodexho.

GAMBIA
FDI INFLOW AS A PERCENT OF GROSS FIXED CAPITAL FORMATION

1990	1991	1992	1993	1994	1995	1996	1997	1998	1999	1900	average
20	12	17	15	13	20	22	29	31	64	60	28

The country was politically stable most of the decade. Population growth has been one of the world's fastest. Life expectancy is 54 years and adult literacy is 40 percent.

Steady rates of FDI accelerated in recent years in the hospitality sector. Other foreign investment information is sketchy.

CAMBODIA
FDI INFLOW AS A PERCENT OF GROSS FIXED CAPITAL FORMATION

1990	1991	1992	1993	1994	1995	1996	1997	1998	1999	2000	average
0	0	17	19	16	24	36	35	28	24	23	20

Cambodia has struggled for decades to overcome the bloody rule and terrible management by the Khmer Rouge. Elections in 1993 established a basis for stability. Life expectancy is 58 years and adult literacy is 70 percent.

FDI is diversified, with most interest in tourism, forestry, and textiles. East Asian and Southeast Asian investors are the most prominent.

29.3 PER-CAPITA CHANGES IN OUTPUT AND CONSUMPTION

We should try to estimate the behavior of the possibility frontier during the decade. Was it improving? If so, were improvements passed along to consumers?

As a first approximation let us consider population growth relative to output growth. For the decade of the 1990s, output per capita did grow in Lesotho and Cambodia. It seems to have declined slightly in Gambia and Angola. Thus, only Lesotho and Cambodia experienced unambiguously improved per-capita possibility frontiers during the decade.

GROWTH OF OUTPUT AND POPULATION—AVERAGE ANNUAL %			
	per-capita growth rate [A minus B]	output growth rate [A] 1990–2001	population growth rate* [B] 1990–2000
Lesotho	3.1	4.0	0.9
Cambodia	2.1	5.0	2.9
Gambia	−0.1	3.4	3.5
Angola	−0.3	2.0	2.3

Source: 2003 World Development Indicators, Table 4.1, 186–88.
*Population Growth rates are from www.census.gov/ipc/www/idbsum.html.

Our concern is deepened when we consider changes in consumption per capita. As we might expect from Angola's poor performance above, the consumption figures there are negative—a decline in per-capita consumption of about 3.5 percent per year. Evidently, most of the local value of the FDI in resource industries benefited the warring factions who controlled the most important national assets.

Lesotho and Cambodia are a surprise. Although per-capita income grew significantly in both countries during the 1990s, per-capita consumption fell. Since the possibility frontier was shifting out, we might surmise the investment/output ratio rose at the expense of consumption and/or the capital/output ratio was higher. In Lesotho, a decline in transfers from abroad probably played a role.

Per-capita household consumption rose only in Gambia even though output per capita failed to rise there. This would seem to be an odd result. In Section 5 we might gain the clue needed to understand this.

CHANGE OF PER-CAPITA HOUSEHOLD CONSUMPTION EXPENDITURE ANNUAL AVERAGE %—1990–2001	
Gambia	1.1
Lesotho	−0.5
Cambodia	−0.7
Angola*	−3.5

Source: 2003 World Development Indicators, Table 4.10, 222–23.
*Angola figure for 1990–1998, from www.ucpress.edu/books/
pages/9577/pdf/Atlas.43-46.pdf.

29.4   POVERTY ELASTICITY OF GROWTH

Our results are disappointing. Only two of the four LDCs with high FDI/gross investment ratios during the 1990s experienced higher per-capita income during that decade. Both of those countries experienced *lower* per-capita consumption. Thus, none of the countries had higher per-capita income *and* consumption.

Most LDCs are known for great inequality in income distribution. It is possible a high degree of inequality dampens poverty-reducing impacts of growth. One way to measure this is the 'poverty elasticity of growth'. If per-capita GDP grows by one percent, by what percent does the poverty headcount decline?

Let us recall something we learned in Chapter 6, on Macroeconomics. According to Lucia Hanmer and Felix Naschold,[2] the poverty elasticity is highly sensitive to the degree of inequality:

when inequality is 'low' (gini < 43): the poverty elasticity = −0.93
when inequality is 'high' (gini > 43) : the poverty elasticity = −0.34

In the first case, a one percent growth of GDP per capita would average more than nine-tenths of a percent decline in headcount poverty; in the second case the impact would average only a *third* of a percent.

We have gini index information for the two countries with per-capita growth during the 1990s—Lesotho and Cambodia. Lesotho's gini is above the '43' threshold while Cambodia's gini is below it. If the share figures for Lesotho are correct, the Gini index is actually greater than 56. We rarely see share figures indicating such extreme inequality. According to this measure, we should have observed a notable decline in poverty in Cambodia. However the fall in consumption per capita suggests otherwise.

			percent share	
	survey year	gini index	lowest 20%	highest 20%
Lesotho	1995	56.0	1.4	70.7
Cambodia	1997	40.4	6.9	47.6

DISTRIBUTION OF CONSUMPTION EXPENDITURE

Source: 2003 World Development Indicators, Table 2.8, 64–65.

The Lesotho story gets even gloomier. A poverty elasticity was calculated between 1986 and 1998. It was only –0.12.[3] That is, a one percent increase in per-capita income reduced the incidence of poverty by about a *tenth* of a percent. There is literally no growth path out of poverty if the elasticity is so low. The circumstances and institutions perpetuating the huge inequality must be addressed.

We can see this from another angle: 80 percent of Lesotho's population is rural, much of that in subsistence agriculture, much of it underemployed. (In recent years, the AIDS epidemic has been added to this challenging mix.) The great inequality and low poverty elasticity are probably found here.

29.5   LEADING SECTORS

Can we detect *any* macroeconomic impact of FDI? Were the leading growth sectors the ones favored by FDI? Here we can give a more positive answer.

In Lesotho the leading sectors were industry and manufacturing. The largest industrial source of growth is the Lesotho Highlands Water Project (LHWP); the largest source of manufacturing growth is the Taiwan-dominated textile industry. The LHWP is run and owned by the government of Lesotho—which means it is not considered FDI—but it is largely financed from foreign sources.

In Angola the leading sector—the only leading sector—was industry. This is largely in off-shore oil, the main concentration of FDI.

In Gambia the leading sectors were agriculture and services. Most of the FDI was concentrated in the latter although there is some in the former.

Cambodia had the broadest and strongest growth, with industry, manufacturing, and services all leading sectors. FDI is found in all of these, targeting breweries, property, tourism, textiles, logging, and precious gems.

Growth of Output—by Sector			Annual average % 1990–2001		
	GDP	Agriculture	Industry	Manufacturing	Services
Cambodia	5.0	1.8	10.2	8.2	6.2
Lesotho	4.0	1.7	7.8	6.2	3.0
Gambia	3.4	5.2	2.5	1.3	3.7
Angola	2.0	0.1	4.0	0.6	−1.0

Source: 2003 World Development Indicators, Table 4.1, 186–88.

However, we may gain more insight into the disappointing conclusions of Section 3 by comparing changes in the agricultural sector with changes in household consumption expenditure:

Consumption per capita moved in the same direction as agricultural output per capita in Gambia, Cambodia, and Angola. The rank order in the consumption column is exactly the same as the rank order in the agriculture column. *The excellent performance of agriculture in Gambia more than compensated for a slight decline in overall output per capita.*

Agriculture is the largest source of employment in LDCs. It is also the heart of social subsistence. Our results remind us this sector should not be overlooked. If it performs well as a leading sector, the roots of progress are strengthened.

Essentials of Subsistence—annual average % changes 1990–2001		
	agricultural output per capita*	household consumption expenditure per capita**
Gambia	1.7	1.1
Lesotho	0.8	−0.5
Cambodia	−1.1	−0.7
Angola	−2.2	−3.5

*Calculated from data above and population growth figures in Section 3. **From Section 3.

29.6   Closer Look at Lesotho

Lesotho was our most promising candidate for positive impacts of FDI. Not only was FDI a high percent of gross investment throughout the 1990s, the per-capita possibility frontier rose significantly. However, we observed a decline in per-capita consumption and we found a low sensitivity of poverty reduction correlated with a very high gini coefficient. Let us take a closer look at Lesotho.

29.6.1   Impacts of FDI, in Context

UNCTAD has provided an excellent *Investment Policy Review* (2003) for Lesotho. We can glean from this some outstanding characteristics of the FDI.

First of all, foreign clothing and footwear companies provide about one quarter of the jobs in the private sector, mostly employing women. This is the most outstanding positive characteristic of the FDI (15).

Almost all of the garment companies are from Taiwan. Most of the technical, supervisory, and managerial staff are foreign. All machinery, fabrics, and accessories are imported; packaging is largely imported, too (16–19).

Even though the modern garment industry was established 16 years ago, there are only two local apparel entrepreneurs. Barriers to entry are low in this industry so we may surmise a dearth of entrepreneurial talent (17). Local entrepreneurship is essential for development. Indeed:

> [E]ntrepreneurial weaknesses limit the ability of Lesotho to 'root' FDI strongly in the local economy, to raise the local content of industrial activity, to attract higher quality FDI (in more complex activities and functions) and to reap spillover benefits from foreign presence. (69)

The following chart of financial inflows may shed some light. Lesotho is greatly dependent upon inflows from miners working in South Africa and official development assistance. *These massively outweigh FDI.* Miners' remittances are equivalent to 23 percent of GDP. They certainly contribute to consumption and imports and probably contribute to working-capital formation. But in the absence of local entrepreneurship, miners' remittances will not fuel an engine of growth.

Selected Capital Inflows to Lesotho—1981–2000
Annual Averages, current US$, millions

	1981–85	1986–90	1991–95	1996–2000
miners' remittance	335	308	359	278
ODA and official aid	98	117	128	73
FDI	5	12	19	29
water and power royalties	0	0	0	15
total	438	437	535	395

Source: Investment Policy Review—Lesotho (Geneva: UNCTAD, 2003), 12.

29.6.2   Is Lesotho Fifth World?

Lesotho is a human development contradiction. Adult literacy is over 80 percent while HIV/AIDS has pushed life expectancy to under 40 years. A third of the adult population is HIV+ and a quarter of the total population is undernourished.

In the year 2000, household consumption was more than 100 percent of gross domestic product. A fifth world country is indicated when the social subsistence exceeds the net output. If household consumption exceeds *gross* output, we can probably surmise such a country is incapable of producing its social subsistence.

Lesotho is the rare country where domestic income is only about 60 percent of national income. Given its great dependence upon miners' remittances and foreign aid we may seriously doubt Lesotho's ability to produce its social subsistence.

29.7   There Is Hope?

Lesotho should have been an excellent candidate for positive impacts of FDI on poverty reduction. FDI averaged 45 percent of gross capital formation for a full decade in labor-intensive businesses and the literacy rate was high. If AIDS had not drastically shortening the lives of many adults, and non-FDI inflows had not shrunk, it is possible we would have observed some poverty-reducing impacts of FDI, even though Lesotho had a very low poverty elasticity of growth.

None of the four countries with high rates of FDI as a percent of gross investment experienced both higher per-capita income *and* higher per-capita consumption. However, changes in per-capita consumption were sensitive to changes in per capita production in agriculture—a common observation, and challenge, in the poorest countries.

Lesotho had the highest literacy rate in the group of four. Angola and Gambia lagged well behind on this indicator. Perhaps we need to ponder a general conclusion found elsewhere:

> The statistical studies suggest that a threshold level of human capital needs to be in place in the host countries before the growth enhancing effects of FDI can be unleashed. Such a threshold level of human capital is to be found mostly in the more developed amongst the developing countries. And it is for this reason statistical studies suggest that FDI is most effective in promoting growth in countries which have achieved a threshold level of development. (V.N. Balasubramanyam, "Foreign Direct Investment in Developing Countries: Determinants and Impacts," OECD *Global Forum on International Investment*, November 26–27, 2001, 9)

Basic education and sound health are prerequisites for effective utilization of a labor force in LDCs. Fundamental weaknesses in one or both can cripple macroeconomic performance and perpetuate a condition of underdevelopment.

30

NATURAL DISASTER—1
—KILLER CYCLONE: A SOCIAL-ACCOUNTING RECONSTRUCTION—

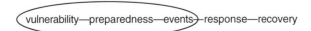

vulnerability—preparedness—events—response—recovery

The Sequence—Risk Factors for Mortality

30.1   PERCEPTIONS OF BASIC NEEDS

Let us begin with a picture. Human beings live in societies within nature. Basic human needs can be identified according to *time*: those that are day-to-day, year-to-year, and generation-to-generation. These are the 1, 2, and 3 below.

The day-to-day needs are called sustenance, *our daily bread*, to use the metaphor of a powerful prayer. The year-to-year needs are the renewal of the social subsistence, cycles of *sowing and reaping*. The generation-to-generation needs are twofold: both the sustainability of a society as well as the life-cycle of human existence *cradle to grave*.

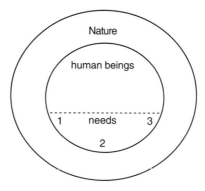

Most of the time, nature follows cyclic patterns that are well known and well adapted to. Sometimes these patterns are interrupted by extreme events. Imagine the circle above called 'Nature' *shaking violently*. Suddenly nothing can be taken for granted. The roots of survival are dangerously exposed. Many lives might be lost and a multitude of people face unspeakable sorrow and suffering. In a state of shock, the homeless and jobless seek sustenance. The social economy has abruptly broken down.

During normal times, the most basic needs are nutrition, shelter, clothing, healthcare, fuel—and the means to acquire them. During disasters, priorities can abruptly change. *Physical safety* often becomes the greatest need. Accurate information is needed to estimate the extent and duration of the threat.

Suppose a powerful cyclone is heading toward the coastal area of a poor country. In order to limit loss of life what are the primary considerations?

First of all, the people potentially affected must have ample warning of the coming storm. If people live in rural pre-industrial conditions, this cannot be taken for granted. With warnings issued and received, people need to prepare for weathering the storm in safe shelter, getting there by whatever means available. During a violent storm, moving to safe shelter is dangerous. If people evacuate at a late stage of the storm's approach, the dangers increase. Even if they reach safe shelter, injury may occur along the way.

30.2   DISASTER-ANALYSIS FRAMEWORK

The study of natural disasters can be seen as a sequence: vulnerability, preparedness, events, response, recovery. Many experts specialize in one of these. Disaster events and response get most of the attention in the press. Vulnerability is the least studied or discussed, but it is the most important because it impinges upon the other four.

Suppose a great cyclone strikes a bay populated by sleepy villages. Many great challenges now define the life of that region. In this case we focus on the second part of the sequence. There are a lot of issues here:

What is the magnitude and extent of the disaster? Whose lives have been lost or are still at risk? What response is needed immediately? How will relief goods and services be acquired, transported, and distributed? What temporary arrangements can bring some normalcy to the victims who have lost housing? How are the destitute going to survive? What will become of debt burdens that are now unpayable? What are the best ways to approach reconstruction? How long will this take? How are these different challenges going to be financed? How effective are the various response and recovery efforts?

vulnerability—preparedness—(events—response—recovery)

For some purposes, the first part of the sequence holds the key to analysis. If a certain location is historically vulnerable to cyclones, disaster preparedness requires an understanding of the geographic and human vulnerabilities. Who are the most vulnerable populations? How do they get their information? What concerns may inhibit them from seeking safer shelter?

Disaster shelters must be accessible but usually they are only going to serve their function correctly if people are familiar with the buildings because they serve other regular functions—such as schools or houses of worship.

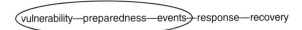

(vulnerability—preparedness—events)—response—recovery

There is another use for the first part of the sequence. Let us consider again the great cyclone we were musing about. In that case, were looked *forward* from the event. Now, in order to understand fatalities from the disaster, we need to look *backward* from the event.

Who survived and who died? Can we detect economic patterns of survival and mortality? Can we detect patterns based upon gender or age? The key to successful analysis is a good understanding of the relevant vulnerabilities. This reveals the risk factors for mortality.

30.3   DISASTER EPIDEMIOLOGY

Epidemiology usually refers to the study of disease patterns in human populations. In the past few decades, the principles of epidemiology have been applied to the study of every kind of disaster, taking into account any situation that might threaten the health or life of vulnerable populations. This creative expansion of methodology has resulted in the field of disaster epidemiology.

Bangladesh has long been the center of disease and disaster studies. The country is beleaguered by water-related disease and death. Water floods in from the north, comes up in storm surges in the south, falls in torrents from the sky, is arsenic-contaminated in the wells, and carries numerous diseases. When I lived in Dhaka I bought a bottle of water called 'Life' at a pharmacy. It made me seriously ill for days. 'Life' contained the seeds of death.

Three times in recent memory—1988, 1998, and 2004—most of the country was flooded. This led to a great loss of property and a long disruption of daily life. However, in Bangladesh, cyclones are the greatest threat to life.

At least half a million Bangladeshis have perished in cyclones since 1960. One cyclone took about 138,000 lives in late April 1991. According to the article we study in detail, 95 percent of the coastal households surveyed received the official cyclone warning, but only 13 percent sought shelter before the storm surge. In most cases, they underestimated the danger. Many feared falling victim to looters. In keeping with the national culture, many surrendered their futures fatalistically to the 'Will of Allah'.

An 11 person team, lead by C. Bern, prepared a 'Risk Factors for Mortality' analysis of that storm for the *Bulletin of the World Health Organization* (1993). In their words:

> [W]e conducted a rapid epidemiological assessment of two cyclone-devastated areas to identify factors that might have determined why some people survived and others did not. (73–74)

The authors of the risk-factors study (hereafter RFS) state their hypothesis:

> We hypothesized that survival would be related to the ability of individuals to reach a reinforced structure in good time, and would thus be associated with housing type, timely receipt and understanding of the cyclone warning, and how early in the course of the storm individuals sought shelter. (74–75)

Their article has four parts: Introduction, Survey Methods, Results, and Discussion. We are concerned with presenting their results in a transparent way as an example of clear social accounting. This is not an easy task. The results are presented in a jumble, typos are frequent, and the data has gaps.

Their results begin with mortality. Following our model, we begin with identifying vulnerability.

30.4   SURVIVAL ACCOUNTING

The sample population surveyed in the RFS lived on the Bay of Bengal, in the direct path of the storm. Most of this area floods during storm surges. The scarce 'high ground' is relatively expensive and is generally only available to institutions and the best-off families. Only 2 percent lived in brick or concrete housing, possibly multistorey, designed to withstand the fury of a cyclone. Thus, the population was subject to a double life-threatening vulnerability: location and housing.

TABLE 1: CORE VULNERABILITY

27	live in safe houses	(*pukka*: brick or concrete)
1094	live in unsafe houses	(*kutcha*: bamboo and thatch)
1121	total sample population	

According to the RFS, the cyclone warning occurred at night. The reader is left with the impression that everyone in the sample population was at home at the time and that the entire storm episode occurred at night. The 'prewarning' information below and the housing information above are the same.

Table 2 is based upon Figure 2 in the RFS, with corrections for typos there. They divide the situation into four periods: prewarning, warning, approach of the storm surge, and impact of the storm surge.

TABLE 2: VULNERABILITY DURING DISASTER EPISODE

	prewarning	warning	approach	impact
in safe shelter	27 (2%)	40 (4%)	151 (13%)	385 (34%)
at risk	1094 (98%)	1081 (96%)	970 (87%)	736 (66%)

Table 2 is explained in the RFS in the following way:

> In response to the warning, which most respondents reported hearing 3–6 hours prior to the storm surge, only 40 individuals (4%) sought and reached safe shelter. When the flood waters first reached the area, 10–60 minutes before the storm surge, 151 persons (13%) were in safe shelter. In all, 385 persons (33%) [sic] had reached safe shelter by the moment of impact of the storm surge; none of these people died. (75)

That paragraph ends with this somber sentence: "In contrast, of the 736 persons at risk, [according to survivors] 162 (22 percent) drowned in the flood waters" (75). We use the last column of Table 2 with this statistic to construct a T-account of mortality and survival:

TABLE 3: MORTALITY AND SURVIVAL

1121	population		736	at risk	
− 162	died	(14%)	− 162	died	(22%)
959	survived		574	survived at risk	
			+ 385	in safe shelter	
			959	survived	

30.5   PEOPLE IN SAFE SHELTER

We now focus on the people who reached safe shelter by the time of impact. Table 4 is constructed out of information presented on pages 75–76 of the RFS. "By far the greatest number of people in safe shelter were those who sought refuge in small public buildings such as markets, schools and mosques. A few private *pukka* homes also provided shelter to immediate neighbours" (77). But: "No one took shelter in a neighbor's [superior] house until the impact of the storm surge" (76).

TABLE 4: PEOPLE IN SAFE SHELTER—BY BUILDING TYPE

in public building	219	(57%)
in neighbor's home	90	(23%)
in designated cyclone shelters	51	(13%)
in own home	25	(6%)
	385	(100%)

Five cyclone shelters existed in the survey area. Two of them were well used "while the other three were almost unused because high-water precluded access to them, even before the impact of the storm surge" (76). (The RFS recommendation addresses this issue: "All new schools, community centers, health clinics, and mosques in coastal areas should be . . . two- or three-storeyed, reinforced structures . . . designated . . . as . . . shelters" [77].)

A demographic breakdown of Table 4 is constructed below from information contained in Figure 3 of the RFS—constructed after recalculating erroneous percent computations on that figure.

More males reached safe shelter than females. The ratio is almost two-to-one for people 40 years or older! However, more young girls reached safe shelter than young boys. Table 5 would be more informative if we had data showing population figures for the entire area before the cyclone. Without that information we cannot judge how representative the survey population was.

TABLE 5: PEOPLE IN SAFE SHELTER—BY GENDER AND AGE

females	180	(47%)
males	205	(53%)
Total	385	(100%)
females age < 10	67	(37%)
female age 10–39	95	(53%)
female age ≥ 40	18	(10%)
Total	180	(100%)
males age < 10	63	(31%)
males age 10–39	107	(52%)
males age ≥ 40	35	(17%)
Total	205	(100%)

30.6   PEOPLE AT RISK

We now consider the people who did not go to safe shelter or tried to reach it and failed. This most crucial section was difficult to piece together because of severe gaps and ambiguities in the RFS.

The RFS identifies four locations for people at risk but does not account for them fully. On Table 6, numbers are given for 'swept away' and 'floated on some object'. We should note that the number swept away (285) exceeds by more than a hundred the number who died (162).

It is not possible to record numbers for those who 'sought high ground' or 'took refuge in trees' since that data is not included in the RFS. Also: was all *kutcha* housing destroyed during the storm or rendered entirely useless? The RFS does not say. But we may guess that most of those who 'floated on some object' were clinging to the wreckage of their homes or to floatable household goods.

TABLE 6: PEOPLE AT RISK

swept away	285	(< 39 %)
floated on some object	179	(24 %)
sought high ground	?	
took refuge in trees	?	
Total	736	(100%)

Mortality rates are supplied (on 75 of RFS) and are recorded below in Table 7. The 'swept-away' category warrants particular consideration. According to Tables 6, of those at risk, just under 39 percent were swept away. According to Table 7, of the 285 people swept away, just over 39 percent died. We can calculate the number as 111 (out of the 162 who died). The RFS does not tell us how the 'swept-away survivors' survived.

TABLE 7: MORTALITY RATES FOR PEOPLE AT RISK (%)

swept away	> 39
sought high ground	22
floated on some object	15
took refuge in trees	11

Women and children were identified as the groups most likely to die if they did not reach safe shelter. Women over the age of 40 and children less than 10 had the highest mortality rates. We cannot tell if the second category of women was in the range of 40–59 or included all women over 40. Elderly men were not mentioned at all. They, too, are likely to have been high risk and high mortality.

TABLE 8: MORTALITY RATES FOR HIGH-RISK GROUPS (%)

women aged > 60 years	40
women aged > 40 years	31
children aged < 10 years	26
men aged > 60	?

30.7   FOLLOW-UP COMMENTS

I wrote the first draft of this chapter in Honolulu, in February 1995, soon after my beloved Kobe was devastated by a terrible earthquake. After presenting the paper to a group of international public health students, I had a chance meeting with a gentleman from Bangladesh, in the Hale Manoa dorm at the East-West Center. He was having his early morning meal, following the custom of Ramadan; I was having a coffee. After some small talk, I asked him some questions about the Cyclone of 1991. He answered my questions clearly. Although I cannot verify his comments, they were very interesting. We talked for more than an hour.

Consistent with the RFS, he said that the mortality rate was high because people failed to respond to the warnings in time—they were 'complacent because of past false alarms'. On further questioning, information emerged showing some cultural and economic logic behind the villagers' behavior:

(1) Most poor villagers were reluctant, for economic reasons, to abandon their animals. Moving them to safe shelter during the storm was difficult and dangerous. The RFS is silent on this. However, as stated in the RFS, they were concerned about other property, especially clothing and kitchen goods.

(2) The cyclone hit eleven days after the Festival of Animal Sacrifice (which occurs two moons plus ten days after Ramadan, during the last month on the Islamic Calendar). Based upon an episode from the life of Abraham, the sacrifice of goats is central to celebrating the festival throughout Bangladesh. *If the cyclone had hit a few weeks earlier, the loss of life would have been much greater* since the people most at risk in poor housing— 98 percent of the population!—would have been greatly reluctant, for religious reasons, to abandon their goats.

(3) The shelters were, basically, strong boxes with windows. No provision was made for communal preparation of food, no water was stored and sanitation was poor. Few people would go into such a place until desperate.

(4) The poverty of villages and villagers was possibly *understated* by the housing statistic (2 percent in safe housing, 98 percent at risk). They were without electricity, had little access to TV, newspapers were rare, and, while radios were common, batteries were expensive. No local income was adequate for buying a safe house. The cyclone-safe houses were built from incomes earned in a richer Islamic country or in a Bangladeshi city.

Finally: How did the swept-away survivors survive? People pulled out to sea, or pulled under, could not survive. But the gentleman from Bangladesh suggested a novel idea, one essentially biblical: the storm surge may have *thrown some people up*, on to higher ground.

31

NATURAL DISASTER—2
—KATRINA DESTROYS NEW ORLEANS—

The Wikipedia entry for Hurricane Katrina is excellent. Anyone interested in more information should start there:

http://en.Wikipedia.org/wiki/Hurricane_Katrina

WINDOW ON PERSONAL VULNERABILITY	ORLEANS PARISH	LOUISIANA	UNITED STATES
population—2003 (millions)	0.47	4.5	290
population growth—1990–2000 (%)	−2.5	6	13
population growth—April 2000–July 2003 (%)	−3.2	0.6	3.3
African American—2000 (%)	67	33	12
median household income—1999 ($)	27,133	32,566	41,994
persons below poverty line—1999 (%)	28	20	12
students eating free/subsidized meals (%)*	77	—	—
fourth-graders proficient in reading (%)*	13	—	—
eighth-graders proficient in reading (%)*	5	—	—

Note: http://quickfacts.census.gov (percentages rounded in most cases) (accessed October 1, 2005).
Los Angeles Times, September 17, 2005.

31.1 THE BIG EASY

> Though providing protection from weaker storms, the levees would also trap any water that gets inside—from breach, overtopping or torrential downpour—in a catastrophic storm.
>
> "Filling the bowl" is the worst potential scenario for a natural disaster in the United States, emergency officials say. ("Washing Away—Part 2: The Big One," *Times-Picayune*, June 24, 2002)

In 1718, Jean Baptiste le Moyne, Sieur de Bienville created a settlement on a sliver of marshland between the Mississippi River and Lake Pontchartrain. It proved to have both economic and strategic value. Being on a natural flood-plain and prone to heavy rainfall, only the higher ground was used at first. Much of the area between the river and lake was a geographic bowl. No sane person would consider building a city there.

As commerce grew, so did the settlement. Bit by bit, marshland was drained and put to use. New Orleans was well situated to serve as a port for the products brought down the Mississippi River. Eventually this included large quantities of cotton, grain, and sugar. There was never a conscious decision to build a city there. It happened gradually, over a long period of time.

The United States acquired New Orleans in the Louisiana Purchase of 1803. The city was home to French, Spanish, English, African, and Creole peoples. During the War of 1812, the British navy failed in their assault on the city.

By 1840, the city had 100,000 residents. At the time of the Civil War, New Orleans was the second largest city in the South, after Baltimore. It was captured early in the war without a battle, sparing it the scars of fighting.

After the Civil War, European immigrants and former slaves poured in. Black musicians nicknamed it the Big Easy because they could find work there.

Each time the population expanded, flood protection was a key concern. Pre-industrial methods of land reclamation and floodwalls gave way to industrial methods. This enabled further population growth. In the 1920s, the modern system of water pumping and levee building was developed.

Hurricane Betsy caused much flooding in 1965. Defenses could not with-stand the impact of a stronger storm. Although defenses were strengthened, population growth, the destruction of natural barriers against hurricanes, and the gradual sinking of the city itself left it terribly exposed to the Big One.

The social pattern was also disturbing. With almost 500,000 residents, New Orleans was two-thirds black, one-quarter poor, and two-fifths illiterate!

If Mother Nature wanted to show America her might, this was the Big Easy.

31.2   Vulnerability

A major hurricane could decimate the region, but flooding from even a moderate storm could kill thousands. It's just a matter of time. ("Washing Away—Part 2: The Big One," *Times-Picayune*, June 24, 2002)

New Orleans was well known as the most *probable* catastrophic natural disaster facing the country. It is important to first consider aspects of vulnerability.

31.2.1   Physical Vulnerability

A great deal of the city is below sea level and is likely to flood if there are levee breaches. This vulnerability affects some upper-income areas but affects large low-income areas at the bottom of 'the bowl'. The government claimed the levee system could withstand a Category 3 hurricane. But the natural defenses have been badly weakened decade after decade by land uses detrimental to marshes and island barriers.

Due to natural and human causes, the entire delta region of southern Louisiana is sinking into the Gulf of Mexico. The Gulf is about 20 miles closer to New Orleans than it was during Hurricane Betsy in 1965. As the Mississippi delta sinks, saltwater flows farther inland, destroying the marsh ecosystem. Canal building, drilling, and dredging speed up the breakup of marshes. At one time the marshes absorbed much of the energy of a storm, reducing wind speed and storm surges. Now the city is catastrophically vulnerable to *any* direct hit.

As natural protections deteriorate, man-made defenses sink and weaken. While the land, including the city, has been sinking, the sea level has been rising. During the past century, this combination has added several feet to all storm surges. There is currently no defense against a surge from a major storm. The winds from such a strong direct hit can damage almost any structure in New Orleans.

31.2.2   Human Vulnerability

The population of New Orleans has been shrinking steadily for decades:

> in 1960: 628,000 city residents, 37 percent black
> in 2000: 485,000 city residents, 67 percent black

In the shrinkage, it had gone from majority white to majority black.

According to the website of the New Orleans Convention and Visitors Bureau, the *illiteracy* rate in the city was 38 percent.

The median household income was smaller than Louisiana's (one of the poorest states in America) and about 40 percent smaller than the median income in United States. Over a quarter of the population lived below the poverty line. Most students ate free or subsidized meals. Many families depended upon public welfare to survive.

The city was a legendary murder and drug capital. Police corruption was common. Louisiana was considered the third most corrupt state in the nation.

Some of the lowest land was entirely occupied by blacks. The Lower Ninth Ward was more than 98 percent black and more than one-third lived in poverty: 35 percent of black households did not have a car.

Even among the employed, living paycheck to paycheck was common. Many adults had no checking or savings account. Emergency savings were small.

These vulnerabilities were ripe for a strong storm: much of the population of New Orleans was seriously undereducated, had income and employment insecurity, lacked net assets, lived on terribly vulnerable land, were immobile, and had no coherent social protection system to turn to during times of danger.

31.2.3   *FAIR WARNING—EFFORTS TO EXPLAIN THE DANGER*

After the near miss by Hurricane Georges in 1998, there were various attempts to draw attention to the city's unique exposure.

An award-winning assessment was published in June 2002, as a five-part series in *The Times Picayune*. Named 'Washing Away', it covered five topics: (1) In Harms Way, (2) The Big One, (3) Exposure's Cost, (4) Tempting Fate, and (5) Cost of Survival. In "The Big One," they warned:

> Hundreds of thousands would be left homeless, and it would take months to dry out the area and begin to make it livable. But there wouldn't be much for residents to come home to. The local economy would be in ruins.

'Washing Away' emphasized the possibility of catastrophe from a modest-sized hurricane because of the loss of wetlands between New Orleans and the Gulf of Mexico. Insurance risks and costs received due attention. Many public and private buildings were uninsured, either because of redlining or poverty.

Well-known publications also gave 'filling the bowl' some dramatic attention:

—*Popular Mechanics*, "New Orleans Is Sinking" (September 2001)
—*Scientific American*, "Drowning New Orleans" (October 2001)
—*National Geographic*, "Gone with the Water" (October 2004)

The Natural Hazards Center in Boulder, Colorado, published an article in their "Disasters Waiting to Happen Series" called, "What if Hurricane Ivan Had Not Missed New Orleans?" (November 2004).

A NOVA program on Public TV covering the most important issues found in the publications above, in a January 2005 episode.

Finally, in this limited survey, FX aired a docudrama in June 2005 on possible economic impacts of the Big One hitting the city. As a clever blog writer said, "By the time there's a *docudrama*, I think you've had adequate warning."

31.3   PREPAREDNESS

Beyond terrorism, this was the one event I was most concerned with always. (Joe M. Allbaugh, the former Bush campaign manager who served as his first head of FEMA)

New Orleans dodged the bullet twice in recent years—first Hurricane Georges in 1998 and then Hurricane Ivan in 2004. Both storms were on a collision course with the city, prompting evacuations. Both storms changed course and struck land to the east of the city with minor effects in New Orleans.

Before we look at the physical and human preparedness as of August 2005, we should give some attention to those near misses. They tell us much about the mentality of 'preparedness'.

31.3.1   *FAIR WARNING—NEAR MISSES*

Soon after Hurricane Ivan, Mike Davis wrote a scathing article titled "Poor, Black and Left Behind." The first three paragraphs are worth quoting in full:

The evacuation of New Orleans in the face of Hurricane Ivan looked sinisterly like Strom Thurmond's version of the Rapture. Affluent white people fled the Big Easy in their SUVs, while the old and car-less—mainly Black—were left behind in their below-sea-level shotgun shacks and aging tenements to face the watery wrath.

New Orleans had spent decades preparing for inevitable submersion by the storm surge of a class-five hurricane. Civil defense officials conceded they had ten thousand body bags on hand to deal with the worst-case scenario. But no one seemed to have bothered to devise a plan to evacuate the city's poorest or most infirm residents. The day before the hurricane hit the Gulf Coast, New Orleans' daily, *The Times-Picayune*, ran an alarming story about the "large group . . . mostly concentrated in poorer neighborhoods" who wanted to evacuate but couldn't.

Only at the last moment, with winds churning Lake Pontchartrain, did Mayor Ray Nagin reluctantly open the Louisiana Superdome and a few schools to desperate residents. He was reportedly worried that lower-class refugees might damage or graffiti the Superdome.

After the near miss by Hurricane Georges, a proposal was made to establish a public bus system for emergency evacuation. A different approach was preferred. Faith-based organizations were enlisted to develop a ride-sharing program. This had the support of some emergency managers, NGOs, and local universities. Dissenters were powerless to influence policy.

After the near miss by Ivan, this approach was still preferred over a public system. It was 'less bureaucratic' than a system requiring the city to devise and test a sound public bus evacuation plan and the state to devise and test a sound public shelter plan in the interior of Louisiana.

31.3.2 PHYSICAL PREPAREDNESS

The *quadruple* danger—sinking city, sinking levees, loss of wetlands protection and increased hurricane activity—was well known. Levee-system inadequacies were well documented. Even so, flood protection was long under funded.

After 9/11, the funding was cut several times. In 2003, federal funding was greatly reduced. In 2004, the Army Corp of Engineers received less than 20 percent of their requested budget—enough to pay salaries. The funds were diverted to homeland security and the Iraq war. This trend continued in 2005.

31.3.3 HUMAN PREPAREDNESS

In 1997, Congress ordered FEMA to develop an evacuation plan. The money was diverted to a causeway bridge study. In 1999, Congress strengthened its request, ordering 'an evacuation plan for a Category 3 or greater storm, a levee break, flood or other natural disaster for the New Orleans area'. That money, too, went to the causeway commission. In both cases, the intent of Congress was to provide a way out for most vulnerable populations.

The official New Orleans 'disaster preparedness' guidelines were equally useless to the most vulnerable residents of the city. The page on 'general evacuation guidelines' tells people to 'take your disaster supply kit' and 'if you need a ride, try to go with a neighbor, friend, or relative'.

What was this disaster supply kit?

DISASTER SUPPLY KIT—Assemble the supplies you might need. Store them in an easy-to-carry container. Include:

• A supply of water for drinking and cooking. (One gallon per person per day). Stored in sealed, unbreakable containers. • A supply of non-perishable packaged or canned food, and a non-electric can opener. • A change of clothing, rain gear and sturdy shoes. • Blankets or sleeping bags (1 per person). • A first aid kit and prescription medications. • An extra pair of eyeglasses, contact lens supplies. • A battery-powered radio, flashlight and plenty of extra batteries. • Credit cards and cash in a water proof container. • An extra set of car keys. • A list of important family information; the style and serial number of medical devices such as pacemakers. • Special items for infants, elderly or disabled family members, such as extra diapers, hearing aids, and medical certification. • Books, magazines, cards, toys and games. • Important documents in water-proof containers. (Insurance Policies) • Photographs or videotapes of personal property as well as an up-to-date inventory of items (include serial numbers). • Hygiene supplies. • Shovel, axe and other useful tools. • Fire extinguisher. http://www.cityofno.com/portal.aspx?portal=46&tabid=14 (accessed September 11, 2005)

How could *any family* store such a kit in an 'easy-to-carry container'? How could such a list have *any use* to the disabled, ill, elderly, car-less, or poor?

31.4 Events

[I]t should have been a blinding flash of the obvious to everybody that when you order a mandatory evacuation, you can't expect everybody to evacuate on their own. These are people who don't have credit cards; only one in 10 families at that level in New Orleans have a car. (Colin Powell, speaking to Barbara Walters, September 9, 2005)

We divide the events section into three parts: Warning and Evacuation, Katrina Strikes East of the City, and Post-Katrina Chaos.

31.4.1 Warning and Evacuation

Early morning Saturday, August 27, Katrina reached Category 3. The Hurricane Center predicted a direct hit on New Orleans sometime on Monday. The storm nearly followed that path, sparing the city a direct hit before making landfall.

The governor asked President Bush to declare a federal state of emergency. The president granted her request. The federal emergency declaration authorized the Department of Homeland Security and FEMA to coordinate relief. The state police set up 'contraflow' on the main highways. It took about four times the usual period to reach destinations such as Jackson or Houston.

The voluntary evacuation gave way to a mandatory call. The Superdome was opened for shelter on Sunday morning. Katrina was upgraded to Category 4, then 5. The Hurricane Center issued stark warning of catastrophic damage to New Orleans and other areas in the path of the storm. Poor folk—left behind.

31.4.2 Katrina Strikes East of the City

Katrina came ashore as a Category 3. Hurricane force winds started to hit the city at 5 am. At 9 am the eye passed to the east of the city. Top wind speeds were estimated at 135 mph. The city was still entirely within the hurricane-force wind zone at 11 am, as Katrina moved north at 15 mph.

At 8:14 am the National Weather Service reported a levee breach on the east side of the city, along the Industrial Canal. Floods of 8–10 feet, it said, were expected in the Ninth Ward and St. Barnard Parish. This news became known to the *only* FEMA worker inside the city. He reported the breach to the head of FEMA by email. Michael Brown claimed he was unaware of any levee breach for at least another 24 hours! He did not read email carefully and ignored information from agents in the field.

In a stunning blow to relief capacity, the headquarters of the Louisiana National Guard flooded. They were located on some of the worst land! For the first 24 hours, the HQ was engaged in saving *itself* from the floods! There is no evidence anyone in Washington—or, on TV!—knew or cared.

There is something bizarre and troubling in this situation: *neither* decisive piece of information became known that day via TV news. Levee breaches were reported in the *Miami Herald* online Monday afternoon but they were not reported by network news until Tuesday. The debacle of the National Guard went unnoticed by TV News—and thus it went unnoticed in general.

These two decisive events—levee breach and National Guard HQ flooding—should have been reported by newswires and network news *immediately*. The chaos and bungled response efforts both derive their inevitability here. Network TV's lack of effectiveness or professionalism is seen in that, first, they were thrilled to play with the wind, then, they were happy to report *the places they go to* were okay!

31.4.3 POST-KATRINA CHAOS

Early Tuesday morning, A FEMA coordinator in Baton Rouge said, "I don't want to alarm everybody that, you know, New Orleans is filling up like a bowl. That's just not happening." In a sense he was right. It already had happened. By Tuesday afternoon, 80 percent of the city was underwater.

City officials opened the Convention Center and instructed exposed residents to gather there. Conditions at the Superdome deteriorated rapidly. On Wednesday, TV reported extensively on the desperate situation at the Convention Center where 20,000 were stranded. Chris Lawrence said on CNN:

> [T]his convention center is right in the heart of downtown . . . picture any downtown where . . . you live, Main Street, wherever. The main building, there's a dead body that has been sitting out there for two days. They put a blanket over him. These people are hungry. They're tired. They've got nowhere to go. They've got no answers, and they've got no communication whatsoever.

This went unnoticed by the FEMA director while TV covered it for hours! On Nightline, Ted Koppel asked Brown, "Don't you guys watch television? Don't you guys listen to the radio?" Brown replied, "We learned about it factually today that that's what existed."

Relief efforts swung into gear sometime on Friday, four days late but much welcome. On Sunday FEMA reported the complete evacuation of the Superdome and Convention Center. It claimed to have evacuated 150,000 people. *The Times-Picayune* said that day, in a blistering open letter to Bush:

> Every official at [FEMA] should be fired, Director Michael Brown especially . . .
>
> Yet, when you met with Mr. Brown Friday morning, you told him, "You're doing a heck of a job." That's unbelievable.
>
> There were thousands of people at the Convention Center because the riverfront is high ground. The fact that so many people had reached there on foot is proof that rescue vehicles could have gotten there, too . . . No expense should have been spared. No excuses should have been voiced. Especially not one as preposterous as the claim that New Orleans couldn't be reached.

NATURAL DISASTER—2   291

31.5 RESPONSE

It is extremely important that a commission independent of the executive and legislative branches analyzes the Katrina disaster and the events leading up to it. (Kathleen Tierney, director, Natural Hazards Center, University of Colorado)

We concentrate on the response failure at every level of government, beginning with the city itself. Mention must also be made of the inability of the national media to bring vital information to public attention in a timely way.

31.5.1 CITY-GOVERNMENT FAILURE

Just as Colin Powell said, it is a blinding flash of the obvious that a mandatory evacuation can only be fully effective if the city provides transportation for those without the means. The faith-based method will not work for at least three reasons: (1) the better-off families are likely to focus on plans to save themselves, (2) the better-off families need space in their vehicles for their 'disaster-supply kit', and, (3) the better-off families cannot be expected to pay hotel charges for extra passengers even if there is space in their vehicles.

31.5.2 STATE-GOVERNMENT FAILURE

The evacuation failure also falls on the state government. While the city should have established an evacuation system for vulnerable populations based upon public transportation, it could not provide shelter for them outside of the city. Shelter in the interior of the state had to be organized at the state level. Given the large vulnerable population, this would have required detailed planning.

After Katrina hit, the Louisiana National Guard failed to respond. At the time, the diversion of Guard personnel and equipment to Iraq was widely commented on. While relevant, this was not the decisive factor. *The National Guard headquarters flooded and was preoccupied with saving itself!* This came to light a month after Katrina, on September 28, 2005 in the *New York Times*:

> The morning Hurricane Katrina thundered ashore, Louisiana National Guard commanders thought they were prepared to save their state. But when 15-foot floodwaters swept into their headquarters, cut their communications and disabled their high-water trucks, they had their hands full just saving themselves.
>
> For a crucial 24 hours after landfall on Aug. 29, Guard officers said, they were preoccupied with protecting their nerve center from the waves topping the windows at Jackson Barracks and rescuing soldiers who could not swim. The next morning, they had to evacuate their entire headquarters force of 375 guardsmen by boat and helicopter to the Superdome.

One needs to wonder who located the Louisiana National Guard HQ on the worse land from the point of view of its most critical mission!?

31.5.3   FEDERAL-GOVERNMENT FAILURE

Although the potential for this disaster was always recognized by FEMA, the federal government commitment to building and maintaining the levee system was undermined by years of under funding. Once the city flooded, a massive federal response was essential and it was not forthcoming.

Upon request of the governor, the White House issued a pre-Katrina Declaration of Emergency. The districts named in the declaration were the *least likely* to suffer from the storm. The wrong 'half' of the list was published.

It took FEMA more than 24 hours to recognize the flooding of the city. FEMA never recognized the flooding of the National Guard HQ—thus it never acknowledged the complete inability of the state to respond to the crisis. At each step, the director of FEMA was worse informed than the average viewer of television news. FEMA's pathetic response reflected his ignorance.

Although Katrina hit on a Monday, President Bush made his first statement on Wednesday. On Friday, his ignorance of events was so vast an aide had to show him a DVD containing television news clips. The same day he praised the FEMA director. In fact, significant assistance only began to pour in that day.

There were numerous reports of FEMA interfering with private relief efforts by competent organizations. Federal red tape was so severe, other states could not effectively respond. Some of the 'responders' sent by Washington *after* Katrina struck had to take a two-day training course before deployment!

Perhaps none of this should be surprising. FEMA was considered a well-run agency before 2001. After that, unqualified political cronies staffed the top positions. FEMA's mission was degraded when the Department of Homeland Security absorbed it. Poor funding further undermined it.

President Carter founded FEMA in 1979, based upon three commitments: (1) it would be led by disaster-management experts, (2) it would be an independent agency, and (3) it would be adequately funded. The Bush administration negated all three, to the detriment of New Orleans and the disgrace of America.

31.5.4   MEDIA FAILURE

Last, the information catastrophe: two deadly events were not reported on and analyzed *the day of the hurricane*: the breach of levees and the flooding of the Louisiana National Guard Headquarters! This is where the media lost the thread of the story. Instead they went on about troops in Iraq and bad planning. Yes, the disaster planning was terrible. But these two events defined the failure.

The media's failure should be investigated internally and by a public panel appointed by Congress. Local media did much better during that terrible week. It should get praise and more of the national airtime during disasters.

31.6   RECOVERY

> Given this kind of catastrophe . . . do you rebuild it? . . . Especially since we are below sea level and it can happen again the next week . . . Planners need to think about that: Do we repeat Bienville's mistake? (Walter Maestri, Jefferson Parish emergency director, quoted in "Washing Away—Part 1: In Harm's Way," *Times-Picayune*, June 23, 2002)

The recovery tasks are enormous. We begin with the levees. Prudent reconstruction of the city depends upon them. Then we discuss the port. After that we have a page on the poor followed by a page on the rich.

31.6.1   LEVEE SYSTEM

Inside the system of levees lurked inferior materials and inadequate designs. Breaches occurred under Category 1 conditions, well below the design goal of Category 3 protection. This may be a huge scandal for the Army Corps.

The levee system is greatly weakened by Katrina. Even restoring the levees to their previous level of protection will be difficult and time consuming. The immediate goal is to restore the system then improve it.

It took a generation to get the levees supposedly to a Category 3 standard—only to learn that weak spots were broken by the indirect hit of a large and strong storm. It is not certain the levees can achieve a higher level of protection unless the wetlands and barrier islands are restored to some extent. In the quest for Category 5 protection, a $30 billion project is under discussion.

Making the levees taller will add weight, causing them to sink faster. For every additional vertical foot they must be widened three feet. This will require the purchase of adjacent land, adding greatly to the cost.

31.6.2   PORT ACTIVITY

As the fourth largest port in America, New Orleans is vital to commerce based upon the Mississippi River. It used to move more than 11 million tons of cargo per year. Katrina obliterated 30 percent of the port, with extensive damage to roads and bridges. It is a high priority for federal funds. Restoring the port is also vital for restarting the local economy.

Cold storage and concrete production were knocked out. Perhaps half of the production and processing activities will be relocated off of the floodplain. Some of the port activities can be moved to smaller ports in the area.

The port currently operates at less than its former capacity. Full restoration is expected during 2006. Rebuilding and relocation costs will be at least one billion dollars.

31.6.3   IMPOVERISHED EVACUEES

City residents are scattered across America. Because the flooding of lowlands was widespread, they range from the illiterate poor to the previously well off who have lost everything. They now suffer additional indignities as there is no system in place to deal with them effectively.

After Hurricane Katrina hit, one-fifth were housed in shelters while four-fifths were housed in hotels. They are now scattered to the winds, with no comprehensive housing plan in place. The illiterate poor might fall through the cracks of this system because of their inability to deal with paperwork.

Immediately after the storm, FEMA purchased $1.5 billion dollars of RVs and mobile homes. Their plan to create trailer parks stalled while they try to deal with land leases, zoning laws, local opposition, and policy issues.

Rental vouchers are the better method, if illiterates receive assistance. Trailer parks are likely to re-create ghetto patterns. The goal should be the establishment of a stable residence in a location of their choice, with education and employment opportunities nearby. The Department of Housing and Urban Development should replace FEMA. It is better suited to run such a program.

A generous resettlement fund—perhaps $50,000 per evacuee—is needed by the people. Many of the evacuees need classes in literacy and small-business accounting. They need access to stable employment or access to small-enterprise credit.

31.6.4   LOWLANDS

Of the tens of thousands of buildings in Louisiana uninhabitable after the storm, the majority are in the lowlands of New Orleans. Strong arguments can be made against rebuilding many of them and possibly most of them.

Flood and hurricane risks are so great, private-insurance companies are unlikely to underwrite policies. The federal government should not be expected to do so.

Even if reconstruction loans and insurance coverage were available, the new structures would have to meet both flood and hurricane codes. This would require the construction of reinforced structures on well-designed stilts. They would be expensive to build and expensive to rent or own. Even middle-class families could not afford such housing—let alone the poor.

On this basis, only the wealthier lowlands are likely to be rebuilt. This would include Lakeview, even though it is prone to severe flooding. Lowlands adjacent to higher ground can probably be raised, although at great cost.

Equity considerations should impel us to support generous resettlement funds for displaced residents who have little hope otherwise. Environmental considerations should induce us to support the return of lowlands to nature. New aquatic parks could help revitalize and diversify tourism and become a new source of local employment.

31.6.5 *View from the Highlands*

The well-off residents of the dry Uptown neighborhoods perceive the opportunity to influence reconstruction plans and profit from the flurry of construction activity. They also see this as an opportunity to change the demographic, geographic, and political realities of the city.

The tendency to want to rebuild a smaller but more modern New Orleans has been reinforced by a map published on the front page of *The Times-Picayune* (Thursday, November 3, 2005). It came with a long two-tone headline:

> An 1878 map reveals that may be our ancestors were right to build on higher ground . . . Almost every place that was uninhabited in 1878 flooded in 2005 after Katrina.

The huge underclass, atrocious public schools, and high crime rates have been swept away by the floods. They are unlikely to be allowed back. The following statistics highlight the most important demographic facts of the past generation along with a forward-looking estimate that would satisfy the Highlands view:

in 1960: 628,000 city residents, 37 percent black

in 2000: 485,000 city residents, 67 percent black

in 2006: 200,000 city residents, 30 percent black
projected in 2016: about 300,000 city residents, 30 percent black[?]

The hurricane has accelerated the shrinkage while reversing the racial balance. Economic and geographic circumstances will result in a smaller and whiter population. White-flight to the suburbs might be reversed some.

Although the view from the highlands can be seen as insensitive, elitist, and possibly racist, downsizing is prudent. The levee system might be precarious *always*. Evacuation of a large population might *always* tax the road system and any public evacuation plan. A population ceiling might be necessary. Bienville's mistake cannot be undone but it should not be compounded again.

31.6.6 *Relief and Recovery Spending*

The lethargic underresponse by Bush was replaced with an extravagant promise, pledging 'one of the largest reconstruction efforts the world has ever seen.' A $200 billion price tag did not sit well with fiscal conservatives. Project design is a daunting task and there are many disagreements about what reconstruction projects should cost and what should get priority.

Although there has been considerable public discussion in the city regarding priorities, the final priorities will probably emerge out of private discussions and deals. The pattern of spending has already been set to prefer cronies at federal, state, and city levels. Fighting over the total budget and its allocation is fierce. There is a lot at stake. Fortunes are being made and lost.

31.7   THE BIG UNEASY

Hurricane Katrina did more than physical damage; it was a blow to our self-image as a nation. (Paul Krugman, "The Big Uneasy," *New York Times*, September 23, 2005)

Every aspect of this disaster should make us uneasy. There are a lot of 'could haves' in this sticky situation. Flood damage could have been prevented if the levee system had received the funds promised by the federal government. Even if the funding had been available, the levee system was itself suspect in terms of materials used and the reliability of levees when under stress. The levee system in spots catastrophically *underperformed*.

Many of the people stranded could have been evacuated before the storm if the city and state had prepared for it. Faith-based 'evacuation initiatives' failed while none based upon science or social science were seriously considered.

The posthurricane response could have begun sooner if the state national guard had placed its HQ outside of the floodplain. Assistance from other states could have been useful if federal red tape had not gotten in the way. The federal response could have been credible if FEMA had had professional management. The scattered poor could have better life prospects if they had access to generous resettlement funds plus educational and employment opportunities.

The scattered illiterate poor are getting nowhere in the new maze they call life. This is a scattered uneasy without a voice, forgotten by the media, entangled in terrible services from 'authorities'.

Throwing more than one hundred billion dollars at reconstruction should make us more uneasy. The small-scale looting after Katrina is possibly being replaced by looting on a grand scale. Billions of dollars are pouring into one of the most corrupt states in America, intended for one of the most corrupt industries—construction. Huge contracts are going to companies known for their high level political connections. The money pouring in is so large small players can get rich, too.

Finally, the *perpetual* physical vulnerability of New Orleans should make our unease intense. According to posthurricane data, Katrina produced winds of only 95 mph over the east end of Lake Pontchartrain and about 65 mph over the west end. Is there any sanity in fully rebuilding on the flood-prone lowlands? Some common sense is needed.

Ominously, Katrina was *not* necessarily the Big One. A direct hit from a Katrina-class hurricane would inflict huge damage from wind as well as water, smashing wooden housing and glass buildings in the highlands. It would force almost everyone to consider scaling down the city forever. But Katrina *was* big enough to expose layers of rot near the surface of the American Dream. Ag shame!

32

ALTERNATIVE DEVELOPMENT

SARVODAYA	GRAMEEN BANK
5: Assist Other Villages	
4: Access Economic Services of SEEDS	
3: Incorporate Sarvodaya Shramadana Village	3: Life-Cycle Services
2: Social Infrastructure Building	2: Housing Loan
1: Psychological Infrastructure Building	1: Working-Capital Loan
ARIYARATNE'S	YUNUS'S
FIVE-STAGE VILLAGE RENEWAL	BANK SYSTEM FOR THE POOR

32.1 FOURTH WORLD PROBLEM

In this section we have given much of our attention to nations who successfully escaped from the poorworlds. What about countries mired in the vicious cycles of fourth world poverty? Let us turn our attention to that problem.

We use our familiar diagram, with consumption per person in years zero and one. As usual, OA and OB are subsistence per person and point C represents the two-year subsistence condition. The curve DE depicts the possibility frontier of this poor country. Point F shows equal consumption both years. This country satisfies the production-survival condition.

It fails the distribution-survival condition because the median person consumes at point G, at about 80 percent of its share of the social subsistence. The median person is undernourished, undereducated, and undercared for. This is an exact picture of the fourth world problem.

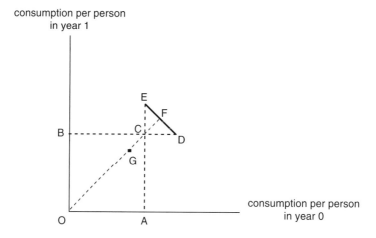

How stable is this situation? It appears to be quite stable. Productivity is high enough to avoid collapse while the deprivation of the masses may be low enough to avoid revolution. The restricted income and income-earning potential of the masses create a strong constraint on increasing effective demand.

Constraints on improving the possibility frontier are powerful. Population booms and undernourishment can and do occur together. This strains the per-person possibility frontier. A population explosion can sink it.

The low-level of human development translates into terrible quality control. In industrial sectors things are seldom done properly the first time and corrupt inspectors bless the misadventures. 'Most of the water pipes don't leak, most of the fuse boxes have fuses. That's good enough!'

The collapse of the possibility frontier cannot be ruled out. It is often maintained, in part, by the inflow of funds from donor agencies and citizens living and working abroad. If one or both of these sources dry up, the country might collapse into the fifth world.

32.2   Two Views on Development

We may now identify two views on development.

The 'orthodox' view concentrates on improving the possibility frontier, mostly through capital accumulation and technical change. This is often a *GO-approach* (governmental organizations). In recent years, it has significantly morphed into a very capitalistic *BO approach* (business organizations). In fact, they both have a role to play.

The 'alternative' view focuses on uplifting people living below subsistence. It involves programs aimed at basic needs, including access to nonexploitative credit. This is often an *NGO-approach*. The core principle is *human development with economic opportunity*.

These two approaches are often taken as rivals. Sometimes their leaders are antagonistic. Since many NGOs exist because of GO/BO failures, this hostility is understandable. But if they each do their jobs they are allies, and not rivals.

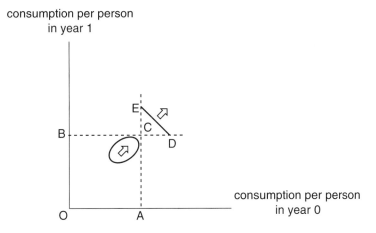

What is the best way for BOs and GOs to improve the possibility frontier? Through building and maintaining *infrastructures*: physical (energy, transportation, communications) and social (education, health, administrative). That increases per-capita income and employment. But it also increases the complexity of the social subsistence. These infrastructures become a necessary part of social reproduction. If they fail they will fall, and mighty will be the crash! But if they succeed entrepreneurs can create prosperity.

The great NGOs were born out of the creative personal recognition of dire human need. Professor Mohammad Yunus saw poor women in need of working capital. He resolved to assist them in a business-like way by establishing *social collateral* as the initial principle of the Grameen Bank. The founder of Sarvodaya in Sri Lanka, Dr. A.T. Ariyaratne, saw impoverished villages in need of help and self-improvement. He discovered ways to use *sharing* as a vehicle for village upliftment. NGOs can suffer from all the diseases of modern organizations, but the good ones can do a lot of good. In this chapter we take a look at both of these great movements.

32.3 SARVODAYA SHRAMADANA

The word Sarvodaya was coined by Mahatma Gandhi, while in South Africa, to mean 'the welfare of all'. It began as his Gujarati translation of John Ruskin's *Unto This Last* (1860). Eventually, Sarvodaya embodied Gandhi's hopes for India's suffering poor. It was a vision of decentralized society based upon simplicity, sanctity of labor, and nonviolence. It was summarized in his saying, 'Plain living and high thinking'. During Gandhi's lifetime, Sarvodaya never progressed beyond a list of goals. His successors failed to bring it to life.

In Sri Lanka, A.T. Ariyaratne was inspired by Gandhi's example and vision and began experiments in 1958 to help poor villages outside of Colombo. He, along with students and colleagues at a Buddhist high school, would ask villagers to identify their greatest collective need. Ariyaratne used his persuasive energy to get the needed material inputs donated. With materials in hand, the villagers, Ariyaratne and members of his High School, donated their labor to complete the task. Everything was based upon *sharing* what one could. Sarvodaya grew from those original community-development camps.[1]

Ariyaratne reinterpreted *Sarvodaya* to mean 'the awakening of all'. He adopted the word *Shramadana* that means 'sharing human energy'. So his movement, Sarvodaya Shramadana means 'the awakening of all through sharing'.

In order to harness the success of initial Sarvodaya Shramadana projects, Ariyaratne had the villages form peer groups—children, youth, mothers, elders, and farmers. Each group could suggest Shramadana projects. Eventually the mother's groups developed the most solidarity and were given the task of establishing and maintaining preschools.

In 1968, Sarvodaya launched the One Hundred Villages program. It surpassed all expectations. On May 3, 1972, an Act of Parliament incorporated the Sarvodaya Movement. This allowed the village organizations to form legal entities—Sarvodaya Shramadana Societies. These registered and incorporated organizations took on responsibility for certain village needs, like water and sanitation. By the late 1970s, Sarvodaya was a well-established institution.

At the same time, Ariyaratne was writing practical and philosophical essays, in the context of his Buddhism. His perceptions were akin to the Green Movement taking root in Europe at the same time. Franz Schumacher, the author of *Small is Beautiful* (1973), was among his early foreign supporters.

The Sarvodaya Shramadana Movement is working toward decentralization of economic and political institutions—the fulfillment of Gandhi's dream. In the villages joining Sarvodaya, people are encouraged to have faith in simplicity, truth, and nonviolence. Participants in Shramadana are fond of saying, 'We build the road, the road builds us.' The Sarvodaya approach to village renewal is intended to transform thinking, acting, and being.

32.4   SARVODAYA'S FIVE-STAGE MODEL

Although Sarvodaya was successful at helping villagers reform their communities, most attempts at income-generating activity ended in failure. In 1985, Dutch consultants studied this problem. Based upon their recommendations, Sarvodaya created the Sarvodaya Economic Enterprise Development Services (SEEDS), in 1986. A professional staff was recruited.

SEEDS has three parts: banking, enterprise services, and training services. With the inauguration of SEEDS, a five-stages model emerged. SEEDS was placed atop Ariyaratne's brilliant social base. These stages are:

Stage 1: Psychological Infrastructure Building: An initial Shramadana camp is conducted. This brings about a needed village improvement through cooperative activity. The main goal is to change defeatist patterns of thinking.

Stage 2: Social Infrastructure Building: Peer groups are formed. Foremost members are given leadership training on child-care, health, nutrition, and sanitation. A village child-care center is established.

Stage 3: Incorporate Sarvodaya Shramadana Village: This entity gives organized leadership to village-level activities that lead to higher living standards. The Society can hold property, open bank accounts, and enter into written contracts. The primary goal becomes the satisfaction of basic needs.

Stage 4: Access to the Economic Services of SEEDS: Members of Sarvodaya villages save, invest, borrow, improve existing enterprises, start new ones, repay loans, and evolve their own village development bank. Technical, extension, and training services are available.

Stage 5: Assist Other Villages: The village is both able to meet the costs of its own services and extend help to weaker neighboring villages. In addition, it is able to cooperate with other villages in mutually beneficial tasks.

Sri Lanka has about 35,000 villages. More than 4,000 are incorporated Sarvodaya villages. More than 3,000 of those villages access the services of SEEDS. About 1,000 villages have their own Sarvodaya Development Bank.

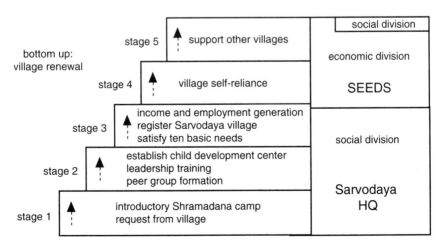

32.5   GRAMEEN BANK

The Grameen Bank traces its origin to a microcredit project in a very poor village organized by Professor Muhammad Yunus in 1976. Since then, Grameen has developed into a multifaceted Bank, issuing billions of dollars of small loans to mostly landless and illiterate women throughout Bangladesh. Grameen has become a center of new thinking, with many attempts at replication around the world. It has achieved this distinction because of its focus on satisfying basic human needs through a brilliant mixture of microcredit, women's solidarity, basic life-style education, and a dedicated workforce.[2]

The seeds were sown during a famine. At that time, Yunus was teaching economics at Chittagong University. He was stunned by the desperate condition of people all around him and the bankruptcy of the economics he was teaching.

In conversations with people producing handicrafts, he learned they earned almost nothing because of severe exploitation by the trader/moneylender they were essentially bonded to. When Yunus made an inquiry at a local bank he was told 'the poor are not credit worthy' because they do not have collateral. Yunus did have collateral, so he took out loans on behalf of a few dozen people in that village. They repaid him. Yunus renewed and expanded the cycle. They repaid him. Each time the bankers said, 'When you get big it won't work'.

The Universal Declaration of Human Rights is a cornerstone of Grameen:

> Article 25: Everyone has the right to a standard of living adequate for the health and well being of himself and his family, including food, clothing, housing and medical care, and necessary social services, and the right to security in the event of unemployment, sickness, disability, widowhood, old age or other lack of livelihood in circumstances beyond his control.

In other words: human beings have a right to their share of the social subsistence. Yunus draws some strong conclusions from this line of thinking. In making the case that *credit is a human right* he observes:

> Poverty, to me, is the denial of all human rights . . . No matter how sacred those rights are . . . to the impoverished, it makes no sense, has no meaning . . . I am saying that credit should be accepted as a human right because that's the beginning of all the human rights . . . credit opens up the difficult extreme by allowing self employment . . .
>
> http://www.pbs.org/speaktruthtopower/b_yunus.htm (accessed November 15, 2006)

In order to secure this right it is necessary to create well-designed financial services exclusively for the poor, applied through a specialized delivery system by well-trained personnel. Such programs must be simple, direct, consistent, and based upon business principles. They must be able to withstand hostility from vested interests. They must have feedback mechanisms to identify and correct design flaws. Professor Yunus was just the man for the job.

It was Yunus' genius to realize that a banking system could be founded without physical collateral. The illiterate poor have skills: listening, memory, survival, and occupational. Within well-designed programs they pull their weight.

Grameen Bank member are organized in self-selected groups of five. They pledge to support each other, thus creating the bonds of social collateral. Six groups join to create a 30-person center. The members of a center build the meeting place. This project is the first result of their collective identity. Leadership positions are determined by election, but in every five-year cycle each member of a group will experience the role of leader.

Obligatory center meetings—and loan repayments—occur each week. The groups assemble before the bank worker arrives. They open the meeting with their Four Principles: 'Discipline, Unity, Courage and Hard Work is Our Motto!' During the meeting they discuss current issues and problems. All bank business is conducted openly. Decisions are made on the basis of consensus.

During the meeting members recite their social welfare constitution—the 16 decisions. An abridged version is found on the next page.

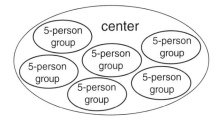

If a newly formed group conforms to the rules, two members receive loans. If they repay their weekly installments, two more members receive loans. The fifth member receives a loan after the other members establish timely repayment records. The group chairperson is usually the last to receive a loan. A second set of loans is issued after the successful repayment of the first set.

In addition to working-capital loans, well-established members are eligible for housing loans. These are applied to a cost-effective design pioneered by Grameen. The design is intended to withstand typhoon winds.

There are three kinds of Bank field offices: branch, area, and zonal. A Branch office is responsible for up to 60 centers within walking distance. About 80 percent of the Bank's staff work in branches. *The Branch is the fundamental profit-making unit.* It charges 20 percent annual interest to borrowers and gets its money at 12 percent from the zonal office. Branch workers can receive a share of the profits.

An area office supervises about 10 branches. A zonal office (usually located in a government district capital) monitors and evaluates about 10 area offices. At the top of the Grameen Bank is the head office, in Dhaka.

Members must maintain deposits and are the owners of the Bank. Founded in 1983, Grameen does not require donor funds.

THE 16 DECISIONS OF GRAMEEN BANK MEMBERS

---

1   Follow the four principles: discipline, unity, courage, and hard work.
2   Bring prosperity to our families.
3   Repair our houses and work toward constructing new houses.
4   Grow vegetables year round, eat plenty of them, and sell the surplus.
5   During plantation seasons, plant as many seedlings as possible.
6   Keep our families small. Minimize our expenditures. Look after our health.
7   Educate our children and ensure they can pay for their education.
8   Always keep our children and the environment clean.
9   Build and use pit-latrines.
10 Drink tubewell water or boil water or treat it with alum.
11 No dowry. No child marriage.
12 Neither inflict injustice on anyone, nor allow anyone to do so.
13 Collectively undertake bigger investments for higher incomes.
14 Always be ready to help each other. Help anyone in difficulty.
15 Help restore discipline in any center suffering a breach.
16 Do physical fitness exercises. Take part in social activities collectively.

32.6 GRAMEEN BANK 2

By 1995, the Bank had more than 2 million members. Cracks began to appear in the strict application of the standardized set of rules. The most serious problem was the weekly repayment requirement. This was applied even in the face of family tragedy. In addition, long-term member/borrowers began to chafe under this rule and were upset because competitor NGOs were more flexible.

That year many borrowers boycotted center meetings and repayments. This was organized by husbands and local politicians. Up to this point, Grameen had been effective at neutralizing opposition through solidarity. The one-size-fits-all approach was losing its simplicity value and emerging as a design flaw.

Grameen began to move slowly toward reform when a terrible flood devastated Bangladesh in 1998. At one point nearly 80 percent of the country was under water. Half the country was under water for 10 weeks.

Grameen Bank extended new loans in order to replace lost houses and income-generating activities. These loans were in addition to outstanding loans from the preflood period. Soon the financial burden was too great for many borrowers. Some centers were collapsing. Reform of repayment rules was an urgent task.

In a flurry of creative activity, Grameen Bank designed and tested a major reform program, with some new features. The process began in the spring of 2000. Two years later Grameen Bank 2 emerged as the next-generation bank.

With some humility Yunus has written:

> Please rest assured that the poor people are not going to create any trouble. It is us, the designers of institutions and rules, who keep creating trouble for them. One can benefit enormously by having trust in them ... (www.grameen-info.org/bank/bank2.html)

The new system revolves around 'basic' and 'flexible' loans. The borrower begins with the basic loan but may convert it to flexible terms if needed. If a borrower leaves the system entirely the outstanding balance is written off. This should relieve the great tension caused when borrowers fall behind.

The 'Grameen Generalized System' allows for customization. Loan duration, timing, and repayment schedules can all be customized. Weekly repayment is still required but the amount may vary to reflect peak and lean business seasons.

Members now keep three required savings accounts: personal, special, and pension. The pension fund's popularity is a great internal source for new loans. A loan-insurance savings account has been added to cover untimely death.

The bank now offers higher education loans to students from Grameen families. It also provides scholarships, with at least one available to each branch.

Finally, all rules have been suspended for destitute women. Groups are encouraged to mentor them until they can join a group of their own.

32.7 BRIGHT LIGHTS FOR THE POORWORLDS

The Grameen Bank spread rapidly in Bangladesh and has been replicated elsewhere. It provides needed services in a simple, transparent, and effective way. Grameen Bank 2 demonstrates the maturing of the microfinance industry.

The creation of financially viable banks for the poor is a milestone in history. Professor Yunus was justly awarded the Nobel Peace Prize. His 'action research' is so great he should win the prize in Economic Science too.

Replication and sustainability, however, cannot be taken for granted. Every poor country has feudalistic and corrupt interests who stand in the way of progress. But, by focusing on well-designed financial services in a nonviolent and business-like way, the regressive power elites can be neutralized.

Although Grameen Bank is not organized as a 'stages model', with the development of Grameen Bank 2 we can perceive three interconnected levels: At the bottom are regular loans initially backed by social collateral later backed by 'trust'. Next are housing loans. Finally, a new level covering life-cycle needs—education for children, pensions, and loan insurance.

SARVODAYA	GRAMEEN BANK
5: Assist Other Villages	
4: Access Economic Services of SEEDS	
3: Incorporate Sarvodaya Shramadana Village	3: Life-Cycle Services
2: Social Infrastructure Building	2: Housing Loan
1: Psychological Infrastructure Building	1: Working-Capital Loan
ARIYARATNE'S	YUNUS'S
FIVE-STAGE VILLAGE RENEWAL	BANK SYSTEM FOR THE POOR

My search for truth in macrofoundations has taken me to Sarvodaya and its brilliant five-stage model. It is a very great achievement in alternative development. Sarvodaya has survived many great challenges. It has expanded incorporation to over 10 percent of Sri Lankan villages, mostly on a shoestring budget. After the tsunami, it was the most effective network on the island!

Sarvodaya Shramadana might be able to help millions of people in the poorworlds. It might help them find a path to solve the subsistence problem by way of village renewal.

A Sarvodaya Shramadana society would not require a high ratio of net output to social subsistence to satisfy basic needs and nurture able human beings. *Sarvodaya might become a powerful vehicle to deliver Senian 'capabilities'.*

Africa, specially, is crying out for solutions to grave problems. Gandhi coined the word Sarvodaya while living in Africa. Has the time come to return the word to Africa—as Sarvodaya Shramadana and SEEDS?

Dr. Ariyaratne and Professor Yunus are true godsons of Mahatma Gandhi. A Buddhist, a Muslim, and a Hindu—three bright lights for the poorworlds.

When the Son of Man comes in his glory, and all the angels with him, then he will sit on the throne of his glory. All the nations will be gathered before him, and he will separate the sheep from the goats, and he will put the sheep at his right hand and the goats at his left.

Then the king will say to those at his right hand, "Come, you that are blessed by my Father, inherit the kingdom prepared for you from the foundation of the world; for I was hungry and you gave me food, I was thirsty and you gave me something to drink, I was a stranger and you welcomed me, I was naked and you gave me clothing, I was sick and you took care of me, I was in prison and you visited me."

Then the righteous will answer him, "Lord, when was it that we saw you hungry and gave you food, or thirsty and gave you something to drink? And when was it that we saw you a stranger and welcomed you, or naked and gave you clothing? And when was it that we saw you sick or in prison and visited you?"

And the king will answer them, "Truly I tell you, just as you did it to one of the least of these who are members of my family, you did it to me."

Matthew 25: 31–40

NOTES

INTRODUCTION

1. David C. Colander, "The Macrofoundations of Micro," *Eastern Economic Journal* 19 (1993): 447–57. See also, Colander, ed., *Beyond Microfoundations: Post Walrasian Macroeconomics* (New York: Cambridge University Press, 1996). The Appendix contains an annotated bibliography.
2. The idea behind vicious-cycle diagrams is old. In email correspondence, Professor Kahn recalled learning the first diagram as a student. A clear verbal statement is found in Ragnar Nurkse, *Problems of Capital Formation in Underdeveloped Countries* (Oxford: Basil Blackwell, 1953), 4–11. For a complex version well-worth reading, see Michael P. Todaro, *Economic Development in the Third World*, 4th ed. (New York and London: Longman, 1989), 91–94.

CHAPTER 1: SOCIAL SUBSISTENCE

1. The use of subsistence as an analytic concept has nearly been forgotten. For a doctrine-historical survey see: Krishna Bharadwaj, "Subsistence," *The New Palgrave: A Dictionary of Economics*, vol. 4, edited by John Eatwell, Murray Milgate and Peter Newman (London: Macmillan Press Ltd., 1987), 543–45.

CHAPTER 2: LIFE EXPECTANCY

1. The classic work on life expectancy is Louis Israel Dublin and Alfred J. Lotka, *Length of Life: A Study of the Life Table* (New York: The Ronald Press Co., 1936). See also: James C. Riley, *Rising Life Expectancy: A Global History* (Cambridge; New York: Cambridge University Press, 2001).
2. Condorcet championed the highest ideals of the French Revolution but fell victim to its brutal side. His book was published posthumously in 1795 and was quickly translated into English. It is divided into ten 'stages', starting with "Men are united in tribes" and ending with "The Future progress of the human mind." The tenth chapter/stage contains passages of awesome foresight mingled with naïve passages predicting the triumph of equality. Antoine-Nicolas de Condorcet, *Sketch for a Historical Picture of the Progress of the Human Mind*, translated by June Barraclough (London: Weidenfeld and Nicolson, 1955), 173–202.
3. Francis Fukuyama, *The End of History and the Last Man* (New York: Free Press; Toronto: Maxwell Macmillan Canada, 1992), 39.
4. "Altered Flies Live Twice as Long" (BBC News, December 15, 2000), http://news.bbc.co.uk/hi/english/sci/tech/newsid_1071000/1071910.stm

CHAPTER 3: POPULATION

1. For the three population diagrams, see: Europe: William Langer, "The Black Death," *Scientific American* 210, no. 2 (February 1964): 117. England: E. A. Wrigley, R.S. Davies, J.E. Oeppen, and R.S. Schofield, *English Population History from Family Reconstitution, 1580–1837* (Cambridge; New York: Cambridge University Press, 1997), 614. Ireland: "Ireland's Population in the Mid 1800's," http://www.mapspictures.com/ireland/history/ireland_population.htm (accessed March 1, 2006). For additional information on England, see: G. Talbot Griffith, *Population Problems of the Age of Malthus* (Cambridge, UK: At the University Press, 1926), 183, 189, and 198–207. For additional information on Ireland, see: Cormac O Grada, *Ireland A New Economic History 1780–1939* (Oxford: Clarendon Press; New York: Oxford University Press, 1994), 200–01 and 225.

2. An outstanding source on political ecology is Thomas F. Homer-Dixon, *Environment, Scarcity and Violence* (Princeton: Princeton University Press, 1999). See also "Key Findings [Chapter 7]," *Ecoviolence: Links among Environment, Population, and Security*, edited by Thomas Homer-Dixon and Jessica Blitt (Lanham, MD: Rowman & Littlefield, 1998), 223–28.

CHAPTER 4: PRODUCTION-SURVIVAL CONDITIONS

1. Isabel V. Sawhill, "Poverty in the U.S.: Why Is It So Persistent?" *Journal of Economic Literature* 26 (September 1988): 1076. Italics added.

CHAPTER 5: PRODUCTIVITY LIMITS

1. Nobuo Okishio, "Notes on Technical Progress in Capitalist Society," *Cambridge Journal of Economics* 1, no. 1 (1977): 93. Okishio attributes this analysis to the German edition of Marx's *Critique of Political Economy* (1859).

CHAPTER 6: MACROECONOMICS

1. Lucia Hanmer and Felix Naschold, "Are the International Development Targets Attainable?" *Stiglitz Summer Research Workshop on Poverty, Washington DC* (World Bank: WRD on Poverty and Development 2000/01: July 6—July 8, 1999), 5.

2. The World Bank has *finally* recognized the extraordinary impediment to development caused by wealth and income inequality. See: *World Development Report 2005: Equity and Development* (New York: Oxford University Press, 2005). That report noticeably lacks a developed theoretical model and diagrams are scarce.

CHAPTER 14: ECOCIDE

1. For another well-considered view on this topic, see Jared Diamond, *Collapse: How Societies Choose to Fail or Succeed* (New York: Viking, 2005).

Chapter 19: Abuse of Macrofoundations

1. George Sylvester Viereck, *Glimpses of the Great* (New York: The Macaulay Co., 1930), 214.
2. Leon Tabah, "Alfred Sauvy: Statistician, Economist, Demographer and Iconoclast," *Population Studies* 45 (1991): 353–57.
3. Alfred Sauvy, *General Theory of Population*, translated by Christophe Campos (New York: Basic Books, 1970), 51–59 and 341–47. First published in French in 1952.
4. From a speech by J.W. Kauwahi, delivered on January 1, 1867. Malcolm Naea Chun (translator and editor), *Must We Wait in Despair: The 1867 Report of the `Ahahui La`au Lapa`au of Wailuku, Maui on Native Hawaiian Health* (Honolulu: First People's Productions, 1994), xxx–xxxi.

Chapter 21: Guns and Butter

1. Recent literature on North Korea is large. One might care to start with: Bruce Cumings, *North Korea: Another Country* (New York: New Press, Distributed by W.W. Norton, 2003), or, Young Whan Kihl and Hong Nack Kim, eds., *North Korea: The Politics of Regime Survival* (Armonk, NY: M.E. Sharpe, 2006).

Chapter 29: Foreign Direct Investment

1. My interest in this topic was stimulated by many discussions with Robert Grosse. See his article (and the book containing it): "Poverty and MNEs in Emerging Markets," *Multinational Corporations and Global Poverty Reduction*, edited by Subhash C. Jain and Sushil Vachani. (Cheltenham UK; Northampton MA: Edward Elgar, 2006), 286–98.
2. See endnote 1 to Chapter 6.
3. Julian May, Benjamin Roberts, George Moqasa, and Ingrid Woolard, "Poverty and Inequality in Lesotho" (CSDS Working Paper No. 36, April 2002), 8.

Chapter 32: Alternative Development

1. For an overview of the Movement, from its inception until recent years, see some of the writings of the founder: *Sarvodaya Shramadana: Growth of a People's Movement* (Colombo: Kularatne, 1970) and *Schumacher Lectures on Buddhist Economics* (Ratmalana: Sarvodaya Vishva Lekha Publishers, 1999).
2. Yunus does not write much but in his writings every word counts. See *Grameen Bank, As I See It* (Dhaka, Bangladesh: The Bank, 1994). The bank produces training manuals. An early one, if not the first, is David S. Gibbons ed., *The Grameen Reader* (Dhaka, Bangladesh: Grameen Bank, 1992).

BIBLIOGRAPHY

Acsadi, G.Y. and J. Nemeskeri. *History of Human Life Span and Mortality*. Budapest: Akademiai Kiado, 1970.

Ariyaratne, A.T. *Sarvodaya Shramadana: Growth of a People's Movement*. Colombo: Kularatne, 1970.

———. *Schumacher Lectures on Buddhist Economics*. Ratmalana: Sarvodaya Vishva Lekha Publishers, 1999.

Bailey, Ronald. "Billions Served [Interview with Norman Borlaug]." *Reason Online* (April 2000). http://reason.com/0004/fe.rb.billions.shtml (accessed October 10, 2004).

Balasubramanyam, V.N. "Foreign Direct Investment in Developing Countries: Determinants and Impacts." *OECD Global Forum on International Investment*, November 26–27, 2001.

Bentham, Jeremy. *Principles of the Civil Code*. University of Texas at Austin: Classical Utilitarianism Web Site. http://www.la.utexas.edu/research/poltheory/bentham/pcc/index.html

Bern, C., J. Sniezek, G.M. Mathbor, M.S. Siddiqui, C. Ronsmans, A.M.R. Chowdhury, et al. "Risk Factors for Mortality in the Bangladesh Cyclone of 1991." *Bulletin of the World Health Organization* 71, 1 (1993): 73–78.

Bharadwaj, Krishna. "Subsistence." In *The New Palgrave: A Dictionary of Economics*, vol. 4, edited by John Eatwell, Murray Milgate, and Peter Newman. London: Macmillan Press Ltd., 1987, 543–45.

Borlaug, Norman. "The Green Revolution, Peace, and Humanity." *Nobel Peace Prize Lecture, December 11, 1970*. Official Website of the Nobel Foundation. http:// nobelprize.org/peace/laureates/1970/borlaug-lecture.html (accessed October 10, 2004).

Broswimmer, Franz J. *Ecocide: A Short History of the Mass Extinction of Species*. London; Sterling, VA: Pluto Press, 2002.

Chen, Cheng. *Land Reform in Taiwan*. Taipei: China Publishing Co., 1961.

Childe, V. Gordon. *Man Makes Himself*. New York: New American Library, 1951. First published in 1936.

Chun, Malcolm Naea, trans. and ed. *Must We Wait in Despair: The 1867 Report of the `Ahahui La`au Lapa`au of Wailuku, Maui on Native Hawaiian Health*. Honolulu: First People's Productions, 1994.

Clark, John Bates. *The Distribution of Wealth: A Theory of Wages, Interest and Profits*. New York; London: Macmillan, 1899.

Colander, David C. "The Macrofoundations of Micro." *Eastern Economics Journal* 19 (1993): 447–57.

Colander, David C., ed. *Beyond Microfoundations: Post Walrasian Macroeconomics.* New York: Cambridge University Press, 1996.

Condorcet, Antoine-Nicolas de Caritat, marquis de. *Sketch for a Historical Picture of the Progress of the Human Mind.* Translated by June Barraclough; with an introduction by Stuart Hampshire. London: Weidenfeld and Nicolson, 1955. First published in French in 1795. First translated into English in 1795.

Cumings, Bruce. *North Korea: Another Country.* New York: New Press, Distributed by W.W. Norton, 2003.

Diamond, Jared M. *Collapse: How Societies Choose to Fail or Succeed.* New York: Viking, 2005.

———. *Guns, Germs and Steel: The Fates of Human Societies.* New York: W.W. Norton, 1997.

Dublin, Louis Israel and Alfred J. Lotka. *Length of Life: A Study of the Life Table.* New York: The Ronald Press Co., 1936.

Dyson, Tim and Cormac O Grada, eds. *Famine Demography: Perspectives from the Past and Present.* Oxford; New York: Oxford University Press, 2002.

Easterbrook, Gregg. "Forgotten Benefactor of Humanity." *Atlantic Monthly* 279, no. 1 (January 1997): 75–82.

Fogel, Robert William and Stanley L. Engerman. *Time on the Cross: The Economics of American Negro Slavery.* Boston: Little, Brown, 1994.

Fukuyama, Francis. *The End of History and the Last Man.* New York: Free Press; Toronto: Maxwell Macmillan Canada, 1992.

———. *Our Posthuman Future: Consequences of the Biotechnology Revolution.* London: Profile Books; [New York]: Farrar Straus & Giroux, 2002.

Galtung, Johan, Tore Heiestad, and Eric Ruge. *On the Decline and Fall of Empires: The Roman Empire and Western Imperialism Compared.* Tokyo: United Nations University, 1979.

Gibbons, David S., ed. *The Grameen Reader: Training Materials for the International Replication of the Grameen Bank Financial System for Reduction of Rural Poverty.* Dhaka, Bangladesh: Grameen Bank, 1992.

Goalstone, Clifford David. "On a Macrofoundation of Macroeconomics." *Kobe-Gakuin Economic Papers* 20, no. 3 (1988): 149–61.

———. "On a Macrofoundation of Macroeconomics: Part 2." *Kobe-Gakuin Economic Papers* 21, no. 1 and 2 (1989): 75–88.

———. "On a Macrofoundation of Macroeconomics: Part 3." *Kobe-Gakuin Economic Papers* 22, no. 2 (1990): 97–115.

———. "Sir James Steuart and the Rehabilitation of Classical Economics." *Korea Review of International Studies* 3, no. 1 (2000): 91–105.

Goldstone, Jack A. *Revolution and Rebellion in the Early Modern World.* Berkley: University of California Press, 1991.

Goulet, Denis. *Survival with Integrity: Sarvodaya at the Crossroads.* Colombo, Sri Lanka: Marga Institute, 1981.

Griffith, G. Talbot. *Population Problems of the Age of Malthus.* Cambridge, UK: Cambridge University Press, 1926.

Grosse, Robert. "Poverty and MNEs in Emerging Markets." In *Multinational Corporations and Global Poverty Reduction*, edited by Subhash C. Jain and Sushil Vachani. Cheltenham UK; Northampton MA: Edward Elgar, 2006, 286–98.

Gurr, Ted. "On the Political Consequences of Scarcity and Economic Decline." *International Studies Quarterly* 29, no. 1 (1985): 51–75.

Hanmer, Lucia and Felix Naschold. "Are the International Development Targets Attainable?" *Stiglitz Summer Research Workshop on Poverty, Washington DC.* World Bank: WRD on Poverty and Development 2000/01, July 6–July 8, 1999.

———. "Attaining the International Development Targets: Will Growth be Enough?" *Development Policy Review* 18 (2000): 11–36.

Hicks, John Richard, Sir. *The Social Framework: An Introduction to Economics.* Oxford: The Clarendon Press, 1943.

Homer-Dixon, Thomas and Jessica Blitt, eds. *Ecoviolence: Links among Environment, Population, and Security.* Lanham, MD: Rowman & Littlefield, 1998.

Homer-Dixon, Thomas F. *Environment, Scarcity and Violence.* Princeton: Princeton University Press, 1999.

Kahn, James R. *Economic Approach to Environmental and Natural Resources*, 3rd ed. Mason, OH: Southwestern Press, 2005.

Kantowski, Detlef. *Sarvodaya: The Other Development.* Delhi: Vikas Publishing House, 1980.

Katz, Richard. *Japan, the System that Soured: The Rise and Fall of the Japanese Economic Miracle.* Armonk, NY: M.E. Sharpe, 1998.

Kihl, Young Whan and Hong Nack Kim, eds. *North Korea: The Politics of Regime Survival.* Armonk NY: M.E. Sharpe, 2006.

Krugman, Paul. "The Myth of Asia's Miracle." *Foreign Affairs* 73, no. 6 (November/December 1994): 62–78.

Langer, William. "The Black Death." *Scientific American* 210, no. 2 (February 1964): 114–21.

Malthus, Thomas Robert. *An Essay on the Principle of Population*, 1st ed. Edited with an introduction by Geoffery Gilbert. Oxford; New York: Oxford University Press, 1993. First Published in 1798.

———. *An Essay on the Principle of Population*, 6th ed. London: J. Murray, 1826.

———. *Parallel Chapters from the First and Second Editions of An Essay on the Principle of Population.* New York, London: Macmillan and Co., 1895.

May, Julian, Benjamin Roberts, George Moqasa, and Ingrid Woolard. "Poverty and Inequality in Lesotho." *CSDS Working Paper No. 36* (April 2002): 1–49.

Meek, Ronald L. *The Economics of Physiocracy: Essays and Translations.* London: George Allen & Unwin, 1962.

Mill, John Stuart. *Principles of Political Economy: With Some of Their Applications to Social Philosophy* [microform]. London: J.W. Parker, 1848.

Motiur Rahman, PK. Md. *Poverty Issues in Rural Bangladesh.* Dhaka, Bangladesh: University Press Limited, 1994.

Nurkse, Rangar. *Problems of Capital Formation in Underdeveloped Countries.* Oxford: Basil Blackwell, 1953.

O Grada, Cormac. *Ireland A New Economic History 1780–1939.* Oxford: Clarendon Press; New York: Oxford University Press, 1994.

Okishio, Nobuo. "Technical Changes and the Rate of Profit." *Kobe University Economic Review* 7 (1961): 85–99.

———. "Notes on Technical Progress and Capitalist Society." *Cambridge Journal of Economics* 1, no. 1 (1977): 93–100.

———. "Mr. Goalstone's 'Macro Foundation of Macro Economics.'" *Kobe-Gakuin Economic Papers* 23, no 2 (1991): 1–11.

Place, Francis. *Illustrations and Proofs of the Principle of Population.* Boston and New York: Houghton Mifflin Co., 1930. First published in 1822.

Polanyi, Karl. *The Great Transformation.* New York, Toronto: Farrar & Reinhart, 1944.

Ricardo, David. *An Essay on the Influence of a Low Price of Corn on the Profits of Stock* [microform]. London: Printed for John Murray, 1815.

Riley, James C. *Rising Life Expectancy: A Global History.* Cambridge; New York: Cambridge University Press, 2001.

Rostow, W.W. (Walt Whitman). *The Stages of Economic Growth: A Non-Communist Manifesto,* 3rd ed. Cambridge [England]; New York: Cambridge University Press, 1990. First Published in 1960.

Ruskin, John. *Unto This Last: Four Essays on the First Principles of Political Economy.* London: G. Allen, 1906. First published in 1860.

Sachs, Jeffrey. *The End of Poverty: Economic Possibilities for our Time.* New York: Penguin Press, 2005.

Samuelson, Paul Anthony. *Economics: An Introductory Analysis.* New York: McGraw Hill Book Co., 1948.

Sauvy, Alfred. *General Theory of Population.* Translated by Christophe Campos. New York: Basic Books, 1970. First published in French in 1952.

Sawhill, Isabel V. "Poverty in the U.S.: Why Is It So Persistent?" *Journal of Economic Literature* 26 (September 1988): 1073–119.

Schumacher, Ernst Friedrich. *Small Is Beautiful: Economics as if People Mattered.* New York: Harper & Row, 1973.

Sen, Amartya Kumar. *Poverty and Famines: An Essay on Entitlement and Deprivation.* Oxford: Clarendon Press; New York: Oxford University Press, 1981.

———. *Development as Freedom.* New York: Knopf, 1999.

Senior, Nassau William. *Two Lectures on Population, Delivered before the University of Oxford, in Easter Term, 1828* [microform]. London: J. Murray, 1831.

Smith, Adam. *An Inquiry into the Nature and Causes of the Wealth of Nations.* Edited with an introduction by Kathryn Sutherland. Oxford; New York: Oxford University Press, 1993. First published in 1776.

Soto, Hernando de. *The Mystery of Capital: Why Capitalism Triumphs in the West and Fails Everywhere Else.* New York: Basic Books, 2000.

Steuart, Sir James. *An Inquiry into the Principles of Political Economy.* Edited with an introduction by Andrew S. Skinner. Chicago: University of Chicago Press, 1966. First published in 1767.

Tabah, Leon. "Alfred Sauvy: Statistician, Economist, Demographer and Iconoclast." *Population Studies* 45, no. 2 (July 1991): 353–57.

Todaro, Michael P. *Economic Development in the Third World,* 4th ed. New York and London: Longman, 1989.

Townsend, Joseph. *A Dissertation on the Poor Laws, by a Well-Wisher to Mankind* [microform]. London: Printed for C. Dilly, 1786.

United Nations Conference on Trade and Development. *FDI in Least Developed Countries at a Glance: 2002.* New York and Geneva: UNCTAD, 2002.

———. *The Least Developed Countries Report 2002: Escaping the Poverty Trap.* New York and Geneva: UNCTAD, 2002.

———. *Investment Policy Review: Lesotho.* Geneva: UNCTAD, 2003.

Viereck, George Sylvester. *Glimpses of the Great.* New York: The Macaulay Co., 1930.

Winch, Donald. "Darwin Fallen among Political Economists." *Proceedings of the American Philosophical Society* 145, no. 4 (2001): 415–37.

World Bank. *World Development Report 1993: Investing in Health.* New York: Oxford University Press, 1993.

———. *World Development Report 1994: Infrastructure for Development.* New York: Oxford University Press, 1994.

————. *World Development Report 2000/01: Attacking Poverty.* New York: Oxford University Press, 2000.

————. *World Development Report 2003: Making Services Work for the Poor.* New York: Oxford University Press, 2003.

————. *World Development Report 2005: Equity and Development.* New York: Oxford University Press, 2005.

Wrigley, E.A., R.S. Davies, J.E. Oeppen, and R.S. Schofield. *English Population History from Family Reconstitution, 1580–1837.* Cambridge; New York: Cambridge University Press, 1997.

Yunus, Muhammad. *Grameen Bank, As I See It.* Dhaka, Bangladesh: The Bank, 1994.

———— with Alan Jolis. *Banker to the Poor: Micro-Lending and the Battle against World Poverty.* New York: PublicAffairs, 1999.

INDEX OF SUBJECTS

INDEX OF PEOPLE

INDEX OF PLACES